The *Self*
Does Not Die

D1729649

The *Self* Does Not Die

Verified Paranormal Phenomena from Near-Death Experiences

Titus Rivas, MA, MSc,

Anny Dirven, and Rudolf H. Smit

Foreword to the Dutch edition by Stan Michielsens
Foreword to the English edition
by Robert G. Mays, BSc, and Suzanne B. Mays, AA

English edition edited by Janice Miner Holden, EdD
Translation by Wanda J. Boeke

Project management and editorial
oversight by Robert G. Mays, BSc

IANDS Publications

International Association for Near-Death Studies, Durham, NC

International Association for Near-Death Studies (IANDS)
2741 Campus Walk Avenue, Building 500
Durham, North Carolina 27705-8878
www.iands.org

ISBN-13: 978-0-9975608-0-0

Cover design and photo by Rudolf Smit.
Photos of Dr. Miguel Ángel Pertierra Quesada and Robert F. Spetzler
courtesy of Wikimedia Creative Commons.
Photo of Michael Sabom courtesy of HarperCollins.
Photo of Elizabeth Fenwick, Peter Fenwick,
and Pim van Lommel courtesy of Rudolf Smit.
Photo of Lloyd W. Rudy and Mike Milligan from
"Dr. Lloyd Rudy, Famous Cardiac Surgeon, Talks About the Importance
of Oral Systemic Health," courtesy of http://oralsystemiclink.pro/.
Photo of Jan and John Price courtesy of the QUARTUS Foundation.
Photo of Eben Alexander's sister Betsy courtesy of Eben Alexander III.
Photo of F. W. H. Myers from Morgan, S. R. (1950).
Index to psychic science. Swarthmore, PA.
Illustration of neocortex by Henry Vandyke Carter from Gray, H. (1918).
Anatomy of the human body. Philadelphia, PA: Lea and Febiger.
Illustration of EEG burst suppression courtesy of IEEE Xplore.
Passage in Case 1.9 (pp. 16–20) from Sartori, P. (2008).
The near-death experiences of hospitalized intensive care patients: A five year clinical study.
Lewiston, UK: Edwin Mellen Press. Courtesy of Penny Sartori and Edwin Mellen Press.
Passage in Case 9.4 (pp. 208–211) from Farr, S. S. (1993). *What Tom Sawyer learned from
dying.* Norfolk, VA: Hampton Roads. Courtesy of Bruce Lawson, son of Sidney Farr.
Unless otherwise noted, photos are courtesy of the subject.

For Mary Rose Barrington

In memory of Anny Dirven, Johanna Wols-Van Bemmelen,
Wim Stevens, Cica Rivas, Guusje Rivas, Mesut P., and Pam Reynolds

What if you slept
And what if
In your sleep
You dreamed
And what if
In your dream
You went to heaven
And there plucked a strange and beautiful flower
And what if
When you awoke
You had that flower in your hand
Ah, what then?

—Attributed to Samuel Taylor Coleridge

The defenders of materialism today are indeed screaming
and kicking ever more loudly, perhaps because of a total lack
of evidential support for their respective ideology.
—Neal Grossman, PhD
Foreword to *Science and the Near-Death Experience* by Chris Carter

There is documented evidence that supports the patients' testimony.
—Penny Sartori, PhD, RGN
The Near-Death Experiences of Hospitalized Intensive Care Patients

Doubts about the validity of the NDE can be safely
dispatched on purely scientific grounds.
—Kenneth Ring, PhD, and Evelyn Elsaesser Valarino
Lessons from the Light

When the experience occurs in the circumstances of cardiac arrest and
the objective period of death, I think *near*-death experience would
more accurately be termed the *actual*-death experience, or ADE.
—Sam Parnia, MD
Erasing Death

Contents

Foreword to the Dutch Edition
by Stan Michielsens

The free encyclopedia *Wikipedia* describes parapsychology as the discipline that investigates the existence and causes of psychic abilities, as well as the possibility of life after death, using scientific methods. Parapsychological phenomena refer to phenomena caused or experienced by living beings that cannot fully be explained by known natural laws or natural forces.

This book investigates near-death experiences through parapsychology and categorizes these experiences into various paranormal phenomena. The authenticity of this investigation is based on third-party witness statements. The value and the significance of this book lie in the finding that during a near-death experience, certain facts can arise that are part and parcel of parapsychological phenomena. They thus confirm particular phenomena that belong to the investigative purview of this discipline.

Innumerable words have already been spoken and written about the authenticity of near-death experiences. Is there a real experience that takes place independently of physically bound activity, or is it, after all, a spasm, a last manifestation of the final end of a dying human being? At times, this debate gets emotional. But in scientific thinking, the emotional factor must, as much as possible, be sidelined so its potential to bias results is minimized. So why do emotions keep coming up in this debate? One possible explanation is the fact that many scientists have relied on the same hypothesis for 20, 30, or 40 years: that the brain produces consciousness, so that when the brain dies, consciousness dies. They have become intimately attached to this hypothesis and seeing it confirmed time and again by colleagues. It is difficult to cast doubt on a value that is so deeply entrenched. If they were to accept the evidence for the authenticity of near-death experiences, their hypothesis would be undermined, and the foundation would be pulled out from under their life's work! It would mean that people had been on the wrong track all their lives! That would be unimaginable! It is very human and understandable that people respond emotionally under such circumstances. However, para-psychological phenomena exist, even if they cannot be proven by exclusively materially oriented scientific methods. It is to be hoped that all this emotion will dissipate and that people will continue to work toward a universally acceptable consensus. For, in the future, there will also be people, even scientists, who will set their egos aside in talking about their near-death experiences because what they went through surpasses their outlook and mind-set, as we now ascertain with neurosurgeon Eben Alexander III. Under the influence of such experiences, some scientists are showing more interest in these phenomena and are including them in their research projects. We can only welcome this development!

But now that emotions have been mentioned: People who have had near-death experiences also experience intense emotions. Because near-death experiences are typically felt to be not only real but hyperreal, they stand out powerfully in experiencers' minds. They leave deep, lifelong traces, causing drastic lifestyle changes in some cases. Hallucinations or dreams, which usually distinguish themselves in vagueness, do not bring about this kind of change. In this book, more than 70 cases (in this English edition, more than 100 cases) are discussed. With each case, I stopped for a moment and attempted to imagine what that experience had meant for that person and what it still means! Some scientists speak of these experiences as if they were anecdotes. According to Merriam Webster, an anecdote is a "story, tale, or yarn." In French, one speaks of "une petite histoire" or "a nice little story." Sounds cute and fun, but for many experiencers, this is *the* story of their lives! However, a child has to be given a name, no matter how limited that name might be in fully describing the child. So we will call these phenomena "cases."

Finally, I find that the researcher-writers of this book have carefully selected and meticulously checked their sources. They did not spare any effort to gain maximum certainty concerning authenticity and completeness. I know from experience that they are very strict about maintaining the discipline they impose on themselves. Despite their strict scientific method, the book reads very smoothly. One reason is that the vocabulary they used is not academic; in addition, their formulations are lucid, and the sequencing is very straightforward. And by making use of cases, they also invite the reader to participate.

This book is an important contribution to gaining insight into the multifaceted nature and complexity of near-death experiences. This phenomenon has lots of commonalities, after all, such as its parallelism to the essence of the great religions and their mystical experiences as well as its place in para-psychology as is demonstrated in this book. However, the phenomenon surely also encompasses still other important aspects that demand thorough investigation. I am thinking, for example, of a moral-philosophical approach that, to my knowledge, has yet to be addressed: the next challenge for anyone who is called and feels qualified to explore this theme!

March 22, 2013
Stan Michielsens is former chair of Limen /
International Association for Near-Death Studies, Flanders, Belgium.

Foreword to the English Edition
by Robert G. Mays and Suzanne B. Mays

This book is like a collection of precious jewels that have been sorted out and set into different sections of a display case, showing different levels of brilliance and color, different degrees of uniqueness and beauty. As such, the book is a valuable catalog of important cases of paranormal phenomena from near-death experiences (NDEs) that have been investigated, confirmed, and documented by researchers over the years.

To the two of us, many of these jewels are old, familiar friends. In our study of NDEs over the past 40 years, we have come across many of these jewels in our reading together as interesting, even fascinating, cases of paranormal phenomena. They are familiar friends because we have studied and pondered them, replayed them in our minds, argued about them, and written about them.

We first encountered several of these jewels in Raymond Moody's 1975 book, *Life After Life*. They included the basic features of NDEs: the feeling of peace, the separation from the physical body, the sense of hyperreality, meeting deceased loved ones, encountering a great being of light, having a "life review" of the events of one's life, returning to one's body, and later finding corroboration of aspects of the experience by oneself or from others.

These last jewels—the perceptions and other information the near-death experiencer (NDEr) received during the experience that were later confirmed by other witnesses—were of the greatest interest to us because they suggested that these experiences are not only subjectively but also objectively *real*, that NDEs are, in fact, a taste of what it is like to die and, therefore, they suggest that the *self* does not die when the physical body dies.

A few years after Moody's book, we came across two additional jewels of this type in George Ritchie's (1978/2007) book, *Return From Tomorrow*. In his NDE, Ritchie experienced being out of his body, flying eastward across the frozen plains of east Texas at night in December 1943. He flew over a large river and saw a city on the opposite shore, where he decided to stop and ask directions at an all-night café. Because no one could see him, Ritchie returned to his body in the army hospital at Camp Barkley, near Abilene, Texas. There he encountered a brilliant Being of Light who led him into a transcendent realm. Near the end of his transcendent journey, Ritchie was led through an unusual sphere-shaped building where a catwalk led over a tank filled with water.

A while after his recovery, Ritchie and two army buddies were driving back to Texas, and they passed through Vicksburg, Mississippi. Ritchie felt that the city looked very familiar, and he found himself across the street from the café he had stopped at in his NDE 10 months earlier. In 1952, nine years after his NDE, Ritchie was looking through the December 15 issue of *Life* magazine and came across an artist's drawing of a sphere-shaped building with catwalk and tank that was being built in Schenectady, New York, to hold a naval nuclear submarine engine under development. Ritchie had "walked" through this building and over the catwalk 9 years earlier during his NDE.

These two jewels from George Ritchie's NDE—accurate physical perceptions 525 miles from his physical body and an accurate precognitive vision—as impressive as they are, however, do not have sufficient "beauty" to be included in this book's display case because they lack one key element— namely, clear confirmation from an independent source. This book includes only paranormal cases that meet this higher standard. Nevertheless, as a result of our own detailed research into Ritchie's case, summarized at the end of Chapter 2, we became convinced that NDEs are real experiences of a transcendental nature.

To be sure, while the paranormal cases in this book *do* have third-party confirmation, they only *suggest* that the core of one's being survives physical death. In science, there is no *proof* of any proposal, only greater evidence leading to an ever-stronger sense of certainty about the proposal. For the question of survival, the evidence of an autonomous self can only be indirect, because the self cannot be observed physically. The evidence presented in this book, nevertheless, strongly suggests that the self is something that is objectively real and that it survives physical death.

In our study of NDEs, we have been dismayed that these instances of paranormal phenomena are scattered over dozens and dozens of books and research articles, covering now more than 40 years of research. And most of the cases have "disappeared" from common discourse in the field of near-death studies.

Even worse, the NDE research community and skeptics alike have preferred to focus on only a handful of favorite cases, ending up—in our view—flogging and reflogging a few long-dead horses, thereby unequivocally proving, we suppose, that at least *some* creatures can survive physical death, repeatedly.

By far, the most popular cases to argue about have been those of Pam Reynolds (Case 3.29 in the book) and the Dentures Man (Case 3.7), with that of Maria's Tennis Shoe (Case 2.3) "running" a distant third. The result has been that some researchers cite one or two such cases to demonstrate the possibility that the mind can exist independent of the brain, while skeptics cite these same cases with different interpretations to demonstrate the exact opposite.

The arguments on both sides then turn on the very narrow specifics of just these few cases: Could Pam Reynolds have physically heard the conversation she accurately reported, even though she was deeply anesthetized at the time? Could the Dentures Man have constructed a mental model of the crash cart where the nurse put his dentures, even though he was in a coma when the nurse placed them there? Could Maria, prior to her cardiac arrest, have overheard nurses talking about a tennis shoe outside on a window ledge, even though her English was limited and no one reported such a conversation having occurred?

We share the hope with the authors that this collection of the strongest, verified paranormal cases, gathered together in one place for the first time, will change the discourse in this field from the specifics of a few isolated cases to the phenomenon of NDEs *viewed as a whole*.

A Compendium of Paranormal Cases From Near-Death Experiences

In May 2012, we received an e-mail from Titus Rivas that he, Anny Dirven, and Rudolf Smit were compiling cases of NDEs with independently verified veridical (accurate) aspects. From a number of sources, including more than 100 case descriptions NDE researcher Jan Holden had compiled for her chapter on veridical perception in NDEs in the 2009 *Handbook of Near-Death Experiences*, they had thus far collected 50 such cases. Did we know of any recent or obscure cases of this type? We responded with several suggestions for additional cases, a few of which were new to them. We were later delighted when their book in Dutch with 78 cases appeared in October 2013.

We felt that an English-language version of their book would be very important to enable a broader dissemination of this collection among researchers, and Robert assisted the authors to arrange for a publisher. When a mainstream publisher was not forthcoming, Robert persuaded the non-profit International Association for Near-Death Studies (IANDS), where he serves on the board of directors, to undertake fund-raising and publishing the English edition.

For IANDS, as the foremost supporter of NDE research and disseminator of information about NDEs, this was a natural step to take, although its first step in the field of publishing. IANDS provided about 20% of the funding for this project, and the rest has come from many, many donors—members of IANDS, near-death experiencers, researchers, and the general public—all of whom see the real value of this book for this field.

Indeed, the book is a compendium of the strongest, verified paranormal cases, conveniently classified and cataloged together, with the relevant references for further investigation. With the collection of similar cases together, researchers can readily focus on the common elements of related cases.

Explaining *All* Aspects of *All* Near-Death Experiences

NDEs share a number of striking characteristics—namely, hyperreal perceptions, a locus of perception outside the physical body, veridical perceptions of the material and transmaterial realms, indelible memory formation of the experience, and the experience evidently at times occurring when there is no brain function. Theorists have offered two opposing hypotheses to explain these characteristics: (1) electrical activity in the person's brain produces these effects in NDEs, or (2) the person's mind or consciousness has separated in some way from the body, and these effects result.

One effort to shed light on these hypotheses was the 3-year, $5 million "Immortality Project" led by John M. Fischer, distinguished professor of philosophy at the University of California, Riverside (n.d.). The project began in 2012 and funded scientific, philosophical, and theological studies of the possibility of the afterlife.

In a 2014 paper critiquing Pim van Lommel's (2013) theory of nonlocal consciousness, Benjamin Mitchell-Yellin and Fischer conceded that any *complete* explanation of NDEs must account for *all* aspects of *all* NDEs. This principle means that all the elements and all the details of each different NDE need to be accounted for and consistent with the explanation.

Considering the variety of conditions that NDEs occur in—from the NDEr being completely healthy (a near-death-like experience) to being in cardiac-arrest death—this principle appears to present a daunting task for the first explanatory hypothesis that the brain's electrical activity produces consciousness. Such an explanation would need to account for all the paranormal phenomena that are documented in this book.

Two-thirds of the cases in this book (Chapters 1–3) describe instances of accurate, verified perceptions in which the NDEr should not have been able to perceive the object or event through ordinary physical senses. In these cases, one of several physical conditions existed: The person's vision was blocked, the object was out of the physical line of sight or at a distance, or the person was unconscious or clinically dead. These cases present a serious challenge to the brain-production hypothesis.

As incredible as it may seem, the most parsimonious explanation, in our view, is that the NDE *is* what it appears subjectively to the NDEr to be—namely, that the person's mind or seat of consciousness in fact separates from the physical body in an NDE and reunites with it when the person is revived. This explanation can account for all the paranormal characteristics of NDEs and all the paranormal cases described in this book.

Are Near-Death Experiences Objectively Real?

The power of this collection of paranormal cases is seen in the ability to address questions that could not be approached adequately with only one or two cases. With several similar cases, the particular paranormal aspect can be generalized and the argument can be made that the paranormal aspect is *real* in some meaningful sense.

Long before this book was published, we had sought to answer the question: Are there *objective* validations that NDEs are real, that a nonmaterial aspect of the person actually separates from the physical body? If, in the NDEr's *subjective* experience, the mind or locus of consciousness separates from the body while still perceiving the material realm, there should be some *objective* evidence whereby another person reports an objective effect that confirms the separate "mind-entity."

Indeed, such paranormal cases exist, and we had, in our studies, assembled several cases in which objective evidence was suggested. But the cases we found were relatively weak, and we were unsure whether other important instances of this sort had been lost in the ever-increasing NDE literature.

Indeed, it turns out that there was an entire class of cases of which we were completely unaware. When we received the outline of this book's contents, this new type of case—which we call "apparitional NDEs"—just popped out.

In the end, we found *two* types of cases in this book that seem to us to be most evidential in suggesting that the NDEr's sense of separation is objectively real. The first type of case we call a "shared NDE"; one case of this type is included in this book (Case 3.32).

In a shared NDE, a healthy person observes the NDEr's transition out of body and observes other aspects of the event that match the NDEr's subjective experience. Shared NDEs are very similar to *shared-death experiences* (SDEs), as described in Raymond Moody's 2010 book, *Glimpses of Eternity*. In an SDE, a person is dying in the presence of one or several others. These loved ones or friends of the dying person themselves experience elements very similar to an NDE—there is unusual light and music. They may observe a mist or shape leaving the person's body. They are sometimes drawn out of their own bodies and are with the dying person, out of body. They may observe the life review of the dying person. A tunnel may open, and deceased relatives may greet the dying person and escort the person into the tunnel.

In an SDE, the person dies. A *shared NDE* is a similar phenomenon except that the dying person does not die but returns to the physical body and has experienced an NDE.

In Case 3.32, Jan Price was having a heart attack at home. The paramedics were called. She suffered a cardiac arrest on the gurney, and during the paramedics' resuscitation procedure, her husband, John, who was perfectly healthy, observed Jan's solid form leave her physical body and rise up, dressed in a flowing, green gown. Then their recently deceased, beloved dog, Maggi, appeared briefly to John. Jan experienced leaving her body, rising above it, and then her dog appearing. Jan had other veridical perceptions of her resuscitation that were verified by the paramedics.

In this case, the elements of Jan's and John's observations—Jan leaving her physical body and rising up and their deceased dog appearing—matched exactly. So in a shared NDE, another person objectively observes the same things that the NDEr experienced and, in particular, observes the NDEr as a localized, nonmaterial entity that is separated from the physical body.

The second type of case we are calling "apparitional NDEs," of which there are several cases in Chapter 7, both from previous centuries and from contemporary times. The NDEr, while out of body, visits and communicates with a living person, and both accounts are subsequently verified to be consistent with one another.

One of these cases is Olga Gearhardt's (Case 7.3). In 1989, Olga underwent heart transplant surgery. All of her family came to the hospital to await the outcome, except her son-in-law who could not be at the hospital. The heart transplant was successful, but at 2:15 a.m., her new heart stopped beating, and it took 3 hours to resuscitate her heart and then longer still for her to recover consciousness. The son-in-law, who was sleeping at home, awoke at exactly 2:15 a.m., and Olga was standing at his bedside. Thinking that the surgery had not taken place, he asked her how she was. She replied, "I am fine. I'm going to be all right. There's nothing for any of you to worry about." Then she disappeared. The son-in-law wrote down the time and exactly what was said, and he went back to sleep.

When Olga regained consciousness, her first words were, "Did you get the message?" Olga later reported that she had left her body and had tried but was unable to communicate with the family members who were all asleep in the hospital waiting room, so she went to the son-in-law, with whom she succeeded in communicating. Melvin Morse and Paul Perry thoroughly verified these details, including the note the son-in-law had scribbled.

Another "apparitional NDE" case is from physician Laurin Bellg (Case 7.5). In 2011, Dr. Bellg was treating a woman in the hospital intensive care unit who was dying of cancer. The woman refused to have her son visit her in the hospital. The son had been estranged from the family for 25 years because of certain financial deals he had made that had harmed the family. The mother continued to feel a lot of animosity toward her son.

So the son is sitting in a bar one afternoon. His mother is dying, he is deep in remorse and regret, and he is crying. He sees his mother coming into the bar. He is elated and gets up to greet her, but the bar is crowded and his vision is blocked for a moment, and then she is no longer there. The mother wakes up that same afternoon and tells her daughter, "I had the strangest dream. I saw my son in a bar. He got up and started to come to me. I got scared and woke up." Later that evening, the daughter spoke with her brother, who told her about seeing their mother earlier come into the bar and then disappear. The daughter related both stories to Dr. Bellg, who then confirmed the details with both the mother and the son. The details of both stories matched.

In all three of these cases, a healthy person objectively perceives the NDEr as a nonmaterial entity existing independent of the physical body. In these cases, the NDE is not just an event perceived subjectively by the experiencer but is also an observation perceived objectively by a healthy person, and the two perceptions match exactly.

The apparitional NDE cases are particularly compelling because the NDEr has a strong desire to visit another person, the NDEr appears to the person as a physical presence, and the NDEr may communicate something. The interaction is corroborated in all details by both parties. These cases strongly suggest that the mind or spirit of the NDEr has an *objective* existence, especially (a) when the two accounts are corroborated as happening at the same time, (b) when all the observed details of the interaction match, and (c) when information is communicated or the NDEr's presence is made known.

The Power of Numbers

In compiling and organizing these veridical paranormal cases, the authors of this book have made possible analyses such as those described in the preceding section of this foreword. The juxtaposition of similar cases permits a detailed analysis that is often necessary to find the common elements among them and to make valid generalizations.

We believe that because of the paranormal nature of the cases in this book, a healthy skepticism is essential for the reader considering them. For many people, these cases will not fit into their existing conceptual framework or paradigm, whether that is a materialist viewpoint, a fundamental religious viewpoint, or even a "spiritual" viewpoint. These cases will stretch even the most flexible thinking. So in reading these pages, it is important to keep an open mind, exercise intellectual honesty, and let the phenomenon speak for itself.

The opposite—a closed-minded pseudoskepticism—is also a possible response to these cases. In the extreme, pseudoskeptics seek to fit the phenomenon into their existing paradigm by cherry-picking certain facts, dismissing others, and ignoring the rest. Indeed, when one's mind is made up, any alternate explanation must be incorrect and the facts do not need to be considered. The last chapter of this book contains a number of examples of such responses.

The power of a large number of cases of one type, assembled together, makes it exponentially more difficult for pseudoskeptics to dismiss this evidence as mere anecdotes, to write them off as fraud or confabulation, or to make ad hoc arguments that are specific to only one or a few cases. At the same time, the power of a large number of cases with similar characteristics makes the validity of a hypothesis that explains all aspects of all the cases exponentially stronger.

It is our hope that this book will now foster this higher level of analysis and a higher level of discourse in the field of near-death studies.

Chapel Hill, North Carolina

Spring 2016

Robert G. Mays and Suzanne B. Mays are independent NDE researchers.

References

Holden, J. M. (2009). Veridical perception in near-death experiences. In J. M. Holden, B. Greyson, & D. James (Eds.), *The handbook of near-death experiences: Thirty years of investigation* (pp. 185–212). Santa Barbara, CA: Praeger/ABC-CLIO.

Mitchell-Yellin, B., & Fischer, J. M. (2014). The near-death experience argument against physicalism: A critique. *Journal of Consciousness Studies, 21*(7–8), 158–183.

Moody, R. A., Jr. (1975). *Life after life.* Atlanta, GA: Mockingbird Press.

Moody, R. A., Jr. (with Perry, P.). (2010). *Glimpses of eternity: An investigation into shared death experiences.* New York, NY: Guideposts.

Ritchie, G. G. (with Sherrill, E.). (1978/2007). *Return from tomorrow.* Grand Rapids, MI: Chosen Books.

University of California, Riverside. (n.d.). *The science, philosophy, and theology of immortality.* Retrieved from http://www.sptimmortalityproject.com/

van Lommel, P. (2013). Non-local consciousness: A concept based on scientific research on near-death experiences during cardiac arrest. *Journal of Consciousness Studies, 20*(1–2), 7–48.

Introduction

*Scientific research has shown that consciousness can indeed be
experienced independently of the body without brain function.*
—Pim van Lommel, MD, *Consciousness Beyond Life*

This book is intended for anyone with a broad interest in the human mind, near-death experiences (NDEs), and parapsychological phenomena. The approach is scientific and focuses on serious parapsychological evidence. At the same time, no special prior knowledge is necessary to be able to read the book. Our purpose is to examine what comprises the serious case-oriented evidence of parapsychological, or paranormal, phenomena involved in NDEs and to try to draw conclusions from this evidence.

The book came about as a collaborative project facilitated by three organizations: the Athanasia Foundation, the Merkawah Foundation / Near-Death Experience Network, and the not-for-profit association Limen/IANDS Flanders. (IANDS is the International Association for Near-Death Studies that originated in the United States.)

The Athanasia Foundation is a parapsychological, philosophical, and psychological organization, founded in 1996 in Nijmegen, Netherlands, to address questions such as personal life after death, spiritual evolution, reincarnation, and the relationship between body and soul. Titus Rivas and Anny Dirven have been affiliated with Athanasia for many years, as has Rudolf Smit. Under that banner, we conduct our own investigations and study of literature. The Merkawah Foundation was founded in 1988 in the Netherlands to target NDEs and the people who had them, providing information and support in addition to research. In 2014, the Merkawah Foundation became the Near-Death Experience Network. Limen, founded in 1997 in Belgium, is a sister organization to Merkawah.

For many years, apart from a 2-year interlude during which Jacqueline Schippers assumed the tasks, Rudolf Smit has been the editor of Merkawah's publication *Terugkeer* (Return). Since 2003, Smit has encouraged Titus Rivas and Anny Dirven in their production of articles for the journal, which led to the publication in 2010 of the collection *Van en naar het Licht* (From and to the Light).

All three of us are members of what was called the "Science Group," focusing on NDEs and associated topics, which was set up through Merkawah. During one of the group meetings, we proffered the idea that we could put together in book form an overview of the main published NDEs that have possible parapsychological or paranormal aspects. It was to be about the "core" cases in this field. After some time, Merkawah officially gave us the green light to produce such a book, which would be a fruit borne of the collaboration between the two foundations. Limen has worked closely with Merkawah for some time, and so the project is also associated with Limen. This collaboration is tangibly expressed in the fact that the foreword to the original book was written by Limen's chair, Stan Michielsens. His foreword is joined in this English edition by a second foreword by Robert and Suzanne Mays.

The book consists of chapters that each cast light on a different paranormal aspect of NDEs. Every instance involves "anomalous" phenomena that do not fit into a materialistic worldview, in that according to that worldview, consciousness or mind is utterly restricted and determined by what happens in the brain. In most cases, "extrasensory perception," which consists of clairvoyance and telepathy, is involved (Chapters 1 through 4), although there are also chapters on the observations during an NDE of those who have died (Chapters 5 and 6), on the clinically dead patient as observed by others (Chapter 7), on paranormal healing (Chapter 8), and on paranormal abilities as a result of the NDE (Chapter 9). In most instances, a case illustrated only one of our topics, so we presented it in its relevant chapter. If it illustrated two topics, we presented it twice: once in each relevant chapter. We numbered cases by chapter and sequence, such as Case 2.1, 2.2, and so on. A case that appears in two or more chapters is numbered in the context of each chapter; thus the same case might be numbered 2.2 and 3.7—with the latter referring back to previous citations ("Case 3.7 [see also Case 2.2]"). If a case involves observation of events with no outstanding feature, it is titled by the experiencer's name or pseudonym; if it includes a unique feature, the title refers to that feature.

We opted for clear, succinct summaries of the NDEs that we included, obviously highlighting the possibly paranormal elements of the experience.

Whenever appropriate and relevant, we also briefly addressed discussions that have gone on or are still going on in the professional literature regarding particular cases.

The cases in this book are a product of a thorough investigation of the literature, in which we were ably assisted by Ms. Inge Manussen. We also significantly benefited from Janice (Jan) Miner Holden's 2009 overview of cases as well as from our own empirical research, which is more generally provided in *Van en naar het Licht*. Rudolf Smit and Titus Rivas also participated in a yet-to-be-published rating of cases in a study being conducted by IANDS past president Holden.

Our criterion for including a case was that a patient's report of a paranormal phenomenon during an NDE be directly confirmed by at least one other person. We limited ourselves in this book specifically to such confirmed cases. This restriction certainly does not mean that we have no affinity for other cases. As we mentioned earlier, this overview is intended to be a presentation of just the *core* of published NDEs with paranormal aspects.

Janice (Jan) Miner Holden, EdD

Of course, it is possible that we overlooked certain cases. If we have, we call on readers to let us know. We also invite readers who themselves have had—or who know others who have had—NDEs with confirmed paranormal features to send us their accounts.

The book concludes in Chapter 10 with a general discussion and in Chapter 11 with a very interesting broader treatment by Rudolf Smit of the way in which the so-called skeptics have dealt with NDEs.

Controversy

Since the publication of the bestseller *Consciousness Beyond Life* by cardiologist Pim van Lommel (2010), NDEs have captured the imagination more than ever before. In the context of this book, "NDE" refers to an experience someone had while he or she was observed to be unconscious and clinically dead or in another severely life-threatening state. All kinds of experiences in various ways resemble this type of "real" NDE, and we have written about these in *Van en naar het Licht* and elsewhere, but these experiences will not be addressed in this book.

Researcher and author Pim van Lommel has been praised as well as maligned by the media. His supporters and detractors have meanwhile engaged in countless discussions about the most disparate aspects of the phenomenon of NDEs.

Some commentators have focused specifically on the spiritual implications of NDEs, whereas others have been particularly interested in a possible revolution in the scientific worldview. More conventional authors, such as anesthesiologist Gerald Woerlee (2005), psychologist Susan Blackmore (1993), and neurologist Kevin Nelson (2011), have argued on the contrary that NDEs can easily be understood and accommodated with a regular, naturalistic view of human beings. In their view, consciousness and mind depend entirely on the physiological processes in the brain. Such authors consider NDEs to be no more than a kind of reassuring spasm of a dying brain. The brain apparently dishes up an attractive—or, in the less common case of distressing NDEs, a horrifying—illusion of the hereafter for people in the event of a life-threatening situation.

Naturalism here generally means a worldview based on the assumption that all of reality is a product of mindless, physical processes. If there were a mind that could not be reduced to the physiology of the brain, no matter: That mind would still be utterly bound to that physiology. In this theory, it is unthinkable from the outset that people actually leave their bodies mentally during an NDE and that they can then receive accurate extrasensory impressions.

In constructing their theories, skeptics like Gerald Woerlee and Susan Blackmore have explicitly linked them to a rejection of the—in Woerlee's opinion—outdated notion of an immaterial soul. This philosophical position is revealed, for example, by the title of a recent book by Woerlee (2013a): *Illusory Souls*.

One of the central discussions in the professional literature focuses on the question of whether NDEs not only signal the existence of another or broader reality, the way a painting or a dream can, but also are evidence of such a reality in and of themselves. Even though NDEs may often be profound and entail impressions of a spiritual reality usually perceived to be beautiful, are they not rooted in generally accepted psychological processes, just like the average (day) dream is? Or are there aspects to NDEs that would indicate there is more going on than mere imaginings?

Near-Death Experiences and Parapsychology

One can approach these questions either phenomenologically or objectively. According to the first, phenomenological or empathetic approach, one seeks the answer in the lived experiences of those involved. If *they* experienced it this way, they really did, for instance, leave their bodies and step into another dimension; the subjective reality of their experiences already suffices. From such a perspective, scholars go too far when they critically analyze NDEs or wonder whether the experience can be psychologically (never mind neuropsychologically) explained away. This kind of analysis, which calls into question the integrity of a person's subjective experience, disrespects the experiencer; one's subjective experience is considered valid in and of itself and should not be diminished by being challenged.

With the second, objective approach, one examines the empirically objective or intersubjective evidence that will or will not demonstrate the presence of one or more *anomalies*. An anomaly is generally a phenomenon that does not fit into a particular theoretical framework—in this case, *materialism*, a form of naturalism, the proponents of which argue that all of reality is physical.

Within materialism, there are various major schools of thought:

- According to *reductive materialists*, or reductionists, mind and consciousness can be "reduced" to neurological processes in the brain.
- According to *eliminative materialists*, mind and consciousness are antiquated concepts that no longer have a place in today's scientific language. Mind and consciousness do not really exist; they are just "words" that need to be tossed or "eliminated."
- According to *nonreductive materialists*, there is such a thing as a mind or a consciousness, but only as a kind of "holistic" phenomenon that correlates directly to the complex organization of the brain. Just as with other holistic phenomena, mind cannot be reduced to the underlying processes, although the mind depends on the neurological processes on which it is constructed. Mind, in its activity, is restricted by the brain's condition, so if the brain quits, the mind automatically exits the stage.

(This perspective also applies to so-called property dualism, a closely related naturalistic school of thought that equates mind with assumed nonmaterial attributes of the brain. If the brain dies, its assumed nonmaterial attributes also vanish.)

Within these major schools of thought, there are again countless subschools. In one respect, however, all the movements within materialism concur: *No matter what, there is no mind that can actually go beyond the limits of the material brain.*

An anomaly that would counter this central argument must show that the mind *can* extend beyond the limitations of the material brain. An approach that centers on anomalies of this kind is termed a *parapsychological approach*, where parapsychology, or psychic (psychical) research, should be understood in the broadest sense to be the science of anomalies involving mind, consciousness, or soul.[1] This approach requires a nonmaterialistic thought context or ontology (philosophical theory of the ultimate nature of reality) such as interactionist dualism or substance dualism. Proponents of this philosophical perspective hold that there are two kinds of phenomena (dualism)—physical phenomena and nonphysical (mental) phenomena; that nonphysical phenomena interact with the physical ones (interactionism); and that there is a substantial nonphysical being (soul, mind, psyche, consciousness) that can still be there after the death of the body (substantialism). Another ontology that fits well with this parapsychological approach is ontological idealism: the view that everything that exists actually is ultimately and essentially mental or psychic in nature, including the entire physical world. In other words, from this perspective, consciousness is primary, and there is no matter outside the mind or consciousness. To summarize, materialists believe that matter is primary and that all phenomena, including consciousness, are identical to material interactions, whereas ontological idealists believe that consciousness is primary and that the material world is a manifestation of consciousness.

---

1. We use *parapsychology* in its original, broad definition and therefore as a synonym of psychic research, rather than in the narrow, modern meaning of "experimental research into Psi (ESP and psychokinesis)." We are aware that this terminology may be unusual for English-language readers. In the English-speaking world, the term *psychic* (or *psychical*, outside of the United States and Canada) is usually reserved for case-oriented research, including research into phenomena suggestive of survival after death, whereas *parapsychology* is reserved for experimental investigations of the clairvoyant, telepathic, and psychokinetic capacities of the living. However, the term parapsychology, or *parapsychologie* in France, Germany, the Netherlands, was already in use before the present-day, one-sided focus on experimentation and Psi in the living arose.

It should be noted that not everyone uses this definition of parapsychology. Ironically enough, there are also (preponderantly) materialistic viewpoints—such as that of Dutch parapsychologist Dick Bierman, who asserted that parapsychology should not be focused on phenomena whereby the mind operates beyond the limits of the brain. Instead, he and others have argued for expanding the current picture of physical reality so that some parapsychological (or "paraphysical") phenomena will henceforth fit into it. This perspective usually means that, like other materialists, its proponents adhere to the argument that the mind is entirely dependent on the brain, and on the whole they do not entertain evidence that counters this position. For example, a few years ago, Bierman proclaimed that spontaneous cases of consciousness during cardiac arrest, even if the perceptions involved had been verified, could never provide sufficiently solid evidence to change his mind.

Generally, the terms "parapsychological" and "paranormal" can be used interchangeably. However, when combined with specific experiences, we will usually use the term "paranormal"; so we will say "parapsychological phenomena" (phenomena that belong to the field of parapsychology) or "paranormal phenomena," although we will refer to "paranormal perceptions" rather than to "parapsychological perceptions" when we mean extrasensory perceptions. The word combination "parapsychological perceptions" seems to refer instead to a parapsychologist's perceptions or observations rather than to an experiencer's extrasensory perception that involves a parapsychological phenomenon. Examples of parapsychological or paranormal phenomena (in the broad, continental European sense of "phenomena studied by psychic researchers and/or experimental parapsychologists" used in this book) are telepathy, psychokinesis, clairvoyance, (actual) memories of a past life, (real) experiences out of the physical body, healing through visualizations, and (real) contact with those who have died.

It should be noted that a parapsychological approach (according to our definition) certainly does not rule out attention to or respect for people's lived experiences. In fact, it is part of the moral code of bona fide parapsychological researchers, or researchers of psychic phenomena, to always deal with respondents respectfully, not only acknowledging but also honoring their subjective experiences as absolutely real to them.

The main focus of parapsychological, or psychic, research on NDEs is obviously their parapsychological or paranormal aspects. These then are generally aspects that do not fit into a materialistic worldview. The point is to document paranormal phenomena that arise during or as a result of an NDE in the best possible way and to interpret them in a nonmaterialistic theoretical framework.

The English translation of the title of the original Dutch version of this book is "What a Dying Brain Can't Do." That title was inspired by the dying brain hypothesis of materialists like Susan Blackmore (1993). Her theory holds that NDEs are a kind of hallucination that arises as a result of the process of the brain dying. Our title was also inspired by the title of a book by the American philosopher Hubert Dreyfus (1978): *What Computers Can't Do*. In a critique of artificial intelligence, he identified characteristics of the human mind that have no parallels in how computers operate. In this book, we reflect on aspects of NDEs that cannot be explained by current models of how the brain functions—whether that brain belongs to a person who is living or dying.

Focusing on paranormal aspects is very compatible with an interest in other aspects, such as the spiritual message or the psychological consequences of NDEs. Starting with the parapsychological questions themselves, however, researchers focus on paranormal experiences that in principle can be confirmed—wholly or in part—by others. So, in this light, it is not enough for people *themselves* to believe that their NDEs must somehow be called "paranormal." Rather, the paranormal content of their NDEs must be verifiable by one or more witnesses.

A line should be drawn in other respects, too. A spiritual transformation after an NDE or changes in personality might be experienced by many people as "miraculous," but in theory it is still conceivable that "merely" unconscious psychological processes underlie such transformations or changes. In that case, an NDE could be comparable to an extraordinary spiritual dream, hypnotic session, or visualization. Of course, materialists generally acknowledge that such phenomena exist, and there do not appear to be any convincing reasons to consider them anomalies. We therefore decided not to include in this book attention to the transformative aftereffects of NDEs, no matter how miraculous they may be in and of themselves.

Within parapsychology, or psychic research, investigators are open not just to positive evidence but also to the possibility that the description of a specific experience is not accurate. They are absolutely aware that evidence must be verified as much as possible, because the mere presentation of a specific experience is not necessarily correct. Indeed, the professional literature includes cases that were later confirmed to be fraudulent. A recent example concerns the book *The Scalpel and the Soul* by neuroscientist Allan J. Hamilton (2009; Rivas, 2009a). The author feigned having discovered a new NDE case that was extremely persuasive evidentially. In that case, the patient, Sarah Gideon, purportedly observed all kinds of things beyond her physical senses while it was certain that she exhibited no brain activity. Fact-checking revealed that the woman in question did not even exist. Dr. Hamilton had fabricated the account based on well-known existing cases. Prior to this example, at the end of the 1980s, physician Larry Dossey also published a case of a nonexistent patient whom he, ironically, also called Sarah. According to Dr. Dossey, she had been blind all her life, but during her NDE she was still able to watch the medical activities surrounding her resuscitation. In this case, too, she was a fabricated woman who was "composed" of existing patients. Both authors claimed to have put together the nonexistent Sarahs to make readers aware of the spectacular phenomena that really can occur in NDEs. They evidently did not realize that they were mostly giving themselves, and potentially the field of near-death studies, a bad name.

In another case of apparently unintentional fraud cited in the book *Mindsight* (Ring & Cooper, 1999), social psychologist Kenneth Ring and coauthor Sharon Cooper included an appendix (pp. 189–201) that was an NDE account taken from www.nderf.org. They included a short note to the appendix titled "Author's Advisory" that reads:

> Readers are advised to disregard entirely the Author's Note and Appendix in which a case of a blind woman who purported to have an NDE is described. The case, which came to our attention at the last moment, was provided to us by another researcher, Dr. Tricia McGill, who is the only person to investigate it. Subsequent to the publication of this book, however, we discovered, to our chagrin, that this case has fraudulent aspects and is not reliable. Dr. McGill, who offered this account to us in good faith, now believes she was deceived by the woman in question, and has apologized to us for having inadvertently supplied us with an untrustworthy report.

A more recent case of fraud involved the apparently fabricated NDE of Alex Malarkey, who in 2004 supposedly visited heaven as a result of a car accident. Malarkey alleged at the beginning of 2015 that he had not, in fact, had an NDE at all and that the book that was written about it, *The Boy Who Came Back From Heaven* (Malarkey, 2011), was based on pure fantasy. Malarkey indicated that he concocted the story because he craved attention. The book has meanwhile been taken off of bookstore shelves. Another name-related irony in this case is that the word *malarkey* means deceptive communication. Seasoned researchers take all these forms of deception sufficiently into account and do not feel the need to defend overly controversial claims if there are strong indications that the claims are not based on the truth.

Sometimes this requirement of an open yet critical attitude gets confused with the attitude of so-called skeptics. Such skepticism should not be confused with the neutral concept of open-minded criticism. In modern parlance, skeptics are people who believe that there is no such thing as a "miracle" or, in any event, that miracles are not scientifically plausible. Such skeptics may have different backgrounds. Although most skeptics seem to be materialistically oriented, we are also familiar with skeptics who have Christian or Hindu backgrounds and even esoteric skeptics who might have an anthroposophical philosophy of life. These latter adherents appear to have particular trouble with phenomena that might compete with "revelations" or with an esoteric method of knowing ("vision") that they consider to be the only valid source of information about nonmaterial phenomena. Somehow many skeptics—regardless of their particular views on life—share a closed, dogmatic attitude regarding paranormal phenomena. The term "skepticism" still includes both debunkers as well as those having an open, critical, and inquiring attitude; however, members of the latter group come much closer to the actual Greek root of the term skepticism. By contrast to skeptics in the modern parlance, but in line with *skeptic* in the original Greek sense, investigators engaged in parapsychology, or psychic research (in its actual, original sense), are open to the possibility that actual paranormal phenomena may occur in NDEs and that these phenomena might be verified by scientific evidence.

Moreover, parapsychological, or "psychical," researchers usually do not commit the error in their thinking of assuming that *reality itself* coincides with *what can be demonstrated about reality*. The fact that one may never be able to completely examine reality scientifically should not dissuade one from remaining open to new evidence. An important critical stance is a combination of openness and discernment that could be termed "rationality."

Kinds of Evidence

There are roughly two views of the proper scientific method in the empirical sciences. Some researchers argue that in any kind of investigation, one should strive to *stimulate* or elicit phenomena using the experimental method, whereby all the conditions under which the phenomenon occurs are kept under control as much as possible. When, for whatever reason, this procedure cannot be performed in practice, investigators must strive toward an approach that is as close as possible to the experimental method. This, in fact, is the attitude behind the worldwide AWARE (AWAreness during REsuscitation) Study headed up by physicians Sam Parnia, Peter Fenwick, Stephen Holgate, Robert Peveler, and others. Reflecting research methods from five similar studies dating back to the late 1980s, they are attempting to determine whether patients are able during an NDE to see visual targets: pictures placed outside their physical field of vision but presumably within an NDE field of perception. In early 2013, Parnia published a book titled *Erasing Death* in the United States and *The Lazarus Effect* in the United Kingdom, in which he discussed the initial results of this investigation. Several new (not previously published) pieces of evidence for the continuation of consciousness during cardiac arrest that meet our own criterion of external confirmation do, indeed, appear in this book.

Until now, however, not one patient—in this or any of the previous studies—has observed the visual targets. In other words, experimentally, even this most recent study has not yet produced evidence of an experimental nature. Parnia (2013) therefore argued for adapting the experimental setup in a follow-up study. In December 2014, various aspects of Parnia's study that he had reported were reiterated in an AWARE Study report in the peer-reviewed journal *Resuscitation*.

This method involving visual targets, preferred by investigators like Parnia and his predecessors, conforms to earlier experimental (parapsychological) investigation of extrasensory perception during intentionally produced out-of-body experiences (OBEs). During an OBE, a person perceives his or her consciousness to be functioning outside of the physical body; though the experience is usually spontaneous, as during an NDE or circumstances not involved in a close brush with death, some people report they are able to induce the experience at will. Probably the most well-known example of a positive result in investigation of such individuals is that of parapsychologist Charles Tart's research subject, Miss Z, who observed a number containing five digits during an OBE (see "Two Investigations Into Out-of-Body Experiences," https://youtube.com/watch?v=UwmZ1JohClc). Other famous test subjects in this area are Stefan Ossowiecki, Alex Tanous, Ingo Swann, and Keith (Stuart Blue) Harary. Some of the field's best-known investigators are Stanley Krippner, Karlis Osis, and Robert (Bob) Monroe, the last of whom experimented particularly with his own OBEs. In Spain a few years ago, successful out-of-body experiments were conducted by someone using the nickname "qbeac."

According to proponents of the experimental approach, the closer investigators stick to the ideal of experimental research, the more scientific—and, therefore, the more credible—the investigation is. Convinced of this perspective, proponents can go so far as to believe that *only* experimental research can really be called "science." All other kinds of investigation, then, are based on *anecdotes*, which can at best offer a rationale for "real" scientific research, although they themselves are not classified as such research.

Proponents of another view hold that the experimental method simply is not equally suitable for all scientific fields. Some phenomena can rarely, if at all, be summoned on command. For these types of phenomena, it might be better to examine spontaneous cases that are studied or reconstructed as much as possible. According to this view, these different methods are *complementary*, and the experimental method does not constitute the sole or ultimate criterion for scientific research. So, from this perspective, it is wrong to dismiss all the evidence that is not experimental as purely "anecdotal" and thus unscientific. It is possible to document someone's story and to support it with third-party witness statements. From this perspective, the more evidence there is that a particular NDE entails verified paranormal aspects, the stronger that "case" becomes.

We are explicitly among the proponents of this second view. Obviously, we think it is fantastic when evidence of paranormal aspects of NDEs is collected under strictly controlled circumstances. But that does not mean that all other cases automatically become unscientific. There are simply many kinds of evidence, and they can all have scientific value. For Parnia's investigation, this perspective would mean that specific cases of extrasensory perception that, strictly speaking, do not meet his experimental requirements should still be considered scientific evidence.

Reducing scientific evidence to experimental evidence logically implies taking an agnostic position regarding phenomena that cannot be demonstrated experimentally. Notably, if not surprisingly, skeptics usually do not assume this agnostic view, opting instead for a militant naturalism. This stance applies to leading authors like Susan Blackmore, whom we mentioned before, and Kevin Nelson, as well as other current-parlance skeptical spokespersons such as Dick Swaab, Michael Shermer, and the late Rob Nanninga. From a purely rational perspective, however, it is either/or: Either one seriously accepts as evidence case studies of reported phenomena that can be duly investigated as cases or one takes an agnostic position with respect to the reality of those phenomena (Barrington, 1999).

Besides the experimental and case-oriented approach, there is also the possibility of investigating reported NDEs for patterns. Through this process, investigators can, for instance, try to determine just which attributes NDEs might have in common. This method is important for finding out whether something like an NDE phenomenon exists at all. It is also important to be able to systematically compare NDEs with related phenomena such as the preexistence memories of young children (memories of a nonphysical existence as a spiritual being without a physical body, prior to conception or birth) and to compare NDEs across cultures. The possible outcome that they strongly correspond with each other could indicate a common or comparable source or cause of the experiences. We are, however, of the opinion that encountering patterns in large numbers of NDEs is not in and of itself enough to determine whether NDEs have paranormal aspects. Rather, we believe that proper investigation of paranormal aspects must involve evidence at the level of the individual case. We differ in this respect from experts such as radiation oncologist Jeffrey Long (2011) and his wife and colleague, attorney Jody Long, even though we sincerely value their work in other respects.

And finally, we offer this point. Critics of this book should know that we certainly are not under the illusion that we did not make any mistakes in our case summaries. However, if critics do find errors, we request that they ask themselves how important those errors are in light of all the information presented; minor errors presumably would not nullify an otherwise substantial amount of material. In any event, we will correct in any future edition any errata of which we become aware.

References

Barrington, M. R. (1999). *What is proof? The assessment of past events.* Retrieved from http://parapsychologie.ac.at/programm/ss1999/barringt/proof_txt.htm

Blackmore, S. J. (1993). *Dying to live: Near-death experiences.* Amherst, NY: Prometheus Books.

Dreyfus, H. L. (1978). *What computers can't do: The limits of artificial intelligence.* New York, NY: HarperCollins.

Hamilton, A. J. (2009). *The scalpel and the soul: Encounters with surgery, the super-natural, and the healing power of hope.* New York: NY: Jeremy P. Tarcher/Penguin.

Long, J. (with Perry, P.). (2011). *Evidence of the afterlife: The science of near-death experiences.* New York, NY: HarperCollins.

Malarkey, K. (2011). *The boy who came back from heaven: A remarkable account of miracles, angels, and life beyond this world.* Carol Stream, IL: Tyndale Momentum.

Nelson, K. (2011). *The spiritual doorway in the brain: A neurologist's search for the god experience.* New York, NY: Dutton.

Parnia, S. (with Young, J.). (2013). *Erasing death: The science that is rewriting the boundaries between life and death.* New York, NY: HarperCollins.

Parnia, S., Spearpoint, K., de Vos, G., Fenwick, P., Goldberg, D., Yang, J., . . . & Schoenfeld, E. R. (2014). AWARE—AWAreness during REsuscitation—A prospective study. *Resuscitation, 85*(12), 1799–1805.

Ring, K., & Cooper, S. (1999). *Mindsight: Near-death and out-of-body experiences in the blind.* Palo Alto, CA: William James Center for Consciousness Studies at the Institute of Transpersonal Psychology; (2008; 2nd ed.). Bloomington, IN: iUniverse.

Rivas, T. (2009a). *The scalpel and the soul: Encounters with surgery, the supernatural, and the healing power of hope,* by Allan J. Hamilton (Book review). *Journal of Near-Death Studies, 27*(4), 255–259.

Rivas, T., & Dirven, A. (2010a). *Van en naar het Licht* [From and to the Light]. Leeuwarden, Netherlands: Uitgeverij Elikser.

van Lommel, P. (2010). *Consciousness beyond life: The science of the near-death experience.* New York, NY: HarperCollins.

Woerlee, G. M. (2005). *Mortal minds: The biology of near-death experiences.* Amherst, NY: Prometheus Books.

Woerlee, G. M. (2013a). *Illusory souls* [Kindle ed.]. Amazon Digital Services: Author.

Acknowledgments

First of all, we thank Inge Manussen for her excellent work regarding the various cases included in the book. Then we want to explicitly thank a number of people for their inspiration and help, including the late Ian Stevenson, Tyler Scott Anderson, Jan Holden, Jeffrey Long, Toon Pruyn, Ariadne Belmer, Ian Wardell, Larry Kiggundu, George Graves-Sampson, Alian Namaki, Kees van Emmerik, Joop Nauta, Stephan Vollenberg, Bert Stoop, Roland Hoedemaekers, Hicham Karroue, Tilly Gerritsma, Musa van den Heuvel, Robert and Suzanne Mays, Carlos Alvarado, Penny Sartori, Kirti Swaroop Rawat, Lida Uittenbogaard, Wim van Grimbergen, Feniks van Grimbergen, Chris Canter, Chris Carter, Mark Janssen, Jan Kox, Diana Schillemans, Hettie Pols, Max Pols, Mats Tegel, Masayuki Ohkado, Kim Kok, Robin Timmers, Arif Demirbas, Sylvia Lucia, Maria Fernandes Rodrigues, Enrique Vargas, Richard Krebber, Erlendur Haraldsson, Annekatrin Puhle, Frans Gieles, Constantia Oomen, Jime Sayaka, Andrew Paquette, Stephen Woodhead, TG, Pam Reynolds, Robert Spetzler, Karl A. Greene, Bruce Greyson, Laurin Bellg, John Kruth, Norman Hansen, Karen Newell, Eben Alexander, Cherylee Black, L. Suzanne Gordon, Dean Radin, Stephen Braude, Doug D'Elia, Bobbie Ann Pimm, George Weissmann, Emine Fougner, Hiroyoshi Takata, Miguel Ángel Pertierra Quesada, Kimberly Clark Sharp, Baroness Andrea von Wilmowsky, Mike Milligan, Roberto Amado-Cattaneo, Tom Aufderheide, Michael Sabom, Dominique Surel, Vitor Moura, Alex Tsakiris, Wilfried Kuhn, Joachim Nicolay, Monica Williams-Murphy, Òscar Morent, Raymond Moody, Cheryl Moody, Huriye Kacar, P.M.H. Atwater, David Rousseau, Mario Beauregard, Neil Carman, Elizabeth Carman, Abhijat van Bilsen, Antoine Janssen, Hein van Dongen, and (saving the best for last) Corrie Rivas-Wols.

Pim van Lommel, Sam Parnia, Peter Fenwick, and Niclas K. each made a special contribution by actively thinking along with us and discussing the argumentation for particular interpretations of different types of cases.

If people think we mistakenly left them off the list, they are probably right. We apologize!

Thanks to IANDS, Netwerk NDE, and the many donors who donated to cover the cost of producing this English edition.

We are also very grateful to everyone who read the original manuscript critically but with goodwill, including Ruud van Wees, Hans van Geel, and Jacqueline Schippers of the Merkawah Foundation / NDE Network Science Group; Christophor (Bob) Coppes, author and former chair of Merkawah (now Near-Death Experience Network); Jart Voortman; and of course our Dutch publisher, Jitske Kingma of Elikser.

The Authors
Nijmegen / Budel / Zwolle, Netherlands
Spring 2016

A Few Remarks on the English Translation

We are delighted and very proud that people who should know what constitutes a worthy publication apparently found our book interesting enough to be translated into English. Consequently, we owe many thanks not only to the translator, Wanda Boeke, and our Dutch publisher, Jitske Kingma, but also to Robert and Suzanne Mays, Jan Holden, and James Clement van Pelt. They jumped in to get an English version produced that would appeal to an English-language readership as well as to an international audience.

Although the English translation gave us an opportunity to use a new title, the content of the book deviates very little from the Dutch original. Some new passages and quite a few cases have been added, and we made a few changes to correct inadvertently misunderstood details. No cases were dropped from the Dutch edition in compiling the English one. We did shift a few cases to different chapters because, on later review, they fit even better there.

As far as listing sources goes, we always restricted ourselves to the books, articles, video clips, or interviews that addressed a case or theoretical discussion. We did not list the specific numbers of the pages from which we cited—not because we were lazy but because many of our source books have come out in different editions, and we often used translations, so specific page numbers would be accurate for only those sources—to which readers likely would not have access. This is why we are relying on readers to find the citations they want by doing a little digital searching or some page-flipping.

We obviously will not pretend that this new book is now perfect in every way. But we will say that in essence the cases included both here and in the original are at minimum accurately presented and that our arguments are the result of diligent follow-up and mulling.

Only a few weeks before the completion of the English version of our book, on April 5th, our beloved co-author Anny Stevens-Dirven passed away. She was really proud that our work was going to reach a larger public and hoped it would have a real and lasting impact. She was not afraid of death; rather, she was looking forward to being reunited with her late husband Wim Stevens. Both had had a near-death experience, by the way.

Anny Dirven was a very close and loyal friend, and she will be dearly missed by many people. We are convinced she is following and supporting us from the realm of Light. One day we will meet again. Thank you so much for everything, Anny!

Titus Rivas and Rudolf Smit
Spring 2016

CHAPTER 1

Extrasensory Veridical Perception of the Immediate Environment

For these reasons, the autoscopic hallucination does
not appear to be a plausible explanation for the NDE.
—Michael B. Sabom, MD, *Recollections of Death*

From the perspective of parapsychology, or psychic research, one feature is probably most responsible for near-death experiences (NDEs) coming to public attention as a phenomenon with possible paranormal aspects: specific impressions of the material world that near-death experiencers (NDErs) reportedly perceived from a location outside their physical bodies. With this chapter, we begin the presentation of such cases. As a caveat for the entire book, not all well-known cases of NDEs with possible paranormal aspects are included. We included only those cases that came across to us as sufficiently reliable to present credible evidence of paranormal aspects.

Many stories have been published about NDEs in which experiencers had the feeling that they left their bodies and perceived the material world from a location apart from their bodies. During this out-of-body (OB) aspect of the NDE, the NDEr typically perceived his or her own body as well as what was happening in the surroundings in which that body lay and sometimes physical locations away from the body, apparently without using the physical senses—the very definition of *extrasensory* perception. Later, it turned out that what the experiencer saw and heard during the OB aspect corresponded exactly with the determinable facts, meaning that the perceptions were verified as accurate, or *veridical*. Within the professional literature about NDEs, these perceptions are usually considered to be a subcategory of "AVPs"—that is, apparently nonphysical veridical perceptions, a term coined by Jan Holden (2009). The verification can range from weak (verified by the experiencer alone) to strong (verified by a researcher in the course of a study), but the accuracy is verified nonetheless. These types of experiences are probably what most people think of regarding the subject of "paranormal experiences during an NDE." Indeed, most of the cases in this book involve AVPs with extrasensory perception in the form of clairvoyance and telepathy, except for those in Chapter 7 on extrasensory perception in others and a possible case of psychokinesis, and Chapter 8 on paranormal healing of diseases or physical disabilities.

In some cases, the veridical perception of the physical environment appears to have taken place at a point in time when most mainstream neuroscientists would consider the experiencer to have insufficient brain activity for complex, conscious perception to occur. This category of experience contradicts the prevailing scientific theory that all forms of consciousness are entirely dependent on a functioning brain and, specifically, that complex forms of human consciousness are dependent on an active neocortex. Consequently, this category forms an important anomaly that may be of great interest to parapsychologists, or psychic researchers. We will go into this phenomenon further in Chapter 3, so we excluded cases of this type from this chapter.

In this chapter, we present cases of medical patients' NDEs in which we cannot be certain or sufficiently certain of the exact moment of the purported extrasensory perception. In other words, it is conceivable that the NDE did not coincide with clinical death. Of course, this condition does not mean that paranormal perception necessarily occurred *before* the patient's brain stopped functioning or *after* it became sufficiently active again; it simply means that the extent to which the patient's brain was functioning at the time of the veridical perception cannot be determined. Furthermore, although OBEs and NDEs do not depend on a flatlined electroencephalogram (EEG) in order to occur, a flatlined EEG may stimulate the occurrence of an OBE because the flatline condition may lead to a temporary loosening of the psyche, mind, soul, or consciousness from the earthly body.

We furthermore make a distinction in this chapter among (a) cases that were reported by someone other than the NDEr; (b) cases in which the perceptions were confirmed, but only by means of a medical report or file; and (c) cases in which investigators have a statement both from the patient and from one or more witnesses. The probative value of the last category is obviously the greatest, particularly if the witness's/witnesses' statement(s) were made independently of the patient's statement. Cases that have only a doctor's or nurse's statement are also more probative than cases in which only the patient claims to have had paranormal perceptions, a category we intentionally did not want to include in this overview. Within the three subsections of this chapter, we do not present the cases in any particular, ranked order because we find the evidence for all of them to be strong and equivalent in their strength.

Finally, we would like to emphasize again that the book addresses the paranormal aspects of NDEs. This focus usually means that we will leave other stages, aspects, or elements of individual NDEs out of the discussion. This exclusion may, of course, leave unaddressed the broader spiritual meaning of the experiences, but that topic simply is not the subject of this book.

Cases Reported by Third Parties Without a Direct Statement From the Patient to the Investigator

CASE 1.1 Emine Fougner's Father

Emine Fougner, a translator and computer scientist of Turkish descent from Arizona, sent Titus Rivas an e-mail at the end of 2006. From further correspondence in March 2007, he learned some details about the medical condition of her 58-year-old father from Hamilton, Canada. This man ended up in a Canadian hospital for various interventional operations and tests, including undergoing a complicated form of vascular surgery in connection with a fistula. Afterward, Fougner's father told her what he had experienced during his surgery. Fougner emphasized that, in order to spare her father unnecessary distress, it had been decided not to tell him too many details about his impending surgery, so her father was not aware of the various procedures that the doctors and nurses would be performing during the operation. Emine Fougner e-mailed her entire personal contact list a message that we summarize as follows:

> But after the operation (two days after, to be exact, because he had received heavy anesthesia), he described one by one all the procedures that were performed during the operation the way someone who is observing would do. But how was that possible? He was fully anesthetized and was attached to machines on both sides. We know that he experienced an OBE. He said that he knew that he had died at a certain point. He felt his lower jaw grow cold and he couldn't feel the rest of his body; he could only see his chin through which, he said, a shiver passed. He also told us that he could see a group of people who looked like they were soldiers who were coming to get him. He

could hear them and one of them said to the others, "We won't be taking him." With that, his body and soul were united again.

Fougner noted that her father's perceptions truly corresponded with what she heard from the medical staff about the operation. In a later e-mail, Fougner added that her father would never believe in things like that if he had not personally experienced them. He was a changed person after the operation.

SOURCE

Rivas, T., & Dirven, A. (2010a). *Van en naar het Licht* [From and to the Light]. Leeuwarden, Netherlands: Uitgeverij Elikser.

CASE 1.2 Joan La Rovere's Young Patient

Sam Parnia is a physician affiliated with various hospitals in the United Kingdom as well as the Weill Cornell Medical Center in New York City. In his book *What Happens When We Die*, Dr. Parnia reported the case of a U.S. doctor by the name of Joan La Rovere, whom he met personally. Dr. La Rovere told him the following story, which we summarize.

At the time of the case, La Rovere was in England working as a member of a team that went to small local hospitals to pick up sick children who had to undergo treatment by specialists at the Great Ormond Street Hospital in London. One evening she went with the rest of her team to a hospital in Kent, some 20 miles from London, to pick up a 9-year-old girl with a serious kidney disorder. The child was very ill and had to be rushed to the Great Ormond Street Hospital to be treated in its pediatric intensive care unit.

During the ambulance ride, the team got stuck in rush-hour traffic. They were driving as fast as they could, with lights flashing and sirens blaring, but were not making enough headway, so the girl's condition worsened quickly. Suddenly the girl's heart gave out, and she suffered cardiac arrest. La Rovere's team immediately began resuscitation in the ambulance, but despite repeated attempts throughout the long traffic delay, they could not get her heart going again.

Finally, one of the nurses remarked that the girl was dead. She suggested leaving the highway and driving to a local hospital to have a coroner's report drawn up.

La Rovere, however, had an intuitive feeling that they had to continue resuscitation, even though it looked as if they had really lost her. She said, "If she's going to be pronounced dead, it will be at Great Ormond Street and nowhere else." So they continued resuscitation. Although La Rovere had little hope that it would succeed, something inside her told her that she needed to talk to the girl during the resuscitation. She kept reassuring the girl and told her that she should not worry and that everything would be all right.

At about the time that they arrived at Great Ormond Street Hospital, the girl's heart started up again, although she was still in very critical and unstable condition. La Rovere's duties at that time were limited to picking up patients from other hospitals. She did hear from Great Ormond Street Hospital nurses, though, that the girl gradually got better and could finally be discharged from the hospital.

Parnia cited La Rovere with respect to what happened a few months later when the girl visited the hospital to meet everyone who had cared for her:

> During her visit, she asked one of the nurses, "Where is the American doctor who looked after me in the ambulance and who was talking to me during the trip?" She had watched everything from above and had recalled all the details. I was amazed when I heard this, as she'd never even seen me throughout the trip. She had been too ill and had been on a life-support machine.

SOURCE

Parnia, S. (2006). *What happens when we die: A groundbreaking study into the nature of life and death.* Carlsbad, CA: Hay House.

CASE 1.3 Dress Code

The 2003 article "The Nature and Meaning of the Near-Death Experience for Patients and Critical Care Nurses," by U.S. investigators and PhD-level nurses Linda L. Morris and Kathleen A. Knafl, highlights descriptions of nurses' experiences.

One of them concerned a female nurse who witnessed how a patient recognized her. She was giving the patient, a woman, a bath, when the patient remarked, "You were here yesterday." The nurse asked her if she could remember anything. The patient told her that she had seen from above how the team had tried to resuscitate her. She also remembered a conversation between the nurse and one of the doctors about the dress code. The doctor had, in fact, said to the nurse that she was not allowed to wear dresses to work anymore in response to the fact that she had worn a skirt that day.

SOURCE

Morris, L. L., & Knafl, K. A. (2003). The nature and meaning of the near-death experience for patients and critical care nurses. *Journal of Near-Death Studies, 21*(3), 139–167.

Case Reported by the Patient Without Confirmation From a Specific Witness, but Confirmed by the Content of a Medical Report

In this category, we included only one case in which the course of a resuscitation was confirmed by what doctors or nurses recorded in a medical report. We excluded cases that, medically speaking, come across as realistic but the main points of which are not supported by a report of the medical procedures. Also, we did not include cases in which the report merely described a standard procedure.

CASE 1.4 A Heart Shaped Like Africa

A case from the book *Recollections of Death* by U.S. cardiologist Michael B. Sabom concerns a 52-year-old night watchman from North Florida who experienced two heart attacks with cardiac arrest in 1973 and 1975. Dr. Sabom met him for the first time in November 1977 and learned that the patient had had an extensive NDE during his first cardiac arrest in December 1973 (see Chapter 3, Case 3.19). In January 1978, this patient had to undergo open-heart surgery at the University of Florida's medical center. At their next meeting, the patient turned out to have had an NDE during this second surgery as well. During this operation, the patient found himself suddenly above his body. He observed his own body, various medical procedures, and the instruments used. He also caught snippets of conversation that went on during the operation.

The observations did not completely meet the patient's expectations. He was surprised to have seen that his heart was shaped somewhat like the continent of Africa, and there was less blood loss than he had expected. He also saw, for example, that one of the doctors involved was wearing white shoes and was the only one not wearing green scrub covers over those shoes.

Sabom compared the patient's observations with the medical report of the operation. He did not mention any specific witnesses for this case. The cardiologist concluded that many specific details in the report corresponded exactly with the patient's description, including the following consistencies:

1. The patient said, "My head was covered, and the rest of my body was draped with more than one sheet, separate sheets laid in layers." The medical report: "[The body was] draped in the customary sterile fashion."
2. Patient: "I could draw you a picture of the saw they used." Medical report: "The sternum was sawed open in the midline."
3. Patient: "The thing they used to separate the ribs with. It was always there. . . . It was draped all around you, but you could see the metal part of it. . . . That thing they held my chest open with, that's real good steel with no rust, I mean, no discoloration. Real good, hard, shiny metal." Medical report: "A self-retaining retractor was utilized over wound towels."
4. Patient: "One general area to the right or left was darker than the rest instead of all being the same color." Medical report: "The ventricular aneurysm was dissected free. . . . The aneurysm was seen to be very large."
5. Patient: "He cut pieces of my heart off. He raised it and twisted it this way and that way and took quite a bit of time examining it and looking at different things." Medical report: "An incision was made over the most prominent portion of the aneurysm after the heart had been turned upside down in the pericardial wall. . . . The entire aneurysm was resected."
6. Patient: "Injected something into my heart. That's scary when you see that thing go right into your heart." Medical report: "Air was evacuated from the left ventricle with a needle and syringe."
7. Patient: "They took some stitches inside me first before they did the outside." The medical report states: "The wound was closed in layers. . . . The pectoral fascia was reapproximated with interrupted sutures of 2-0 Tevdek . . . subcutaneous tissue was closed with a running suture of 3-0 chromic . . . the skin was closed with 4-0 nylon."

Sabom commented that some details that the patient reported did not appear in the medical report because they concerned aspects that were not essential in an operative summary. According to Sabom, however, these details, too, were accurate in the context of an open-heart operation.

SOURCE

Sabom, M. B. (1982). *Recollections of death: A medical investigation.* New York, NY: Harper & Row.

Intermezzo: Can Specific Descriptions of Resuscitation Procedures Be Explained by Factors Like Prior Knowledge?

Perceptions during NDEs of specific correct details about doctors or nurses involved in a resuscitation procedure usually provide enough evidence to justify the conclusion that those perceptions cannot be attributed to chance hits or prior knowledge. Both cardiologist Michael Sabom and medical investigator and PhD-level nurse Penny Sartori have examined more generally whether NDErs' descriptions of resuscitation procedures are, on average, more correct than the descriptions of cardiac patients who have not had NDEs. If NDErs' accounts were not more correct, it would follow that their perceptions were the result of chance or prior knowledge.

As material for comparison, Sabom used a group of cardiac patients not reporting NDEs who had never been resuscitated. For her investigation, Sartori used a group of patients who had likewise never reported an NDE but had been resuscitated. Despite the difference in comparison groups, both investigators determined that the NDErs' descriptions were markedly more correct and believable than those of the comparison groups. For example, the NDErs reported many more accurate details, and the comparison groups of patients without near-death experiences made greater errors in their descriptions. These latter patients did not know, for instance, on which parts of the body the electrical "pads" (small, self-adhering cushions) or "paddles" (metal disks) of a defibrillator were placed, or they thought that an electric shock was a standard component of the procedure. Some patients from the comparison groups had no idea about resuscitation procedures at all, and others had a distorted notion that was based on popular TV shows.

Both investigators concluded from their studies that normal factors like prior knowledge, guesswork, or pure coincidence do not offer an acceptable explanation for correct extrasensory perceptions of resuscitation procedures. In her blog of October 5, 2011, Sartori wrote: "Anomalous well documented cases like this cannot be explained by current scientific explanations."

SOURCES

Sabom, M. B. (1982). *Recollections of death: A medical investigation*. New York, NY: Harper & Row.

Sartori, P. (2008). *The near-death experiences of hospitalized intensive care patients: A five year clinical study*. Lewiston, UK: Edwin Mellen Press.

Cases Reported by the Patient and Confirmed by Witnesses

CASE 1.5 A Surgeon Taking Flight?

In New England, van driver Al Sullivan underwent an emergency operation at age 56 at the Hartford Hospital in Connecticut. He was having heart arrhythmias at work, and when he was examined at the hospital, one of his coronary arteries became blocked, requiring him to undergo immediate surgery. During the operation, he felt himself leaving his body. He had the feeling of rising up and, in doing so, seemed completely surrounded by a kind of thick, black smoke, until he finally rose to a kind of amphitheater that he was unable to enter. There was a wall between him and the theater, and behind it a particularly bright light was shining. He managed to hold on to the wall and to look over it. To his surprise, he saw his body in the lower left, lying on a table and covered by light-blue sheets. He also saw how he had been cut open to expose his chest cavity. He saw his heart and also his surgeon, who had explained to him prior to the operation what he was going to do. This surgeon looked a little perplexed. It even seemed like he was "flapping" his arms as if trying to fly.

Then Sullivan moved beyond the material, physical realm in what is called the transmaterial aspect of his NDE, in which he saw deceased loved ones (among them his mother, who had died young) and a glorious, yellow light, all the while experiencing overwhelming feelings of warmth, joy, love, and peace.

MOMENT OF DEATH

Finally, Sullivan was resuscitated. As soon as he was able to speak again, he shared the experiences he had had during the operation with his cardiologist, Anthony LaSala. The latter attempted to ascribe the experiences to the medication, however. It was only when Sullivan described how the heart surgeon, Hiroyoshi Takata, had flapped his elbows as if he were trying to fly that Dr. LaSala's attitude changed. He wondered who could have told Sullivan about this, considering it was in fact a personal habit of Takata's. When Dr. Takata was not operating, he wanted to avoid contaminating his hands, so he would lay his palms flat on his chest and direct his assistants by pointing with his elbows.

According to Sullivan, LaSala told Takata what Sullivan had observed during the NDE, but Takata, rather than focusing on the perceptual anomaly, took the information as personal criticism of the quality of his surgical care of Sullivan. Takata said, "Well, you're here, you're alive, so I must do something right!" His defensive response raises the question of how many veridical accounts may have been overlooked or hidden as a result of surgeons' concerns about professional competency or legal liability.

In the fall of 1997, investigator and psychiatrist Bruce Greyson interviewed both LaSala and Takata. Takata could not specifically confirm that he had "flapped" his elbows during the operation on Mr. Sullivan, but he did acknowledge that this was a general habit with him. The habit stemmed from the desire not to touch anything with his sterile hands as he carried out an operation.

LaSala confirmed that Sullivan had spoken with him shortly after the operation about his NDE. He also confirmed that Takata does have the strange habit of "flapping" his elbows, adding that he never saw any other surgeons do anything like that.

In a video reenactment of this case, Sullivan's eyes were taped shut, and there was a sterile drape over his head that blocked any possible physical perception of Takata. These conditions were explicitly confirmed by LaSala who said (2:47), "Even if he was conscious, it would be impossible for Al to see Dr. Takata's stance or arm movement because Al is behind a drape that blocks the vision of the patient and his eyes were taped shut." Assuming that pointing with one's elbows does not produce sounds discernable in the bustle and equipment-related noise of an operating room, Sullivan's perception could not be attributed to hearing.

In addition, an investigative team consisting of psychologist Emily Cook and psychiatrists Bruce Greyson and Ian Stevenson also determined that Sullivan had most likely really been unconscious and under total anesthesia at the moment Takata had flapped his arms. They drew their conclusion from Sullivan's own report of his NDE. Sullivan specifically claimed that Takata exhibited the behavior while he was the only one standing near Sullivan's opened chest, which was being held open by metal clamps, while two other surgeons were busy on Sullivan's leg. This last observation made Sullivan wonder during the NDE itself because he did not understand the connection between a leg and the heart operation. Only later did he learn that a leg vein is often used for bypass procedures during heart surgery.

Even though Takata's strange behavioral pattern took place in the operating room itself, the investigators could not imagine how the totally anesthetized and unconscious Sullivan could ever have observed the pattern with his normal physical senses.

In early April 2004, Titus Rivas was in e-mail contact with Hiroyoshi Takata. Takata informed Rivas that a Japanese TV crew had meanwhile filmed him. A few years later, in 2009, Professor Masayuki Ohkado translated for us what Takata had said during an interview with the well-known Japanese journalist Takashi Tachibana, as included in the latter's book titled "Near-Death Experiences" (in English). The main passages from the translated interview with Takata read:

> I have often heard from other doctors a case in which the anesthetic wears off during the operation and the patient hears the doctors' conversation and I myself have had such patients. But I have never encountered one in which the patient describes such details of the operation as if he/she saw the process. Frankly, I don't know how this case can be accounted for. But since this really happened, I have to accept it as a fact. I think we should always be humble to accept the fact. In sum, I think science has not yet sufficiently revealed the ability of human beings. There exists in this world something that cannot be captured by science or mathematics.
>
> There are those who will not accept this but I think their attitude is not humble in front of the fact. [. . .] Though I am a doctor, I don't think science is omnipotent. I have been thinking that there are spiritual aspects in this world. So I was not surprised to come up with such a phenomenon. I cannot account for it, but I have to admit that such things do happen.

In the video reenactment mentioned above, Takata stated (2:38), "I cannot explain how he saw these things under the complete sleep of anesthesia."

SOURCES

Cook, E. W., Greyson, B., & Stevenson, I. (1998). Do any near-death experiences provide evidence for the survival of human personality after death? Relevant features and illustrative case reports. *Journal of Scientific Exploration, 12*(3), 377–406.

NDEAccounts. (n.d.). Al Sullivan's–NDE–Confirmation of out of body experience. Retrieved from https://www.youtube.com/watch?v=J5_x8U7SR0I

Rivas, T. (2009b). *Uitspraken van Hiroyoshi Takata over de casus van Al Sullivan* [Statements made by Hiroyoshi Takata about the Al Sullivan case]. *Terugkeer, 20*(3), 22.

Rivas, T., & Dirven, A. (2010a). *Van en naar het Licht* [From and to the Light]. Leeuwarden, Netherlands: Uitgeverij Elikser.

CASE 1.6 The Patient From Missouri

Among the cases Michael Sabom included in his book *Recollections of Death* is that of a 42-year-old woman from Missouri. The patient told him that in September 1972, she had undergone a lumbar-disk operation that she had watched in an out-of-body state from the operating room ceiling.

She saw that the operation was taking place in a green room, and it struck her that the operating table was not next to the medical-instrument table but stood at an angle in the room. The patient subsequently also observed how the medical team operated on her and what roles the two doctors played. After her back operation, she apparently went into cardiac arrest, and they sutured the wound so quickly that it was not done very neatly.

After she had regained consciousness, the patient recognized one of the surgeons involved, even though she had never met the doctor in question prior to the operation. She also shared her NDE with a student nurse who confirmed to her the accuracy of her impressions.

Dr. Sabom consulted the medical report and in this way determined that the operation had indeed been performed by the two doctors whom the patient had observed during her NDE. He also ascertained that there were no discrepancies between the observations the patient reported having had during her NDE and the surgical procedures described in the report. In addition, the operation went differently than the patient had expected beforehand. She had thought that her primary doctor would perform most of the surgery, but it was the other doctor—whom she had never met—who did the great majority of the work. (As far as we know, the instance of recognition was unfortunately not confirmed by the doctor involved.)

Sabom, moreover, had a conversation with the student nurse 6 years after the operation. Although she had forgotten many of the details in the intervening time, her story corresponded at least in large part with the patient's story.

SOURCE

Sabom, M. B. (1982). *Recollections of death: A medical investigation*. New York, NY: Harper & Row.

CASE 1.7 A. S. Wiltse

This case dates from the end of the 19th century and was written up by Frederic William Henry Myers in his book *Human Personality and Its Survival of Bodily Death*.

In 1889, A. S. Wiltse, a doctor from Skiddy, Kansas, suffered from typhoid fever. He finally succumbed and fell into a coma. When the attending physician, S. H. Raynes, could not detect any pulse or heartbeat for four hours, Wiltse appeared to be clinically dead.

As the presence of his case here would indicate, Wiltse nevertheless returned to consciousness. He recounted that he had seen with great interest how his body separated from his spirit. He had felt like a jellyfish as far as shape and color were concerned. His mind loosened from his body like a soap bubble loosens itself from the end of a tube. In that shape, he softly fell to the ground. However, he stood up as a complete but transparent figure, and he noticed that he walked straight through people. He described in detail "with the interest of a doctor" all that he experienced in his out-of-body state.

The following aspects of his experience are important to our purpose in presenting this case. He saw his body lying on a sofa. Two women, kneeling to his left, were crying. After he had regained consciousness, it turned out that the two women had been his own wife and sister—but during the NDE itself, he had not recognized them. Although during his NDE Wiltse had repeatedly tried to let all those in the room know he was as alive as ever, all his attempts failed.

F. W. H. Myers

After it was all over, Wiltse described his extrasensory perceptions of the room and his body's condition during the NDE. He asked witnesses to describe in their own words to what extent his perceptions had been correct. Wiltse sent witness statements—signed in the presence of a notary—to the investigator Richard Hodgson.

The details that Wiltse had observed regarding the room, the people who were there, and the way in which his body had lain either were confirmed by witnesses or were at least not denied by them. Myers included witnesses' written statements in his book.

SOURCE

Myers, F. W. H. (1903). *Human personality and its survival of bodily death*. London, UK: Longmans, Green.

CASE 1.8 Nancy

In the book *Mindsight: Near-Death and Out-of-Body Experiences in the Blind* by social psychologist Kenneth Ring and coauthor Sharon Cooper, Nancy's case figures prominently. In September 1991, Nancy was 41 years old when she was admitted to a hospital in California for a biopsy. Unfortunately, something went wrong with the procedure: A blood vessel, the superior vena cava, had been nicked. The surgeon panicked and stitched the vessel shut, which hindered circulation. After Nancy had revived, she noticed that she could not see anymore. She let the nurses know and was rushed on a gurney to an elevator. When her gurney slammed into the elevator, she had an OBE. She was in a life-threatening situation because the blood supply to important organs had been impeded.

During her OBE, and in spite of her loss of sight, she could see that her face was covered by a breathing pump and that her body lay under a sheet. She also saw that the people around her were all in a panic. Moreover, she could see two men standing in the corridor who looked shocked—namely, the father of her son and her boyfriend at the time, Leon. After her resuscitation, the doctors were unable to restore her sight.

Dr. Ring and Ms. Cooper consulted her medical file and interviewed the two men she had seen. Nancy attached a lot of value to statements made by Leon, by now her ex-boyfriend—in particular what he said in an interview on April 2, 1995. His version of the events corresponds with Nancy's for the most part. For instance, he confirmed that he was in a kind of state of shock when he learned what had happened to his then girlfriend. His statement also revealed that he and her son's father had, in fact, stood together in the corridor.

The investigators could not determine with certainty that Nancy was already totally blind when she had the NDE or whether her blindness arose only some time later. However, they did conclude that under the given circumstances, the patient would, in any event, not have been able to observe with her physical eyes what she saw during her OBE.

SOURCE

Ring, K., & Cooper, S. (1999). *Mindsight: Near-death and out-of-body experiences in the blind*. Palo Alto, CA: William James Center for Consciousness Studies at the Institute of Transpersonal Psychology; (2008; 2nd ed.). Bloomington, IN: iUniverse.

CASE 1.9 A Pink Lollipop

In 2006, Penny Sartori, along with colleagues Rev. Paul Badham and Dr. Peter Fenwick, published a case report in the *Journal of Near-Death Studies*. In this case, which occurred in the hospital where Sartori worked in Wales, two different phenomena occurred: a paranormal observation and a miraculous healing of physical ailments. Thus this case also appears in Chapter 9; here we address only the first phenomenon. Sartori also reported on this patient in her book *The Near-Death Experiences of Hospitalized Intensive Care Patients*, where he is designated as Patient 10.

Patient 10 was a 60-year-old white male who was recovering from an emergency intervention in connection with intestinal cancer. After the operation, he felt terrible; he was suffering from sepsis and the failure of various organs. Nevertheless, after 5 days, he seemed to be improving. He no longer needed medication to keep his blood pressure at normal levels, and his kidneys started functioning normally again, so his kidney treatment was discontinued. He was improving so rapidly that the medical team, especially his physiotherapist, encouraged him to leave his bed and sit in a nearby chair to help him begin to regain muscle tone. Within about five minutes after he sat down in the chair, his respiratory rate increased considerably, and the oxygen content in his lungs had dropped from its former normal level of 96% or higher to 70% or 86%. Because it was feared that cardiac arrest was imminent, the patient was immediately returned to his bed, whereupon the patient lapsed into a deep, unconscious state, with his eyes shut and with him failing to respond to verbal commands or quite painful stimulation.

The patient's condition deteriorated, and everyone tried to figure out what was going on. Various medical procedures were performed in an attempt to improve his condition. Meanwhile, the physiotherapist on the team worried that she was responsible for what had happened. The woman was standing nervously on the other side of the privacy curtain, intermittently poking her head around the curtain to see how the patient was doing. Once the patient's condition had stabilized, they noticed that he was drooling. Sartori cleaned the patient up. First, she used a long suction catheter and then a wet, pink sponge on his mouth. After about half an hour, the patient began to blink his eyes and move his arms and legs. He was still unable to respond to commands, however. Three or four hours after the incident, the patient had fully regained consciousness.

Once the patient had revived, the medical team on duty walked toward his bed. He made an excited attempt to tell the doctors something. He could not speak because he was hindered by a breathing apparatus. He was given a board with letters, on which he spelled out, "I died and I watched it all from above."

As soon as the patient no longer needed the breathing apparatus and had recovered his voice, Sartori did an in-depth interview. We cite a few passages from her article. The patient told Sartori:

> They wanted me to get out of bed, with all my tubes in me and sit in the chair. They insisted, especially one sister. I didn't want to because I felt so weak; then eventually I got out. All I can remember is looking up in the air and I was floating in a bright pink room. I couldn't see anything; I was just going up and there was no pain at all. [. . .] It was unusual; I went up. . . . It was so painless; there was no pain. . . . I was so happy. . . . I was enjoying myself. But looking back, I could see everybody. I was happy, no pain at all, until I felt somebody going to my eye. I looked back and I could see my bed, my body in the bed. I could see everything that was happening on the floor. I saw doctors when I was up there; I was looking down and could see the doctors and even the sister, what she was actually doing in the ward. It was marvelous; I could see nurses around me and the doctors. I was still going up in the air and I could feel somebody going like this to my eye. [He raised his finger up to his eye.] I eventually looked back and I could see one of the doctors pulling my eye, what for I didn't know. One doctor was saying, "There's life in the eye."
>
> I could see everybody panicking around me. The blonde lady therapist boss, she was panicking; she looked nervous because she was the one who got me out in the chair. She hid behind the curtains, but kept poking her head around to check on me. I could also see Penny, who was a nurse. She was drawing something out of my mouth, which looked to me like a long, pink lollipop, like a long, pink thing on a stick—I didn't even know what that was.

[. . .] Eventually, I felt myself coming slowly back into my body. I went in my body on the bed and I was in terrible pain; the pain was worse then than it had ever been before. All these cables were in me, as they were before I went up. I couldn't speak because I had tubes in my throat and my nose. [. . .] I heard voices down below but couldn't make out what they were saying. Only thing . . . something about my eye, life there. . . . I don't know what he meant by that.

> PS: I remember that. It was the consultant actually, and he looked in your eye and he shone a torch [flashlight] and he said, "Yes they [the pupils] are reacting, but unequal."

A moment later:

> PATIENT: You were there, Penny, and two doctors. But you with the lollipop, sponge, yes, like a mouth wash.
> PS: I can remember doing that, but at the time you were completely unconscious and your eyes were closed.
> PATIENT: Well, I could see that, as plain as I can see you now. [. . .]
> PS: Did you hear me say that I was going to clean your mouth?
> PATIENT: No, I didn't hear anything. I was just looking back and could see you doing something with my mouth and seeing this long, pink thing.

Sartori wondered whether her patient's OBE could be reduced to a mental model that he had constructed from what remained of his sight, sounds, and instances of touch. She wrote about this possibility in the same article:

> This patient had been in the ITU [Intensive Therapy Unit] for eight days prior to the experience and was very familiar with the layout of the unit and the daily routine. At this point, it is pertinent to examine the features of his OBE separately. [. . .]

> 1. *The doctor shining the light in his eyes.* The doctor who checked his pupils was the consultant anesthetist, who entered the ITU for the first time that day, just as the patient's condition deteriorated. The junior doctors were unavailable; subsequently the consultant reviewed the patient. When the patient's condition stabilized following the administration of fluid to

increase the blood pressure, the junior doctors arrived and the consultant returned to his office until he began the ward rounds later that afternoon. The consultant checked that the patient's pupils were reacting by shining a light into them. He remarked, "Yes, they're reacting, but unequal." The patient reported hearing the doctor saying, "There's life in the eye" or "something like that." This was inaccurate, although this highlighted his interpretation of what was said and was a good comprehension of what the consultant meant.

The patient was unconscious by the time the consultant reviewed him, and remained unconscious when the consultant left the bedside. It was only as the ward rounds approached the patient's bed area four hours later that he regained full consciousness and excitedly tried to communicate what he had experienced. The patient correctly identified the consultant as having shone the light in his eyes, rather than one of the junior doctors with whom he was familiar. The patient was deeply unconscious at this time and had not previously seen the consultant that morning, although he had seen the other junior doctors. However, it is possible that he heard the consultant's voice at the time of unconsciousness, which may have contributed to the construction of a mental model.

2. *The nurse cleaning his mouth.* When the patient had been put back to bed, he had drooled from the side of his mouth. Once his condition had stabilized, the nurse cleaned his mouth. He knew who his nurse for the day was, and was familiar with the nursing procedures to be performed. He knew that his mouth was cleaned by using a pink sponge dipped in water. When performing any nursing procedures, the nurse always explains her actions, even if the patient is unconscious. He could therefore have heard the nurse explain her actions, although he adamantly denied having done so, and could also have felt her cleaning his mouth. However, because he had drooled, a long suction catheter, normally used for endotracheal suction, was used to clean the oropharyngeal secretions from the back of his throat.

This long catheter was used in preference to the shorter, hard, plastic Yankauer sucker, as it is softer and more comfortable for the patient; this is not the usual procedure, as most nurses use the Yankauer sucker. After his mouth was cleaned, a moist pink sponge was put into his mouth to freshen it up. The pink sponge is not long, as the patient reported, but the suction catheter that was used first was long. He could therefore have "seen" both pieces of equipment. Also, the secretions cleaned away were pink in color.

3. *The physiotherapist "poking her head around the curtains."* The patient also reported seeing the physiotherapist looking very nervous and "poking her head around the curtains" to see if his condition was improving. The same physiotherapist was on the ward rounds at the time he reported the experience. She had been on duty all day, and the patient was aware of this fact. It is possible, but not confirmed, that she inquired verbally about the patient's condition, as she was "poking her head around the curtains." Thus the patient could have heard her asking, which could have contributed to the construction of a mental model. The patient's eyes were closed throughout the period the physiotherapist was checking on his condition. However, if his OBE was a mental reconstruction, it is surprising that the patient should report her to be "poking her head around the curtains, looking very nervous." It would be more likely that he would construct a view of her standing closer to the bedside, without the need to "poke her head around the curtains."

Was His OBE a Mental Reconstruction?

Could a mental model have been constructed during the four hours it took for the patient to regain full consciousness? Could it have been his brain's attempt to make sense of what had occurred through the senses, especially residual sight, sound, and tactile stimulation? The discrepancy between what the consultant said ("Yes, they're reacting, but unequal") and what the patient reported he said ("There's life in the eye") could be accounted for by the possibility that he was confused, and so unable to pay full attention to verbal cues. This would suggest that "viewing" the situation with such clarity would not be possible if it was due only to a mental model reconstructed from what he could hear and feel. If the mental reconstruction was based on what he could hear, then it would be expected that he would accurately report the verbal cues he had heard.

Despite these discrepancies, the patient's description of what happened while he was unconscious was extremely accurate and was reported immediately as soon as the patient regained full consciousness. It is possible that some of the information could have been gained from the senses, but that is an incomplete explanation for the detailed events described by the patient and witnessed by the senior author. The experience remained vivid and accurate when recalled on follow-up on several occasions from one year to five years after the experience.

Did the NDE Happen as the Patient Was Regaining Consciousness?

[. . .] It is possible to say that the experience of observing the nurse cleaning his mouth with what looked like a pink lollipop, and observing the doctor shining a light into his eyes, must have happened at least three hours before the patient regained full consciousness. As the medical records show, the patient was deeply unconscious with his eyes closed at the time when those events occurred, and the experience of undergoing those events must have been contemporaneous with their occurrence rather than happening four hours later while the patient was regaining consciousness.

SOURCES

Sartori, P. (2008). *The near-death experiences of hospitalized intensive care patients: A five year clinical study.* Lewiston, UK: Edwin Mellen Press.

Sartori, P., Badham, P., & Fenwick, P. (2006). A prospectively studied near-death experience with corroborated out-of-body perceptions and unexplained healing. *Journal of Near-Death Studies, 25*(2), 69–84.

CASE 1.10 J. S.

Canadian neurologist Mario Beauregard, together with several colleagues, published an open letter in the journal *Resuscitation* in January 2012. In it he described a case of an adult female patient, whom he referred to as J. S., from the Hôpital du Sacré-Coeur, affiliated with the University of Montreal. This patient had undergone what is called a deep hypothermic circulatory arrest, or DHCA, for 15 minutes. This is an "arrest" procedure in which, for operative purposes, the body is cooled substantially and the heart is artificially stopped. Thus, in this case, the word "arrest" refers to temporarily stopping the body's processes completely. In this case, DHCA was required for replacement of part of J. S.'s aorta.

Dr. Beauregard came across this case in the context of his retrospective study of patients who from 2005 to 2010 had conscious experiences during their artificial cardiac arrests. He discovered a total of three cases of this type, of which J. S.'s case appears to have been the most significant.

J. S. was 31 weeks pregnant when she felt totally out of breath and weak. She was brought to the hospital, where, first, a caesarian was performed, enabling her son to enter the world in good health. Then she was taken to an operating room, where she was anesthetized in preparation for surgery to repair an aortic dissection by replacing her ascending aorta. While this surgery was going on, she could not see what kind of equipment was behind the operating table by normal sensory means.

Following the surgery, J. S. explained that during the operation on her aorta, she had had an OBE during which she was easily able to observe a nurse handing over medical instruments to the surgeon. She also observed the equipment for anesthesia and ultrasound that were located behind her head. Furthermore, she experienced feelings of peace and joy and saw a bright light. Beauregard's team succeeded in verifying the descriptions that J. S. gave of the nurse and the equipment. The surgeon in question confirmed that they were correct.

SOURCE

Beauregard, M., St-Pierre, É. L., Rayburn, G., & and Demers, P. (2012). Conscious mental activity during a deep hypothermic cardiocirculatory arrest? *Resuscitation, 83*(1), e19.

CASE 1.11 Naomi

A patient of critical care physician Laurin Bellg's, whom she called Naomi in her recent book *Near Death in the ICU*, had a cardiac arrest resulting from a heart attack. The medical team used every means at hand, including cardiopulmonary resuscitation (CPR) and administering electrical shocks, to get her heart started again and to stabilize her heart rhythm. The process was very difficult, and, during the course of these attempts, the patient even had a second cardiac arrest. In the end, her coronary artery turned out to be blocked. When the blockage was removed, her heart was still too weakened to circulate the blood. This caused her lungs to function less optimally, and so she had to be put on artificial ventilation.

As soon as Dr. Bellg had decided that the patient could be taken off the ventilator, Naomi wanted to share an NDE with her. Naomi said:

> I saw everything. I saw it all. I saw my mom who died, I saw angels, saw you working on me, all the other doctors, me in the ER [emergency room]. [. . .]
>
> In the ER I was aware again, but this time it seemed different. I couldn't figure it out at first, then I realized I was up above my body watching everyone

rush around. I saw them pumping up and down on my chest and putting a breathing tube in my mouth. I saw my closed eyes and how limp I was with one arm hanging off the bed.

Then she described feeling herself no longer in the ER but in a space that appeared to be an operating room. "There was a large light overhead and different medical personnel than she had seen in the ER." After that, she experienced being in the intensive care unit (ICU).

Bellg wrote the following about this case:

She described it to me and, astonishingly, even reminded me of something I had forgotten. [. . .]

She saw members of the resuscitation team try to tilt her whole body sideways to put a long flat board under her and me saying, "Whoa, whoa, whoa, my stuff," as I grabbed the things I had set on top of the sterile field to prevent them from falling onto the floor. She couldn't understand the long plank, so I explained to her that it is called a backboard.

"It helps us do more effective chest compressions to circulate blood if there is a hard surface under the body as we press down," I went on to explain. "Otherwise, your body would sink into the soft mattress and the pumping wouldn't be nearly as effective." She nodded that this made sense to her, but I remained amazed that she had been aware of that happening and saw me reacting to the shifting field by grabbing my supplies to keep them from falling off the bed when I knew, for a fact, that she was totally unconscious.

SOURCE
Bellg, L. (2015). *Near death in the ICU.* Appleton, WI: Sloan Press.

CASE 1.12 Carlita

Carlita (not her real name), a 38-year-old Latina, was suffering from the consequences of meningitis, for which she had been treated with antibiotics. Unconscious, she finally ended up in Laurin Bellg's ICU. It was not long before it was discovered that she had pneumonia and sinusitis as well. Even though these "offenders" did not provide sufficient reason, she still had not regained consciousness days after admission and treatment. Dr. Bellg took the patient's limp hand and pressed her thumbnail down on the nail bed at the cuticle to see if the patient would react. There was absolutely no response. She also tested eye reflexes, which were normal.

Only after the 13th day in the ICU did Carlita start to respond, and she progressed each day. When she was transferred from the ICU to the neurology ward, Bellg went by to see her. When the doctor introduced herself, Carlita said she remembered her. On Bellg's invitation, she shared that she had observed Dr. Bellg examining her while she had been out of her body. She said:

> I figured you were probably seeing how I was doing. You came around to the same side of the bed where I seemed to be standing and started pushing buttons on a large machine. Then I watched you pick up my hand and pinch my finger. I thought it was strange and wondered why you would do that. [. . .]
>
> I saw all the things the nurse did to me—tickling the bottoms of my feet with a stick and rubbing my chest with her knuckles. Then I saw you shine a light in my eyes and move my head from side to side while the nurse held my eyes open. [. . .] It was very strange watching the two of you do those things to me and I didn't feel a thing. I saw you shine the light but, from where I was standing, I didn't see a bright light shining in my eyes.

Bellg explained to Carlita why they had done what they had done.

In this case, the visual observations certainly cannot be explained by tactile stimuli, because it was these very test stimuli to which the patient showed absolutely no response.

SOURCE
Bellg, L. (2015). *Near death in the ICU.* Appleton, WI: Sloan Press.

CASE 1.13 The Scissors and the Needles

In a 2014 online interview, Spanish physician Miguel Ángel Pertierra Quesada, of the otolaryngology department of the Regional Hospital in Malaga, Spain, talked about one of his patients who had an OBE during an operation and who observed very specific elements, such as various medical instruments.

In his book *La Última Puerta* (The Last Door), Dr. Pertierra elaborated on this case. It involved a middle-aged woman, a heavy smoker who was extremely obese and who had serious bronchial symptoms. She had had trouble breathing for several days in a row in conjunction with infections in her airways. It was determined that there had to be an obstruction or a narrowing of her upper respiratory tract that was impairing her breathing. She was in very bad shape, exhibiting tachycardia and profuse sweating. Her dire condition required her to be operated on right away or she might die. But despite how quickly the team tried to save her, she went into secondary respiratory failure and cardiac arrest.

It took Pertierra only a few seconds to open her trachea with a scalpel. He then requested a special type of forceps, a trivalve tracheal dilator. This instrument looks like a pair of scissors from the back, and like the long beak of a wading bird from the front, but with three beaklike prongs being visible instead of two. When the jaws open, they create an opening that enables introduction of the cannula through which the patient will be able to breathe.

The doctor succeeded in introducing the cannula to artificially ventilate the woman. The problem was not yet solved, though, because the patient's lung had meanwhile collapsed. The team therefore tried to reduce pressure on the chest. Pertierra and one of the anesthetists stuck special needles into her chest cavity. The needles that are most suitable in such situations are orange needles labeled number 14. Fortunately, the excess air indeed escaped from her chest, the way air is let out of an air mattress. The patient was then kept sedated in order to optimize her recovery and to avoid her experiencing unnecessary pain. She was then transferred to the intensive care unit.

Once the patient had revived, she repeated over and over in what seemed like an obsessive delirium that she had seen all the members of the medical team, as well as "the light." Some time later, Pertierra went to see her. While the patient shut off the ventilation hole with her finger from time to time so she could speak, she said as she exhaled, "Doctor, I could see from outside, I could see you. I need to talk to you. I have seen many things I must tell you about." However, not wanting to tire her, the doctor reassured her that they would talk in detail when she was better. Some days after that, there was a second conversation about her NDE. She told the doctor that during her experience, she was suddenly no longer lying on the operation table but had found herself behind Pertierra. She said (authors' translation):

> I saw you stick out your arm and cut my neck from the top down with a scalpel. Then you asked for something, I don't remember exactly what you said, it was a number. They opened a little case and gave you a really strange pair of scissors that opened downward in three parts. You stuck the scissors

into the hole you made in my neck and you put a white plastic tube in there. After that you hooked something up to me, a kind of rubber, like electric tubing that electricity cables run through.

Then something happened. I don't know what it was. I saw my body and I heard all kinds of noises coming from the monitors. You were all talking and listening to my heart. After that you all asked for something and poked huge needles into me that were orange where they were widest. That hurt the most. It was strange, what you guys did after that seemed to be about somebody else, but I noted that it was being done to me, lying there, although I saw all of you from at least one meter away, something very strange.

Finally, she felt as if she were rising up to a light, after which she awoke in the ICU.

According to Pertierra, her observations had no normal explanation. In an effort to find an explanation, he asked her whether she—or even one of her family members—might know something about the practice of medicine. This was not the case, however.

Dr. Miguel Ángel Pertierra Quesada

What made the case so extraordinary, in Pertierra's mind, was that the patient observed extremely specialized medical instruments that hardly anyone outside the otolaryngological field would be familiar with. On top of that, she could not have heard anyone say the color of the needles because the color is not mentioned when someone asks for one.

Although it appears as if she experienced physical sensations during the acute moment of pain, that by itself still does not begin to explain how, in her condition, she could have seen correct images of unfamiliar medical instruments.

SOURCES

Astorga, J. V. (2014, November 9). Miguel Ángel Pertierra: "No entusiasmo a la profesión médica de forma oficial pero sí individualmente" [Miguel Ángel Pertierra: "No enthusiasm from the medical establishment, just individuals"].

Diario Sur–Málaga. Retrieved from http://www.diariosur.es/malaga/201411/04/
miguel-pertierra-entusiasmo-profesion-20141104221417.html

Pertierra, M. Á. (2014). *La última puerta. Experiencias cercanas a la muerte* [The last
door: Near-death experiences]. Madrid, Spain: Ediciones Oberón.

CASE 1.14 The "Mayo" Scissors

A good number of years ago, Miguel Ángel Pertierra became involved in the treatment of a male patient who was extremely obese. The man had to be operated on, but it was very difficult to find a suitable vein for a plastic catheter that would administer his medication and IV fluids. Artificial ventilation provided by a mask also proved to be an issue because it did not provide enough oxygen to maintain a sufficient blood-oxygen level. It was too late to take any other course of action, so an attempt was made to introduce a tube through his mouth and into his trachea. The man had a proportionately small mouth that unfortunately contained a fleshy tongue, so it was practically impossible to succeed with the intubation. Several anesthesiologists tried and failed.

At the time, Dr. Pertierra was in another room, preparing for a procedure on another patient, when a nurse burst into his operating room, calling for an otolaryngologist. Pertierra hurried out of the room with the nurse, while she breathlessly recounted that they had been unable to intubate the patient, things were bad, and the patient was dying. At that very moment, Pertierra was still wearing a device on his head, a medical headlight that consisted of an adjustable plastic headband with a little light mounted on the front of it. When he arrived at the patient's side, Pertierra rapidly performed a tracheotomy.

A few days later, the doctor was once again called to assist with this same patient when it was time to replace the tube and plug the opening in the trachea. Once Pertierra had done so, he and the patient ended up talking.

The patient told Pertierra that he recognized him. He had observed the entire operation from the side. After the anesthetist had told him that he was to go to sleep, he suddenly saw that he was in a group of people dressed in green who were standing around his body. He heard the monitors and saw that the team was busy working on him. Pertierra narrated the following conversation with the patient (authors' translation):

> "I saw one of them tell a nurse that she had to notify the head doctor in the emergency room or the one in the operating room, and she shot out of the room.

"A few seconds later, you came walking in. It struck me the way everybody turned their head in your direction, that you had some gadget on your forehead, and that you asked for a scalpel and a pair of Mayo scissors, I think. I didn't know there was a type of scissors for every month of the year [mayo is Spanish for May], even though we're not exactly in May."

I think you could tell by looking at me that I was perplexed. Mayo scissors are special surgical scissors known for their durability and we mostly use them because they're bent at the tip. The name has nothing to do with the month of May. [. . .]

"What a tube you were going to stuff into me. When I saw what you wanted to stick into my neck, I thought it wouldn't fit and it looked like one of those sword swallowers, although in this case it was a rubber tube.

"It seemed like I was just somebody who was there, although of course I'm not used to seeing things like that. Just the sight of blood makes me sick, but that didn't happen this time.

"And one of the last things I remember is that the anesthetist who put me to sleep hugged you. That doesn't surprise me, though, because you could see the relief on that poor man's face."

SOURCE

Pertierra, M. Á. (2014). *La última puerta. Experiencias cercanas a la muerte* [The last door: Near-death experiences]. Madrid, Spain: Ediciones Oberón.

Remarks

From the cases in this chapter, we found it convincing that during their near-death experiences, patients are able to have correct, verified perceptions, or AVPs, of specific events in or attributes of their immediate environments that most likely cannot be explained by (residual) activity in their physical senses. Because of the specificity of their reports, often of elements that exceeded their knowledge at the time and/or contradicted their expectations, chance is not an acceptable hypothesis; neither are prior knowledge or the mental reconstruction of events.

The convincing nature of this evidence is revealed not only by the condition in which the patients were when they lost consciousness but also by the fact that some observed details and events took place beyond the patients' normal sensory range. In the next chapter, we will present cases in which the paranormal perceptions involve things entirely beyond the normal scope of the physical senses.

CHAPTER 2

Extrasensory Veridical Perception of Events Beyond the Reach of the Physical Senses

These perceptions are hard to explain by a residual awareness on the part of the body or hallucinations that only by chance correspond with the facts.
—Michael Nahm, PhD, *Wenn die Dunkelheit ein Ende findet* (When the darkness comes to an end)

In Chapter 1, we presented cases of veridical perception of phenomena that were in the immediate vicinity of the near-death experiencers' physical bodies such that the involvement of the physical senses in the perception, though highly improbable or even seemingly impossible, could not be definitively ruled out. In this chapter, we present near-death experiences (NDEs) that include perceptions of events that occurred beyond the range of the normal physical senses. Thus sensory perception of the events would have been impossible even if the physical senses had been functioning normally. In most cases, the perception was of phenomena located at a distance from the physical body. However, this category also includes cases in which the near-death experiencer (NDEr) perceived phenomena in the vicinity of the physical body but beyond the reach of the physical senses.

As mentioned in Chapter 1, cases in which we are reasonably sure that perceptions occurred during cessation of measurable electrical brain activity are included in Chapter 3. With the cases in this chapter, we are not sufficiently certain that cardiac arrest occurred or, if it did, of the moment of cardiac arrest; cases involving greater certainty in this regard appear in Chapter 3.

Cases Reported by Third Parties Without a Direct Statement From the Patient to the Investigator

CASE 2.1 A Letter From the Venezuelan Assistant

This case comes from the website of radiation oncologist Jeffrey Long and his wife and colleague, attorney Jody Long: the Near Death Experience Research Foundation (NDERF; http://www.nderf.org).

Ricardo Ojeda-Vera came from Venezuela, but in 1977 and 1978, having concluded his studies in England, he was working in Germany as an assistant to the head physician of the hospital on a lake called the Tegernsee. The hospital was very well known at that time and specialized in treating terminal cancer patients. Ojeda-Vera was responsible for coordinating therapeutic procedures. It was terribly hard work, and the staff was under enormous pressure.

He was living in a flat in a small house in Rottach-Egern/Weissach. One evening, he was sitting at his desk after work. He wrote a long letter to his mother in Caracas in Spanish, his mother tongue. He told her about all the pressure he was under at work and what he thought of living in a foreign country. He also described the landscape around the Tegernsee.

The next day, he made the ward round together with the head physician. As part of his responsibilities as coordinator, it was his job to pass by all the ward units. At each separate unit, the doctors and head nurses would come to them. In this way, they passed alongside all the beds as they always did. In one of the rooms, there was a patient with a carcinoma in one of her breasts, which had metastasized into her lungs, liver, and bones. The assistant had hardly had any contact with her until then, because, as was customary, it was primarily the head physician who would speak with her. While they were reading the lab results, the patient suddenly turned to Ojeda-Vera and said, "That was a beautiful letter you wrote your mother yesterday." All those present were able to hear this remark and looked at Ojeda-Vera in surprise, which embarrassed him because they might easily conclude that he just went around showing his personal letters to the patients. Although he remembered that he had written his mother a letter, he did not understand how the patient could be aware of this fact.

Two hours later, after finishing the round, he asked her what she had meant. She responded that from the content of the letter, she had realized how fond he was of his mother, and she described in detail exactly what he had written. When he kept asking her how she was able to know this, the patient finally told him that she had looked down on him from the ceiling. She knew he had written the letter at a desk and that he had worn a green bathrobe. Ojeda-Vera asked her if she spoke Spanish. It turned out she did not know any Spanish, but she knew what he had written, nevertheless. She even described what his pen looked like, how things were arranged on his desk, the writing pad he had used, even his Roman-style chair. The patient died 3 days later. Ojeda-Vera, moreover, had not felt any particular bond with the patient. However, he called this the most impressive experience he had ever had.

We included this experience in the first category because it is not an NDE investigator's report but, rather, a personal statement from Ricardo Ojeda-Vera himself. Also, because Ojeda-Vera did not say whether, at the time of her veridical perception, the patient was in the kind of acute condition usually associated with an NDE, the experience might have been an NDE or a closely related type of experience known by various terms such as deathbed vision or nearing-death awareness. Both types of experience occur in individuals who are close to death; in this case, the patient was terminally ill and died within days of her experience. Either way, the case can be regarded as an experience involving telepathy, due to the patient's paranormal knowledge of the contents of Ojeda-Vera's letter.

SOURCES

Ojeda-Vera, R. (n.d.). Roseann's DBV: Report by Ricardo Ojeda-Vera. *Near Death Experience Research Foundation.* Retrieved from http://www.nderf.org/NDERF/NDE_Experiences/roseann_dbv.htm

Speer, C. (2007, December). Sterbebettvisionen [Deathbed visions]. *NTE-Report: Informationsbrief des Netzwerk Nahtoderfahrung, 5*(3), 4–5. Retrieved from http://www.netzwerk-nahtoderfahrung.org/images/Bilder/Dokumente/newsletter/oeffentlich/NTE-Report3-07.pdf

CASE 2.2 A Penny on the Cabinet

Linda L. Morris and Kathleen Knafl, both PhD-level nurses, interviewed 19 nurses about their experiences with patients who had been close to death or who had had an NDE. The nurses reported all kinds of experiences, such as a visible glow around a patient shortly before the patient's death, perceptions of "angels" at the deathbed, and paranormal dreams about patients. One nurse told of a patient who had had an out-of-body experience (OBE) during cardiac arrest. She said:

> So she [the patient] described this whole scene. And I says, "Well, where were you?" And she says, "I was, like, flying above everybody." And so, she described, typical of what you would see if you're doing, like, we'd do CPR

on her. Now, I'm not there. I'm just describing what she's saying. And then she said something that was kinda funny. She said, "There was a penny on top of one of the cabinets but you'd have to climb up to see." And I happened to mention this to another nurse who talks about things like I do. And she actually looked up there and found it.

SOURCE

Morris, L. L., & Knafl, K. A. (2003). The nature and meaning of the near-death experience for patients and critical care nurses. *Journal of Near-Death Studies, 21*(3), 139–167.

CASE 2.3 Maria's Tennis Shoe

Social psychologist Kenneth Ring and NDE researcher Evelyn Elsaesser Valarino discussed a case from 1977 about a U.S. migrant worker named Maria. Maria was admitted to the cardiac ward of Harborview Medical Center in Seattle after a heart attack. Three days after admission, Maria had a second attack. She had an OBE, during which she observed her resuscitation from above and saw how printouts spilled out of the machines that were monitoring her bodily functions and onto the floor, even ending up under her bed. Among other things, she saw a man's left tennis shoe located outside on a ledge near a window on the third floor. After resuscitation, Maria described the shoe in detail for a social worker, Kimberly Clark Sharp. Sharp recently explained to Titus Rivas how they had communicated:

> Maria told me about the shoe—and other experiences while she was out of body—in Spanish, with some English words. For big explanations, a translator was usually on hand, but not at that time. All I had was high school Spanish, but between Maria's poor English and my poor Spanish, and using our hands and facial expressions, we communicated okay. But it took a long time.

Maria told her that the tennis shoe was dark blue, that the material was worn over the little toe, and that one lace end was tucked under the heel. Maria asked Sharp to look for the shoe, thereby confirming her story. Sharp then went to the third floor, looked out all the windows to see if she could see the shoe, and pressed her face against the pane. Finally, she found the shoe, but from inside she could not see the worn-out fabric or the shoelace. Sharp retrieved the shoe from the window ledge, and the description in fact turned out to be correct.

The case is often cited and also received attention from skeptics like Keith Augustine. He passed the case off in 2007 as a kind of urban legend. According to Augustine, investigators Hayden Ebbern, Sean Mulligan, and Barry L. Beyerstein had already demonstrated in the 1990s that Maria could have obtained her information in a normal manner. According to these investigators, prior to Maria's second heart attack, she could have picked up certain details consciously or unconsciously, such as by overhearing hospital personnel discussing the shoe. She would have been able to guess other details, according to them, because they were very predictable. These events would be very difficult to imagine, however, because as Sharp wrote in a 2007 journal article, "[Maria] spoke very little English, certainly not the level that would have been required to comprehend the details of a shoe's appearance and location in the building."

Ebbern, Mulligan, and Beyerstein, moreover, themselves placed a shoe on a ledge on the third floor of the building to determine to what extent it could have

Kimberly Clark Sharp, MSW

been observed from outside. According to them, the shoe was very visible in a normal way from the ground floor, and this would have been even more the case in 1977, considering that in the 1990s, there was a construction site nearby. According to the investigators, it was therefore more than likely that someone had seen the shoe (in an utterly normal manner) and had talked about it, which Maria could in turn have unconsciously overheard.

They also tested Sharp's claim that the shoe was readily visible from inside but only if one's face were pressed against the windowpane. According to them, this action was not necessary at all because the shoe was visible from various spots in the room. In other words, even people on the ward could have seen the shoe and talked about it. In addition, these investigators claimed that the specific details that Sharp reportedly could not see through the window were actually totally visible. They also pointed out that the social worker only wrote a preliminary report 7 years after the incident, which could have led to distortion. According to Augustine, Maria's case was probably (unconsciously) embellished.

In 2007, Sharp herself responded to this challenge to the facts as she knew them. The investigators who had tried to rule out her claims appear to have been rather dishonest and rude in collecting their information. More importantly, however, Sharp addressed their criticisms point by point with information directly opposing their claims. She insisted, for instance, that the characteristics of the shoe could not be seen from inside. The spot that the investigators had used for their experiment did not coincide with the specific spot from which Sharp had looked. And as for whether or not Sharp embellished the story, she claimed that over the years her own version had, on the contrary, grown less distinct because she had forgotten that (according to Maria) a Nike logo had been visible on the shoe near the ankle.

Incidentally in discussions of paranormal cases, "Maria's Tennis Shoe" often morphs into "Kimberly Clark Sharp's Tennis Shoe." This shift probably has to do with the fact that the social worker herself also had an NDE and even wrote a book about it.

SOURCES

Augustine, K. (2007). Does paranormal perception occur in near-death experiences? *Journal of Near-Death Studies, 25*(4), 203–236.

Ring, K., & Valarino, E. E. (1998). *Lessons from the light: What we can learn from the near-death experience*. New York, NY: Insight Books.

Rivas, T. (2008a). Artikelen uit het zomernummer 25(4) van het *Journal of Near-Death Studies* van 2007 [Articles from the summer issue, 25(4), of the *Journal of Near-Death Studies* of 2007]. *Terugkeer, 19*(1), 24–28.

Sharp, K. C. (1995). *After the light: What I discovered on the other side of life that can change your world*. New York, NY: William Morrow; (2003; 2nd ed.) Lincoln, NE: iUniverse.

Sharp, K. C. (2007). The other shoe drops: Commentary on "Does paranormal perception occur in NDEs?" *Journal of Near-Death Studies, 25*(4), 245–250.

CASE 2.4 The New Shoelaces

Social psychologist Kenneth Ring and PhD-level nurse Madelaine Lawrence described the case of a patient of Joyce Harmon's, a surgical intensive care unit nurse at Hartford Hospital in Hartford, Connecticut.

Harmon, at the time of the patient's NDE, had just returned from vacation the week before. During that vacation, she had bought new shoelaces that had a plaid pattern, and she happened to be wearing them her first day back at the hospital. That same day, she was busy resuscitating a patient, a woman whom

Kenneth Ring, PhD

she did not yet know. She administered medications to her. The resuscitation was successful, and the next day Harmon by chance saw her again, and they had a conversation.

The patient said spontaneously, "Oh, you're the one with the plaid shoelaces!" Harmon was dumbfounded and felt the hairs on the back of her neck stand up. The patient told her that she had seen the shoelaces from above when she died.

SOURCE

Ring, K., & Lawrence, M. (1993). Further evidence for veridical perception during near-death experiences. *Journal of Near-Death Studies, 11*(4), 223–229.

CASE 2.5 The 12-Digit Number

The documentary *Beyond the Light* highlights a case reported by Norma Bowe, PhD, a professor in the College of Education at Kean University in Union, New Jersey, and a registered nurse. When Bowe was employed as a nurse in ERs and ICUs, she dealt with many patients. She was regularly confronted by fatalities.

In the neurology ICU, she once encountered a patient with a stitched-up head wound who had had an OBE. The woman came to Nurse Bowe's unit in a coma. She remained in a coma for several weeks. During that time, she had a cardiac arrest from which a team resuscitated her after repeated attempts in the ER.

When the patient came out of her coma, she was unhooked from the apparatuses that had kept her alive. The patient claimed that she had had an OBE, during which she had observed the room from above. Because Bowe was familiar with this kind of story, she did not attach much significance to it, and so she was only half-listening to the patient. The patient, however, turned out to be suffering from an obsessive-compulsive disorder that centered on remembering numbers, and this feature did catch Bowe's attention. The patient compulsively tried to commit to memory every number she came across. The woman claimed that during her OBE, she had imprinted in her memory the serial number of the respirator, which was to be found on the top of the machine. At the time, respirators were some six feet in height. The patient chanted the number, comprising 12 digits. Bowe and her colleagues wrote the number down but thought no more of it.

One day, the respiratory specialist came to take the machine from the room because the patient did not need it any more. A custodial staff member was therefore called to dust the top of the respirator. A ladder was needed to reach it. The man who dusted the machine proceeded to read out exactly the same number as the one the patient had observed from above. (Bowe seems to imply that this happened after she had asked for the number, although it can also be understood that the custodian simply recited the number of his own accord.)

SOURCE

NHNE Near-Death Experience Network. (2012). *Beyond the light* [Motion picture]. Retrieved from http://nhneneardeath.ning.com/video/beyond-the-light

Cases Reported by the Patient and Confirmed by an Investigator or Others Involved

CASE 2.6 The 1985 Quarter

Physician John Lerma worked for 10 years at the renowned Texas Medical Center Hospice at The Medical Center of Houston, Texas, and has written about visions that the dying may have. In his book *Into the Light*, Lerma highlighted the following case, which was instrumental in his decision to pursue a career as a hospice physician.

At the time of this case, Dr. Lerma was working as an intern at a hospital in San Antonio, Texas. One night, several patients were brought to the hospital for emergency treatment, including Ricardo, aged 82, a man who had collapsed while eating dinner. Lerma tried to resuscitate this patient directly. After the first electrical shock, the patient's heart rhythm appeared to restore itself. Ricardo slowly awoke and mumbled something about "the light" and about an

OBE. He also made a comparison with a roller coaster. Ricardo was still bothered by chest pain, so in order to distract him, Lerma asked the patient to tell him more about the roller coaster. Ricardo then described a classic, beautiful NDE, including meeting angels who told him that he would survive. After this short conversation, the patient had another cardiac arrest. The team tried to resuscitate him again by means of a shock, but that did not work this time. Only when Lerma delivered an epinephrine injection into the patient's heart was heart rhythm restored. On the cardiac ward, cardiologists tried to stabilize his heart rate and rhythm. Finally, it was determined that Ricardo had undergone a major infarction, and his heart subsequently responded well to various medical treatments.

The next day, Lerma went to see the new patients and saw Ricardo waving at him and motioning that the doctor should come see him first. He thanked Dr. Lerma for his efforts and also referred to the conversation about the near-death experience. Ricardo told Lerma the kinds of life lessons he had retained from the NDE. Lastly, he asked the intern to help him to prove that his experience had been more than a kind of dream. The patient said:

> When I was out of my body and floating up above the trauma room I spotted a 1985 quarter lying on the right-hand corner of the 8-foot-high cardiac monitor. It was amidst the dust as if someone had put it there for this very reason. Dr. Lerma, could you please check for me? It would mean so much to me.

Subsequently, Lerma took a ladder to the ER. He climbed up the ladder, in the presence of nurses. Lerma wrote, "To our total amazement, there it was, just as he had seen it, and even the year was right: 1985." He argued that there appeared to be only two possible explanations for the correct description of the quarter: Ricardo had placed the quarter there himself, or he was able to truly see the coin in his out-of-body state. He mentioned that Ricardo, from a medical point of view, had not been in any condition to climb a ladder for years. Lerma also could not establish a link with anyone who worked in the ER.

SOURCE

Lerma, J. (2007). *Into the light: Real life stories about angelic visits, visions of the afterlife, and other pre-death experiences.* Wayne, NJ: Career Press / New Page Books.

CASE 2.7 Major Scull

Neuropsychiatrist and neurophysiologist Peter Fenwick and his wife, Elizabeth Fenwick, reported the NDE of Major Scull. During a hospital treatment, Major Scull experienced an OBE in which he floated up to the upper-left-hand corner of his intensive care room. He observed his own body from there. He could also observe, through the windows at the top of the walls of his room, the reception area outside the unit. He suddenly saw his wife, Joan, waiting at the receptionist's desk in the reception area. Her presence there was strange because it was not visiting hours. Joan was talking to someone sitting behind the desk, and she was wearing her red pantsuit. The next thing Scull knew was that he was back in his bed, and the moment he opened his eyes, he saw that his wife was at his bedside and that she was, in fact, wearing the red pantsuit.

The Fenwicks argued that it is hard to imagine that this situation involved no more than coincidence, because Scull observed not only that she was wearing particular clothing but also that she was at the hospital outside of visiting hours. In addition, they emphasized that he was not familiar with the intensive care unit or the reception area because he had not been out of his room since admission into the hospital. The door to his room was closed, so he could not have observed his wife by normal means.

From left to right: Elizabeth Fenwick, Peter Fenwick, MBBch, PhD, and Pim van Lommel, MD

The investigators interviewed his wife, Joan, and asked her whether she often wore the red pantsuit or whether he was particularly fond of it. Neither was the case. Joan was an artist and decided to wear red that day on purpose. This was not a color she often wore, but she thought red was a cheerful color that would be the right thing to cheer up her husband.

SOURCE

Fenwick, P., & Fenwick, E. (1995). *The truth in the light: An investigation of over 300 near-death experiences.* London, UK: Headline (2012, reprint). Hove, UK: White Crow Books.

CASE 2.8 Dan O'Dowd

In 1979, Dan O'Dowd was 29 years old and co-owner of a Hollywood video company, when one day he was hit head-on by a drunk driver on the Pacific Coast Highway along California's coast. Over the next 2 years, 50 operations followed. During one at Cedars-Sinai Medical Center in Beverly Hills that lasted almost 15 hours, Dan had an NDE. Suddenly, totally lucid and awake and no longer under the influence of narcotics, he saw a straight line on the monitor. Then he felt himself soar upward and was looking down at his body. He looked on in astonishment as the doctors declared him dead.

The patient then went into the hallway outside the operating room and observed that his family was being informed of the failure of the operation. Then he was back in the operating room and observed the doctors there, still busy resuscitating him—possibly against their better judgment. To his surprise, he saw that they placed defibrillation paddles on his body and were trying to stimulate his heart with electric shocks. He recalled:

> One guy grabbed those big thumpers and someone puts some gel on me and I'm looking down and I look terrible dead. Then they put those big shockers on me and blast away. The first time nothing. The second time it started me back up and immediately I could feel myself being sucked back under the anesthesia. And out.

O'Dowd later talked of what had happened to him during the operation. His surprised family confirmed that doctors had indeed told them what Dan had seen and heard. Surgeon Mohammed Atik, who headed up the Cedars-Sinai surgical team that worked on O'Dowd, was perplexed. He stated in an article in the *Los Angeles Times* that he did not want to contradict O'Dowd, but that he did not have a medical explanation for the experience.

SOURCE

Tiegel, E. (1983, March 30). His "deaths" transformed the course of his life. *Los Angeles Times*.

CASE 2.9 Mr. O.

Michael Sabom described in *Recollections of Death* the case of Mr. O., a 60-year-old retired manual laborer. Dr. Sabom interviewed him for the first time in August 1977 after he had learned that the man had had an NDE in July 1976 in connection with a heart attack with cardiac arrest. The man observed the procedures involved in his resuscitation, but unfortunately, Sabom did not succeed in tracking down his medical file so as to confirm various details. Mr. O., however, also saw his wife during his OBE, along with his eldest son and eldest daughter, standing beside the doctor in the corridor, crying.

Sabom interviewed Mr. O.'s wife, who had not planned to visit her husband because it was expected that he would be able to go home the next day. Their eldest son and daughter unexpectedly stopped by to see her, and, having the time, they decided to surprise Mr. O. with a joint visit. They did not call him before they went but arrived unannounced at the hospital and walked down the corridor that led to his room. At that moment, it turned out there was a lot going on near his room, and they were stopped by a nurse about 10 rooms away from his room.

The wife recognized her husband's gray hair and knew something was wrong. She saw that he had just been wheeled out of his room and that a number of doctors and nurses were working on him. His face was turned away from her, and she could just see the top of his head. He was then wheeled directly to intensive care on another floor without passing her or the children.

Three days later, Mr. O. had recovered to such an extent that he could tell his wife what had happened. In her words:

> He seen everything. He seen them working with him. And he told me he seen us standing down at the end of the hall. And he couldn't have seen us because his head was facing us [the face pointed the other way]. He couldn't have seen us. . . . He swore he'd seen us, and I said he couldn't have. And even if he had just been laying there in the hall without the heart attack or anything he couldn't have recognized us from the distance. . . . And what was funny was that I wasn't always with the same people. We have six children, and they're all grown. So he couldn't have known who I was with or that I was even there. And he told me who was there. . . . He said he seen us standing there talking to the doctor. And we were. . . . And when he told me the different things that he had seen, it's always the same. He never changes it.

Sabom also interviewed the daughter who had been at the hospital that evening. She was not able to remember many of the details of this particular visit anymore but did recall that she had arrived with her mother and brother moments after her father had unexpectedly had a cardiac arrest.

SOURCE

Sabom, M. B. (1982). *Recollections of death: A medical investigation*. New York, NY: Harper & Row.

CASE 2.10 The Glass Neck of the Medicine Vial

In his book *The Light Beyond*, physician, philosopher, and NDE investigator Raymond Moody described the case of an older woman whom he had resuscitated. While she was on an exam table in the ER, he had applied external (closed) heart massage to her. The female nurse assisting Dr. Moody ran into another room to get a vial of medication that they needed. It was a glass-necked vial that should be held in a paper towel while breaking off the top so as to avoid getting cut. When the nurse returned, the glass neck had already been broken off so that Moody was able to use the medication right away.

When the patient regained consciousness, she looked at the nurse with great kindness and said, "Honey, I saw what you did in that room, and you're going to cut yourself doing that." The nurse was shocked. She admitted that in her haste to open the vial, she had broken off the neck with her bare hands.

The patient recounted to the two of them that she had followed the nurse back into the room to see what the nurse was doing during the resuscitation.

SOURCE

Moody, R. A. Jr. (1996). The light beyond: The experience of almost dying. In L. W. Bailey & J. Yates (Eds.), *The near-death experience: A reader* (pp. 25–38). New York, NY: Routledge.

CASE 2.11 The Red Shoe

The following case was investigated by social psychologist Kenneth Ring and PhD-level nurse Madelaine Lawrence and appeared in their article "Further Studies of Veridical Perception during Near-Death Experiences." It shows a remarkable consistency with Case 2.3 about Maria's tennis shoe—a point that the investigators themselves explicitly acknowledged. This appears to be the kind of meaningful coincidence known as "seriality." Seriality involves a series of incidents that strongly resemble one another without there being a causal connection between those events. It is evident, for instance, in the form of the common occurrence that in their practices, doctors and other medical practitioners regularly encounter multiple patients with the same type of ailment, one shortly after the other.

This case occurred in 1985 and concerns the NDE of a woman who wishes to remain anonymous and who was examined by Kathy Milne, a nurse at Hartford Hospital in Hartford, Connecticut.

Following up on a phone conversation with professor Ring on August 24, 1992, Milne described the NDE in a letter to him dated October 19, 1992. While the patient saw that her body was being resuscitated, she was pulled up through the various floors of the hospital. She was finally viewing Hartford's skyline from above the roof. She had a beautiful view. "She marveled at how interesting this view was and out of the corner of her eye she saw a red object. It turned out to be a shoe. . . . [S]he thought about the shoe . . . and suddenly she felt 'sucked up' a blackened hole."

Milne stated that the rest of this patient's story shares similarity with other NDE stories. Milne shared her story shortly thereafter with a resident who responded with derision and incredulity. Later that day, however, the same man asked a custodian to give him access to the roof—where he recovered the red shoe. He brought the red shoe back inside the hospital. His disbelief had vanished.

As it turned out, Milne had never heard of the case of Maria's tennis shoe (Case 2.3 in this book). She was therefore particularly surprised that there already was a story that so strongly resembled her patient's experience.

SOURCE

Ring, K., & Lawrence, M. (1993). Further evidence for veridical perception during near-death experiences. *Journal of Near-Death Studies, 11*(4), 223–229.

CASE 2.12 Tony

Physician Barbara R. Rommer of Fort Lauderdale, Florida, investigated the case of Tony, the husband of Pat Meo, a nursing supervisor at Rommer's own Holy Cross Hospital. Tony had to undergo a complex open-heart operation in Milwaukee, Wisconsin, in 1993, some 1,250 miles from Fort Lauderdale.

During the operation, his heart was arrested for 30 minutes, and he went into a coma that lasted for 2 weeks. During his NDE, he "floated" back to his house in Fort Lauderdale. Later, he told his skeptical wife, Pat, how he had seen that the person looking after their house was having sex there with an unknown girlfriend. He described what the girlfriend looked like in detail.

Pat considered the experience as nothing more than a dream, but the man who was looking after the house confirmed the accuracy of Tony's observations. What really convinced Pat, however, was the description Tony had given of the mail strewn all over their dining room table. He had seen a Danish office supply catalog lying there, that, according to Pat, they had absolutely never written away for. To her utter surprise, they had indeed received the catalog in question that one time.

In addition to these paranormal observations, Tony also had a vision of life after death, and when he was sent back, a higher being shared with him the exact date of his death. His mission in life until that time would be to bear witness to his NDE. Over a year after his death, Pat found a small piece of paper in one of her husband's desk drawers. Written on it was, "Return date: August 29," the date that corresponded exactly with the day he had died.

SOURCE

Rommer, B. R. (2000). *Blessing in disguise: Another side of the near death experience.* St. Paul, MN: Llewellyn.

CASE 2.13 A Middle-Aged Muslim Woman

Sam Parnia in his book *What Happens When We Die* related the case of a middle-aged Muslim woman who shared her NDE with him. The patient had been admitted to the hospital for interventional surgery. During the operation, she noticed that she was looking at her body below from a ceiling-corner location, and she realized she had died.

The woman told Dr. Parnia:

> I could see outside the operating room, and the doctors were telling my family that I had died. I felt very frustrated, as I felt comfortable [up] at the ceiling and wanted to tell them I was fine. There was complete peace. There was a bright, warm light everywhere. I was really distraught by the fact that my family was so upset and they were all crying. It was very frustrating . . . then the next thing I knew, I was in pain and back in my body.

Parnia had a conversation with the woman's son. The son confirmed to Parnia that the entire family had indeed been told that the woman had died.

SOURCE

Parnia, S. (2006). *What happens when we die: A groundbreaking study into the nature of life and death*. Carlsbad, CA: Hay House.

CASE 2.14 The Smoking Grannies

In 1994, 17-year-old Michaela of Homer City, Pennsylvania, was on vacation with her family. Unfortunately, she was the victim of a serious car accident caused by the driver of a large truck. She was flown to an ER by helicopter. She was not the only family member who was hurt, but her injuries were the gravest. She had suffered serious brain injury and wounds to her arms. The doctor who gave Michaela trauma treatment in the helicopter, Scott Magley, did his utmost to save her, but she still slipped into a coma on arrival at the hospital.

In this condition, Michaela had an NDE with a panoramic review of her past along with a peek into her future. Afterward, she found herself up in the corner of the hospital room from where she looked down on her own body. Then Michaela saw her parents sitting in the hospital cafeteria, with both her grandmothers sitting across from them. In a YouTube clip, she recounted:

> My dad is a smoker and he said he was gonna have a cigarette because he just wanted to get some breathing room and get out of there. And it was funny because my grandmother, my mom's mom, who would never, has never and would never, have a cigarette in her life, was like, "Oh, I need one too. I'm gonna have one too." And then my other grandma was like, "Yeah, me too."

Two weeks later, Michaela awoke from her coma. She told her astonished mother that both her grandmothers had suddenly started smoking in the hospital cafeteria. This event was explicitly confirmed by her mother in the same clip.

SOURCE

NDEAccounts. (2014). *Michaela's-NDE-Meeting with her future family*. Retrieved from https://www.youtube.com/watch?v=EydWO5vqT80

CASE 2.15 Chester

Chester (not his real name) was a 74-year-old retired foundry worker who had had a heart attack. He was first resuscitated in the Appleton, Wisconsin, hospital ER and then transferred to the ICU where critical care physician Laurin Bellg worked. Even though it had been determined that his coronary arteries were completely clean and his heart was working properly again, he still had three more cardiac arrests over the next 2 days. They were triggered by a condition known as ventricular tachycardia, and the medical team had trouble stabilizing his heart rhythm even with large doses of medications and the implantation of a defibrillator.

Later, after it was discovered that Chester had developed pulmonary fibrosis during his working life, he came to the hospital for a follow-up visit to set up a plan to monitor the development of this lung disease. When Dr. Bellg met him again on that occasion, he spontaneously told her about an NDE. It involved OBEs during which Chester noticed that he could direct his OBEs.

Bellg wrote this about Chester's NDE:

Equally curious, Chester found he could also perceive thought and hear conversations between loved ones from a great distance away. He recalled a distinct conversation between his wife and daughter that, based on the subject matter, was later corroborated and found to have been held down the hall in the family waiting room, well out of earshot of the ICU. They were discussing an unusual tree just beyond the waiting room window—its odd shape, fringy foliage, and distinct reddish color. I told Chester that I know that tree and it is a strange one, but he never saw it visually, and there is really no way he could have from where he was in the ICU or where he was when he left the hospital. It is only visible from a certain waiting room courtyard—one he's never been to. He heard them discussing the possibility of taking some leaves from the tree to try to identify it. He also heard them laughing about whether or not it would be considered theft of hospital property if they just took a small cutting. His wife and daughter were shocked when he recounted the conversation to them. How could he possibly have known about that?

He had also heard his two-year-old grandson fussing and crying, then laughing and talking about a green tractor knocking down a wall he had assembled from a set of blocks. His daughter confirmed she had bought the tractor for him in the hospital gift shop to keep him entertained while they waited and that he had been using it to knock over blocks. Again, this all took place in the waiting room, far removed from where Chester lay tenuously trying to stay in a normal heart rhythm. He could hear the conversations clearly, hear his grandson playing with the tractor and blocks, even though he had never seen them and had no way of knowing at the time about these new toys.

In personal correspondence to Robert and Suzanne Mays, as well as Titus Rivas, Bellg added:

I have confirmed [these details] with Chester (not his real name), his wife and his daughter. [. . .] I [knew] him to be in the ICU and not mobile on the days his wife, daughter and grandson were in the waiting room. He was never [physically] in the waiting room.

This NDE could also have been included as a case in Chapter 9, because Chester also claimed that his vision and hearing had considerably improved after the NDE. Unfortunately, this improvement completely disappeared in 3 weeks, before this claim could be assessed medically.

SOURCE
Bellg, L. (2015). *Near death in the ICU.* Appleton, WI: Sloan Press.

CASE 2.16 Don

Don (fictitious name) had been involved in a terrible car accident, which left him with multiple fractures, so that at the hospital in Appleton, Wisconsin, he was immobilized in traction. In addition, his lungs had been bruised, and he had suffered a severe heart contusion and a head injury. Because he was unconscious from the head trauma, and considering the injury to his lungs, plus his broken bones, he was put on artificial ventilation. While he was being stabilized in the ICU for the necessary operations, he remained unconscious, and he literally had nowhere to turn. Nevertheless, he had the impression that he was able to observe and address a female nurse. Considering that she did not respond and then just walked out of the room, he got the feeling that she was ignoring him on purpose. Frustrated by this action, he got out of bed (in his experience) and followed her so as to give her a piece of his mind. At the physical level, though, this activity was utterly impossible because he could not turn over, never mind get out of bed.

Don did not just have some sort of hallucinations but correctly observed all kinds of details about his surroundings that he could not perceive with his eyes or ears because these veridical perceptions were beyond the range of his physical senses.

Laurin Bellg wrote the following about Don's experience:

We know *exactly* what night this happened because the red-headed woman he was looking for was a visiting nurse who had finished her two-month stint of time with us by working a night shift—*that* night shift—before moving on to her next assignment in another city.

Don described getting out of bed and leaving his ICU room through its sliding glass doors. Not seeing anyone, he followed the sound of voices around the corner until he found a group of nurses sitting at a central station, chatting and working on the computers. It was a work center he later described in perfect detail that he couldn't possibly see from his room. Walking up to them, he spotted his nurse and started talking to her, but she did not even acknowledge his presence. [. . .]

I asked him to tell me more about the area he had observed and who he had seen. He described the nursing station perfectly. [. . .] He also described the nurse with the short, wavy red hair who had already moved on to another hospital, long before he was awakened from sedation and removed from the vent.

Although Dr. Bellg suggested to Don that he had had an OBE, this possibility made no sense to him, despite the fact that he had been in traction and totally immobilized at the time of his experience with the nurse.

SOURCE
Bellg, L. (2015). *Near death in the ICU.* Appleton, WI: Sloan Press.

CASE 2.17 Carole

Carole (not her real name), another one of critical care physician Laurin Bellg's patients in Appleton, Wisconsin, was an elderly woman who was suffering from severe sepsis that was affecting several vital organs at the same time. Her kidneys in particular had been affected and, as is normal under the circumstances, would constantly signal her to urinate. However, at the ICU, her urine was being drained through a tube in her bladder. Because Carole was unconscious at this stage, the fact that she could urinate freely could not be explained to her.

Carole had an OBE while she was completely sedated and unconscious. The patient had seen a female nurse and tried to draw her attention for assistance with urinating. The nurse appeared to ignore her completely (similar to Don's experience in the previous case). She finally became so frustrated that she got out of bed in search of a bathroom.

After Carole had regained consciousness, she shared her experience with Dr. Bellg. Carole told her:

> I got up and went to ask someone else where the bathroom was. I saw a receptionist and asked her for directions, but she ignored me, too. I got her name though. [. . .] It was Meg [fictitious name], and she had short, spiky blond hair with dark roots.

Bellg wrote:

> Now, I was really intrigued. Meg only worked part time, and the last time I had seen her working was a couple of days prior to the patient waking to tell me about her experience. She wasn't working the day Carole and I talked. In the days before she was removed from the vent and able to converse with me, Carole was definitely still under deep sedation with a tube in her bladder. Plus, she was on the vent at the time and would not have been able to talk in the way that she was recounting she had. There would have been no possible way for her to climb out of bed and leave her room in order to converse with the secretary she described so accurately. Curiously, she perceived herself as not only observing people we could confirm were there and their actions, but she was also able to feel as if she was actually communicating verbally and walking around.

In response to a question from Robert Mays, Bellg did not completely rule out the possibility that Carole had already seen Meg at some point. However, she found it highly unlikely because Meg only worked at the hospital part time. Furthermore, on August 2, 2015, she wrote:

She did see Meg and described her accurately. [. . .] She said that she had her name. My impression by her description of the other events of the day is that she had seen her badge. I know that she was only wakened from the medically induced coma when Meg was not working.

In response to the question, "Specifically, did you confirm that Meg's location and actions matched Carole's descriptions?" Bellg wrote, "Yes. Primarily because I know the staff so well and generally I know when Meg works."

Just as with Don's experience in the previous case, Bellg's suggestion did not succeed in convincing Carole of the possibility that she had had an OBE.

SOURCE

Bellg, L. (2015). *Near death in the ICU.* Appleton, WI: Sloan Press.

CASE 2.18 Helen

Helen (fictional name) was involved in a very serious car accident. Both of her ankles were broken, and it was a long, difficult procedure to free her from her car. She was unconscious when they tried to get her out of the vehicle, and she regained consciousness only hours after the accident. In spite of all this, she had clear, vivid memories of how she had gotten out of her car in a kind of panic shortly after the collision in order to assess the damage and to determine whether everyone had come through unscathed.

Helen shared her experience with Laurin Bellg, who was directly involved in her care. Dr. Bellg wrote the following about Helen's NDE:

She knew how many vehicles were involved—there were four—and that one was a gray, floral delivery van with company decals on the side, comprised of blue writing superimposed on a spray of red roses. That was correct. This was also something she shouldn't have actually known because she was unconscious at the time.

She described walking over to a dark green, four-door sedan that was smashed against her hood at a sharp angle where it had hit her from the left side, after running a stop sign. She described the dark-haired man with a beard, slumping over the steering wheel, moaning. She correctly detailed that the impact of the two vehicles—her car and the bearded man's—had been the initial catalyst that had created a pile up when the delivery van that was behind her and the white suburban behind it couldn't stop in time. She noted that the van had slammed into the back of her, causing her car to be wedged, like an accordion, between the green vehicle and the van. This left her pinned in and unable to move—physically, that is.

The white suburban merely rear-ended the delivery van behind Helen, and the driver seemed none the worse for wear. Helen pointed out that it was the driver of this vehicle that she had *heard* making the call on her cell phone to emergency services, as clearly as if she were right beside her. This was also correct. The driver of the least damaged, white suburban made the initial call for help.

Helen was unresponsive and trapped in her car, according to the paperwork.

Her consciousness, however, seemed to have surveyed the scene and remembered it accurately from a vantage point, not just outside of her vehicle, but also actually outside of the physical body itself, which was still trapped in the car. She knew the driver of the delivery van was relatively unharmed but unable to open his door, which was rendered unusable by the impact.

She also knew that, after placing the 911 call, the driver of the white suburban was rushing frantically from vehicle to vehicle to survey the damage. She saw her reach into the green sedan, weaving her arm underneath the injured driver, to turn off the engine that had already started to generate billowing smoke from underneath the wrinkled hood. Hearing him groan, she then leaned in to comfort him, rubbing his back in a soothing gesture. Helen heard the lady trying to reassure him that he would be okay and help was on its way.

She also saw the woman in the passenger's seat beside the bearded man crying, obviously upset. Seeing that the owner of the white suburban was focused on the driver, Helen walked over to the passenger side of the car and tried to offer comfort and support to the crying woman through the shattered window, but she didn't answer. She didn't even seem to notice her. Helen assumed it was because the lady was so upset. She thought this was understandable and, in that context, didn't think it strange that the woman didn't answer back or even take notice of her.

It was then that she heard the wailing sirens of approaching police cars and ambulances. She took that as a cue to get back to her own vehicle so that they could all be properly cared for. Walking back to her own car, a sudden realization stopped her in her tracks—she was looking at a woman, apparently unresponsive, in the driver's seat of her car and realized that *she* was that woman.

She was simultaneously standing outside of her own car, looking at what appeared to be *her* body trapped in the driver's seat of a very damaged vehicle. It took her a while to orient to the fact that she was looking at her own body while somehow being separate from it. In doing so, she eventually came to the sobering reality that if she was outside of her body, looking at her self trapped in the heap of mangled metal, then she must be dead. Nothing else made sense.

The official police report indicated Helen was quite entangled in the debris of her car and that it took nearly thirty minutes to extricate her. It was unclear, at the time, exactly what was injured or broken, but, soon enough, the odd angles of her ankles revealed the truth of her injuries and that was what was called into the hospital ahead of her arrival. Not only was she trapped in the rubble of the car, both of her ankles were clearly broken, and she was observed, by experienced rescue workers, to be unconscious at the scene. There is no physical way that she would have been able to get out of her vehicle, let alone walk around and report with such great accuracy what she later described. [. . .]

She told us details she couldn't possibly have been aware of unless she was awake and walking around, observing from the specific angles she described—especially when she saw her own body in the driver's seat of her car.

SOURCE

Bellg, L. (2015). *Near death in the ICU.* Appleton, WI: Sloan Press.

Remarks

Just as with the cases in Chapter 1, the cases included in this chapter show that patients have observed objects, people, and events correctly during their NDEs, although such ability cannot be satisfactorily explained by physiological processes. Even if the physical senses of these patients had been functioning adequately so as to make normal sensory perception possible, this state of affairs still could not explain the correct observations in these specific cases. Evidently, NDErs are not only able to have veridical perceptions of their immediate environments but their perceptions can also utterly exceed the reach of their normal senses. As far as this aspect is concerned, these perceptions are similar, for instance, to perceptions of successful human test subjects in the so-called remote viewing parapsychology experiments of investigators like Russell Targ and Hal Puthoff (1978). In such experiments, people attempt, within a controlled setting, to gain paranormal impressions of randomly chosen remote locations.

An even more direct parallel—outside the context of NDEs—is seen in cases of spontaneous remote perception during OBEs. In this context, in an article about the case of Sylvia Lucia in their collection "From and to the Light" (*Van en naar het Licht*), Anny Dirven and Titus Rivas (2010a) focused on confirmed paranormal perceptions during an OBE. In this case, Sylvia Lucia, a Frisian author, found herself in the place where an old school friend, a woman she had not seen in years, now lived. The perceptions during her OBE specifically corresponded with reality in various aspects and have been confirmed by the school friend and the friend's son. Sylvia Lucia observed, for instance, a bus garage, gas pumps, details of an apartment, and the physical appearance of the friend's son. Chance and self-deception do not seem appropriate as explanations for these experiences.

Another example concerns author and artist Graham Nicholls's account of his verified observations involving the Alexander Nevsky Cathedral in Tallinn, Estonia, during an OBE. His story is confirmed by his partner, Triin Tõniste, whom Nicholls had told in detail about his impressions before he tried to verify them on site. Both talked about this experience in two sequential video clips on Graham Nicholls's account on YouTube (2013).

In addition, Robert and Suzanne Mays (2010) systematically investigated whether the "long-distance" perceptions from 1943 of the well-known NDEr George Ritchie were correct. Considering that over 60 years had elapsed by the time they conducted this investigation, we decided not to include their positive findings as a case in this book. However, we do have great respect for their interesting detective work.

A key feature of Ritchie's NDE was that he "flew" due east by the position of the North Star to his left in the clear night sky. Mays and Mays wrote the following about their findings:

> The correspondence of three aspects of Ritchie's account with likely correlates in the physical world, *all at the exact same latitude,* makes a strong case that his perceptions were in fact veridical:

- Ritchie described leaving the rear door of a ward building that was near the x-ray department of the station hospital. There was a ward building, whose rear door was [located] at the appropriate latitude, which was likely near the hospital's x-ray department.
- Ritchie described passing over a town with multiple blinking caution lights at intersections. The main street in Tyler, Texas, ran directly east-west and lay just north of the appropriate latitude. At the time, Tyler had four traffic lights along this path that were set to caution blinking at night.
- Ritchie described arriving directly over an all-night café in a city by a very large river with a large bridge, which he later recognized was Vicksburg, Mississippi. There was a café at the appropriate latitude at 1501 Levee St. matching the description Ritchie gave and matching the story of his return visit to Vicksburg. Although Ritchie later saw and recognized the building and his later perceptions could have influenced his written accounts, his *recognition* matched the reality in nearly all details (rectangular building, front door flanked by two windows, telephone pole with a guy wire nearby, situated by a large river with a large bridge nearby) and matched other details which were very likely the case (Pabst blue neon sign, all-night operation).

[. . .] The fact that three key aspects of the account have likely corre-lates at the exact same latitude and that Ritchie reports having traveled east strongly suggest that an *objective*, albeit unusual, event occurred. It is highly unlikely that Ritchie could have imagined events, or had *déjà vu* of experi-ences, with such strong physical correlations: a particular ward building rear door, a particular street with multiple caution lights, and a particular café in a city on the far shore of a large river. It is highly unlikely that Ritchie could have fabricated such an account where the details have now been shown to be so highly correlated and where one of the aspects (the caution lights) was mentioned apparently only in passing.

In this chapter, we presented cases of veridical perception in NDEs under the circumstances that what the NDEr perceived was out of range of the five physical senses. However, in these cases, whether or not cardiac arrest was involved, we could not be certain of the temporal correspondence between the medical condition and the perceptions. In the next chapter, we present cases in which that temporal correspondence seems clear.

REFERENCES

Mays, R. G., & Mays, S. B. (2010). *Investigation of George Ritchie's NDE OBE.* Retrieved from http://selfconsciousmind.com/ritchie/

Nicholls, G. (2013). *Verified out-of-body experience—with author Graham Nicholls.* Retrieved from https://www.youtube.com/user/shahmainetwork; part 1 at https://www.youtube.com/watch?v=bCEivV6RhEI; and part 2 at https://www.youtube.com/watch?v=F-qjAVBIk4g

Rivas, T., & Dirven, A. (2010a). *Van en naar het Licht* [From and to the Light]. Leeuwarden, Netherlands: Uitgeverij Elikser.

Targ, R., & Puthoff, H. E. (1978). *Mind-reach: Scientists look at psychic abilities.* New York, NY: Delacorte.

CHAPTER 3

Awareness and Extrasensory Veridical Perception During Cardiac Arrest and Other Conditions Seemingly Incompatible With Consciousness

In cases such as these, we can't say that the experience was happening
at the beginning or the end of the cardiac arrest, as the patients
recalled details of what was happening during the cardiac arrest.
—Sam Parnia, MD, *What Happens When We Die*

Evidence from studies of the brain during cardiac arrest do not in
general support the suggestion that the brain is "severely impaired"
but "functioning" during cardiac arrest. All brain stem reflexes are lost
immediately after cardiac arrest and do not typically return even with
cardiopulmonary resuscitation until after the heart has been re-started.
—Sam Parnia, MD, in a letter to the journal *Resuscitation*

According to philosophical materialists, human consciousness depends directly on the activity of the brain, specifically in the cerebral cortex. From this perspective, complex mental processes, such as perception, thought, and memory, arise from the activity of the neocortex—the portion of the cortex that is more pronounced in humans but that also plays an important role in other animals. During cardiac arrest, the brain activity of the cortex is shut down within an average of about 15 seconds to such an extent that, according to materialists, no complex conscious experiencing can occur after this point. Nevertheless, in dozens of cases of near-death experiences (NDEs), people report such conscious experience precisely when it would be assumed, from a materialist standpoint, to be impossible. These cases are the focus of this third chapter.

Please note that our focus is not on cardiac arrest as such but on the effect that cardiac arrest has on the brain: the total loss of cortical activity ("flat line" on an electroencephalogram [EEG]) that, according to materialists, would be incompatible with the presence of any type of consciousness.

NDEs that occur while the cardiac arrest patient's cortex is either inactive or not active enough to explain clear, complex experiences can be subdivided into various kinds. Division into the separate categories involves the degree to which the timing of the NDE during a clinical death can be confirmed by third parties. In a certain sense, each sequential category provides slightly stronger evidence than the preceding category provided.

In the first category, the NDE in all probability occurred during the cardiac arrest but without this conclusion being supported by specific extrasensory veridical perceptions. Cases 3.2 through 3.5 belong to this category. Cases 3.2 and 3.5 involve young children who spontaneously started talking about an out-of-body experience (OBE) during a clinical death—without anyone having told them that they had almost died. In the remaining cases, patients regained consciousness immediately after a cardiac arrest and reported what they had just experienced. For the cases in this category, it is not a matter of specific observations verified later but, rather, an indication of consciousness during the clinical death.

In the second category, witnesses reported cases of NDEs involving extrasensory veridical observations of striking characteristics of objects, living beings, or incidents directly linked to the cardiac arrest, but investigators did not speak directly with the near-death experiencers (NDErs). Cases 3.6 through 3.18 belong to this category.

In the third category, patients reported veridical perception during an NDE confirmed not by a witness but by a medical report that investigators obtained. Cases 3.19 through 3.22 belong to this category. The fourth category consists of cases with veridical perceptions during a cardiac arrest in which investigators were in contact with both the NDEr and one or more witnesses. Cases 3.1 and 3.23 through 3.36 belong to this last category.

Before we proceed with the cases, we want to address the matter of American cardiologist Fred Schoonmaker of Denver, Colorado, who is said to have collected countless confirmed cases of NDEs during cardiac arrest. If we had been able to locate these cases, we would have included them in this chapter. Unfortunately, despite our best attempts, we were unable to do so. Our investigation began with the website of the Dutch organization Skepsis, where it is stated that an article about Schoonmaker's work appeared in *Anabiosis*, the forerunner to the *Journal of Near-Death Studies*, in 1979 (Vol. 1, No. 1, pp. 1–2). Skepsis placed the article, in

English, below a Dutch translation of a 1990 presentation by Susan Blackmore (http://www.skepsis.nl/bde-blackmore.html) in which she referenced it. Others have attributed the article to John Audette, one of the founders of the International Association for Near-Death Studies (IANDS) that publishes the journal, although Blackmore attributed it to Dr. Schoonmaker himself.

According to the anonymous Skepsis article, Schoonmaker claimed to Raymond Moody and John Audette that he had examined more than 2,300 patients who were in life-threatening states and that more than 1,400 of them had had an NDE. In at least 55 of his cases, flat-lined electroencephalographic brainwave recordings (EEGs) were even recorded. Schoonmaker told them he was writing a book about his findings, but apparently he never followed through.

A further clue was provided in a newspaper article that was mentioned on the Skepsis website and that investigator Robert Mays found for us. The March 24, 1977, article from the Burlington, North Carolina, *Times-News* described a lecture that one of Schoonmaker's research partners had given on their joint research on NDEs. The partner was Loren Young, PhD, a theologian, author, and industrial counselor. Although the article contributed to our impression that Schoonmaker had been involved in serious NDE research, it did not provide further evidence for his extraordinary claim.

Naturally, we really wanted to get hold of the original article in *Anabiosis*, so Anny Dirven and Titus Rivas contacted IANDS in 2010. Rhonda Bailey, IANDS's office manager, replied by e-mail, letting them know that, as far as she was able to determine, the article in question had never been published in *Anabiosis*. Ms. Bailey had reviewed the IANDS *Index to the Periodical Literature on Near-Death Experiences, 1877 Through 2005*. When Dirven and Rivas pressed her, it turned out that the first issue of *Anabiosis* had come out not in 1979 but in 1981. The editorial board had in fact planned a piece about Fred Schoonmaker for that first issue, but it had been postponed until December of that year. Evidently, the plan was never carried out. Bailey even plowed through a number of issues for Dirven and Rivas, but the article did not appear in these either. She therefore concluded that Skepsis had posted an unpublished text in English that never officially appeared in *Anabiosis*.

In addition, Rudolf Smit found a reference by American pediatrician Melvin Morse to a conversation that the latter had had with Schoonmaker in 1993. Schoonmaker allegedly discovered no fewer than 2,000 patients whose EEGs had been recorded, and more than 300 patients supposedly had reported having an NDE during a flat-lined EEG. Schoonmaker himself referred to the (unpublished) article in *Anabiosis*! Morse did state that Schoonmaker remained very vague during the conversation, though, and that he was more interested in recording EEGs in dying patients than in NDEs.

Jim van der Heijden subsequently determined that, according to Google Books, Schoonmaker was also supposed to have talked with American NDE researcher Kenneth Ring about his investigation (as revealed by Susan Blackmore in *Dying to Live*, 1993, p. 133). It turned out to be about someone who had been born blind and who could list the accurate number of people who were in his room during his NDE. Schoonmaker did not report any further details. Because we were unable to locate any of Schoonmaker's alleged cases, we were unable to include them here.

Before we proceed to the cases, we provide some information about terms related to cardiac arrest that will appear throughout this and subsequent chapters. According to various entries in *Wikipedia* (a source we acknowledge is not always accurate but appears accurate on the following points), ventricular fibrillation (VF) is a condition in which there is uncoordinated contraction of the cardiac muscle of the ventricles in the heart, making them quiver rather than contract properly so that there is no pump function; as a result of VF, blood no longer circulates, and the body's tissues no longer receive oxygen. From the onset of VF, the victim loses consciousness within approximately 10 seconds. If this arrhythmia continues without intervention for more than a few seconds, it will likely degenerate further into asystole (nicknamed "flatline" on the electrocardiogram—the complete absence of heart function), and after 5 minutes, irreversible brain damage or brain death occurs. As a consequence of cardiogenic shock, sudden cardiac death (SCD) will result in a matter of a few more minutes. Cardiac arrest can often be reversed by a forced electrical shock through the heart from a defibrillator, such as an automated external defibrillator (AED).

We begin with a typical case containing both consciousness and veridical perception.

CASE 3.1 Observing an Amputation

Jean-Jacques Charbonier, a French anesthetist-ICU doctor at the Capio Clinique Saint-Jean Languedoc in Toulouse, France, became known for his work in the area of NDEs and life after death. In the documentary *Untimely Departure: Near-Death Experience* (a translation of the French-language documentary *Faux Départ—Enquête sur les EMI/NDE*), he mentioned a relevant case of a patient of his:

I operated on a woman under general anesthetic. And when she woke up, she described her operation as if she had been on the ceiling. Not only that, she also described the operation that took place in the next theater, the amputation of a leg. She saw the leg; she saw them put the leg in a yellow bag. She couldn't possibly have invented that and she described it as soon as she woke up. I checked afterwards and the operation had indeed taken place in the next theater. A leg had been amputated at the very same time that she was under anesthetic, and thus totally disconnected from the world.

SOURCE

Barkallah, S. (Producer & Director). (2015). *Untimely departure* [motion picture, English translation]. Berre l'Etang, France: S17.TV 2015. Retrieved from https://www.s17.tv/documentaires/faux-depart.html

Cases of Consciousness During a Cardiac Arrest but Without Specifically Verifiable Observations

CASE 3.2 John's Drawing

This case is derived from the book *What Happens When We Die* by physician Sam Parnia. Dr. Parnia received a letter from a grandmother with the following content:

John's heart had stopped. . . . There was a lot of commotion. They were pressing on his chest and he was lifeless and blue. They put him in an ambulance and took him to hospital. . . .

[After he had been discharged from hospital] one day, during the course of play, he said, "Grandma, when I died, I saw a lady." He was not yet three years old. I asked my daughter if anyone had mentioned anything to John about him dying, and she said, "No, absolutely not." But over the course of the next few months, he continued to talk about his experience. It was all during the course of play and in a child's vocabulary.

He said, "When I was in the doctor's car, the belt came undone, and I was looking from above." He also said, "When you die, it is not the end. . . . A lady came to take me. . . .

"There were also many others who were getting new clothes, but not me, because I wasn't really dead. I was going to come back."

John's parents also noticed that he would draw the same thing again and again. As he grew older, his drawings became more complex, and a balloon, among other things, showed up in them. When he was asked about this balloon, he said, "When you die, you see a bright lamp and . . . are connected by a cord [as a balloon is tied to and held by a string]."

Crucial in this NDE is that it probably started when the boy was clinically dead, specifically when he was en route to the hospital in the ambulance.

SOURCE

Parnia, S. (2006). *What happens when we die: A groundbreaking study into the nature of life and death.* Carlsbad, CA: Hay House.

CASE 3.3 Penny Sartori's Patient 4

The book *The Near-Death Experiences of Hospitalized Intensive Care Patients: A Five Year Clinical Study* by Penny Sartori, PhD, RGN, includes a case of consciousness during a cardiac arrest. It involves a patient whom Sartori referred to as "Patient 4." This woman, on the cardiac ward, had ventricular fibrillation that caused cardiac arrest. She remembered afterward that her husband had been sitting by her bed and then that she had had a vision of hell and, dovetailing with that, a distressing NDE. After this experience, she suddenly found herself lying in her bed again.

Once this patient had been resuscitated, she immediately regained consciousness and did not receive any calmatives or sedatives. She was certain that her NDE had occurred between the moment at which her husband had sat at her bed and the moment she came to again. Considering the patient regained consciousness immediately after resuscitation, this means that the experiences she had must have occurred during her cardiac arrest.

SOURCE

Sartori, P. (2008). *The near-death experiences of hospitalized intensive care patients: A five year clinical study.* Lewiston, UK: Edwin Mellen Press.

CASE 3.4 Penny Sartori's Patient 7

This case also derives from the book *The Near-Death Experiences of Hospitalized Intensive Care Patients* by PhD-level nurse Penny Sartori. It involves a man whom Sartori referred to as "Patient 7." During the time this man was clinically dead, his NDE did not include a material aspect—that is, perception of the material world from a position outside his physical body. However, according to Sartori, it did include a transmaterial (beyond the material world) aspect: He saw his deceased father and found himself in a large room, between two thin lines that seemed to function as a kind of barrier that he could not cross.

Sartori concluded that the NDE occurred during cardiac arrest because the patient was only briefly unconscious and immediately regained consciousness after the cardiac arrest had been resolved.

SOURCE

Sartori, P. (2008). *The near-death experiences of hospitalized intensive care patients: A five year clinical study*. Lewiston, UK: Edwin Mellen Press.

CASE 3.5 Marney S.'s Daughter

On their Near Death Experience Research Foundation (NDERF) website, Jeffrey and Jody Long presented the account of a mother, Marney S., who wrote about her daughter's NDE.

When the little girl was 2 years old, she had an unexpected cardiac arrest and was unconscious for at least 4 minutes. She was resuscitated at a hospital with the help of a defibrillator. Her mother wrote:

A few months after being released from the hospital, she told our then 12 year-old daughter, "I'm all better now." Our older daughter responded with, "You are? How do you know that?" Our 2 year-old said, "God told me." A few weeks later, we were sitting around the campfire as a family roasting marshmallows when our daughter told us, "God came to see me when I was at the hospital. He carried me up to the sky when the doctors were putting something on me. He told me I was all better now and took me back to the hospital." She was very upset that she had to return to the hospital. She really wanted to go.

Her mother thought the statement that they laid something on her (body) was a reference to the defibrillator pads, but the little girl's story is not that specific. Nevertheless, it seems clear that the NDE did occur during cardiac arrest.

SOURCE

Marney S. (n.d.). *Marney S's daughter's NDE*. Retrieved from http://www.nderf.org/
    NDERF/NDE_Experiences/marney_s_daughter_nde.htm

Cases Reported by Third Parties Without a Direct Statement From the Patient

CASE 3.6 Sue Saunders's Patient

At the end of the 1970s, Sue Saunders, a respiratory therapist at Hartford Hospital in Hartford, Connecticut, assisted in the ER with a difficult resuscitation after a cardiac arrest in a man in his 60s. When the patient lost consciousness and showed no heartbeat, she tried administering oxygen to him. About halfway through the resuscitation process, however, someone else took over, and Saunders left to attend to another duty.

A few days later, Saunders saw the resuscitated patient again at the ICU. He greeted her with the words, "You looked so much better in your yellow top. . . . Yeah, I saw you. You had something over your face and you were pushing air into me. And I saw your yellow smock."

This observation turned out to be absolutely true. She had worn the yellow work smock only during the resuscitation, and she had had a mask over her face. She had taken part in the resuscitation efforts after he had lost consciousness and left before he had regained it. Saunders was so impressed by these statements that it gave her goose bumps.

SOURCE

Ring, K., & Lawrence, M. (1993). Further evidence for veridical perception during
    near-death experiences. *Journal of Near-Death Studies, 11*(4), 223–229.

CASE 3.7 The Man With the Dentures

The patient whom we now know as "the man with the dentures" and "the dentures man" became famous as a result of a well-known article in the field of near-death studies authored by Dutch cardiologist Pim van Lommel and his coinvestigators and published in 2001 in the medical journal *The Lancet*. The case was not part of their own investigation, but the authors reported it as an illustration of a patient who had had an NDE when such an experience should have been impossible according to conventional neuropsychological opinion.

The case derives from 1979. The patient in question shared his experience at the time with a male RN who wishes to be referred to as TG. TG was talking about this case with a colleague, and eventually this colleague got in touch with coauthors van Lommel and Vincent Meijers. In 1991, Meijers interviewed TG's colleague. It was not until a few years later, in February 1994, that TG himself was interviewed. This interview by Ap Addink, a member of the Merkawah Foundation staff, led to an unpublished manuscript of which van Lommel and his coauthors wrote up an abstract for their *Lancet* article.

The case was also included in van Lommel's 2007 bestseller *Eindeloos Bewustzijn*, published in English in 2010 as *Consciousness Beyond Life*. Around that time, one of van Lommel's other coauthors, Ruud van Wees, shared with Rudolf Smit that he still had documents from the 1990s about the case. Shortly after this, we (Smit, Rivas, and Dirven) tried to contact both TG and his colleague. This attempt led to phone conversations in 2008 and finally a long interview by Titus Rivas of TG at his home. Rivas, together with Dirven and Smit, prepared the interview for an article in *Terugkeer*. Smit (2008b) used the phone conversations and the article a short while later for his own English-language report for the *Journal of Near-Death Studies*. Dirven and Rivas also tried to establish the identity of the man with the dentures, but this was not possible, as nearly 30 years had transpired since the patient's cardiac arrest.

At the end of 1979, TG worked at the old Canisius Wilhelmina Hospital in Nijmegen, Netherlands, as the senior nurse on the resuscitation team. He received a phone call from ambulance personnel late one evening about a man with a massive heart attack. The man was found unconscious, stone cold, and apparently clinically dead out in a meadow in the Ooij region near Nijmegen. In the ambulance, they tried to resuscitate him, but failed, so the patient was brought into the hospital, ashen gray, with livor mortis (in which blue-black discoloration occurs where blood pools in the lowest areas of a corpse) and blue lips and nails. He exhibited no blood circulation. The patient was a tall, slender man, about 44 years old, and he was probably a rebar worker.

After arriving at the hospital, TG took over the resuscitation, along with two female nurses in training. At that moment, the patient still had no heart rhythm. TG laid the man on a bed in order to position him under a Thumper mechanical CPR device to massage the heart. He inspected the man's mouth in order to place an airway tube in it to prevent the tongue from sagging back into the throat. This action was important because he had to place a ventilation mask on the man's face. During this inspection, TG ascertained, to his surprise, that the patient still had his upper denture in. He thought this was strange, because although the man had already received artificial respiration in the ambulance, the denture evidently had not been noticed. TG removed the upper denture and laid it on a crash cart that had been constructed by the hospital's own building and grounds department. It was a simple metal cart on wheels, with two fixed shelves and a wooden pull-out shelf. On the cart were all the medications and infusion fluids that would be needed for the resuscitation so that everything was out in view and at hand. TG laid the denture on the pulled-out wooden shelf. At that moment, there was still no heart rhythm or blood circulation.

Sometime later, a resident internist came to assist the team, and still later, a cardiologist also came to help. The resuscitation was very difficult, and the team even debated quitting the effort. TG regularly checked to see whether the patient's eyes were reacting normally to light, but the man retained "dead" pupils—unresponsive to light. The team continued the resuscitation effort only because of the man's relatively young age. Not until after over an hour of resuscitation did the patient have enough blood circulation again so that he could be rolled to the ICU. He was still unconscious. In the ICU, he was kept in an artificially induced coma for some time.

About a week later, the patient was back on the cardiology ward. TG had the task of distributing medications there one day:

> And then I opened the door to the room. The man sees me coming in, and I can still see his face, like really surprised and pointing at me. "Hey! But you, you know where my dentures are!" And I say, "How's that?" "Well, you were there when I came in," he says, and I say, "Yes, that's right." I say, "But I still don't know where the dentures are. I'll look for them."
>
> Later that evening, I went back to the man, and I asked him, "Tell me, how could you have known that?" So, then he describes how I take the dentures out of his mouth and place them on a little shelf in a cart with all kinds of bottles on it. And he can still hear the clinking of those bottles. He told me he saw that. He described how I laid them on a little pull-out shelf.
>
> He described it from a high place from where he looked down on us and from a corner so that he could see the whole room. He also described the little counter that was in an alcove. He couldn't [have seen] that from his

bed, lying down, because there were curtains in front of it, halfway. And the position in which he was lying all that time was on his back with his head facing the ceiling, with his eyes closed. I only opened his eyelids to look at the pupil reflex. The rest of the time, his eyes were shut. And he described [the scene and events] to me very clearly. He also described the two young ladies who were there with me. They were my colleagues.

The very important thing was that he also saw and heard our doubt. And we did express our doubt during the resuscitation, like, "So, what should we do now? We've been busy for such a long time already, and still no heart rhythm, still no blood pressure. Shouldn't we stop?"

The patient mentioned two anxious moments during the resuscitation. When he had left his body and had seen himself lying there, he felt a pain at some point from the pressure of the CPR device. He tried to make it clear to the team that they had to stop what they were doing. "Stop that, because I'm still here!" A little while later, when the team was debating about quitting their efforts, the man became scared. "Guys, don't stop, because I'm still here!" In neither case was the patient able to get through to the team. The patient did not describe any transmaterial aspect to his NDE—perceiving and/or interacting with entities and/or environments beyond the material world—but only an extensive material aspect in which he observed the material world from a position outside of his physical body.

TG was very impressed by the patient's story. After all, he was well aware of how poor the man's condition had been. At the time that TG took the upper denture out of the man's mouth, he had not yet turned on the CPR device. TG is therefore certain that at that moment there was still insufficient blood circulation to bring the patient back to any level of consciousness. In addition, the man certainly could not have seen anything because each time TG opened one of his otherwise closed eyelids and shone a bright light on the pupil, it was light-rigid, that is, unresponsive. Even if the patient had been able to see anything at all, purple patches would have appeared in his field of vision the moment TG exposed his eyes to light, in which case, the patient would not have been able to observe anything else very well.

As part of his interview of the patient, TG established that the patient had no normal prior knowledge of the resuscitation room or the crash cart, and his correct observations were far too specific to be based on chance. Considering all the facts, TG believed it was absolutely impossible to "explain away" this

NDE using accepted neuropsychological theory. TG's conviction had remained unchanged for some 30 years when Rivas interviewed him in 2008. There was no change in TG's certainty when skeptical anesthesiologist Gerald Woerlee tried fitting the experience into his materialistic worldview.

Smit and Rivas had exchanges with Dr. Woerlee in 2008 and 2010, supported by Dirven, van Lommel, Jim van der Heijden, and others in *Terugkeer* and IANDS's *Journal of Near-Death Studies*. Woerlee reasoned that the patient had been undercooled and therefore only seemed to be worse off than he actually was; at the hospital, TG supposedly turned the CPR device on and did not take the dentures out of the man's mouth until after that. All of these actions would have sufficiently restored blood circulation so as to enable conscious experiences. According to Woerlee, this sequence of events was not only more acceptable medically, but it also corresponded to what TG had initially presented in an interview. However, in his own response in *Terugkeer*, the nurse emphatically denied Woerlee's account of events. TG never meant to say that he first turned on the CPR device; rather, his intention had been to account for all the procedures that had been employed during the resuscitation, which he had listed in a random order. Without the sequence of events TG adamantly contended took place—that he first took the dentures out and *only then* turned on the device—it would be hard to understand why he would still be so impressed by this case decades after it had occurred.

Woerlee also argued that the patient could have seen TG's face when the nurse was testing his eye reaction, but as was stated, the man had light-rigid pupils and could not see anything at that time. If he saw anything, it would have been the bright light TG shone into his eyes—and then the purple afterimage. Woerlee also claimed that the patient felt the denture being taken out of his mouth. However, according to TG, this is simply impossible because at that time the man could not have had any form of consciousness (according to standard materialistic theories). The same thing applies to hearing sounds. Smit challenged Woerlee to set up an experiment where test subjects had to correctly describe a comparable situation solely on the basis of sound. Woerlee did not, however, take up the challenge.

Finally, Woerlee made use of the fact that the patient had talked of pain under the CPR device. This perception was enough proof for Woerlee that somehow there was, again, sufficient blood circulation. Once again, TG disagreed. We ourselves consider it possible that this perception involved a kind of psychogenic pain that was generated because the patient was shocked, as it were, by what he was perceiving by extrasensory means. But even if Woerlee were correct on this point and the pain were "normal," it still does not explain the OBE that was already under way *before* the Thumper had been turned on. Woerlee was not impressed by our counterarguments and considered his explanation final. On one of his websites, he set up a separate page about the case (http://www.neardth.com/denture-man.php).

In this context, TG wrote in an article in *Terugkeer* in 2008:

I understand that Mr. Woerlee, being a physician, wants to be able to explain the entire event using research that has been conducted, situations that have been described and proven, and past research on comparable events. For medical practitioners, it is evidently intolerable and thus also not true if things happen that they themselves cannot explain on scientific grounds.

SOURCES

Rivas, T. (2008c). Enkele reacties op het stuk van Gerald Woerlee [A few comments on the paper by Gerald Woerlee]. *Terugkeer, 19*(4), 9.

Rivas, T., & Dirven, A. (2010a). *Van en naar het Licht* [From and to the Light]. Leeuwarden, Netherlands: Uitgeverij Elikser.

Smit, R. H. (2008a). Corroboration of the dentures anecdote involving veridical perception in a near-death experience. *Journal of Near-Death Studies, 27*(1), 47–61.

Smit, R. H. (2008b). De Geleerde en de Last van het Geleerde [The scholar and the burden of what has been learned]. *Terugkeer, 19*(4), 1–2.

Smit, R. H., & Rivas, T. (2010). Rejoinder to "Response to 'Corroboration of the dentures anecdote involving veridical perception in a near-death experience.'" *Journal of Near-Death Studies, 28*(4), 193–205.

TG (2008). Commentaar op Woerlee door A-verpleegkundige TG [Comments on Woerlee by registered nurse TG]. *Terugkeer, 19*(4), 8.

van der Heijden, J. (2008). Wat écht is voelt gewoon échter aan dan wat niet écht is [What is *real* simply feels more *real* than what is not *real*]. *Terugkeer, 19*(4), 13.

van Lommel, P. (2008). Reactie op 'de man met het gebit' naar aanleiding van het artikel "Een gesprek met TG over de Man met het gebit" door Titus Rivas [Response to the "Man with the Dentures" on occasion of the article "Een gesprek met TG over de Man met het gebit" by Titus Rivas]. *Terugkeer, 19*(4), 10–12.

van Lommel, P. (2010). *Consciousness beyond life: The science of the near-death experience.* New York, NY: HarperCollins.

van Lommel, P., van Wees, R., Meyers, V., & Elfferich, I. (2001). Near-death experience in survivors of cardiac arrest: A prospective study in the Netherlands. *The Lancet, 358*(9298), 2039–2045.

Woerlee, G. M. (2010). Response to "Corroboration of the dentures anecdote involving veridical perception in a near-death experience." *Journal of Near-Death Studies, 28*(4), 181–191.

CASE 3.8 The Clumsy Nurse

In the "Comments" section to an online *Telegraph* article from September 18, 2008, "Andy" posted an account. Andy was the head nurse at a cardiac ward in East Lancashire, England, from 1982 to 1984. During that time, he regularly spoke with patients who had had NDEs.

One NDE really stuck with him. An older gentleman on the ward had suffered cardiac arrest, so he had had to be resuscitated immediately. The nurse fumbled when this happened. He dropped a kidney tray holding a full syringe of cardio stimulants. He quickly prepared another syringe while the attending physician chided him for his clumsiness.

The patient finally responded well to the resuscitation and was immediately brought to intensive care. Three days later, he was transferred back to the cardiac ward. He told the nurse about his NDE. From above the bed, he had seen how the resuscitation had proceeded. He mentioned the syringe incident and the doctor's chiding. He even knew that the syringe that had fallen had rolled under a bedside locker.

SOURCE

Salter, J. (2008, September 18). Scientists study "out of body experiences." *The Telegraph*. Retrieved from http://www.telegraph.co.uk/news/uknews/2980578/Scientists-study-out-of-body-experiences.html#dsq-content

CASE 3.9 The Hair Clip

In 2012, intensive care nurse Baroness Andrea von Wilmowsky of Pöcking, Germany, reported to Pim van Lommel the following case from her nursing days. The following account is translated by Wanda Boeke from von Wimowsky's own German-language book:

One day a woman with a severe heart attack was admitted to our ward for resuscitation. Resuscitation efforts had already been attempted for a time en route to the hospital, but it didn't look like there was much of a chance of her surviving. She was already clinically dead. At first we didn't really know whether we should continue resuscitation, but did it anyway. It became the most chaotic resuscitation I've ever witnessed.

There were too many people, and they kept stepping on each other's feet and getting in each other's way. An IV bottle was swept off the table in the middle of this chaos and smashed to pieces.

I was a newlywed at the time. My husband had cut a hair clip in the shape of a rose for me out of plywood. I was wearing the hair clip that particular day. The thing must somehow have slid out of my long hair and fallen on the floor. Once on the floor, it was broken when somebody stepped on it. I noticed I was missing the hair clip once the resuscitation had been successfully accomplished.

Our patient lived, but no one thought that she would survive in the long term. She was still completely unconscious when I left for a three-week vacation after that shift. When I first returned to work after that vacation, I saw the patient again. Things were still not going well for her, but she was conscious, and now and then we were even able to talk with each other. At some certain point, out of the blue, she asked me, "What happened to your pretty rose hair clip?" I replied that the hair clip unfortunately had broken not too long ago.

Something about that question perplexed me. There was something odd about it. But, I always had a lot to do, so I didn't think about it anymore. My subconscious must have done so, though, because about three days later as I was riding home on my motorcycle on a country road, it hit me: There was no way she could have seen that hair clip, was there!?

This was so disturbing to me that I had to slam on the brakes and come to a screeching halt. It was shocking! I almost couldn't stop thinking about it until my next shift started, and then I asked her right away how she knew about my clip. In response, she told me the following: During the resuscitation she had had an out-of-body experience in which she hovered in a corner of the room near the ceiling. She had gazed down on the whole scene from above, although she knew that she was actually lying there down below and that we were working on her. But this didn't worry her one bit. She observed everything. She also saw who had stepped on my hair clip and was able to give me a description of the "culprit." It was a doctor, and I didn't have a clue about any of this until that moment! She had also seen the glass bottle fall on the floor and smash to pieces.

Her story made me speechless! Then she told me even more. In this most unusual situation she had seen an extremely bright light and experienced an extraordinary sense of joy—a feeling she had never had before in her life until then! All of her questions had been instantly answered. She had felt utterly happy and at one with the world—and precisely at that moment we had pulled her back into her pain-riddled body! She didn't thank us for that.

Years later I realized: This patient had told me about a near-death experience, in the middle of the 1980s in East Germany!

SOURCE

von Wilmowsky, A. (2012). *Segelfalter* [Sail swallowtail; e-book]. Amazon Digital
   Services.

CASE 3.10 NDE Reported by a Dutch ICU Staff Member

Titus Rivas received several written responses to an interview with the Dutch paper *De Gelderlander* in connection with the case of "The Man With the Dentures" (Case 3.7). One of them came from an ICU staff member who wanted to remain anonymous. He described an NDE of which he had firsthand knowledge:

Right after a successful resuscitation, the patient, a photographer with a fresh transverse spinal cord lesion and heart rhythm disorder, was able to provide a detailed account of what had been done by whom in the preceding minutes. He saw this from a corner up high in the room. Considering that he was totally unconscious, he really baffled the entire team, an anesthetist and three or four nurses. It was talked about a lot afterward, without embarrassment, not like a taboo, but as a remarkable story.

The observations at the time were clear as a bell. From a corner up in the top of the room he saw each person clearly busy with their activity. For instance, someone holding a black balloon near his head. This was the bag on the bag valve mask. Somebody who pressed down on his chest. And then a lot of fussing around his bed, lots of people. He named the people, by name, too, and stated where they were in the room. Considering that someone with ventricular fibrillation doesn't have any blood circulation in his brain and therefore drops into unconsciousness, I consider it improbable that he was still able to perceive through his senses. My colleagues at the time have retired or moved on since then.

Unfortunately I can't say anything more about this. The name of that patient I can no longer recall. The patient was just as surprised as we were; he spends his years utterly dependent in a wheelchair. At the time, he was about 40, but I don't know if he's still alive. It was too long ago to be able to provide more details.

SOURCE

Rivas, T., & Dirven, A. (2009). Twee bijna-doodervaringen gemeld naar aanleiding van een oproep in De Gelderlander over "de man met het gebit." [Two near-death experiences reported in response to an announcement in *De Gelderlander* about "The Man with the Dentures"]. *Terugkeer, 20*(3), 9.

CASE 3.11 Lloyd Rudy's Patient

In July 2011, the account of the famous retired American cardiothoracic surgeon Lloyd W. Rudy (1934–2012) was uploaded on YouTube. After some

Lloyd Rudy, MD, and Mike Milligan, DDS

Internet searching, we figured out that the segment was part of an interview with Mike Milligan during the First Scientific Session of the American Academy for Oral Systemic Health (AAOSH), which took place June 24–25, 2011, at the Westin Hotel in Chicago. This conference was aimed at promoting cooperation between dentists and other physicians. The other part of the interview was about the role of oral infection and tooth decay in heart disease and rejection of implanted heart valves, one of Dr. Rudy's specialties. The very popular, human, and humorous cardiac surgeon first worked as a physician at the Sacred Heart Hospital and the Deaconess Hospital in Spokane, Washington, but later started a cardiac surgery program in Great Falls, Montana.

In the interview, Rudy discussed a patient who, on Christmas Day, as a result of an infection in his mouth, had an infection of his heart valve. Due to the exceptional significance of this case, the full transcript of his statement about this patient follows.

RUDY: We had a very unfortunate individual who on Christmas Day had, from an oral infection, infected his native valve [gestures to indicate a valve of the heart, with "native" referring to the patient's biological valve rather than an artificial, prosthetic valve]. If your native valve has the slightest defect, whether you were born with it or you developed it later—it calcified a little and the valve leaflets don't move or whatever—the body recognizes that as something abnormal that it's got to take care of. So that's what happened to this man, and one of my junior partners was on call, and he had to do an emergency valve resection.

Once we were able to accomplish the repair of the aneurysm and the replacement of the valve, we could not get the person off of the bypass. Every time the four or five liters of blood that we were pumping around his body we would reduce down to two or three, he'd begin to weaken and his blood pressure would go down, and so on. To make a long story short: We simply couldn't get him off the heart-lung machine. Finally, we just had to give up. I mean, we just said: We cannot get him off of the heart-lung machine, so we're going to have to pronounce him dead. So we did that.

And so the anesthesiologist turned his machine off and the bellows that were breathing for the patient stopped. That machine was quiet. The anesthesiologist went into the surgeon's lounge. He hadn't eaten anything all day so he went in to have a sandwich. Then the people who usually clean up the instruments and all that were coming in and taking away all these tools. And my surgical assistant closed the patient in a way that a postmortem exam could be done, because anyone who succumbs on the table by law has to have an autopsy. So he closed him up briefly, with a couple or three wires here and a big stitch to close his soft tissue.

Well, that machine that records the blood pressure and the pulse and the left atrial pressure and all the monitoring lines and things continued to run the paper out onto the floor in a big heap. Nobody bothered to turn it off. And then we put down a trans-esophageal echo-probe, which is just a long tube that has a microphone on the end of it, and we can get a beautiful picture on a monitor of the heart beating. Well, that machine was left on, and the VCR-tape continued to run.

Well, the assistant surgeon and I went in and took our gowns off, and gloves and masks and things, and came back, and we were in our short-sleeve shirts, and we were standing at the door, kind of discussing if there was anything else we could have done, any other medicines we could have given, whatever, to have made this a success. And as we were standing there—it had been at least 20 minutes. You know, I don't know this exact time sequence, but it was close to 20, 25 minutes, that this man recorded no heartbeat, no blood pressure [gestures to indicate the monitoring machine's continuous paper readout], and the echo showing no movement of the heart, just sitting there.

And all of a sudden, we looked up—and this surgical assistant had just finished closing him—and we saw some electrical activity. And pretty soon, the electrical activity turned into a heartbeat. Very slow, 30, 40 [beats] a minute. And we thought, "Well, that's kind of an agonal thing"— and we see that, occasionally, that the heart will continue to beat even though the patient can't generate a blood pressure or pump any blood. Well, pretty soon we look, and he's actually generating a pressure. Now, we're not doing anything; I mean, the machines are all shut off. And we'd stopped all the medicines, and all that.

And so I start yelling, "Get anesthesia back in here!" and, "Get the nurses!" And to make a very long story short, without putting him back on cardiopulmonary bypass, a heart-lung machine, and stuff, we started giving him some medicines, and anesthesia started giving him oxygen. And pretty soon he had a blood pressure of 80, and pretty soon a blood pressure of 100, and his heart rate was now up to 100 a minute, you know.

He recovered and had no neurologic deficit. And for the next 10 days, two weeks, all of us went in and were talking to him about what he experienced, if anything. And he talked about the bright light at the end of the tunnel, as I recall, and so on. But the thing that *astounded* me was that he described that operating room, floating around, and saying, "I saw you and Dr. [Amado-]Cattaneo standing in the doorway with your arms folded, talking. I saw the . . . I didn't know where the anesthesiologist was, but he came running back in. And I saw all of these Post-its sitting on this TV screen." And what those were, were any call I got, the nurse would write down who called and the phone number and stick it on the monitor, and then the next Post-it would stick to that Post-it, and then I'd have a string of Post-its of phone calls I had to make. He described *that*. I mean, there is *no way* he could have described that before the operation, because I didn't have any calls, right?

MILLIGAN: No, and he's sitting, he's *lying* on the [gestures to indicate surgical table]—so he must have been floating?

RUDY: He was up there. He described the scene, things that there is no way he knew. I mean, he didn't wake up in the operating room and see all this stuff.

MILLIGAN: No.

RUDY: I mean he was out.

MILLIGAN: Right.

RUDY: And was out for, I don't know, even a day or two while we recovered him in the intensive care unit. So what does that tell you? Was that his soul up there?

MILLIGAN: It's hard to know, but it certainly brings that possibility into play.

RUDY: It always makes me very emotional.

On January 23, 2013, British correspondent Stephen Woodhead pointed out to Rudolf Smit an online comment by the cardiac surgeon Roberto Amado-Cattaneo of Great Falls, known as Dr. Cattaneo to his U.S. colleagues. In response to the video in which Rudy talked about the case, Dr. Amado-Cattaneo wrote:

Dr. Rudy's description of this event at the time of this patient's surgery is absolutely correct. I was the other cardiac surgeon that he refers to in the video. [. . .] The patient's description of his experience is as Dr. Rudy described it word by word. People should interpret this according to their own beliefs, these are the facts.

On January 28, 2013, Titus Rivas contacted Amado-Cattaneo by e-mail and, in consultation with two NDE researchers, former IANDS president Jan Holden and psychiatrist Bruce Greyson, asked him a number of questions between the end of January and mid-February. Amado-Cattaneo wrote Rivas back the following:

This case happened some time late 1990's early 2000's. I do not know the patient's identity anymore. Neither do I think we can find out, unfortunately. It has been too long and I do not have any records of that case anymore. My role was that of assistant surgeon. I was in the case from beginning to end. I did witness the entire case and everything that my partner Dr. Rudy explained in the video. I do not have a rational scientific explanation to explain this phenomenon. I do know that this happened. This patient had close to 20 minutes or more of no life, no physiologic life, no heart beat, no blood pressure, no respiratory function whatsoever and then he came back to life and told us what you heard on the video. He recovered fully.

I do not think there was something wrong with the monitoring devices. The reason is that there are different types of monitors and they were left on. We could see a flat line, the monitor was on but not recording electrical activity in the heart. When he started coming back, we could see at first a slow beat that eventually evolved into something really closer to normal. The same with the ultrasound scan placed inside the esophagus, we saw no heart activity for the 20 minutes or so, machine still on, and then it started showing muscle movement, that is, contractility of the heart muscle that eventually turned into close to normal function, able to generate a blood pressure and life. The reason we saw him coming back is that fact, that the monitors were on and so we saw him regaining life, when this happened we restarted full support with drugs, oxygen etc.

This was not a hoax, no way, this was as real as it gets. We were absolutely shocked that he would come back after 20 or more minutes, we had pronounced him dead on the operating room table and told the wife that he had died.

I have seen people recover from profound and prolonged shock, but still having life, in this case there was no life. (R. Amado-Cattaneo, personal communication, January 28 and 30, 2013)

Subsequently, Rivas sent Amado-Cattaneo several additional questions suggested to him by Holden and Greyson about the veracity and normal explicability of the patient's statements and about the location of the monitor with the Post-it messages, respectively. Amado-Cattaneo replied:

I do not believe he said anything that we questioned as being real, we thought all along his description was quite accurate regarding things he said he saw or heard. Patients' eyes are always shut during surgery, most of the time they are taped so they do not open since this can cause injury to the corneas. (R. Amado-Cattaneo, personal communication, February 13, 2013)

There are many [pieces of] non-sterile equipment in an operating room including monitors. Monitors are close range so surgeons can "monitor different parameters through the case." The messages to Dr. Rudy I believe were taped to a monitor that sits close to the end of the operating table, up in the air, close enough for anybody to see what is there, like the patient, for example, if he was looking at it. (Dr. R. Amado-Cattaneo, personal communication, February 15, 2013)

At the end of January 2013, Amado-Cattaneo told Smit's correspondent, Woodhead, that the case had occurred not in Great Falls, Montana, but in the period that he and Lloyd Rudy had worked at the Deaconess Hospital in Spokane, Washington. (Both apparently also later worked in Great Falls.)

Anesthesiologist Gerald Woerlee attempted to dismiss this case as one that could be fit perfectly into his materialistic worldview. He wrote in an online article:

> There is an unusual medical event called the [sic] "The Lazarus Phenomenon." The [sic] "The Lazarus Phenomenon" is a situation where a person spontaneously recovers heartbeat, blood pressure, breathing, and consciousness after periods of absent heartbeat lasting sometimes as long as 26 minutes. [. . .] This phenomenon was known and reported during 1994 [. . .]—a period dating before this man was operated and spontaneously recovered heartbeat after 20 minutes of absent heartbeat. Subsequent reviews of this phenomenon [. . .] also seem to have escaped the attention of those involved with describing and reporting this case.
>
> There are multiple explanations for the surprising neurologically intact survival of several of these persons. In some situations, the reason for spontaneous return of circulation is unknown due to lack of details, but that does not mean a paranormal cause. So this fascinating report by Lloyd Rudy is one of the rare, but known cases of the [sic] "The Lazarus Phenomenon." [. . .] This man was only able to report his experiences and observations after recovering evident consciousness and the ability to speak. Accordingly, his experiences and the observations made during his period in the operating theater were remembered experiences and observations. The fact these experiences and observations were recalled memories immediately renders them explicable.

Amado-Cattaneo responded:

> Dr. Woerlee's explanation does not apply to this case. This was not the Lazarus phenomenon, this patient was dead for 25 minutes or more with

no cardiac pulmonary movement or brain function. The brain dies after a few minutes of lack of oxygen, period! This case was 25 minutes at least if not more. I cannot explain it, but it happened and I am a living witness of this case, I was there. Many times in medicine we just do not have the right answers or any answers. One can believe what one wants to believe but this in my mind is a miracle unexplainable by current scientific knowledge.

Regards,

Dr. Roberto Amado-Cattaneo

On September 16, 2015, Amado-Cattaneo sent Woodhead another e-mail in response to the question of whether the patient might not have been able to perceive something with his physical eyes without anyone noticing. Had they, perhaps, already removed the tape from his eyes? If so, what were the implications, then, regarding the question of whether or not his veridical observations could be determined to be normal? Amado-Cattaneo wrote:

We always remove the tapes at the end of the surgery before the patient is transferred to ICU. I am sure this was the case and if so he was so out loaded with anesthetics and other sedatives, that there is no way in the world that he could have seen or be aware of anything.

SOURCES

American Academy for Oral Systemic Health. (2011, June 24–25). *Dr. Lloyd Rudy, famous cardiac surgeon, talks about the importance of oral systemic health* [2-part interview]. Retrieved from http://oralsystemiclink.pro/heart-attack-stroke/1st-scientific-session-of-the-academy-for-oral-systemic-health/

Bale Doneen Method. (2012, May 1). *Making headlines: News & Press: In memoriam— Dr. Lloyd Rudy, Jr.* Retrieved from http://www.baledoneen.com/announcements/in-memoriam-dr-lloyd-rudy-jr

Heritage Funeral Home & Crematory. (2012). *Lloyd William Rudy, Jr. | 1934–2012 | Obituary.* Retrieved from http://www.meaningfulfunerals.net/fh/obituaries/obituary.cfm?o_id=1464561&fh_id=11479

Rivas, T., & Smit, R. H. (2013). Brief report: A near-death experience with veridical perception described by a famous heart surgeon and confirmed by his assistant surgeon. *Journal of Near-Death Studies, 31*(3), 179–186.

Woerlee, G. M. (2014b). *Rivas and Smit & a near-death experience reported by Lloyd Rudy*. Retrieved from http://www.neardth.com/lazarus.php

CASE 3.12 Lifeless Like a Mannequin

We were steered toward this case, which took place in Australia, by the constant alertness of British correspondent Stephen Woodhead. An Australian paramedic who calls himself "Frank" shared the following experience on his website.

Frank and another paramedic responded to an emergency call involving a 49-year-old man who had developed chest pain. When the duo arrived on the scene, they found that the man had collapsed and stopped breathing. He was, in fact, in asystole, a condition in which, as Frank explained, "there is absolutely no electrical activity . . . a sign that the person has been in cardiac arrest for a while and has little hope of survival." The two paramedics called for backup. Then they settled down to the business of resuscitating the man, including performing CPR and intubation and administering intravenous adrenaline. The backup team arrived, and efforts continued. In total, the resuscitation had been underway for 30 minutes when one of the senior paramedics asked, "Okay, what do you guys reckon? Shall we call it?"

According to the account, Frank's partner that day was a "new probationer," or rookie paramedic. Frank responded to the other senior paramedic, saying that the probationer could use more experience with CPR protocol and the team should follow the asystole protocol all the way through. On hearing this, the senior paramedic laughed and said, "Hey, if you want him to get more experience in CPR, there's a maniquien [*sic*] back at the station, he's got just as much chance resuscitating it [as] this guy."

Frank had the distinct feeling that the man who had just been compared to a practice mannequin must have been in an out-of-body state and "heard" the senior paramedic's cynical remark and "decided" he did not yet wish to die. What happened next was a miracle, according to Frank.

> We had a miraculous spontaneous return of circulation (this virtually never happens—and patients still rarely live long term after this much down time). We expedite him to hospital. Two days later we found out that they had stented his heart and that he had been extubated and was neurologically intact in cardiac ICU. No way, we think—good for him!

A paramedic's job involves countless dire situations involving people with life-threatening injuries. What is a critical event in the life of a victim may simply be another case for the paramedic. Thus, after learning the patient had survived intact, Frank did not give the case another thought until early one morning, months after the successful resuscitation of the 49-year-old man, when someone knocked at the department door and addressed Frank by name. The man introduced himself as "John" and said they had met a couple of months prior. The paramedic could not immediately place John. On seeing Frank's confusion, John helpfully remarked that his heart had not been working. As Frank recalled the case, John said, "I want to thank you for giving me an extra 10 minutes of CPR . . . even if it was only so that your rookie could practice CPR."

Paramedic Frank apologized, without wondering how John could have known that the CPR had been continued for another 10 minutes. But John clarified anyway:

> I was there . . . you see . . . I saw the whole thing . . . and I remember Jack saying that he wanted to "call it" and you saying that your probationer needed extra work on his CPR anyway, so you may as well keep going.

Frank was naturally shocked to hear that his feeling at the time that the victim had been out of body had been correct and that the victim had "heard" the senior paramedic talking was also correct. Frank was fascinated. He asked John whether the latter remembered anything else.

> Well, I remember that the other paramedic suggested that there would be just as much likelihood of resuscitating the manequien [sic] back at the station as resuscitating me . . . and it was about then that I realised that this was serious and that if I wanted to live . . . I was going to have to get back in that body . . . and the next thing I know . . . I'm in hospital a few days later.

Frank was so impressed with this statement from a man who had been in asystole that he made sure to recount the case to the other paramedics who had been at the scene that day—and to share the account on his website.

SOURCE
Frank. (2010–2013). *Out of body*. Retrieved from http://www.emergencymedical paramedic.com/out-of-body/

CASE 3.13 Tom Aufderheide's Patient

In his book *Erasing Death*, Sam Parnia reported the account of Tom Aufderheide, MD, a leader in the area of resuscitation technique research. Dr. Aufderheide's story involves the first patient whom he resuscitated when he was a brand-new doctor.

The patient had a cardiac arrest, and Aufderheide felt that he had been given great responsibility because he was on his own. He thought, "How could you [the more experienced doctors] do this to me?" Aufderheide tried to resuscitate the patient using a defibrillator, but the man would just have another attack. It went on like this from about 5:00 a.m. until 1:00 p.m. At about that time, hospital staff came to bring the patient his lunch. Considering the patient was unconscious and Aufderheide was famished, the doctor decided to eat the patient's lunch.

Finally, many hours later, the patient's condition did stabilize. About 30 days afterward, the day before the patient was to be discharged, he addressed Aufderheide. He told the doctor that he had had an NDE. At the end of his story, he said, "You know, I thought it was awfully funny . . . here I was dying in front of you, and you were thinking to yourself, 'How could you do this to me?' And then you ate my lunch!"

In 2013, Aufderheide was a professor of emergency medicine and director of the Resuscitation Research Center at the Medical College of Wisconsin. Rivas sent him an e-mail that Aufderheide answered on September 30, 2013. The doctor confirmed the accuracy of Parnia's presentation in *Erasing Death* and revealed that his patient's observations had in fact been far more extensive. The man had told him that during his NDE he had been able to witness a conversation in the hallway between Aufderheide and the patient's wife and that he had observed a cardiac monitor that was outside of his physical field of vision.

Aufderheide pointed out that the patient's paranormal impressions started at a time when the patient's resuscitation had not even been started yet. The patient received the thought that popped up in the doctor's mind ("How could you do this to me?") before the resuscitation had begun. Aufderheide wrote Rivas, "That got my attention, and to this day I have no explanation."

SOURCE

Parnia, S. (with Young, J.). (2013). *Erasing death: The science that is rewriting the boundaries between life and death*. New York, NY: HarperCollins.

CASE 3.14 The Old Rancher and the Paddles

In his book *Parting Visions*, pediatrician Melvin Morse included the case of a nurse's patient, an old rancher with a heart condition. The nurse had been edu-cated in South Dakota. It was her first day in the ICU when the rancher suddenly had a heart attack and flatlined. The team grabbed a defibrillator and hooked it up as best they could. In their haste and due to their lack of experience, the paddles were incorrectly placed, so the device did not operate well. Finally, the paddles were reversed so that they were able to restart the man's heart.

Morse wrote:

> They later spoke to him, and asked him about their efforts to help him. He smiled gently at them, and told them that in fact they had nothing to do with his successful recovery. He told them that in fact Jesus was responsible for his return to life. And the proof he said is that your machine that you thought you shocked me with was unplugged the entire time.
>
> The students returned to the room that they resuscitated him [in] and found to their amazement that the old rancher was absolutely correct. The machine was unplugged and clearly had been unplugged throughout their attempts to resuscitate him.

SOURCE

Morse, M. L. (with Perry, P.). (1996). *Parting visions: Uses and meanings of pre-death, psychic, and spiritual experiences* (rev. ed.). New York, NY: HarperCollins.

CASE 3.15 The Man Who Could Read a Name Tag

In the book *The Light Beyond* by Raymond Moody, the following case is pre-sented, deriving from a doctor who had gotten in touch with Dr. Moody.

A 49-year-old man had a massive heart attack. The attendant physician tried his utmost to resuscitate the man, but after some 35 minutes, the doctor gave up. He had already started filling out a death certificate when someone pointed out to him that there still seemed to be life in the patient. The doctor again tried resuscitating the patient, and this time the attempt was successful.

The next day, the patient in question was able to tell the doctor in great detail what had happened in the emergency room. What the doctor found truly remark-able was that his patient was able to describe a nurse who came to assist him. The man described her "wedge" hairstyle and was even able to state her last name:

Hawkes. He had read that name on her name tag during his OBE. He had further-more also observed how this nurse had rolled a cart down the hall with two things on it that looked like table tennis paddles, corresponding to the "electroshocker" that was in fact used in the resuscitation. According to the doctor in question, the patient would be able to state these details only if he had actually observed them.

SOURCE

Moody, R. A., Jr. (with Perry, P.). (1988). *The light beyond*. New York, NY: Bantam Books.

CASE 3.16 Richard Mansfield's Patient

In his book *What Happens When We Die* Sam Parnia included a case from a col-league: the seasoned cardiologist Richard Mansfield.

Dr. Mansfield told Dr. Parnia that during one night shift, he had been called regarding a cardiac arrest. Together with other members of the medical team, he rushed to the patient, a 32-year-old man who had no pulse, was not breath-ing, and had a flat EKG (electrocardiogram). The team kept attempting to resus-citate the man, although there seemed to be little chance of saving him. They intubated the patient, and he was administered oxygen and 3-minute cycles of heart compression and adrenaline. He also received atropine, but his EKG remained flat and he did not exhibit any pulse. The team continued with the resuscitation for over half an hour, but when their efforts failed, they lost hope that the patient could still be saved. Considering the patient was 32 years old, they decided to keep going for a short while until it was clear that they could not succeed. Mansfield, as team leader, made the decision to stop the resusci-tation. Before they stopped, he looked at the monitor once more to determine that it and the connections were functioning properly and that the patient still had no pulse. Then the team stopped and accepted that the patient had unfortunately died. They all thought that the outcome was terrible, because he was still so young.

Mansfield left the patient in the room with the nurses, who prepared him for his family. The doctor went to the nurses' station. He made notes in the patient's medical file. While he was busy with this, Mansfield realized he could not remember exactly how many ampules of adrenaline they had given him. About 15 minutes later, he returned to the room to check the number of ampules.

In the room, Mansfield looked at the patient and noticed that the man did not look quite as blue as when Mansfield had left the room. The patient looked pinker, which the doctor thought was very strange. With some hesitation, Mansfield walked over to the patient and checked his groin for a pulse. To Mansfield's amazement, the patient turned out to have a pulse. This meant that the medical team had to resume the resuscitation. Finally, they succeeded in stabilizing the man, and he was then transferred to the intensive care unit, presumably without yet having regained consciousness.

After the cardiac arrest, the medical team was convinced that the patient's brain had suffered injury. However, about a week later, Mansfield was in this patient's room and, to his surprise, not only had the man fully recovered, but he had not incurred any brain damage either.

Mansfield described to Parnia what happened next:

> He told me everything that I had said and done, such as checking the pulse, deciding to stop resuscitation, going out of the room, coming back later, looking across at him, going over and rechecking his pulse, and then restarting the resuscitation. He got all the details right, which was impossible because not only had he been in asystole and had no pulse throughout the arrest, but he wasn't even being resuscitated for about 15 minutes afterward.
>
> What he told me really freaked me out, and to this day I haven't told anyone because I just can't explain it. . . . I also know that I definitely checked the monitor, the leads, the gain [this is a technical means of checking that the flatline is truly flat], and the connections as well as the pulse before stopping. I just can't explain it, and I don't think about it anymore.

SOURCE

Parnia, S. (2006). *What happens when we die: A groundbreaking study into the nature of life and death.* Carlsbad, CA: Hay House.

CASE 3.17 James's Grandfather

Someone calling himself James shared the following NDE on September 3, 2015, on the NDERF website, run by Jeffrey and Jody Long. The account involves the NDE of his grandfather, who died in 1985. Grandson James wrote:

> He was 70 years old when he had a heart attack in 1980, and his heart stopped for a full minute on the operating table. [. . .] When he woke up in the intensive care unit (ICU), he grabbed my mother's hand and intently poured out

his story. He said that in the NDE, he was floating above his body and felt very peaceful. He saw his two daughters and his wife below him, "huddled together." He told my mom with much emotion, that he didn't die because, "You wouldn't let me go." He also said he'd never be afraid of death as a result of his experience.

What I find unique about my grandfather's NDE is the fact that he couldn't have known and nobody told him, that my mother, her sister and my grandmother actually were in the hospital chapel. They were one floor below him and were praying for him to live at the very moment he was on the operating table when his heart stopped. I think the fact my grandfather said he could actually see his family "huddled together" while they actually were together praying for him to live is pretty convincing evidence that he temporarily left his body when his heart stopped.

My mother also told me that she was the one praying aloud, while holding my aunt and grandmother's hands during the time my grandfather's heart stopped for a minute. My grandfather didn't even tell his own wife about his NDE first. Instead, he told my mother first. He was specifically saying "You," referring to my mother, "Wouldn't let me go." I think because she was the one leading the prayer. I think my grandfather's NDE falls in the most rare category of those in which the person reports leaving their body and seeing things that actually were occurring during their NDE.

SOURCE

James. (2015). *James grandfather's NDE.* Retrieved from http://www.nderf.org/NDERF/NDE_Experiences/james_gpa_nde.htm

CASE 3.18 The Key Fob

Physician Miguel Ángel Pertierra Quesada, in his book *La Ultima Puerta* (The Last Door), described an experienced and renowned older surgeon who, during a discussion about NDEs, brought up a case he had witnessed himself. Dr. Pertierra's colleague recounted the following:

There was a case that had a great impact on me concerning a patient with a serious infection. We had to perform surgery on him, and halfway through the operation he had a cardiac arrest following an abrupt drop in blood pressure.

It seemed as if he wouldn't come out of it, but after a little while the green ECG [electrocardiogram] monitor began tracing patterns that were compatible with a weak but constant heart rhythm. This case concerned a middle-aged man.

The team was able to finish up the operation, and after rounds, the surgeon was able to speak with the patient. The man addressed him as follows (authors' translation):

"Hello, Doctor, I'm so happy to see you again," he said. "I really wanted to thank you for saving my life. I know that the whole team contributed, but you were the one who did it. But there is one thing I've been wondering about," he said in a very low voice. "Please excuse my indiscretion, but I know that when you were operating on me I had a cardiac arrest and I almost didn't come out of it. What I don't know is whether this was a dream or reality. As the resuscitation was going on, I saw the way everybody was really busy and concerned about saving my life, but at a certain moment I saw something that drew my attention, and I'd like to know whether it was true. Could I ask you about that?"

The surgeon was somewhat perplexed at his patient's question, but he said that the patient could certainly ask questions. "Do you remember somebody picking up the brown leather key fob that had fallen out of the pocket of your scrubs while you were trying to save my life?" The surgeon was taken aback and hardly knew what to say to his patient. He did remember that a nurse had found it on the floor of the OR. He admitted that it was true that the key fob must have fallen out of his pocket while they were busy with the cardiopulmonary resuscitation. The surgeon recalled that the fob looked exactly as the man had described it. But how did his patient know this?

"Because I saw it fall," the patient said with conviction. "I was able to observe perfectly from my vantage point that it fell out of your pocket without your noticing. I was really wondering if this was a figment of my imagination or if it really happened. But now you've answered that. I thought for a long time that my mind was playing tricks, that it was a reflex of my brain, a fabrication, but now I see that it wasn't, that the incident was real: That day my soul left my body."

Pertierra asked his colleague whether the patient had seen anything else. The surgeon replied that the man "gave a complete description of the operating room and of the way we were, aside from the incident with the key fob."

SOURCE

Pertierra, M. Á. (2014). *La última puerta. Experiencias cercanas a la muerte* [The last door: Near-death experiences]. Madrid, Spain: Ediciones Oberón.

Cases Reported by the Patient Without Confirmation of a Witness, Although Confirmed by a Medical Report

CASE 3.19 A Night Watchman's First NDE

A case from the book *Recollections of Death* by American cardiologist Michael Sabom (1982) concerns the same 52-year-old night watchman from North Florida as in Chapter 1, Case 1.4, who survived two heart attacks with cardiac arrest in 1973 and 1975. Dr. Sabom first met him in November 1977 and learned that the patient had had an extensive NDE during his first cardiac arrest in December 1973. He had seen himself lying on the floor in a semi-fetal position and was also able to see that the floor was a black-and-white tile floor. Two or three people had lifted him onto a metal cart. His legs had been strapped to the cart, and he had been wheeled down the hall, with the cart making a lot of noise. He had eventually seen what looked like a table on which something lay, which he later learned was the defibrillator. He had observed the way the medical personnel had given him an electric shock. It seemed as if the voltage were too high, because his body had jumped some two feet off the table. After that, they had given him a second shock, at which he returned to his body.

In an out-of-body state, he had been able to see the details of his resuscitation. He had seen a small screen that looked like an oscilloscope. It made the same line over and over. A plastic tube that he described as looking like an oil can spout had been inserted into his windpipe. Two round metal disks had been placed on his chest, one considerably larger than the other, and one of the medical personnel had used two hands to stick a needle into his chest—an action that reminded him of an Aztec human sacrifice. The team members had also attempted to place an IV in his left hand but were unsuccessful because the hand had been crushed. (After the resuscitation, they placed an IV in his right hand.) They had pounded him heavily on the chest several times.

Sabom consulted the medical report of the resuscitation, which the patient had not seen, and it showed that the patient's very detailed observations during the NDE corresponded nicely with the recorded events. Considering that the report did not specify that the team had administered medication straight into the patient's heart, Sabom determined that in this case, because an IV hookup had been impossible, the team likely had done what was often done in the early 1970s: They employed a somewhat risky but effective method of direct injection into the heart muscle to quickly administer medication to the patient.

Michael B. Sabom, MD

Sabom got to know the patient better and determined that the man barely had any medical knowledge; among other things, he objected to the customary term "paddles" for the "metal disks" of the defibrillator. During his interview of the patient, when Sabom probed his memory in a way that did not lead him, the patient provided numerous additional details of the resuscitation; the fact that he required some probing convinced the cardiologist that the patient was not motivated by a desire to show off medical knowledge.

SOURCE

Sabom, M. B. (1982). *Recollections of death: A medical investigation*. New York, NY: Harper & Row.

CASE 3.20 Mrs. M.

Another case from Sabom's (1982) *Recollections of Death* involved Mrs. M., a homemaker who was 60 years old when Sabom interviewed her in August 1978. In January of that year, she had been admitted to a neurosurgery ward for serious back pain. During Mrs. M.'s admission in the morning, she had gone into cardiac arrest in her room. During her subsequent NDE, she was able to clearly observe all the procedures that were performed to resuscitate her, along with the equipment used, such as the ventilator and the crash cart. She observed how the medical team pounded her chest and placed IVs, although she did not feel any pain when these procedures were performed. Mrs. M. had also been able to see the way they placed a ventilator mask on her face, lifted her eyelids to look into her eyes, felt her pulse, and took blood from her hand. Furthermore, she had heard a doctor say that she was to be transferred to the intensive care unit, and she had seen a young nurse grab all her personal belongings and put them in bags and suitcases, although the transfer did not take place in the end. Mrs. M. had also seen the doctors and nurses who had come into her room.

Sabom studied the medical report and concluded that Mrs. M.'s description corresponded with the recorded procedures. The blood sample from her hand, for instance, was specifically mentioned in the report. Sabom seemed to have been struck by the remarkably realistic description of the resuscitation.

SOURCE

Sabom, M. B. (1982). *Recollections of death: A medical investigation*. New York, NY: Harper & Row.

CASE 3.21 The Automatic External Defibrillator

In his book *Erasing Death* (*The Lazarus Effect*, UK edition), Sam Parnia (2013) reported only one case that was directly connected to his AWAreness during REsuscitation (AWARE) Study and met our criterion of external confirmation. The case derives from 2011 and concerns the first NDE-related OBE that was encountered in that investigation. It also turns out to be the only case in the report published in 2014 on the first phase of the AWARE Study that met our criteria for this book.

A 57-year-old social worker landed in the Southampton General Hospital in Hampshire, England. He suffered from diabetes and, having become unwell, had been brought to the hospital by ambulance. Preparations to insert a catheter were being made when he went into ventricular fibrillation and had a cardiac arrest. On the ward where this happened, an automated external defibrillator (AED)—the emergency heart-shocking device also found in public places—was available. Specially designed for medical lay persons, an AED is easy to use and can ascertain ventricular fibrillation by itself.

After the resuscitation, the patient told Dr. Parnia about his NDE. What looked like a female angel had motioned to him that he should go up with her, but the patient thought he could not do that. The next minute, though, he was looking down at his own body. The patient saw people standing around him and witnessed that they tried to defibrillate him twice. He could clearly hear an automated voice saying, "Shock the patient, shock the patient." He also specifically observed which people were present, where they were standing, and what they looked like.

Parnia unfortunately could not find anyone who could confirm the man's observations, but he was able to access the patient's medical file. He reported that, according to the medical file, the defibrillator that had been used was an AED, which, as soon as it detects fibrillation, actually does have a voice that says "shock advised," after which it prepares to administer an electrical shock and then directs the user when to administer it. According to the file, this machine was used twice.

SOURCES

Parnia, S., Spearpoint, K., de Vos, G., Fenwick, P., Goldberg, D., Yang, J., . . . & Schoenfeld, E. R. (2014). AWARE—AWAreness during REsuscitation—a prospective study. *Resuscitation, 85*(12), 1799–1805.

Parnia, S. (with Young, J.). (2013). *Erasing death: The science that is rewriting the boundaries between life and death.* New York, NY: HarperCollins.

Cases Reported by the Patient and Confirmed by Third Parties

CASE 3.22 Dominique Surel's Ex

At the end of 2010, in the members-only portion of the Society of Scientific Exploration website, we came across a message from Dominique Surel of Denver, Colorado. Her ex had clinically died in the mid-1970s but had been successfully resuscitated. After he had regained consciousness, he had been able to describe not only how the doctors had tried to resuscitate him but also what had been happening in the room next door and what had been said there.

In an e-mail, we asked Surel for more details. She responded that both the doctors and the nurses verified what her ex had seen and heard in both rooms during his clinical death. She could still remember the way a nurse talked about the NDE in her presence. It showed that her ex had really observed certain situations and witnessed conversations that had taken place in the adjoining room. Surel ruled out that the patient could have observed all of this by normal, sensory means (D. Surel, personal communication [e-mail], November 29, 2010).

SOURCE

Surel, D. (2010). [Untitled entry]. Retrieved from members-only section at https://
    www.scientificexploration.org/

CASE 3.23 An Exceptionally Smooth Resuscitation

In his book *Recollections of Death*, cardiologist Michael Sabom (1982) recounted a
January 1979 interview he had with Mr. J., a 46-year-old laborer from a small American town in northern Georgia. In January 1978, Mr. J. had had a heart attack with
cardiac arrest for the second time, during which he had had an NDE. The patient
observed his resuscitation only visually, without feeling anything. He saw how
everybody stood back for the nurse who resuscitated him. He also saw them give
him only one shock on his chest and what the defibrillator that was used looked
like. From up above, Mr. J. also observed the heads of the doctors and nurses, along
with the room in which he was lying. He also saw a sink, his bed, and two machines.
Mr. J. saw his wife, too, standing outside the door to his room, crying.

Sabom consulted the medical file of the resuscitation and read that the
resuscitation had gone exceptionally well and smoothly. This description corresponded with the patient's observation that he received an electrical shock only
once. His observations of the defibrillation agreed with the standard procedure.
Sabom also sought to get in touch with the patient's wife. She could still remember that she had, in fact, cried when her husband experienced cardiac arrest. She
also confirmed that the patient's descriptions agreed with the resuscitation, as
she herself had observed it through the glass partition wall.

SOURCE

Sabom, M. B. (1982). *Recollections of death: A medical investigation*. New York, NY:
    Harper & Row.

CASE 3.24 The Jacket and the Tie

Cardiologist Maurice S. Rawlings (1991), affiliated with a diagnostic center in
Chattanooga, Tennessee, described a case of a hospital patient who was suffering from recurring chest pain and severe depression. She happened to be a nurse
herself by profession. Dr. Rawlings was asked to examine her, but when he arrived
at the hospital, she was not in her room. Rawlings finally found her unconscious
in the bathroom. She had tried to commit suicide by hanging. She had put a collar
on herself—a collar used to support the neck—and then hung the collar on a coat
hook on the bathroom door. After that, she had slowly bent her knees and finally

lost consciousness. Her tongue and eyes looked swollen, as did her face, which also had a dark bluish color. Rawlings lifted her off the coat hook and laid her on the floor. He ascertained that she had enlarged pupils, and he could not hear a heartbeat when he placed his ear to her chest. He administered external heart massage and mouth-to-mouth respiration. Her roommate alerted some nurses to come and help. The patient was then administered oxygen through a ventilation mask. When electrocardiography was performed, however, the EKG showed a flat line, indicating that electroshock would not have helped—that is, the heart was in asystole, not in ventricular fibrillation that could respond to electroshock. She then also received several medications.

Finally stabilized, the patient was brought by gurney to the intensive care unit, where she remained in a coma for 4 days. On the second day or so after she had awoken from her coma, Rawlings asked her whether she could remember anything about what had happened. The patient stated that she had observed all the effort he had gone through for her. She remembered that he had taken off his brown plaid jacket and tossed it on the floor and that he had loosened his tie, which had brown and white stripes on it. She also remembered that the nurse who came to help him had looked worried. She recalled that Rawlings had asked the nurse to get an Ambu bag (a mask with a balloon to give a patient artificial ventilation) and an IV catheter and that two men with a gurney had come. All these memories were correct, and Rawlings stressed that the patient was clinically dead when she observed these things.

The patient recovered completely and even returned to nursing work. As it happened, she could not remember her suicide attempt at all and experienced no suicidal thoughts.

SOURCE

Rawlings, M. (1991). *Beyond death's door*. New York, NY: Bantam Books.

CASE 3.25 Stopping the Resuscitation

This case concerns a 73-year old man with pressing chest pain, also one of Maurice Rawlings's patients. Before the man had entered Dr. Rawlings's office, he had collapsed in the hall and hit his head on the wall. The man took a few more coughing breaths but then stopped breathing and experienced cardiac arrest with ventricular fibrillation.

A difficult resuscitation followed. Five times the man sat up, pushed every-one away, tried to stand up, only to collapse. In fact, this sequence meant that he was clinically dead six times in a row. Fortunately, the sixth time the pattern stopped, and the patient regained consciousness completely.

The man told Rawlings afterward that he remembered the doctor, just before the sixth resuscitation attempt, saying to a colleague, "We'll try one more time. If the shock doesn't hold this time, let's quit!" He confronted Rawlings, "What did you mean, 'We'll quit'? That was *me* you were working on." The patient's memory in this case, too, was absolutely correct. Rawlings asserted that it was physically impossible for the man to have been able to hear him because the man was clinically dead at that moment.

SOURCE

Rawlings, M. (1991). *Beyond death's door.* New York, NY: Bantam Books.

CASE 3.26 The Blue-Striped Tie

Rawlings (1991) also reported a case of an overweight, middle-aged man whose high blood pressure had repeatedly led to heart attacks with cardiac arrest. He had been clinically dead more than once and had had several NDEs.

Rawlings discussed two of this patient's NDEs, of which one meets the criteria of this chapter section. The patient reported that during the cardiac arrest, he had had an OBE in which he saw two nurses enter the room. One of them was wearing a rose on her uniform. Two more nurses and one orderly entered. Then the patient noticed that his attending physician had also been called back in. The patient wondered why, because he felt just fine.

The doctor took off his coat so he would be able to relieve the nurse who was compressing the patient's chest. The man noticed that the doctor was wearing a blue-striped tie. The room became dark, and the patient had the feeling he was rapidly moving through a dark hallway. Then he was brought back by a tremendous electrical shock to his chest.

Rawlings ascertained that the patient's specific observations, including the number of those present and their actions and the clothing they were all wearing, including the rose and the tie, corresponded with the facts. He concluded from the sequence of the actions that the patient must have been without heartbeat and unconscious during his entire NDE.

SOURCE

Rawlings, M. (1991). *Beyond death's door.* New York, NY: Bantam Books.

CASE 3.27 Sandra do Nascimento

A retired Brazilian psychiatrist named Sandra do Nascimento had had diabetes, heart symptoms, and kidney problems for some time when she finally experienced a cardiac arrest. Subsequently, she had an NDE in which she observed what two doctors and a nurse did to resuscitate her. Then she experienced the powerful presence of a light and a feeling of peace and joy. After the resuscitation, according to her cardiologist, Fernanda Lanzoni, do Nascimento kept bringing up her NDE.

Three days later, the patient recognized a heart surgeon, Leonardo Miana, who had actually been involved in the resuscitation. Do Nascimento had never seen this doctor prior to her cardiac arrest. She addressed him by his first name, Leonardo (a typical Brazilian custom), and she knew he had made an incision during the resuscitation. She was moved to tears on seeing him again and stressed that he had saved her life. A year later, do Nascimento also recognized the other doctor who had assisted Dr. Miana during the resuscitation, and she also addressed him by his first name. Both doctors were particularly impressed by the recollections, and Miana determined that no one could have told do Nascimento any details about the resuscitation.

Later, in response to this and other cases, Miana became actively involved in a Brazilian project in connection with the international AWARE Study. He is currently affiliated with the Santa Casa de Misericórdia de Juiz de Fora, a hospital associated with the Universidade Federal de Juiz de Fora (UFJF) in the city of the same name, Juiz de Fora, in Southeast Brazil.

SOURCES

Pinto, L. F. S., & Raimundo, J. (2011). *Menina ressuscitada em hospital reconhece médico que a salvou* [Resuscitated girl in hospital recognizes doctor who saved her]. Retrieved from http://g1/globo.com/globo-reporter/noticia/2011/09/menina -ressuscitada-em-hospital-reconhece-medico-que-salvou.html

Seara Espírita. (2012). *Cirurgião cardíaco fala sobre experiência de quase morte* [Cardiac surgeon speaks about a near-death experience; interview in Brazilian Portuguese with Leonardo Miana]. Retrieved from http://youtu.be/zpUh5sI2Keg

CASE 3.28 Mark Botts

In his book *Closer to the Light*, Melvin Morse (1990) described the case of young Mark. Mark had been afflicted throughout infancy with tracheomalacia—a floppy windpipe. When he was just 9 months old, he developed serious bron-chiolitis and had to have an emergency tracheotomy, during which he experi-enced cardiac arrest. The doctors worked some 40 minutes to resuscitate him. After the resuscitation, no one ever told Mark that his heart had stopped and that he had been clinically dead.

At the age of 3, Mark saw a Christmas pageant that brought up memories he had of the emergency operation, and he suddenly started talking to his mother about it. He talked of having seen the nurses and doctors bending over him as they tried to wake him up. He had flown out of the room and seen his grandpa and grandma crying while they held each other. He had the impres-sion that they thought he was going to die. Then he saw a long, dark tunnel, and he crawled up it. At the end of it, he saw a bright light toward which he kept moving. Finally, he found a brightly lit place where he ran around in fields with God. After that, God asked him if he wanted to go back home. Mark said no, but God told him that he would be allowed to come back to see him some other day. Mark had clear recollections of his NDE until he was 5 years old, according to Morse.

This case appears not only in Morse's (1990) book but also in Kenneth Ring and Evelyn Elsaesser Valarino's (1998) *Lessons From the Light*. There it is revealed that the boy's full name is Mark Botts and that he retained memories of his NDE even as a teenager. The impressions that Mark received during his OBE of specific events in the physical world turned out to correspond with the facts. Ring and Valarino quoted his mother:

> People would say to us: "How could you believe a child telling you something that had happened to him at nine months old?" And I'd say: "How can you *not* believe when he can tell you where you stood and when it's impossible to see you? How can you not believe him when the things he said happened, when there was no way he could have known it?"

Ring and Valarino added:

> Mark's story, while it may stretch our notions of what children may remem-ber when very young, quite obviously cannot be easily set aside as mere fantasy. There are just too much data that support it.

SOURCES

Morse, M. L. (with Perry, P.). (1990). *Closer to the light: Learning from the near-death experiences of children*. New York, NY: Villard Books.

Ring, K., & Valarino, E. E. (1998). *Lessons from the light: What we can learn from the near-death experience*. New York, NY: Insight Books.

CASE 3.29 Pam Reynolds

During his Atlanta Study, cardiologist Michael Sabom (1998) came across the case of a 35-year-old American singer-songwriter, Pamela (Pam) Reynolds (1956–2010).

In 1991, Reynolds had been diagnosed with a large saccular aneurysm—a sac-like bulge in the wall of a brain artery that is prone to rupture—at the base of her skull under her brain stem. If such an aneurysm does rupture, it leads to hemorrhaging that can affect the adjacent brain stem and result in death. The size and location of the aneurysm made it impossible to remove the bulge by means of a routine neurological intervention. For this reason, Reynolds was sent to neurosurgeon Robert Spetzler at the Barrow Neurological Institute in Phoenix, Arizona. Dr. Spetzler is a pioneer of the method known as hypothermic cardiac arrest, nicknamed the standstill operation. In such an operation, someone's body temperature is dropped to between 59° and 63° F (15° to 17° C). Both heart rate and breathing are stopped, and the blood is drained from the head. In this way, normal physiological processes that could cause serious complications are avoided during operations on the brain, the major arteries, or the heart. From a biological viewpoint, the patient comes very close to death in this procedure, with the understanding that he or she will be roused back to life at the end of the operation.

Once Reynolds was brought into the operating room, she received anesthetics, pain killers, and muscle relaxants, after which she was completely unconscious. Reynolds was hooked up to a machine that took over her breathing. Earbuds equipped with two little loudspeakers were inserted into her ears. The loudspeakers emitted 11 clicks per second at 95–100 decibels in one ear and loud white noise in the other; periodically, the clicking sound was switched to the opposite ear to avoid hearing damage. The earbuds were molded to completely fill her ear canals and then covered with gauze to keep them in place so that all other sound was blocked out. An anesthetist monitored her closely, including keeping track of her EEG to measure her brain activity and, particularly, possible reactions of her brain to the clicking sounds. Such reactions can indicate that the brain is inadvertently still active, even if there is an otherwise flat EEG. Her eyes were taped shut, her head was clamped in place, and the rest of her body was covered with sterile drapes.

After this, neurosurgeon Spetzler began the actual operation on the aneurysm. At the same time, cardiac surgeon Camilla Mican monitored a bypass machine connected to Reynolds's groin artery, a standard technique that is part of the total standstill operation. Her blood was pumped out of her body, cooled, and pumped back in. In this way, the entire body was cooled down. The heart function was taken over by the machine as well. Finally, the bypass machine was turned off and the aneurysm was removed without any complications. Then the machine was turned back on and used to pump blood back into the body and raise body temperature back to normal. Normal heart function was restored, tubes that had been inserted were removed, and the wounds were stitched up.

Early in Spetzler's part of the procedure, just before the cooling down part began, he used a surgical saw to open Reynolds's skull. She later reported that this was when her NDE began. While Spetzler operated the saw, Reynolds perceived a sound that she identified as a musical note (a high natural D). She felt that she popped out of her body and floated above the operating table. The further she left her body behind, the clearer the tone became. Then she observed the doctors working on her body. Her vantage point was just over Spetzler's shoulder. She saw him holding a tool that looked like an electric toothbrush. The thing made a sound that Reynolds found unpleasant, and she observed that it had a groove on top where it appeared to go into the handle. She thought the tool looked like a drill. It had interchangeable blades that resembled bits, and these bits were kept in a small case nearby that looked to her like a socket wrench case. She heard the sound of the saw grow louder. She did not see exactly where the saw bit in, but she did hear something being sawed into. Reynolds then heard someone say that the arteries in her right groin were too small, and somebody else answered that they should try the other side (her left groin). She thought the fuss around her lower body was strange because this was a brain operation, and she did not understand the need for an incision in the groin to connect her to the bypass machine in preparation to cool, then later warm, her blood.

Sabom tried to determine to what extent Reynolds's description of the beginning stage of the operation corresponded with the facts. He contacted Spetzler and was able to see the surgeon's report of the operation.

The correspondences were so major that even Spetzler himself could not offer any normal explanation for them. For instance, Reynolds accurately presented the exchange about her arteries. This perception was physically impossible because the exchange, even if she had been normally conscious, would at the very least have been distorted due to the ear buds.

Pamela Reynolds

Neurosurgeon Karl A. Greene, at the time a newly minted doctor who was involved in the operation, meanwhile also confirmed that Reynolds's experiences were inexplicable. His confirmation came during a conversation with journalist and author Judy Bachrach (2014). She wrote:

> The doctor found it impossible to believe what he had just heard. The surgical saw did in fact look like an electric toothbrush; it emitted a high-pitched sound, and some of its blades were kept in what looked like a toolbox. One of Pam's femoral arteries had been too small to connect to the heart-lung machine, and there had been some discussion about that before a decision was made to try the other femoral artery.

According to author Chris Carter (2011), Stephen Cordova, a technician who worked at the institute at the time, explained to Sabom how the work had been performed, adding that at the time they used to play loud music in the operating rooms. According to Cordova, it was therefore extremely unlikely that Pam Reynolds could have physically heard the exchange.

In response to online discussions with skeptics such as Gerald Woerlee, whom we have mentioned, and to an article of his (2011) in the *Journal of Near-Death Studies*, various opponents of the materialist viewpoint, such as Rudolf Smit, Kristopher Key, and Michael Prescott, themselves tested whether they would be able to follow conversations under such circumstances. This certainly was not the case. At most, what could be caught through the din of the clicks were a few snippets, with no understanding of what was really being said. Smit (2012) described his findings in a letter to the editor of the aforesaid journal. In a reply, however, Woerlee thought it evident that Reynolds was in a better than average position to distinguish sounds because she was a musician. We are of the opinion, however, that no one can negate the din of the clicks, not even someone who is musically trained. Smit addresses this topic in more detail later in this book (Chapter 11).

In another skeptical explanation, Woerlee claimed that Reynolds could have heard through her bones that the surgical instruments were opening her skull, because bones are sound conductors. But this hypothesis does not in any way offer an explanation for the fact that she could hear the spoken exchange.

The descriptions, too, of the saw and the small case containing parts were too similar to reality to be ascribed to pure chance. Both Reynolds and Spetzler confirmed this point to Rivas by e-mail in August 2003, describing everything step by step again so as not to leave any questionable inaccuracies of presentation in the most significant primary sources. Normal explanations, such as foreknowledge, were explicitly rejected by Spetzler. In the BBC documentary *The Day I Died* (Broome, 2006), he asserted:

> I don't think that the observations she made were based on what she experienced as she went into the operating room theater. They were just not available to her. For example, the drill and so on, those things are all covered up. They're not visible. They were inside their packages. You really don't begin to open until the patient is completely asleep so that you maintain a sterile environment.

In one e-mail to Rivas, Spetzler recounted that Reynolds's description was remarkably accurate. To Smit, he added, "She was under EEG burst suppression [a clear sign that the brain is not active but in a state of deep unconsciousness], which is incompatible with anesthetic awareness" (R. Spetzler, personal communication, 2013; see Chapter 11, Note 2).

Dr. Greene wrote Rivas the following about this matter:

> Mrs. Reynolds' NDE-consciousness during the *first phase* involving the bone saw, electrophysiological activity in the central nervous system was more likely than not to have been so profoundly suppressed that Mrs. Reynolds would not have had such a well-formed conscious experience of the use of a bone saw and its sequelae. (K. Greene, personal communication, July 7, 2015)

This point is important, because at this stage, Reynolds indeed had not yet undergone cardiac arrest, but she was fully, unquestionably anesthetized and, according to orthodox models, had too little cortical brain activity to expect any form of consciousness whatsoever, and that is our concern in this chapter.

Reynolds (personal communication, August 2003) wrote Rivas that her accurate observations cannot be explained by normal foreknowledge. Prior to the operation, she had received only a summary explanation of what was going to be done. Considering it was a new procedure, she could not have had access beforehand to written information about the surgical procedures that would be performed—and there was no information online, as the Internet was in its infancy. Reynolds thought it was totally ridiculous that some people assumed that she would have gotten a tour of the operating room and been shown the medical instruments before the operation—which she felt would have been so scary, she might never have gone through with the operation.

She also emphasized to Rivas that she could not after the fact have reconstructed the brief exchange that took place during the early phase of the operation, because she had not known prior to surgery that an incision would be made in her groin, and for 2 days following surgery, she was still unaware of this part of the procedure because the pain in her head was so great that she did not feel the pain in her groin. Reynolds added that before the operation, she had never read a book or article about NDEs and that she had been skeptical about the nature of her own NDE until Sabom investigated further. She thought that NDEs were caused by disruption to the cerebral processes and adjusted her opinion only when Sabom revealed his research results.

Sabom (Broome, 2006) himself stated:

> She looked at the bone saw that was being used to cut open her skull. I didn't have any idea what this thing looked like. She described it as an "electric toothbrush," which I thought was ridiculous. I had to send off for a picture of the saw to Fort Worth, Texas, to confirm whether or not what she said it looked like actually was accurate. And I was astounded when I saw the picture. It indeed does resemble an electric toothbrush.

There also happens to be a slight discrepancy with the actual shape of the saw: It has something resembling a groove, but this groove is on the bottom of the device, not on the handle. The mention of this detail testifies to Sabom's integrity. Unfortunately, this discrepancy on Reynolds's part has led some skeptics to declare her observations to lack all credibility.

Following the observations in the OR, Reynolds suddenly experienced "a presence," and she saw a small point of light that drew her to it. Reynolds (Broome, 2006) said:

> The closer I got to the light, I began to discern different figures, different people, and I distinctly heard my [deceased] grandmother call me. [. . .]
>
> And I saw an uncle who passed away when he was only thirty-nine years old. He taught me a lot; he taught me to play my first guitar. And I saw many, many people I knew and many, many I didn't know, but I knew that I was somehow, in some way connected to them.
>
> I asked if God was the light and the answer was, "No, God is not the light, the light is what happens when God breathes." [. . .]
>
> At some point in time, I was reminded that it was time to go back. [. . .] My uncle was the one who brought me back down to the body. But then I got to where the body was, and I looked at the thing, and I for sure did not want to get in it, because it looked pretty much like what it was, as in: void of life. And I knew it would hurt so I didn't want to get in. But he kept reasoning with me, he says: "Like diving into a swimming pool, just jump in." No. [laughs] "What about the children?" You know what? I think the children will be fine. [laughs] [. . .] He pushed me; he gave me a little help there. [. . .]
>
> I saw the body jump. I saw it do this number [lurches chest forward]. And then he pushed me, and I *felt* it do this number [lurches chest forward again].

If this second phase of Reynolds's NDE really took place during the actual operation on her aneurysm, then it poses a big problem for the materialistic worldview. At that moment, with her heart stopped and the blood drained from her brain, there was *with absolute certainty* no brain activity anymore that could "support" conscious mental function. It did not become clear to us until 2015 that this second stage must have actually arisen while Reynolds could not have experienced any consciousness according to materialist models. Reynolds claimed that she heard the song "Hotel California" during her resuscitation. She also observed how she was "shocked" twice in the process of restarting her heart.

Greene responded to this point in his interview with Bachrach (2014): "The music the doctors had played had indeed included 'Hotel California.' And, of course, the heart—her heart—had to be restarted twice." We wish to point out that—as the various cases in this book illustrate—a patient may need anywhere from one to multiple shocks to reinstate normal cardiac rhythm; there is no standard. Reynolds had no clue that specifically two shocks might be necessary in her case.

Greene confirmed this interesting fact again in an interview for a *National Geographic* program (Sherry, 2008). He said, "She knew her heart had to be stimulated twice to restart. She shouldn't have known that. . . . She was physiologically dead. No brain wave activity, no heartbeat, nothing. No blood inside her body of any consequence. She was dead."

In a July 7, 2015, letter to Titus Rivas, Greene wrote:

There was no blood flow at the time that Pam recalled seeing her body jump, as her body moved as a result of electrocardioversion to restart her heart and, therefore, initiate recirculation of blood to her entire body, including her brain.

A very helpful and diligent English-speaking friend of ours, Stephen Woodhead, wrote us the following regarding Reynolds's case:

When Pam was being rewarmed (on circulatory by-pass), her heart fluttered back to life as expected, but at a severely hypothermic temperature of 27 degrees C (a temperature at which consciousness is not possible coming up from a lower temperature) her heart went into ventricular fibrillation, which is cardiac arrest, which is heart stoppage, no pump action. Two shocks were administered to normalise sinus rhythm as the surgeons were preparing to cut open her chest to give mechanical heart massage.

Pam saw the body jump from a position at the ceiling with her uncle. He then pushed her (apparently) and she entered her body and FELT the second jump. So Pam was somehow AWARE during cardiac arrest and an additional hypothermic coma, still full of barbiturates and apparently still with the BAER functioning [no auditory brainstem response, indicating complete absence of brain activity]. Is it reasonable to suggest she could have been conscious in a normal way in this state?

Skeptics such as Blackmore and Woerlee have asserted that experiences like Reynolds's can never occur during a flat EEG, so they must always occur before or after, when the brain shows enough activity to allow neurologically for the presence of consciousness. Reynolds's own subjective experience within her NDE indicates, however, a *continuum* between the paranormal perceptions of the operation and the experiences in a transmaterial realm.

In addition, the authors of *Irreducible Mind* (Kelly, Kelly, Crabtree, Gauld, Grosso, & Greyson, 2007) rightfully remarked on the following:

> Even if we assume for the sake of discussion that her entire experience occurred during [. . .] earlier stages of the procedure, brain activity at that time was inadequate to support organized mentation, according to current neurophysiological doctrine.

Greene wrote Rivas in the previously mentioned letter of July 7, 2015:

> From a practical standpoint, Mrs. Reynolds' entire conscious experience could be considered anomalous, in that such conscious experience as described by Mrs. Reynolds does not typically occur in our consensus reality while under the influence of doses of barbiturates that markedly suppress brain electrophysiological activity (burst suppression on electroencephalogram); profound hypothermia (loss of spontaneous electroencephalographic activity, somatosensory evoked potential responses, and brain stem auditory evoked potential responses), and circulatory arrest (complete loss of all electrophysiological activity). Mrs. Reynolds' well-informed account of a conscious experience during profound alteration and suppression of central nervous system activity could all be considered anomalous in this setting.

In a subsequent e-mail of August 1, 2015, to Smit on this subject, Greene emphasized that the anesthesiologist would have detected, reported, and responded to any brain activity if it had occurred at any point in Reynolds's surgical procedure:

> EEG activity is continuously monitored throughout any neurosurgical procedure for which any method of intraoperative monitoring is utilized. To ignore ongoing electrophysiological activity during monitoring for neurosurgical

procedures, as inferred, and overlooking seizure activity in a surgical patient places a provider in the United States of America at risk for medical malpractice! [. . .]

The auditory "clicks" of BAER monitoring are continuously monitored throughout the entire neurosurgical procedure.

SOURCES

Bachrach, J. (2014). *Glimpsing heaven: The stories and science of life after death*. Washington, DC: National Geographic.

Broome, K. (Producer). (2002). *The day I died: The mind, the brain, and near-death experiences*. [Motion picture]. Glasgow, Scotland: British Broadcasting Corporation. Retrieved from http://topdocumentaryfilms.com/day-i-died/ (17.40–32.00 minutes)

Carter, C. (2011). Response to "Could Pam Reynolds Hear?" *Journal of Near-Death Studies, 30*(1), 29–53.

Kelly, E. F., Kelly, E. W., Crabtree, A., Gauld, A., Grosso, M., & Greyson, B. (2007). *Irreducible mind: Toward a psychology for the 21st century*. Lanham, MD: Rowman & Littlefield.

MSNBC (Producer). (2001, April 11). *Back from the dead* [interview with Pam Reynolds]. Retrieved from https://www.youtube.com/watch?v=YO8UVebuA0g

Rivas, T., & Dirven, A. (2010a). *Van en naar het Licht* [From and to the Light]. Leeuwarden, Netherlands: Uitgeverij Elikser.

Sabom, M. B. (1998). *Light and death: One doctor's fascinating account of near-death experiences*. Grand Rapids, MI: Zondervan.

Sherry, C. (2008, January 25). *Neurosurgeon and his story of survival after death*. Retrieved from http://mysterial.org.uk/cgi-bin/index.cgi?action=viewnews&id=444

Smit, R. H. (2012). Letter to the editor: Failed test of the possibility that Pam Reynolds heard normally during her NDE. *Journal of Near-Death Studies, 30*(3), 188–192.

Smit, R. H. (with van Lommel, P.). (2003). De unieke BDE van Pamela Reynolds (Uit de BBC-documentaire "The Day I Died") [Pam Reynolds' unique NDE (from the BBC documentary *The Day I Died*)]. *Terugkeer, 14*(2), 6–10.

Woerlee, G. M. (2011). Could Pam Reynolds hear? A new investigation into the possibility of hearing during this famous near-death experience. *Journal of Near-Death Studies, 30*(1), 3–25.

Woerlee, G. M. (2013b). *Successful test of the possibility that Pam Reynolds heard normally during her NDE*. Retrieved from http://www.neardth.com/failed-hearing-test.php

Woerlee, G. M. (2014a). *Pam Reynolds near death experience*. Retrieved from http://www.neardth.com/pam-reynolds-near-death-experience.php

CASE 3.30 The 11-Year-Old Boy

Morse (1990) discussed the case of an 11-year-old boy who had been suffering for months from blackouts and who was therefore brought to a children's hospital for examination and testing. While the boy and his parents were in the waiting room, he had another blackout followed by a cardiac arrest.

Doctors raced in, and the boy immediately received CPR. He was then laid on a gurney and wheeled to the intensive care unit, where they tried to get his heart going again. The boy had no heartbeat for at least 20 minutes. Even the medication he received was to no avail.

When the doctors tried to resuscitate him one more time, he suddenly came to and said, "That was weird. You sucked me back into my body!" He then immediately lost consciousness again. The boy was brought to an operating room for an operative intervention on his heart. A pacemaker was implanted.

Seven years later, Morse had a conversation with the boy, who was then in high school and working part-time. He had completely recovered from his cardiac arrest. He still recalled the pain of the electrical shock that they had used to resuscitate him. At first he hesitated to tell Morse about his NDE, and the doctor had to promise that he would not laugh at him. The boy remembered that he had been up in a corner of the room and had looked down on his body. He had seen the doctors and nurses working on him and exactly which people these were. He told Morse:

> I could see the doctors and nurses working on me. My doctor was there and so was Sandy, one of the nurses. I heard Sandy say, "I wish we didn't have to do this." I wondered what they were doing. I saw a doctor put jelly on my chest. My hair was really messed up. It seemed greasy, and I wished that I had washed my hair before coming to the hospital. They had cut my clothes off, but my pants were still on. I heard a doctor say, "Stand back," and then he pushed a button on one of the paddles. Suddenly, I was back inside my body.

Morse asserted that many verifiable details appeared in his story:

He related many details about the experiences that could be verified. He accurately described his own resuscitation, as though he really watched it from outside his body.

According to Morse, it is clear that an 11-year-old boy cannot give an extremely detailed description of a resuscitation in an emergency room setting, no matter how much television he watches.

Gary Habermas and J. P. Moreland (2004) summarized the veridical details as follows:

After his recovery, he accurately reported the medical procedures used on him, the locations and colors of the instruments in the emergency room, the genders of the medical personnel, and he even reported their discussions.

SOURCES

Habermas, G. R., & Moreland, J. P. (2004). *Beyond death: Exploring the evidence for immortality*. Eugene, OR: Wipf & Stock.

Morse, M. L. (with Perry, P.). (1990). *Closer to the light: Learning from the near-death experiences of children*. New York, NY: Villard Books.

CASE 3.31 Kristle Merzlock

The case of Kristle Merzlock, described by pediatrician Melvin Morse, appears in different variations in the NDE literature. Sometimes she is referred to as "Katie." Critics can see in the variations in the presentation of the case a reason not to take this NDE very seriously. In the Dutch edition of our book, we played it safe, which means that we intentionally did not include the case in our collection and stated this point explicitly, with an explanation.

Since then, we have come to the conclusion that the arguments of the deniers are not as weighty as they first appeared. Kristle has a Mormon background, and this fact was not always made clear in presentations of the case. We assume that Morse glossed over this point to make Kristle's experiences more acceptable to a broad audience. The controversy surrounds an element of Kristle's NDE in which she met the souls of two as-yet-unborn children in heaven. Whereas spiritual preexistence fits with Mormon views, preexistence does not fit with most Christians' views. Some critics who held a Christian perspective felt deceived because Kristle's Mormon background had not been made explicit so they could have taken this fact into consideration in their assessment of her case. Such details are not relevant, however, to our focus: veridical extrasensory perceptions during a cardiac arrest. Those perceptions remain paranormal whatever the NDEr's religious background. For this reason, we decided after long deliberation to include Kristle's case in this English-language edition.

Kristle was a 7-year-old American girl who appears to have drowned in a swimming pool after having been underwater for about 17 minutes. When she was pulled out of the water, she did not show a heartbeat for 45 minutes. When her comatose body arrived at the hospital, Morse was personally involved in her resuscitation. According to a *Reader's Digest* article reproduced online (Celestial Travelers, 2016):

> Kristle's pupils were fixed and dilated, Morse recalls, and she had no gag reflex. A CAT scan showed massive swelling of her brain. A machine was doing her breathing and her blood pH was extremely acidotic, a clear indication of imminent death. "There was little we could do at that point," Morse says.
>
> So when Kristle survived, emerging from her coma three days later with full brain function, Morse was amazed. More extraordinary still, his worldview was profoundly altered when Kristle recognized him. "That's the one with the beard," she told her mother. "First there was this tall doctor who didn't have a beard, and then he came in." That was true. Morse sported a beard, while Dr. Longhurst [the lanky physician who received Kristle in the emergency room], was clean-shaven.
>
> Kristle then described the emergency room with astonishing accuracy. "She had the right equipment, the right number of people—everything was just as it had been that day," Morse explains. She even correctly recited the procedures that had been performed on her. "Even though her eyes had been closed and she had been profoundly comatose during the entire experience, she still 'saw' what was going on."

On August 10, 2012, Alex Tsakiris of Skeptiko.com interviewed Morse about this case. Following are excerpts from that interview, which has since been removed from the Skeptiko.com archives:

> **MORSE:** So by chance or coincidence or fate or whatever, I happened to be in Pocatello, Idaho, and there was a child there who had drowned in a

community swimming pool. She was documented to be under water for at least 17 minutes. It just so happened that a pediatrician was in the locker room at the same community swimming pool and he attempted to revive her on the spot. His intervention probably saved her life but again, he documented that she had no spontaneous heartbeat for I would say at least 45 minutes, until she arrived at the emergency room. Then our team got there.

She was really dead. All this debate over how close do these patients come to death, etc., you know, Alex, I had the privilege of resuscitating my own patients and she was, for all intents and purposes, dead. In fact, I had told her parents that. I said that it was time for them to say goodbye to her. This was a very deeply religious Mormon family. They actually did. They crowded around the bedside and held hands and prayed for her and such as that. She was then transported to Salt Lake City. She lived. She not only lived but three days later she made a full recovery.

TSAKIRIS: And what did she tell you . . .

MORSE: Her first words, the first words she said when she came out of her coma, she turned to the nurse down at Primary Children's in Salt Lake City. She says, "Where are my friends?" And then they'd say, "What do you mean, where are your friends?" She'd say, "Yeah, all the people that I met in Heaven. Where are they?" [Laughs]

The innocence of a child. So I saw her in follow-up, another one of these odd twists of fate. I happened to be in addition doing my residency and just happened to be working in the same community clinic in that area. My jaw just dropped to the floor when she and her mother walked in. I was like, "What?" I had not even heard that she had lived. I had assumed that she had died. She looked at me and she said to her mother, "There's the man that put a tube down my nose." [Laughs]

TSAKIRIS: What are you thinking at that point when she says that?

MORSE: You know, it's one of those things—I laughed. I sort of giggled the way a teenager would giggle about sex. It was just embarrassing. I didn't know what to think. Certainly, I'd trained at Johns Hopkins. I thought when you died, you died. I said, "What do you mean, you saw me put a tube in your nose?" She said, "Oh, yeah. I saw you take me into another room that looked like a doughnut." She said things like, "You called someone on the phone and you asked, 'What am I supposed to do next?'" She described the nurses talking about a cat who had died. One of the nurses had a cat that had died and it was just an incidental conversation. She said she was floating out of her body during this entire time. I just sort of laughed. And then she taps me on the wrist. You've got to hear this, Alex.

After I laughed she taps me on the wrist and she says, "You'll see, Dr. Morse. Heaven is fun." [Laughs] I was completely blown away by the entire experience. I immediately determined that I would figure out what was going on here. This was in complete defiance of everything I had been taught in terms of medicine.

In *Closer to the Light*, Morse (1990) wrote again about Kristle's veridical extrasensory perceptions, referring to her here as "Katie":

Katie [sic] remembered more. "First I was in the big room, and then they moved me to a smaller room where they did X-rays on me." She accurately noted such details as having "a tube down my nose," which was her description of nasal intubation. Most physicians intubate orally, and that is the most common way that is represented on television.

She accurately described many other details of her experience. I remember being amazed at the events she recollected. Even though her eyes had been closed and she had been profoundly comatose during the entire experience, she still "saw" what was going on. [. . .]

At one point in the voyage, Katie was given a glimpse of her home. She was allowed to wander throughout the house, watching her brothers and sisters play with their toys in their rooms. One of her brothers was playing with a GI Joe, pushing him around the room in a jeep. One of her sisters was combing the hair of a Barbie doll and singing a popular rock song. She drifted into the kitchen and watched her mother preparing a meal of roast chicken and rice. Then she looked into the living room and saw her father sitting on the couch staring quietly ahead. [. . .]

Later, when Katie mentioned this to her parents, she shocked them with her vivid details about the clothing they were wearing, their positions in the house, even the food her mother was cooking.

It appears clear to us that the case of Kristle Merzlock is very comparable to other paranormal cases of this type. We consider it unfortunate that Morse did not always provide complete details of the case, even if he did so out of a belief that the reading public would not appreciate them. This exclusion is, however, something very different from someone presenting an obvious *anomaly* as more interesting or more mysterious than is justified. Insofar as we can determine, there is absolutely no evidence of the latter process in this case. For this reason, we consider the case to be an evidential example of veridical extrasensory perception during a cardiac arrest. Kristle observed procedures, such as introducing a small tube into her nose, that took place while she was clinically dead.

SOURCES

Believe it or Not! #3. (2014). *NDE Kristle Merzlock near death experience of 7 year old girl*. Retrieved from https://youtu.be/RaUN_KcX78o

Celestial Travelers. (2016). *Children and the near death experience: Kristle Merzlock*. From *Reader's Digest*, February 2006; Crossing into another realm. Retrieved from http://kuriakon00.com/celestial/child/kristle_merzlock.html

Morse, M. L. (with Perry, P.). (1990). *Closer to the light: Learning from the near-death experiences of children*. New York, NY: Villard Books.

NBC (Producer). (1989). *Near death experience of 7 year old girl—Dr. Melvin Morse*. Unsolved Mysteries, Season 1, Episode 17. Retrieved from https://www.youtube.com/watch?v=H319Mg5PfyQ

Winfrey, O. (Producer). (2011). *Oprah children's near death experiences Dr. Morse presents*. Retrieved from https://www.youtube.com/watch?v=Cz6mqa1s21s

CASE 3.32 Jan Price

During a walk with her husband, John, near their Texas home in December 1993, Jan Price was bitten by a small dog. Although the dog's owner assured them that the dog had been fully vaccinated, Jan Price became ill shortly thereafter.

On December 30, 1993, at 1:35 p.m., Jan felt very ill, and John called for an ambulance. When the crew arrived and she got on the gurney, Jan had an almost fatal cardiac arrest. In an episode of the TV series *Beyond Chance* on Zone Reality (n.d.), this fact is confirmed by the ambulance crew, Melody and Carl, who resuscitated her. The cardiac arrest lasted about 4 minutes.

While Melody began providing CPR and Carl prepared the paddles to shock Jan's heart, Jan's husband saw her slowly rise up out of her body. In John's words, "She looked just as she did, full-fleshed, not a ghostly apparition, and she was wearing this beautiful green, flowing gown." Jan later reported that at that same moment, she in fact had an OBE:

I just was up above looking down at what was going on there and thinking: "Oh my goodness, this is real. EMS is at my house. That's my body down there on that stretcher, and I'm not in it anymore."

She was also able to describe the specific procedures that the ambulance crew had performed during her resuscitation.

In his interview, John continued, "Our dog who had died three weeks before, our Maggi, suddenly appeared before the gurney and looked at me, and I was, I was just totally amazed." Jan later reported that at that point, "I moved into another space, and that's when my dog Maggi appeared before me."

In her book, Jan (1996) provided more detail:

As the density changed, becoming lighter and finer, I felt that I was being lifted to another level of awareness—and then I found myself in surroundings that appeared to be more substantial—Maggi was there. My beautiful dog, my beloved springer, came to me. She had died less than a month before, and John and I still ached from her absence.

I felt her presence, her love, and she appeared to me as she had when she was in physical form—only younger, more vital. She said: "You know that Daddy can't handle both of us being gone right now."

"Yes, I'm going back," I replied. "Will you come soon?"

"When it is time, we will know. Now I will show you wondrous things. Let's explore together."

So Maggi and I were interacting on a finer wavelength, and although we had dropped our physical vehicles, our bodies were made visible to the senses through an image in the mind projected as form—and she was as real to see and touch as she was when I'd held her in my arms in the physical world.

My friend Maggi and I walked side by side as we had so many times in that other place of being. Without any effort we moved through a realm of ecstatic color. The pulsating, indescribable colors were fluid—energy waiting to be formed. Maggi showed me how to shape forms out of energy by pressing with my mind. If you want the form to hold, you press firmly. This is a highly mental plane, and form is created with no bodily effort. An image of that which you wish to create is held in mind, and through intense focus is brought into expression. You can lock it in, or release it. [. . .]

Without spoken words we shared memories and deep feelings. Much communication over here was silent, although sound was sometimes used simply because it was so pleasant. My heart overflowed with gratitude for the opportunity to have this reunion—and see my loved one so joyously, vibrantly alive in what can truly be called paradise.

After John had seen their dog, Maggi, he also saw five people manifest themselves around Jan's body. "They didn't touch her body, but seemed to be massaging and fanning the energy around it."

Jan's NDE entailed even more experiences in a spiritual world, although we will not be discussing them in the context of this book. After her cardiac arrest, she was flown to the Methodist Hospital in San Antonio, Texas.

In the *Beyond Chance* documentary, the paramedic ambulance crew confirmed that Jan had veridical perceptions during her cardiac arrest. Carl reported:

Jan and John Price

She was able to tell us word for word what we said, everything that we did physically to her, and was able to say it in such detail that it would make you sit back and think. How could she possibly know this? There is no way that Mr. Price could have seen what we were doing to her because our bodies blocked his view. There is only one way that she could have known, and that was to be above us.

Likewise, Melody reported, "I believe that Jan had an out-of-body experience, because she gave us too much information that she could not give us. Where her husband was standing, what I was doing."

Thus this case has at least two paranormal aspects. On the one hand, John had a so-called shared near-death experience that entailed his observation of his wife out of her body and of their dog, Maggi, both elements that corresponded to Jan's own subjective experience. On the other hand, Jan reported veridical observations during her cardiac arrest that were verified by the paramedics who treated her.

SOURCES

Price, J. (1996). *The other side of death*. New York, NY: Ballantine Books.

Viacom Productions. (Producer). (1999, December 19). *Matters of life and death*. Beyond Chance with Melissa Etheridge [Video posted online by NDEAccounts. (2015). *Shared near-death experience—Pet spirit guides*]. Retrieved from https://www.youtube.com/watch?v=lLIYZ_SLuHQ

Williams, K. (2014). *Jan Price's near-death experience with her pet dog*. Retrieved from http://www.near-death.com/experiences/with-pets/jan-price.html

CASE 3.33 Howard

Critical care physician Laurin Bellg, in Appleton, Wisconsin, headed up the team that was treating a chronic alcoholic who had had a cardiac arrest, a patient she called Howard in her recent book *Near Death in the ICU* (Bellg, 2015). She administered magnesium to him, but he also needed to be defibrillated. Only after four attempts did he once again show a normal heart rhythm, even though he still had no pulse. Apparently, a portion of his intestines had been removed 2 days earlier because, as a result of his alcoholism, the blood vessels had become diseased and occluded. The operation had been successful, but afterward he began having withdrawal symptoms. Following resuscitation, he was placed on a ventilator, and it was not until 5 days later that he was sufficiently recovered to begin to be weaned off of it. Meanwhile, on the ventilator and thus unable to talk, he had tried to convey something about an NDE but got no further than spelling out the words "green shirt" by pointing to the letters on a letter board and then pointing at Dr. Bellg. At that moment, she was indeed wearing a green shirt but did not understand why this fact was significant.

Once the patient was off artificial ventilation and able to talk, he described who had been present at his resuscitation, what they had worn, and what they had said. The events he perceived had occurred when he certainly must have been unconscious. Bellg was particularly impressed by the detail of his visual observations, which he had made from up above. He provided a thorough description of the resuscitation from the beginning. Early in his NDE, Howard felt himself shoot out of his head:

> I felt myself rising up through the ceiling and it was like I was going through the structure of the building. I could feel the different densities of passing through insulation. I saw wiring, some pipes and then I was in this other room.

It looked like a hospital but it was different. [. . .] It was very quiet and it seemed like no one was there. There were individual rooms all around the edge and on some of the beds were these people, except they were not people, exactly. They looked like mannequins and they had IVs hooked up to them but they didn't look real. In the center was an open area that looked like a collection of work stations with computers.

Dr. Bellg wrote:

That's when my jaw really dropped. I stole a look at the nurse who looked equally surprised. What we knew that Howard didn't, is that right above the ICU is a nurse-training center where new hires spend a few days rotating through different scenarios. There are simulated hospital rooms around the perimeter with medical mannequins on some of the beds. In the center there is indeed a collection of workspaces with computers. I was amazed, but I was all in and I wanted to hear more.

Then Howard also correctly recounted exactly what Bellg had said during the defibrillation. His attention was drawn most by a lime-green shirt that she had worn that day. She was wearing the same shirt again on the day when Howard had tried to communicate about his NDE by means of the letter board.

SOURCE
Bellg, L. (2015). *Near death in the ICU.* Appleton, WI: Sloan Press.

CASE 3.34 Mr. Müller's Patient

On September 10, 2015, neurologist Wilfried Kuhn of Leopoldina Hospital in Schweinfurt, Germany, forwarded to Rivas an NDE account from psychologist Joachim Nicolay. This account included a statement from a former German perioperative nurse named Mr. Müller. This gentleman wrote the following (authors' translation):

Fifteen years ago, I worked as a perioperative (theater) nurse at a hospital. One day, a young man who had had a motorcycle accident was brought in. It was determined that he had several injuries. I attended at the operation.

As a nurse, it was my responsibility to provide the necessary tools and such. The whole story (the operation plus resuscitation efforts) took about three hours. During that time, the patient kept having cardiac arrests, so he would have to be resuscitated each time.

Over the course of the following weeks, this patient had to be operated on a few more times, so that I dealt with him several times, when he was awake, too. I had the task of transferring him from his bed to the operation table, for instance. The third or fourth time that this happened, a conversation developed between us. He said that he recognized me from somewhere. He told me that the night of his accident, when he was operated on and resuscitated, he had left his body and looked down on this from the ceiling. He told me what we did, for instance what I myself had done, such as placing a defibrillator nearby. He described pretty accurately that I had brought the apparatus to him and that certain actions were then performed. He didn't say that it was a "defibrillator." He said, "You set that apparatus down near me and it was used to administer electric shocks to me." [. . .] He also said that he had received injections of particular medications, he mentioned atropine, among others. Atropine in itself [from a medical point of view] is a standard remedy, but you couldn't assume that he would know that through his own profession or whatever.

SOURCE

Nikolay, J. (2015, September 7). Attachment to email to Wilfried Kuhn, forwarded to Titus Rivas on September 10, 2015.

CASE 3.35 The Assistant Who Became Nauseous

The Spanish otolaryngologist Miguel Ángel Pertierra (2014) described the case of a young man in his 20s who was in a serious car accident. The young man ended up in the ICU with broken bones and countless internal injuries.

Dr. Pertierra became involved in the case because the patient had to have a tracheotomy. The doctor was initially assisted by an inexperienced resident who was eager to help out during the operation. Despite every precaution, the patient's blood pressure suddenly dropped, and he went into a brief cardiac arrest. When the assistant witnessed the patient's cardiac arrest, he found it hard to take, so he had to be replaced by another assistant. The cardiac arrest was quickly resolved. Several tests were done in order to determine whether they could finally operate on the patient. Pertierra and the new assistant performed the life-saving tracheotomy some hours later with no further incident.

Several days later, Pertierra received a request to replace a tube in a patient who had a tracheostomy tube. It turned out to be the same young man, who had meanwhile stabilized nicely. Pertierra explained to the patient that he was going to remove the plastic cannula he had inserted before and replace it with a metal one and that he would also be removing the stitches from the previous operation. When the doctor had performed his work, the patient moved his lips to thank him, also indicating he wanted to speak with the doctor. Pertierra went out and came back with a device and explained to the patient and his family how he could use it to temporarily close off the cannula in order to speak. When the patient had figured out how to do this, he said to Pertierra (authors' translation):

> You're the one who did the operation on my neck, aren't you?
>
> [. . .]
>
> I saw you when my heart stopped. You were wearing green surgical scrubs and were accompanied by a very young boy.
>
> [. . .]
>
> I was beside you. I saw that you had a small table covered with scissors and things I'd never seen before in my life, which I assumed were for the operation.
>
> I thought it was weird that you didn't see me. I even stood right in front of you to see if you saw me, but it made no difference.
>
> I remember clearly that the young guy turned pale when they were resuscitating me, because I saw on the monitor that there were no heartbeat lines anymore, like there were at first. Alarms went off.
>
> [. . .]
>
> I don't doubt for a moment that you were the doctor, and I could even see that after everything on the table had been prepared, they covered it with a green cloth.

Pertierra found it remarkable that all the details the young man told him were accurate. He emphasized that no family member could have informed the patient about these details. At the time, there had been no one in the ICU except the medical team.

A few days later, Pertierra had to perform one last postsurgical procedure on the patient. Preceding it, he asked the young man whether he still remembered what he had told him and whether he remembered any more details.

The young man answered (authors' translation):

Yes, totally, and there's more. I remember some details that I'd like to corroborate with you: After that whole scene, you touched your colleague's mask and lowered it. You told him to breathe slowly and to go sit down. Is that what happened?

This, too, turned out to be correct. Pertierra confirmed that everything had taken place precisely as the young man had described, and this last detail, although rare, does sometimes happen to those who aspire to be specialists.

SOURCE

Pertierra, M. Á. (2014). *La última puerta. Experiencias cercanas a la muerte* [The last door: Near-death experiences]. Madrid, Spain: Ediciones Oberón.

CASE 3.36 Dr. Monica Williams-Murphy's Patient

Monica Williams-Murphy is a board certified emergency medicine physician who practices at Huntsville Hospital in Huntsville, Alabama, in one of the largest emergency departments in the United States. Together with her husband, Kristian Murphy, she wrote the book *It's Okay to Die* (2011). She maintains a website with a blog focusing on the theme of this book—namely, that with the right preparation, it is possible to view death positively and with dignity. In a January 21, 2013, blog post, she shared her own experiences concerning the NDE of one of her patients. She wrote:

I have had the pleasure of listening to someone who has journeyed back from death and arrived with a story to tell. [. . .]

Years ago when I was ripe and round with my 3rd child, I was trudging through a late night shift in the ER when a "code" came in by EMS [emergency medical services]. The patient was a young man in maybe his late 30s, and when the paramedics came around the corner with him they were all sweating from the efforts of professional chest compressions and airway support. I remember that they had been unable to place a breathing tube during transport due to the amount of vomit in the man's airway. I recall, that due to my gestational girth, that I had to squat like a Sumo Wrestler to be able to see into his throat myself, but was able to secure a stable airway as we continued CPR.

I was giving the orders, but our entire team was trying to figure out why he had died, and what we could do to resuscitate him. One of the paramedics stated that he thought that drugs were involved and that this was a potential overdose situation.

So I tried a few more medications on him and unexpectedly, we got a pulse!

After a "successful code" we always go through a very detailed examination of the patient to look for signs and hints of what has been and is going on. As we rolled this young man to examine his back, my charge nurse, Penny, pulled a couple of narcotic patches off. "Here is our problem," she said.

We all shook our heads with a type of disappointment [. . .]

"This is too bad," I sighed while examining his pupils. Nothing about his examination suggested that he would live. He had no visible signs of brain life. Nothing. He seemed to be just a body to me, with a beating heart. I wondered aloud if he could even be an organ donor.

No family ever arrived to check on him, to hear my prognosis that I had practiced in my head. "I think his brain just went without oxygen too long. I am so sorry, but I don't think he will pull through this. We did our best, and I assure you that he is not suffering."

I sent him to the ICU and never heard anything about him again . . .

Until 6 months later.

Again I was on a busy night shift and the place was bursting at the seams. I think the lobby was spilling over into the parking area and I was feeling quite stressed about how I alone was going to get to all of these people who needed my help. In the midst of carrying a pile of charts down a hallway of patients, my charge nurse, Penny, said that something unusual had just occurred in triage. A young man walking with a cane came up to the triage nurse and asked if he could have a word with me. [. . .]

I had not even been walking through the doorframe when this smiling gentleman stood to greet me. "Dr. Murphy, I see that you have had your baby girl! How is she?"

I stopped dead in my tracks, and an eerie uncomfortable sensation rushed over my skin. I didn't know this man, had never seen him in my life (or so I thought) and he was speaking to me in very familiar terms about [me] and my 5 month old child.

I eyed him suspiciously. "Do I know you, sir?" I asked.

He continued to smile but took a seat, a visible effort to ease my apprehension. "Yes, you know me, you just don't remember me. Six months ago you saved my life . . . I came here tonight to thank you personally, and to tell you my story."

[. . .]

He started by saying very matter-of-factly, "I died and you brought me back to life in that room across the hall near the end of last year," as he pointed toward the doorway and correctly toward our resuscitation room.

With great detail he began to report on the events of that evening. "I had become addicted to pain killers because I struggled with a bad back. That night I had taken too many pills and had used some of my uncle's pain patches. . . ." He went on to explain how he somehow knew when he stopped breathing and then left "his body." He recounted how he saw his girlfriend find him and then call 911 while she attempted to start CPR on him. He told me the words that she said and what the paramedics said and did on arrival to his home. He told me how he knew one of the paramedics and that she cried and struggled to do her job performing CPR on him while sobbing at the same time. He explained that he closely followed the events that were going on with "his body" and began to describe in accurate detail what had happened in the resuscitation room in the ER. He told me that we were dismayed that he had overdosed at such a young age. He stated that he watched as Penny, my charge nurse, rolled him over and pulled the two pain patches from his back and he heard her say, "Here is our problem." (Note: He did not state Penny's name but called her "that dark-haired charge nurse.") He recalled that I had talked about "whether he could even be an organ donor or not."

"But, I came back into my body and I lived! And here I am today, but I am a changed man. I don't take pain killers anymore. Now, this cane is my only medicine, it's my only crutch," he said, twirling his cane in the air, smilingly.

His story seemed to have come to an end, but after a brief pause he continued, "But I really only came here tonight to share two things with you." His eyes grew serious.

"First, when I was outside of my body, when I was dead . . . I saw something else . . . I saw that there was light coming from you and from your baby," he was staring up at the corner of the room as if viewing the memory with a sense of wonder.

I stared at him in astonishment.

Then he turned to look directly at me, and with a deeply earnest expression said, "But I really just wanted to thank you personally, face to face for helping to save my life, for being a part of giving me a second chance. I promise you, Doctor Murphy, that I will not waste it. There are things that happened to me when I was dead that I cannot tell you about, but I made a promise to use my life and my time differently." [. . .]

That night this man gave me a gift. This gift was a deepened sense of appreciation for my own life and for the gift of time itself. As a result, I became more keenly grateful for the lives of my children, my husband, my family and the opportunity we have all been given to experience this thing called life together.

In early February 2016, Titus Rivas approached Dr. Williams-Murphy by e-mail about this case and asked her which elements, in her opinion, did not fit into a materialistic worldview. She responded:

The three items which stood out to me as inexplicable from a scientific medical perspective (as we presently know it) were:

1. The patient, after resuscitation, exhibited no pupillary response and had no gag reflex, therefore I thought he was clinically brain dead at the time during which he was in my care and yet he recounted the events in incredible detail as if from a 3rd person perspective.

2. He told me that he saw the sex of my unborn child (a girl), which he wouldn't have known later unless he inquired in the community as to the sex of my child. I did not question this.

3. In theory, he could have heard what we said aloud and recounted it later, but he visually described the room and the "dark-haired nurse" in detail and what she did even when she was not talking. This should have been impossible, as he never spontaneously opened his eyes and had no signs of the visual brain centers working. There were approximately 60 staff members or more in the emergency department. Additionally he described in detail what the specific woman did to him. I cannot imagine that random chance would've allowed him to pick her up from a previously known population and then describe in detail what she did.

SOURCES

Williams-Murphy, M. (2013, January 21). *"I died and you brought me back to life": How one patient's near death experience changed my life.* Retrieved from http://www .oktodie.com/blog/i-died-and-you-brought-me-back-to-life-how-one-patients -near-death-experience-changed-my-life/#sthash.8S8WG4cs.dpuf

Williams-Murphy, M., & Murphy, K. (2011). *It's okay to die* [Kindle ed.]. Amazon Digital Services: The authors and MKN, LLC.

Remarks

Each complex conscious mental activity—such as conscious perception, thought, and memory—that a patient experiences after approximately 15 seconds of a cardiac arrest is totally incompatible with a materialistic view of humans. According to materialism, complex human consciousness depends on neurological activity in the cortex. Although, in the materialist model, other parts of the brain such as the brainstem also play an important role in the "production" of subjective experiences, an active cortex is necessary in humans for functions such as conscious perception, conscious thought, and conscious memory. Thus, from a materialistic perspective, the more cortical activity there is, the more complex consciousness can be, and the less cortical activity there is, the more limited consciousness will be.

In cardiac arrest, the activity of the neocortex is reduced to a minimum within an average of 15 seconds; if the individual's brain is being monitored at the time, this absence of activity is reflected in a flat EEG. Materialists should assume that after a maximum of 20 seconds—and, as mentioned, 15 seconds on average—appreciable consciousness is no longer possible, and complex conscious experience becomes possible again only on completion of successful resuscitation.

RESTORED EEG

In an attempt to invalidate the above information, Gerald Woerlee, in a 2012 online commentary, referred to research that ostensibly showed that in some exceptional cases, as a response to external heart massage (chest compression) in combination with artificial ventilation, even before resuscitation in its entirety has been completed, an EEG can restore itself. In certain instances, the procedure allegedly led to the patient's regaining consciousness. This combination of chest compressions and artificial ventilation is known medically by the term "external cardiopulmonary resuscitation" or "external CPR."

Sam Parnia, however, in an e-mail correspondence with Rivas, explained that the primary case that Woerlee cited—reported by investigator T. J. Losasso, MD (1992)—did not actually document a restored EEG that resulted from external heart massage and artificial respiration. According to Parnia, the EEG was actually reactivated after the patient's heartbeat had recovered, thanks to the administration of atropine and epinephrine (adrenaline), which, according to cardiologist Pim van Lommel, is also a standard procedure in external CPR. Even Woerlee must, in any event, acknowledge that, according to the description of the investigator involved, this type of medication was used *at the same time* as the external heart massage. So, even in this "best case," there is certainly no question of definitive proof of the return of EEG activity in an acute cardiac arrest solely on the basis of external heart massage. According to van Lommel, this case involved a cardiac arrest during a surgical procedure on the carotid artery rather than one resulting from an acute heart attack, so as such, this case is not relevant to the discussion of NDEs during cardiac arrests resulting from heart attacks, which are the focus of this chapter.

Losasso himself appeared to accept that restoring blood circulation in the brain becomes increasingly difficult the longer a heartbeat is absent. In addition, it seems clear from this chapter that there are documented cases in which patients observed things *before* the external CPR had been started or *after* it had been stopped—but in any event before resuscitation was successful. Thus external CPR cannot be responsible for the occurrence of conscious experience during cardiac arrest.

Regarding the remaining cases that Woerlee referred to, Parnia emphasized that none of these patients actually had an acute heart attack. Such patients are sometimes considered to be in acute cardiac arrest even though, in fact, they still have a heartbeat—one too weak for doctors to ascertain a palpable pulse. When such patients are treated with external CPR and then regain consciousness, it can appear as if the external CPR was responsible, whereas, in reality, the presence of a heartbeat throughout played a crucial role. The illusion can be reinforced by the fact that consciousness immediately disappears again if heart massage is stopped.

In these types of cases, the combination of external CPR with the continued presence of a heartbeat leads to improved circulation in the brain so that some patients can even regain consciousness completely. According to Parnia, however, in a real, acute cardiac arrest due to a heart attack, there is too little blood circulation for external CPR alone to restore the EEG activity to a level that—according to materialism (and naturalism in general)—is needed for conscious experience.

Van Lommel confirmed to us the accuracy of Parnia's argument. He explained that the situation Parnia described is called "cardiogenic shock." Heart activity can be seen on the EKG, but there is insufficient blood pressure, as measurable or palpable in the patient's arms or legs. Van Lommel pointed out that one of the cases Woerlee mentioned included discussion of the consequences of acute renal failure, which is a totally different medical condition from an acute myocardial infarction (heart attack). This is why, according to van Lommel, none of these cases is comparable to cardiac arrest resulting from an acute heart attack.

Nevertheless, it is conceivable, at least in principle, that some NDEs that seem to occur during a cardiac arrest are, in fact, still linked to an extremely weak heartbeat. We contend, however, that this possibility *cannot* be the explanation for most of the NDEs in this chapter. Parnia emphasized in this context that NDEs in which the patient regains consciousness during the administration of external CPR are very rare and that recovery of sufficient brain activity through external heart massage and artificial respiration on patients with an extremely weak heartbeat likewise rarely occurs as such. This point has even been acknowledged by Woerlee: He admitted that only *"efficient"* external CPR can lead to such a recovery and that it cannot be assumed that this level of treatment is always the case or is even necessarily the norm.

Neuropsychologist Peter Fenwick also asserted in an e-mail to Rivas that there is absolutely no reason to assume that the findings in the cases Woerlee presented have anything to do with the kind of consciousness that manifests in NDEs during acute cardiac arrest. *For these reasons, the kind of cases that Dr. Woerlee referred to cannot play a role in a satisfactory explanation of the NDEs discussed in this chapter.*

Please note that it is certainly conceivable that, as laypeople, we have presented particular aspects of the foregoing viewpoints of Drs. Parnia, van Lommel, and Fenwick incompletely or even inaccurately. But there is no doubt that all three dispute, on the basis of medical arguments and expertise, that the EEG activity Woerlee cited has no bearing on NDEs during acute cardiac arrest.

This is perhaps a good point at which to add nuance to an argument that sometimes arises among those in the antimaterialist camp. They assert that one should take EEG activity during a clinical death seriously only if one is certain that the EEG activity is linked to consciousness, and then only to consciousness as it arises during an NDE. We disagree. The question is not whether materialists have proven that the occurrence of NDEs during cardiac arrest *must* be explained by cortical brain activity. The question is a different one—namely, whether EEG activity can arise that *could be* responsible for NDEs produced by dying brains. Considering the cases in this chapter, the answer is clearly no. The point is not that materialists have not proven that the remaining brain activity is linked to an NDE. The point is that on the whole, materialists have not provided plausible evidence that during acute cardiac arrest there can ever be sufficient EEG activity to consider an NDE possible as a product of brain activity. Conversely, abundant medical evidence exists supporting the conclusion that an acute cardiac arrest cannot be coupled with sufficient EEG activity to explain the complex contents of NDEs.

As long as the brain functions within the cortex have not sufficiently recovered, it cannot be expected within the worldview of materialism that people can have coherent, complex NDEs. Even if it is assumed that brain activity gradually increases during resuscitation, a consistent, coherent consciousness can be expected only after the resuscitation has been completed. Even then, the patient is typically confusional for at least several minutes or remains in a coma for hours to days and is incapable of conscious mental function.

It is for this reason that the reliability of the kind of case that appears in this chapter is so fiercely challenged by materialists. Unfortunately, this criticism is often put forward at the cost of an honest, sober analysis of these cases.

This chapter shows that there are more than 30 published cases involving the confirmed presence of consciousness, and usually also veridical extrasensory perception, during cardiac arrest. We therefore find it makes little sense to continue to doubt the reality of this phenomenon.

STILL JUST A DYING BRAIN?

Recently, some materialists seem to have expressed a willingness to accept that people can have NDEs during cardiac arrest. However, they continue to contend adamantly that this experience could not possibly happen without supporting activity in the brain. According to them, NDEs might occur during cardiac arrest, but only in connection with the resurgence of neurological activity in the cortex. Here, they are not referring to recovery of brain activity through resuscitation, as in the investigations Woerlee cited, but to *spontaneous* resurgence. Their assumptions in this regard are associated with two recently published investigations: one involving rats and the other involving humans.

In 2013, neurologist Jimo Borjigin of the University of Michigan published the results of an experiment on nine rats. Before we proceed with a description, we would like to make it clear that we morally disapprove of this type of experiment in which animals are maimed or killed, even if the study has scientific value that specifically weakens materialistic hypotheses; for several years, Rivas was an activist against such invasive animal experiments. As they artificially induced cardiac arrest in the rats, the researchers monitored the rats' EEGs. After the rats had died, the researchers observed a surge in brain activity that lasted about 30 seconds and then transitioned to a flat EEG that thereafter remained flat.

In 2009, a team led by Lakhmir Chawla, physician and associate professor of anesthesiology and critical care medicine at the George Washington University Medical Center, published several findings relating to the dying process of seven patients. After these comatose patients were removed from life support and measurements indicated no blood pressure and either no heartbeat or seriously compromised heart function, approximately 80% showed a one-time resurgence of brain activity that lasted a maximum of 3 minutes. Chawla acknowledged that because no complete EEG was recorded, he did not know in exactly which part(s) of the brains the spikes occurred; thus the activity might have been in the brainstem rather than in the cortex. He did not even rule out that a chance effect might have been involved—caused, for example, by some external signal. He therefore acknowledged that the conclusions that might be drawn from his investigation are very limited. Chawla did find it plausible that the spikes derived from the patients' brains, because the separate results from the various patients kept showing the same kind of pattern.

From the results of both investigations, some materialists have drawn the conclusion that NDEs can reside in a resurgence of cortical activity after a cardiac arrest has occurred. But is that explanation sufficient? Obviously, the question here is not whether the deceased animals or persons involved in the studies actually had NDEs or even had conscious experiences. Rather, it is whether, if the brain activity in question did occur consistently with spontaneous cardiac arrest, it could provide sufficient support to consciousness to explain NDEs.

In the case of the animal experiment, it is already clear that this phenomenon of a 30-second surge of brain activity following cardiac arrest cannot explain the NDEs that we reported in this chapter. The researchers' results could, at most, only begin to explain NDEs that started immediately after cardiac arrest, lasted no more than 30 seconds, and involved only perceptions available to the normal senses. The cases presented in this chapter clearly defy these limited conditions.

Regarding the report of the dying process in 7 (later 100) patients (Chawla, 2011; Chawla, Akst, Junker, Jacobs, & Seneff, 2009), van Lommel (personal communication, summer 2013) reminded us that these instances involved a gradual dying process, as opposed to the sudden death that characterizes acute cardiac arrest. We think this is a crucial point to keep in mind. The patients in question were in deep comas when machine ventilation and the administration of medication were stopped, which finally resulted in their deaths.

This point becomes important when considering the question of whether a surge lasting up to 30 seconds, or even as much as 3 minutes, could occur in humans following acute cardiac arrest. Van Lommel (personal communication, summer 2013) indicated that all the research in this area shows that from the onset of acute cardiac arrest in humans, measurable brain activity lasts no more than an average of 15 seconds, involves no spike in activity, and is followed by a consistently flat EEG. In the absence of successful resuscitation, a resurgence of brain activity has never been observed in such patients.

A spike of at most 3 minutes is certainly not enough to explain the presence of consciousness in the cases of NDEs during cardiac arrest discussed here. Moreover, in Chawla et al.'s patients, there is a question of only one surge. The duration of consciousness during an NDE cannot therefore be explained by a series of surges, considering no evidence for this pattern exists at all. The results of these investigations certainly do not offer any refutation of the well-documented fact that people with acute cardiac arrest do not show any (spontaneous) cortical brain activity after an average of 15 seconds.

Furthermore, *should* a (yet to be discovered) cortical activity surge occur in people with cardiac arrest, it would last no longer than a number of seconds or, at most, a very few minutes. Brain activity of this duration is inadequate to explain the cases presented in this chapter.

The focus of this chapter has been cases in which NDErs were documented to have had consciousness and accurate perceptions during cardiac arrest at points in the arrest process when, according to current materialist models, such perceptions should have been impossible. In the next chapter, we will present NDEs involving telepathy.

REFERENCES

Blackmore, S. J. (1993). *Dying to live: Near-death experiences.* Amherst, NY: Prometheus Books.

Borjigin, J., Lee, U., Liu, T., Pal, D., Huff, S., Klarr, D., . . . Mashour, G. A. (2013). Surge of neurophysiological coherence and connectivity in the dying brain. *Proceedings of the National Academy of Sciences, 110*(35), 14432–14437.

Chawla, L. S. (2011, May). *Surges of electroencephalogram activity at the time of death: A case series.* Conference: Science of Consciousness: Brain, Mind, Reality. Stockholm, May 3–7, 2011.

Chawla, L. S., Akst, S., Junker, C., Jacobs, B., & Seneff, M. G. (2009). Surges of electroencephalogram activity at the time of death: A case series. *Journal of Palliative Medicine, 12*(12), 1095–1100.

Losasso, T. J., Muzzi, D. A., Meyer, F. B., & Sharbrough, F. W. (1992). Electroencephalographic monitoring of cerebral function during asystole and successful cardiopulmonary resuscitation. *Anesthesia & Analgesia, 75*(6), 1021–1024.

Woerlee, G. M. (2012b). *Setting the record straight: Commentary on an article by Pim van Lommel "The Failure of Expert Authority."* Retrieved from http://www.neardth.com/setting-the-record-straight.php

CHAPTER 4

Telepathy

I began to realize that shared death experiences have been with us since the
beginning of medicine; it's just that doctors and nurses have been discouraged from
speaking about events that could be considered more spiritual than scientific.
—Raymond A. Moody Jr., MD, *Glimpses of Eternity*

In the preceding chapters, we reported near-death experiences (NDEs) in which patients perceived the physical world apparently without the use of their physical senses. This is in fact one of the two main types of extrasensory perception (ESP): clairvoyance. NDEs also sometimes involve the other main type of ESP: telepathy. NDE-related telepathy can take one of two forms: (a) the NDEr (near-death experiencer) perceiving the mind or consciousness of someone else, and (b) another person perceiving the NDEr's NDE—a phenomenon known as shared-death experience (SDE). Telepathy also plays a major role in the description of a transmaterial domain in which the NDEr has contact with those who have died or with other spiritual entities, but this subject will be addressed in upcoming chapters.

To our surprise, in addition to Case 2.1 in Chapter 2 in which an NDEr had paranormal knowledge of the contents of a letter, we were able to find only three more confirmed cases in which an NDEr reported correct telepathic perceptions of another person's mind. We did find in the literature, however, a considerable number of unconfirmed cases of this type. In other words, NDErs regularly report that, during their NDEs, they experienced telepathic contact with living people such as family members and friends.

Cases of Telepathic Perceptions in the NDEr

CASE 4.1 The Car Accident

In his 1988 book *The Light Beyond,* psychiatrist Raymond Moody described the following case of a young cardiologist from South Dakota.

One unfortunate morning, the cardiologist's car struck another car as he was on his way to the hospital. He was very upset by the accident and worried that the people involved would demand a lot in damages. The doctor was still preoccupied by these concerns when he hurried to the emergency room to resuscitate someone in cardiac arrest. The following day, the man whom he had saved told the doctor that during the resuscitation, he had left his body and had watched the doctor during his work.

The doctor asked his patient what he had seen and was taken aback by the accuracy of the patient's description of what had happened. The patient told him exactly how the medical instruments had looked and in which order they had been used. He described the colors and shapes of the tools and equipment and even the settings of the dials on the various machines. But what really convinced the cardiologist was the following statement. "Doctor, I could tell that you were worried about that accident. But there isn't any reason to be worried about things like that. You give your time to other people. Nobody is going to hurt you."

SOURCE

Moody, R. A., Jr. (with Perry, P.). (1988). *The light beyond.* New York, NY: Bantam Books.

CASE 4.2 The Unuttered Sigh

In Chapter 3, Case 3.13 involved a patient's paranormal observation of a doctor, Tom Aufderheide, who ate the patient's lunch. Aufderheide had been a doctor for only 5 days when the case presented, and he had never before been involved in a cardiac arrest resuscitation. The patient kept having cardiac arrests in the midst of frenzied attempts to resuscitate him. Having been engaged with this patient for a full 6 hours, the doctor was so hungry that when the patient's lunch arrived, knowing the patient was in no condition to eat it, he decided to polish off the patient's lunch himself. The patient later reported this NDE observation to Aufderheide, and he also reported that during his NDE, Aufderheide had thought, "How could you do this to me?" By "you," the novice Aufderheide had meant the more seasoned physicians who had thrown him unassisted into this demanding emergency.

Aufderheide shared this experience at the end of one of resuscitation researcher Sam Parnia's talks at a conference in September 2012. He presented this account publicly to Dr. Parnia and the other audience members. After he finished his story, someone from the audience asked Aufderheide whether he had perhaps shared with the nursing staff the thought that he had been thrown to the wolves, so to speak. His response was, "No, I just thought it to myself and hadn't said a word to anyone else. The thought just glanced past my mind for an instant."

In a September 30, 2013, e-mail to Titus Rivas, Aufderheide indicated that he himself considered the strongest component of this case to be the fact that the patient had telepathically caught his thought ("How could you do this to me?"), because he had not shared this thought with anyone until the patient brought it up. Moreover, the thought had occurred to him before the patient's resuscitation had even begun. He wrote:

> This was a fleeting thought that went through my head as he was initially arresting in front of me; I did not verbalize this thought at the time; I never shared this thought with anyone and I had frankly forgotten about it until he later reminded me. At the time of that thought, he was receiving no resuscitative efforts whatsoever (he had collapsed on the bed, unconscious in VF [ventricular fibrillation], and I was uncertain at the time if he had just fainted or had gone into cardiac arrest; thus no resuscitative efforts had started). This was about 5 am in the morning.

SOURCE

Parnia, S. (with Young, J.). (2013). *Erasing death: The science that is rewriting the boundaries between life and death.* New York, NY: HarperCollins.

CASE 4.3 George Rodonaia

In P. M. H. Atwater's (1994/2009) book *Beyond the Light,* she documented the case of George Rodonaia, a neuropathologist and political dissident in the former Soviet Union. Rodonaia was run over by the KGB in 1976. His death was officially confirmed at the hospital, after which his corpse was placed in cold storage, so that 3 days later there could be an autopsy. In this situation, Rodonaia left his body. First, he saw only darkness, but through positive thoughts, that darkness changed into a steadily more detailed vision of light, from a pinpoint of light into eternally life-creating cells that moved in spirals in complete symmetry. He became one with the light and felt intensely happy.

When Rodonaia thought of his body, he saw it lying in the morgue. He remembered everything that had happened. He was also able to "see" the thoughts and emotions of his wife, Nino, and of the people who had been involved in the accident. It was as if they had their thoughts "inside of him." He then wanted to find out the "truth" of those thoughts and emotions. By expressing a longing for greater knowledge, he was confronted by mental images of existence and thus became acquainted with thousands of years of history.

When he returned to his body in the morgue, he was drawn to a nearby hospital, where the wife of a friend had just had a baby. The newborn was constantly crying. He examined the baby, a girl. His "eyes" were like X-rays that could look right through the little body. This ability enabled him to draw the conclusion that the baby had broken its hip during delivery. He spoke to her, "Don't cry. Nobody understands you." The baby was so astonished by his presence that she immediately stopped crying. According to Rodonaia, children are able to see and hear transmaterial apparitions. The child reacted to him, he believes, because he was "a physical reality" to her.

After 3 days, when the autopsy of Rodonaia's body was just getting under way, he succeeded in opening his eyes. At first, the doctors thought it was a reflex, but Rodonaia appeared to have actually come back from the dead, even though his death and his frigid condition had both been confirmed. He was in poor condition physically, but after 3 days, the first words he spoke were about the baby that urgently needed help. X-rays of the baby confirmed that he was right.

At one point, Atwater interviewed Rodonaia's wife, Nino, who stated that during his NDE, Rodonaia had actually witnessed what *she* had seen. According to Nino, he had actually had telepathic contact with her. In an e-mail dated July 28, 2015, Atwater wrote Rivas the following about this aspect of the case:

> George told me that as part of his near-death experience, among the many things he could do was to be able to enter the minds of all his friends and

find out whether or not they were really friends. During this entry process, he also entered the mind of this wife, Nino. When he did, he both saw and heard his wife picking out his gravesite. As she stood there looking at the gravesite, in her head, she pictured several men she would consider being her next husband. She made a list for herself of their various qualities, pro and con, to decide which one would be the most suitable.

After George revived and his tongue shrunk back to its normal size so George could talk (this took three days), George greeted his wife. He told her about the gravesite scenario. He described everything she saw there. Then he told her everything she thought about while there, the specific men she was considering to be her next husband and [the] list she was making in her mind about their various pros and cons. He was correct in every detail. This so freaked her out that she refused to have much to do with him for a year. I had no sense that this was telepathic, but real, physically real, as if George's mind was physically inside his wife's mind. He saw what she saw. He also saw what she thought.

When I met Nino and both children, I asked Nino if I could talk to her about that incident at the gravesite and her list of qualities of the men she was considering marrying. She described the incident for me and that all of this was done in the privacy of her own mind. She only thought about the men and their various qualities. The list was her own. When her suddenly, newly alive, formerly dead husband talked about that personal moment at the gravesite, named the men she thought about, and then went on to "read" the list back to her that she made for each man, she was utterly shocked at his accuracy and how he could even do this. This shock was felt as if an affront against her right to privacy, the intimate privacy of her own mind. I asked if it was true that she would have little or nothing to do with him for a year. She said, yes, it was true. She could not sleep in the same room with him. When I asked why, her answer was: "I no longer had the privacy of my own mind. This was very hard to take." [. . .]

Nino also confirmed what happened at the hospital, the first words he said after his tongue swelling went down, of his friend's wife having just given birth to a daughter, he told the doctors to get right up to the maternity ward and x-ray that baby's hip, that it had been broken by the attending nurse who had dropped the baby. George was a doctor himself and he described the hip break in detail. The doctors rushed up to the maternity ward, had the baby x-rayed and found the break exactly as described by George. They then confronted the nurse with what they found and she admitted to dropping the baby. She was immediately fired.

We could also have discussed this case in Chapter 3 because it appears likely that Rodonaia experienced the telepathic perceptions during a cardiac arrest. Even though Atwater was not able to have the doctor confirm this specific point, we may accept, thanks to the statement of Rodonaia's wife, Nino, that the case in this respect fits into Chapter 2 as well.

SOURCE

Atwater, P. M. H. (2009). *Beyond the light: What isn't being said about near death experience: From visions of heaven to glimpses of hell.* Kill Devil Hills, NC: Transpersonal. (original work published 1994)

Case of Telepathic Perceptions of Someone Else's NDE

CASE 4.4 Josef

In Bernard Jakoby's 2006 book *Begegnungen mit dem Jenseits* (Encounters with the beyond), he described the case of a 5-year-old boy named Josef who suddenly began screaming in his sleep. His mother wrote (authors' translation):

Bernard Jakoby

I ran into his room and saw that the boy was still half asleep. He had stuck his hands up in the air. He was calling for his favorite uncle, who was doing very poorly after a heart attack. When Josef woke up, he said, "Uncle Michael just fell out of bed. There was a light, and I saw a grown-up, white-haired lady. Uncle Michael kept shouting, 'Mother, Mother!'"

Very worried, I picked up the phone and called Michael, but he didn't answer. The next day my sister-in-law called to tell me her husband had fallen out of bed during the night. The woman my son had seen was undoubtedly Uncle Michael's late mother.

SOURCE

Jakoby, B. (2006). *Begegnungen mit dem Jenseits* [Encounters with the beyond]. Hamburg, Germany: Rowohlt Taschenbuch Verlag.

Remarks

It would be strange, from a parapsychological perspective, if only confirmed cases of clairvoyance and never any confirmed cases of telepathy were reported in NDEs. In this sense, it was to be expected from the start that we would also find one or more of such cases of telepathy. The cases in this chapter show that during an NDE, the NDEr can make telepathic contact with the mind or consciousness of living people, and people can also be in telepathic contact with the NDEr.

CHAPTER 5

After-Death Communication With Strangers

The very fact that there are drop-in cases seems to strengthen the case for survival.
—Stephen Braude, *Drop-In Communicators*

In this chapter and the next, we present several cases of NDE-related after-death communication (ADC). In ADC, a person who is living or near death experiences the presence of a deceased person, usually with communication that occurs telepathically. In a recent systematic review of research published on ADC, Jenny Streit-Horn (2011a) found a total of 35 studies published between 1894 and 2006 that had collectively involved a total of more than 50,000 people who had reportedly experienced ADC—ADCrs—from 24 countries. Thus ADC is a phenomenon well established to have occurred widely across cultures for more than 100 years—actually since early in recorded history. Readers interested in a summary of findings from her review can access it online (Streit-Horn, 2011b).

This chapter comprises five cases in which, during an NDE, a patient experienced ADC with someone whom the near-death experiencer (NDEr) had not known prior to the NDE. Later, the deceased person whom the NDEr had encountered was found to correspond to someone who had actually existed. Thanks to the NDE, the patient had paranormal information regarding characteristics of the deceased, such as the dead person's appearance, personality, and specific experiences during earthly life.

CASE 5.1 Durdana Khan

The following case was described in Ian Wilson's 1997 book *Life After Death: The Evidence*. Durdana Khan was the youngest daughter of A. G. Khan, an army doctor at a Pakistani army base in Kashmir at the foot of the Himalayas. In 1968, when Durdana was 2½ years old, she showed symptoms that indicated viral encephalitis (inflammation of the brain). As a result, she became partially paralyzed, temporarily lost her eyesight, and was constantly in pain. Her chances of survival appeared slim.

One unfortunate day, Dr. Khan was called away from seeing patients because his daughter had apparently died at home. He examined her himself and confirmed that she was clinically dead. His wife laid Durdana on her husband's bed, and he began resuscitating her. He whispered, "Come back my child, come back." Durdana awoke after having been "dead" about 15 minutes.

A few days later, Durdana said that during her clinical death, she had been in a beautiful garden among the stars. There had been apples, grapes, and pomegranates, and there were four streams, each with a different color: white, brown, blue, and green. She had also met her grandfather and heard her father calling, "Come back my child, come back." When she finally did want to go back, her grandfather had said that she would have to ask God. God then asked her whether she really wanted to go back, and she affirmed that she did. So then God told her she should go, and she went back down. She finally came back to her body again on "Daddy's bed."

Durdana's father asserted that she "was in no state to know where she was." Neither she nor her little sisters ever slept in his bed.

Durdana's symptoms turned out to have been caused by a brain tumor. She underwent surgery in Karachi. During her recovery, she went with her mother to visit family. At the home of one of her uncles, where Durdana was visiting for the first time, she raced over to a small table on which there was a photograph. She pointed at the photo and said, "This is my grandpa's mother. I met her in the stars. She took me in her lap and kissed me." This was a photo of Khan's grandmother who had died long before Durdana was born. According to Khan, only two photos of his grandmother existed, and both were in the possession of the uncle. Under the circumstances, she could not possibly have seen the photo before.

Peter Brookesmith, editor of *The Unexplained* book series, made Wilson aware of this story. Brookesmith had been a friend of the Khan family for years and could vouch for their integrity and trustworthiness. We concur with Brookesmith and Wilson that Durdana actually did spontaneously recognize her great-grandmother in a photograph.

SOURCE
Wilson, I. (1997). *Life after death: The evidence.* London, England: Sidgwick & Jackson.

CASE 5.2 Colton Burpo

The following case is not to be confused with the case of Alex Malarkey, discussed in the Introduction, who reported and then recanted an NDE. The case of Colton Burpo was presented in his father's 2010 testimonial, *Heaven Is for Real*.

In 2003, as Pastor Todd Burpo and his family were driving from Imperial, Nebraska, to visit relatives in South Dakota over the July 4th weekend, they passed the Great Plains Regional Medical Center in North Platte where then 4-year-old Colton had undergone an acute appendicitis operation 4 months prior. Colton spontaneously remarked that he remembered the hospital as the place "where the angels sang to me." This was the first time Colton had ever mentioned his NDE.

In March 2003, Colton's appendix had ruptured. According to the attending medical staff, there was a significant chance that he would not survive the surgery. During the operation, the boy had a cardiac arrest. However, the operation was successful in the end.

The boy's NDE was a joyous experience in the presence of Jesus and angels. It also included veridical extrasensory perceptions. He saw that his father was praying, alone, in a little room, while his mother was on the phone in another room. Then he met "Pop," one of his father's grandfathers, whom he later recognized in an old photograph of Pop as a young man. Pop had died when Colton's father was a boy. Colton also noted that his father and Pop had been very close.

Finally, as a result of meeting a deceased sister during his NDE, Colton knew that his mother had lost a child. Understandably, because of Colton's young age and the sensitivity of the topic, his parents had never told him anything about this miscarriage.

SOURCE

Burpo, T., & Vincent, L. (2010). *Heaven is for real: A little boy's astounding story of his trip to heaven and back*. Nashville, TN: Thomas Nelson.

CASE 5.3 Andrew

In Sam Parnia's 2006 book *What Happens When We Die* the case of the then-3½-year-old "Andrew" (pseudonym) is documented. Andrew's mother wrote Parnia that the boy had had to undergo open-heart surgery and 2 weeks later started asking questions about "when he could go back to the beautiful sunny place with all the flowers and animals." Andrew had evidently had an NDE and seen a "floating lady":

> The lady came and got me. She held my hand and we floated up. . . . You were outside when I was having my heart mended. . . . It was okay. The lady looked after me; the lady loves me. It wasn't scary; it was lovely. [. . .] I was awake, but I was up on the ceiling, and when I looked down I was lying in a bed with my arms by my sides, and doctors were doing something to my chest. Everything was really bright, and I floated back down.

A year later, in a television show about a heart operation on a child, Andrew recognized the bypass machine that he claimed had also been used in his own operation. He said he had observed this machine when he was floating up with "that lady." A short while later, his mother let him see an old photo of her own mother at the age she herself was at the time. Andrew said, "That's her, that's that lady."

SOURCE
Parnia, S. (2006). *What happens when we die: A groundbreaking study into the nature of life and death.* Carlsbad, CA: Hay House.

CASE 5.4 Pop-Pop

Posted on the *Angels and Ghosts* website is the case of the 3-year-old son of a woman named Sherry (n.d.). The boy fell into Sherry's mother's swimming pool on Father's Day 1988. Sherry had assumed that like all the other guests there, he had gone down to the basement while she and her mother were talking in the kitchen. When the others came upstairs, her son was not among them. Sick with fear, she immediately ran to the swimming pool, where the boy was floating, unconscious.

Her mother called 911 as the boy began to turn blue. His lips looked purple, and he was not breathing. Sherry wanted to give him mouth-to-mouth resuscitation, but her stepfather pushed her out of the way and took over because he thought she was acting hysterical. After a few minutes, the boy regained consciousness, and the ambulance arrived shortly thereafter. The paramedics were going to bring him to nearby Union Hospital in Elkton, Maryland. En route, the boy lost consciousness again, and one of the ambulance technicians suggested they go to Christiana, Delaware, 20 minutes away. Sherry was beside herself and tried to get from her seat beside the driver to her son in the back of the ambulance. The driver was forced to grab her as he was barreling down the highway.

The boy had to stay overnight for observation at the hospital in Christiana. The next morning, Sherry's mother came to pick them up. They drove to her house, and the first thing Sherry's son asked was, "Can I get into the pool?" His grandmother kept repeating that he was not allowed. Finally, Sherry said, "We should let him. If he's not afraid, don't make him afraid." Wearing his inflatable armbands, the boy immediately jumped into the deep end, whereas he normally stayed close to the steps. Sherry and his grandmother were shocked.

Later that evening, Sherry and her son went home again. They were watching television when the boy suddenly broke down and began to sob so intensely that he could hardly breathe. Sherry thought he would have to go back to the hospital. She told him to calm down so that he could tell her what was wrong. He sobbed, "I just want to go back to heaven with Pop-pop." Sherry asked him what he meant. Her son told her that when he fell into the pool, he had tried to grab on to the inflatable raft. He had attempted to get back to the side but was unable to swim well enough. At first it had hurt a lot when he drowned, but then it became peaceful. There was white light everywhere around him and also around a man he somehow knew to be his great-grandfather, who had died when the boy had been only 10 months old. The man said the boy had to go back because it was not his time yet.

Sherry stressed that among the family they never really talked about this great-grandfather. When she asked her son to describe the man, he did so perfectly. He said that the man was a little bit bald but that he still had some hair on the sides of his head; that he was short; and that although he was not fat, he was kind of stocky.

At his great-grandmother's house, he would pick up all kinds of things and ask her, "This was Pop-pop's, wasn't it?"

Sherry's mother lived close to a cemetery, and her grandson kept going there. At a certain point, he told his mother that he had talked with the Virgin Mary. Mary told him that he would receive a book from his great-grandfather when he was a lot older. Years later, his great-grandmother, who was in a care facility by this time, told both the boy and his mother that his great-grandfather had had a book that he had intended his great-grandson to have, thereby confirming what the boy had said Mary had told him so many years earlier.

SOURCE

Sherry. (n.d.). *My son's drowning NDE*. Retrieved from http://www.angelsghosts
   .com/my-son-s-nde

CASE 5.5 Viola Horton's Extensive Perceptions

This case derives from the books *Beyond the Light* by Raymond Moody (1988)
and *Reflections of Heaven: A Millennial Odyssey of Miracles, Angels, and Afterlife* by
Peter Shockey (1999), as well as various websites. The case concerns a patient
from North Augusta, South Carolina, named Viola (Vi) Horton. We discovered in the translation process that Moody had split the account between two
female patients ("June" and "another woman"), so she is sometimes referred
to in the literature as "June." In the spring of 1971, Horton was in her mid-30s
when she had to undergo gall bladder surgery. A few days after the fairly routine operation, while still recuperating in the hospital, Horton suddenly had a
cardiac arrest.

The patient felt herself leave her body while the doctors tried to resuscitate her. She ended up in the hospital corridor, where she saw a number of
her friends and family members standing around. Upon hearing of her critical
condition, they had gone to the hospital as quickly as possible. Horton tried in
vain to draw their attention. She noted that her daughter Kathy was wearing
different plaids that were mismatched.

She moved on through the corridor and arrived at where her brother-in-law
was. She watched as a neighbor, who also happened to be at the hospital, asked
her brother-in-law what he was doing there and what he was doing that weekend. He said that he had planned to go out of town but that he was now planning to stay around because it looked like Horton was "going to kick the bucket"
and he would have to be a pallbearer. This insensitive remark stuck with her.

Horton then went through a tunnel at the end of which was a colorful
meadow, and she was aware of being guided by beings of light as she moved
through the experience. One being came forward as a baby, claiming that he
was Horton's brother, when as far as she knew she only had two sisters. He
told her to remember how he looked, wearing a tiny cap and dress, socks and
booties, and to provide this description to her father, who would recognize the
infant immediately.

After she regained consciousness, Horton discussed these incidents with
her family and found out that they were all true. Her father acknowledged that

his first child had been a boy and that the baby had died a couple of days after birth. This boy was never talked about among the family. As embarrassing as it was for him and as amusing as it was for her, her brother-in-law confirmed that he had in fact said what she had heard him say to the neighbor during her OBE. Her observation of her daughter wearing mismatched clothing was also correct.

On September 15, 2015, Moody's wife, Cheryl Moody, confirmed to Rivas that in Moody's interviews with the family, they had confirmed the accuracy of each of Horton's perceptions during her NDE.

SOURCES

Moody, R. A., Jr. (with Perry, P.). (1988). *The light beyond*. New York, NY: Bantam Books.

Shockey, P. (Director). (1992). *Life after life: Official documentary with Dr. Raymond Moody*. Cascom International. Retrieved from https://vimeo.com/85524391

Shockey, P. (1999). *Reflections of heaven: A millennial odyssey of miracles, angels, and afterlife*. New York, NY: Doubleday.

Shockey, P. (Director). (2013). *Viola Horton's NDE—light at the end of the tunnel* (NDE Accounts excerpt from documentary *Life After Life*). Retrieved from https://www.youtube.com/watch?v=ihaK0ubzcKg

Shockey, P., & Shockey, S. D. (2014). *Miracles, angels & afterlife: Signposts to heaven*. New York, NY: Open Road.

Remarks

Encounters and communication with unknown deceased persons who later turn out to be specific historical individuals do not occur only in NDEs. Comparable contacts have been reported in connection with memories of a spiritual preexistence before birth (the before-life), with apparitions, and with so-called drop-in communicators during séances: spirits who at that moment are unfamiliar to both the medium and the others in attendance.

Generally, these kinds of cases are seen as particularly strong indicators of actual contact with those who have died. In contrast, those who are not convinced of personal survival after death disagree. One such *nonsurvivalist* explanation of an experiencer's encounter with a deceased person is that the NDEr subconsciously obtains information in the experience through "super-psi."

Super-psi is a hypothesized process whereby a person subconsciously obtains information using a form of extrasensory perception or clairvoyance.

Super-psi is also hypothesized to subconsciously produce physical phenomena using a form of psychokinesis. "Super" refers to the unusually powerful extrasensory abilities the person needs to use subconsciously. Adherents of this view hold that super-psi is simply part of everyone's human nature, so it is part of the NDEr's own mind. According to this view, the NDEr encounters an illusory—but historical—"deceased person," whom the NDEr does not know or recognize, and receives information about the "person" subconsciously, using some form of ESP or clairvoyance.

We argue against a super-psi explanation for the cases in this chapter because the NDEr has no motive, no desire, and no reason to access any super-psi information for a deceased person who is totally unknown to the NDEr. If one never knew the person and did not even know that he or she ever existed, it is pretty remarkable then to go looking for information—normal or paranormal—about that person.

Hence these types of cases indicate that those who have died may themselves seek contact with living people, and the initiative in this respect would come from the deceased. NDEs that contain such encounters demonstrate that these experiences cannot be completely reduced to a kind of beautiful private dream called into being by NDErs' own unconscious minds. It is evidently possible to enter into contact with people who no longer have a material body. This phenomenon implies that the reality that people experience during NDEs is an intersubjective reality to a certain extent—a reality that can be shared with others.

REFERENCES

Streit-Horn, J. (2011a). A systematic review of research on after-death communication (ADC) (Unpublished doctoral dissertation). University of North Texas, Denton, TX.

Streit-Horn, J. (2011b). *Fact sheet: After-death communication.* Retrieved from http://www.coe.unt.edu/sites/default/files/22/129/ADC.pdf

CHAPTER 6

After-Death Communication With Familiar People

The evidence of Visions of the Dying, when they appear to see and recognize some of their relatives of whose decease they were unaware, affords perhaps one of the strongest arguments in favour of survival.
—Sir William Barrett, *Death-Bed Visions*

In the previous chapter, we presented five cases of after-death communication (ADC) in which near-death experiencers (NDErs) had confirmed contacts with deceased persons who were unfamiliar to them. However, encountering familiar people who have died has been reported much more frequently in near-death experiences (NDEs). In itself, the perception of a familiar person who has died does not necessarily have to be considered a paranormal phenomenon. From a purely reductionist perspective, this experience might be the result of a projection of dreamy images from the experiencer's unconscious mind. It does change things, though, if at the moment of the NDE, the NDEr knew the deceased but did not yet know that the person in question had died. In this chapter, we present confirmed cases of this type.

Among scholars, cases in which people living or people near death encountered unknown deceased persons—as in the cases in Chapter 5—or known deceased persons not known to have died—as in the cases in this chapter—have been termed "Peak in Darien" cases. Probably the most famous cases of this type fall into the latter category. The term "Peak in Darien" is a reference to an 1816 sonnet by British poet John Keats entitled "On First Looking into Chapman's Homer." The term is a metaphor for something that is totally unexpected, such as when Cortez's exploration party first gazed upon the expanse of the Pacific Ocean from a mountaintop on the Isthmus of Darien in Panama. The text of the poem runs as follows:

> *Much have I travell'd in the realms of gold*
> *And many goodly states and kingdoms seen;*
> *Round many western islands have I been*
> *Which bards in fealty to Apollo hold.*
> *Oft of one wide expanse had I been told*
> *That deep-brow'd Homer ruled as his demesne;*
> *Yet did I never breathe its pure serene*
> *Till I heard Chapman speak out loud and bold:*
> *Then felt I like some watcher of the skies*
> *When a new planet swims into his ken;*
> *Or like stout Cortez when with eagle eyes*
> *He star'd at the Pacific—and all his men*
> *Look'd at each other with a wild surmise—*
>   *Silent, upon a peak in Darien.*

Japanese scholar Masayuki Ohkado (2013) has criticized the use of the term "Peak in Darien"; two of his points are that the obscure English source renders the term culture-bound and that the term itself is obscure because it does not lucidly describe the phenomenon it supposedly labels. He has suggested replacing the term with new terms that correspond with the two categories just mentioned, namely: encounters with unknown decedent (EUDs; as presented in our Chapter 5), and encounters with known decedent not known to have died (EKDs; as presented in this chapter). As "decedent" is a legal synonym for the more commonly used term "deceased person," we forego the use of acronyms for the sake of clarity and refer in this chapter simply to ADCs with known deceased persons not known to have died.

Before we present four cases of NDE-related ADCs with known deceased persons not known to have died, we present a singular case of ADC in which a living person not near death was accurately informed by a deceased person of the impending NDE of another family member. Although it does not technically belong to the category of the other four cases, we include it here because it seemed to us to be conceptually related most closely to them.

ADC With a Known Deceased Person, With Prediction of an NDE

CASE 6.1 An Apparition Foretells an NDE

Emine Fougner, whose father was the focus of Case 1.1 in Chapter 1, engaged in an extensive e-mail exchange with Titus Rivas and Anny Dirven between the end of 2009 and May 2010 regarding an ADC experience involving her younger sister, Huriye Kacar.

Although Emine's sister's official name is Huriye, Emine often addressed her by her nickname, "Huriş." Huriye was named after a grandmother who was very fond of her. When that grandmother died, Huriye was holding her hand. At the time of the events of this case, Huriye lived in Canada, as did her parents, whereas Emine lived in the United States. Nevertheless, Emine and her sister had a particularly strong emotional bond and considered each other best friends.

In mid-August 2009, Huriye was scheduled to go to the hospital to deliver her second child. On August 7, Emine and her children were watching a movie. She fell asleep during the movie and was awakened at about 1:00 a.m. when one of her children wanted to get into bed with her. Once awake, she was unable to get back to sleep. After some time, the light in the hallway came on. It was a motion-sensor light that was activated by movement and that then turned off automatically after about a half minute without any movement. Emine thought that one of the other children had activated it and that if that child also wanted to crawl into bed with her, there would not be enough room. Strangely enough, she did not hear any footsteps, and no other child entered the bedroom. Emine looked at her watch. Just 11 minutes later, the light in the hall went on again. Again, no one came in, and again there were no footsteps to be heard. Once more, 6 minutes later, the light came on for a third time. Emine looked at her watch and sat up in bed to see who it could be. Once again, there was no one to be seen. She lay back down and then suddenly felt someone tapping her foot. She looked up and, to her utter amazement, saw her grandmother standing there. She said, "Grandma? Is it you?" Right after that, she thought, "You keep waking me up with the lights in the hallway; you should just turn the bathroom light on." The next thing she saw was the bathroom light turning on. By that time, she was thinking, "Holy crap! Oh my gosh! Did I just order my dead grandmother to turn the bathroom light on?"

She was wide awake by now and assumed that tricks were being played on her. She blinked her eyes a few times, but she still saw her grandmother standing there.

"Grandma, what are you doing here?"

"Huriş went to the hospital to have her baby."

"Oh, she wasn't due for another two weeks."

"It's not that. She's going to have a very hard time. Her soul will leave her body."

Emine felt her heart start pounding, and she was very scared. "What?!! Is she going to die?"

"Don't worry, don't worry; she'll recover, don't worry. But she will have a very hard time. Be prepared for it, but she will be okay."

Her grandmother's voice sounded comforting. Then she was suddenly gone. Emine looked at her watch and saw that it was 2:11 a.m. She debated whether to call her sister or her parents, but she was afraid of alarming them unnecessarily, so she decided to wait until the next day. She could not get back to sleep, though, so she went to her computer with a cup of Turkish tea.

At about 6:00 a.m., the phone rang, and Emine saw that the call was from her sister's number. She picked up the phone right away with the words, "So, girl, did you have your baby this morning?" But it was her mother, who said:

Your sister went to the hospital to have her baby at 2:00 a.m. our time. It's 9:00 a.m. here, but we haven't heard anything from her husband. His cell phone is turned off, and I can't reach her at the hospital. Could you check McMaster University Hospital [Hamilton, Ontario] for me?

Emine answered, "Mom, she'll be okay. I'll find out in a little while."

In May 2010, Rivas and Dirven received a written explanation in Turkish from the mother of both women, with a translation into English by Emine. Emine and Huriye's mother wrote:

She [Emine] answered [my phone call], I got surprised. "Did you give birth girl?" she said, and I answered, "It's your mother, dear, your sister went to hospital, and been gone for hours, but we received no information." She told me she wasn't surprised, and that her grandmother came to visit her. I first thought she had a dream, but it wasn't.

That scared me, and I asked her "Did she come to take your sister?" The thought made me cry, but she said "Mom, don't worry, she told me that my sister would have a hard time but not to worry—three times—she will get better, but it will be hard."

Emine had tried reassuring her mother. Then, when she called the hospital, her sister's name was not on file. Considering it was very busy, it might be that Huriye was at St. Joseph's Hospital, also in Hamilton. This turned out to be the case, in fact. Emine got a nurse on the line and asked her to ask her sister to turn her cell phone on. She then also spoke to Huriye herself, who told her that she was feeling another kind of pain than during the birth of her first baby. The nurse had told Emine that they expected Huriye to go into labor in two hours, so Emine promised her sister that she would call back around that time. She called her mother back, and only then told her mother about seeing her grandmother's ghost.

A few hours later, Emine tried to get in touch with her sister again as promised, but her sister's phone was turned off. At that time, the hospital did not want to give Emine any information yet. For four hours, Emine could not find out what was going on with Huriye. Meanwhile, she kept trying to reach her brother-in-law. Only after a number of attempts did he finally answer. He told her, sobbing, that his wife had had a baby girl, Ella Naz, but had lost a lot of blood and was at that moment in the intensive care unit. Not until the next day did the family hear that she was there due to a caesarian section. She had lost a lot of blood, and the bleeding had not stopped. This situation had caused Huriye to go into cardiac arrest. The medical team had made every effort to resuscitate her. They had given her a blood transfusion, a doctor had tried to defibrillate her, and she had been hooked up to a heart-lung machine. At the same time, a surgeon had performed a hysterectomy to remove her uterus.

According to Emine, Huriye's heart had stopped a total of three times, and her mother even thought that it had happened five times. The first time, her arrest lasted 15 minutes. There were complications after the hysterectomy, causing her to bleed heavily again, and she had to be operated on again. During this procedure, her heart arrested, and she had to be resuscitated two more times. Finally, the bleeding stopped, but she was still in coma and remained in intensive care. All the family members were inconsolable and beside themselves from the uncertainty. When Huriye finally regained consciousness, she still had a long road ahead of herself before she achieved complete recovery.

All in all, 17 doctors and 50 nurses had been involved in her crisis. She had to stay in the hospital a total of 12 days.

During the second night that Huriye was in the hospital, Emine's 7-year-old daughter came to her during the night with a story that her great-grandmother had kept playing with the lights. She was really tired of it because she could not go to sleep under those circumstances. Emine brought her daughter back to bed and then started to pray for her sister's recovery. As she did so, she had the feeling that everything would turn out well for her sister in the end.

Emine's mother wrote Rivas and Dirven:

Only Emine's inspirations about her grandmother's visit gave us a glimpse of hope. My daughter is alive and normal today. So many days of not knowing whether my daughter would heal or not could have killed us, but her grandmother must have felt the pain we were going to suffer before we did, and she gave us hope. I don't want to remember those days; it's too hard and painful.

Emine's grandmother had predicted that Huriye's soul would leave her body. When Huriye was sufficiently recovered, Emine asked her whether she had felt anything when her heart had stopped beating. Huriye told her that she had observed the doctors' efforts. She had felt totally alone and found herself in a kind of tunnel. She felt the pain of the doctors' procedures, even though the doctors had told her husband that she would not feel anything. She saw how she had been cut open during the operations and felt the doctors' panic.

Emine asked Huriye to provide Rivas and Dirven with an extensive description of the medical procedures she had undergone. Emine also obtained the medical reports and provided them to Rivas and Dirven. They found that the reports corroborated Huriye's description.

Huriye's water had broken a few weeks earlier than expected, and for some reason this development had made her very anxious. She had had a foreboding that something might go wrong. In the end, that premonition was very correct. She had had to undergo three operations and a hysterectomy for blood loss and other complications regarding the birth. The baby had had to be delivered by caesarian section. Later, Huriye's doctor had confided to her that what she had gone through was extremely rare.

Huriye had in fact had an NDE, and she correctly observed the details of the events that involved the caesarian section. She had been completely unconscious. From above, in an out-of-body state, she had observed the doctor saying, "Her eyes are shut." Her nurse had added, "She's asleep." The doctor and the nurse had placed a green screen below her chest. The doctor had opened her abdomen with a scalpel and pulled the baby, a girl, out of the uterus by her head. At that time, the baby was not yet making any sounds. When the doctor cut her abdomen open, Huriye had cried out (without anyone hearing), "He's cutting me open!" The umbilical cord had been cut, and the baby had been laid on her chest for just a moment before being handed to Nurse Melissa. After that, Huriye had seen nothing for a while.

Subsequently, Huriye seems to have regained consciousness for a time. She remembered seeing her husband's head and the tiny head of her baby trying to suck on his face. He had said to her, "Just look at our daughter. Isn't she beautiful?!" He had held his face close to the baby's, and this had made Huriye cry. Then she lost consciousness again.

From that moment on, she received no further visual impressions of the intensive care unit. A second phase in her NDE was starting, and it had nothing to do with the physical world.

One of the questions preoccupying Rivas and Dirvan was whether the pain that Huriye had felt at the hospital had occurred during the OB aspect of her NDE. It had not. Huriye did report pain, but she felt it only at the times that she was still conscious or had regained consciousness, rather than during her NDE.

SOURCES

Rivas, T., & Dirven, A. (2010a). *Van en naar het Licht* [From and to the Light]. Leeuwarden, Netherlands: Uitgeverij Elikser.

Rivas, T., & Dirven, A. (2010b). De bijna-doodervaring van Huriye Kacar [Huriye Kacar's near-death experience]. *Terugkeer, 21*(3), 6–7.

ADCs With Known Deceased People Not Known to Have Died

CASE 6.2 The Death of a Sister

This case derives from Raymond Moody's (1988) book *The Light Beyond*. Moody presented a talk for doctors at the U.S. Army base in Fort Dix, New Jersey. Afterward, someone came to Moody to share his NDE. The man told Moody:

> I was terribly ill and near death with heart problems at the same time that my sister was near death in another part of the same hospital with a diabetic

coma. I left my body and went into the corner of the room, where I watched them work on me down below.

Suddenly, I found myself in conversation with my sister, who was up there with me. I was very attached to her, and we were having a great conversation about what was going on down there when she began to move away from me.

I tried to go with her but she kept telling me to stay where I was. "It's not your time," she said. "You can't go with me because it's not your time." Then she just began to recede off into the distance through a tunnel while I was left there alone.

When I awoke, I told the doctors [*sic*] that my sister had died. He denied it, but at my insistence, he had a nurse check on [her status]. She had in fact died, just as I knew she did.

Moody contacted the attending physicians. They confirmed that the patient's story was correct.

SOURCE

Moody, R. A., Jr. (with Perry, P.). (1988). *The light beyond*. New York, NY: Bantam Books.

CASE 6.3 Aunt Cilla

In Günter Ewald's 2007 book *Nahtoderfahrungen* (Near-Death Experiences), he described Renate A.'s NDE, as recounted by her husband, Bernd A., from Schleswig-Holstein in Germany. Renate had her NDE in 1993 when the couple lived in Saarland. At that time, Renate had a serious alcohol problem, which Bernd tried to help her with. Due to her alcoholism, her physical condition had seriously deteriorated. On Christmas Day 1993, it caused her to fall into a coma, and she was admitted to a hospital. The attending physician reassured Bernd and sent him back home. There, in his wife's handbag, he found a note from a doctor dated December 15, 1993, to the effect of, "Mrs. A.'s illness is life threatening. Liver cirrhosis. There is acute danger caused by bleeding of esophageal varices (veins)."

The day after Christmas, Bernd received a call and learned that his wife had been transferred to the university clinic in Homburg. He went there as quickly as he could, but on arrival discovered that his wife was not in her room. Renate turned out to be in the recreation room where she could smoke a cigarette. The night before, when the doctors had already given her up for dead, she had had an NDE. She had seen her late father and her aunt Cilla, among others. Both had made sure that she returned to her body because her time had not yet come. What was so exceptional about this case was that both Bernd and Renate knew that Renate's father had died, but they thought that her aunt Cilla was still alive and well.

A week after Christmas, Bernd visited his mother-in-law. She asked him if she could accompany him to the hospital and whether Renate was recovered enough to hear sad news. Renate's mother had received a letter that very day stating that her sister Cilla had died and that she had been laid to rest 3 days before the letter had been written. Counting back the days, this meant that Cilla had died shortly before Renate's NDE.

SOURCE

Ewald, G. (2007). *Nahtoderfahrungen: Hinweise auf ein Leben nach dem Tod?* [Near-death experiences: Indications of life after death?]. Kevelaer, Germany: Topos.

CASE 6.4 Eddie Cuomo

According to Brad Steiger and Sherry Hansen Steiger (1995), physician K. M. Dale reported the case of Eddie Cuomo, a 9-year-old American boy. This boy had suffered a high fever for 36 hours as his parents and medical personnel watched over him. When the boy came to at 3:00 a.m., he told his parents that he had been in heaven. He had seen his late Grandpa Cuomo, as well as Aunt Rosa and Uncle Lorenzo. Eddie's father thought it was embarrassing for Dr. Dale to have to overhear Eddie's story, so he tried to discount the story as some kind of hallucinatory dream.

Then Eddie remarked that he had also seen his 19-year-old sister, Teresa, and that she had been the one to tell him he had to go back. This report unsettled his father, because only two nights before, he had spoken with Teresa, who was a student at a college in Vermont. Eddie's father even asked the doctor to give Eddie a sedative.

Later that morning, Eddie's parents called the college. They learned that just after midnight the previous night, Teresa had been killed in a car accident. College officials had been trying to contact the parents to inform them, but had been unsuccessful—because the parents had spent the night at the hospital with their son, out of communication.

SOURCE

Steiger, B., & Steiger, S. H. (1995). *Children of the light: The startling and inspiring truth about children's near-death experiences and how they illumine the beyond.* New York, NY: Signet.

CASE 6.5 Elisabeth Kübler-Ross's Young Patient

The well-known Swiss psychiatrist and thanatologist, Elisabeth Kübler-Ross, has written about the dying process of young children. One of the examples she cited concerned a little boy who had been in a coma following a car accident that had also involved his mother and his brother, Peter. The boy came out of his coma briefly and told Dr. Kübler-Ross, "Yes, everything is all right now. Mommy and Peter are already waiting for me." He smiled contentedly and then slipped back into a coma from which he never recovered.

Kübler-Ross already knew that the boy's mother had died at the scene of the accident, but as far as she knew, his brother Peter had survived. Peter had been brought to another hospital with serious burns because the car had caught fire before rescuers had been able to extricate him. Kübler-Ross decided she would contact the other hospital to check on Peter's condition. However, as she was about to place the call, she received a call from the other hospital to notify her that Peter had died a few minutes before.

Elisabeth Kübler-Ross claimed to have witnessed this pattern a number of times before, in which a child was not apprised of the death of a loved one but still perceived this person during the child's own process of dying. She concluded that she could not attribute this pattern simply to chance.

SOURCE

Kübler-Ross, E. (1983). *On children and death: How children and their parents can and do cope with death.* New York, NY: Simon & Schuster.

CASE 6.6 Lucky Pettersen

Lucky Pettersen, son of Dana and Bill Pettersen, was born in Julian, California in 1992. When he was 4 years old, he enjoyed helping his mother in her country store, although he spent most of his time at Calico's, a restaurant next door. There, he found a wonderful friend in "Big" Gino Focarelli, the father of the owner of the restaurant, Carl Focarelli. The two would play together for hours. In 1997, 4-year-old Lucky was suddenly struck down by a fever. At first, his parents were told it was just the flu, but a week and a half later, the fever turned out to be indicative of something far more serious. It almost seemed as if Lucky were shrinking, and he became unresponsive. His parents rushed him to the UC San Diego Medical Center. En route, Lucky kept slipping in and out of consciousness. His mother, Dana, thought he might die. Not long after they had arrived at the hospital, the doctors made a devastating diagnosis: Lucky had acute renal failure, cerebral edema (brain swelling) that could lead to severe mental impairment, and a nonfunctioning liver. He had slipped into a coma and was fighting for his life.

Dana ran, screaming, from the unit and called a close girlfriend who had become a widow only 2 months prior. The girlfriend told her that she should pray for someone to bring him back. Dana followed this advice, and prayer calmed her enough so that she was able to call her other (adult) children.

The doctors said that Lucky needed a liver transplant within 12 hours or he would die. One of the doctors, Dr. Ronald Busuttil, stated in a documentary presented by *Beyond Chance*, "You could not find a 4-year-old that was sicker than Lucky. I mean, literally, at any moment he could have died." A trauma helicopter flew Lucky to the nearest transplant facility, the UCLA Medical Center in Los Angeles, more than 100 miles away. There was no liver available, either from a child or from an adult, so a suitable living donor was sought. Lucky's parents turned out not to be suitable donors. Surprisingly, his half brother, 16-year-old Jason, who was considered less compatible than Lucky's parents but who pleaded to be tested in order to save his beloved little brother's life, turned out to be a perfect organ donor.

Part of Jason's liver was removed and transplanted into Lucky's body. According to Dr. Busuttil, because Lucky's condition was so far advanced, even if the transplant was successful, he still only had at most a 25% chance of survival. During the transplantation procedure, Lucky had two cardiac arrests but was able to be resuscitated both times. The transplant appeared to be a success, nevertheless.

Three days later, Lucky woke up. He said to his father, "I'm back." His mother then asked Lucky how he was feeling and what he remembered of the operation. He said that he had had a kind of dream that Big Gino "had walked him back from Heaven." In the documentary, Lucky relates, "I kept on hearing: 'Go back! Go back! Go back!' And it turned out to be Big Gino." It was not until 2 weeks later that Dana realized the accuracy of Lucky's experience and that it was more than a nice dream. On the family's return from the UCLA Medical Center, Big Gino's son, Carl, was finally able to tell Dana that on the same Thursday that Lucky had gone to the hospital and slipped into a coma, Carl's father had died. Both the Pettersens and Carl considered Lucky's experience with Big Gino to have been an answer to Dana's prayer for someone to bring Lucky back to the family.

SOURCE
Viacom Productions. (Producer). (2000). *Medical miracle*. Beyond Chance with Melissa Etheridge. Retrieved from https://www.youtube.com/watch?v=lKxBnUzAke8

Remarks

Experiences containing paranormal information regarding familiar people who have died generally suggest actual contact with the other side as long as the patient was not actively seeking that information. The alternative explanation, that the information was obtained by means of unconscious clairvoyance, is, in such cases in particular, even more unacceptable.

In Case 6.1, there is an unexpected, correct prediction, and in Cases 6.2 to 6.6, the fact is that the NDEr could not have known that the person in question had died. Just as in the cases in the previous chapter, those in this chapter indicate communication with the dead.

Anesthesiologist Gerald Woerlee has argued that not all cases involving encounters with deceased people not known to have died are equally strong. Some of them might be based on chance or normal foreknowledge, for instance. Someone who was involved in a serious car accident might, in theory, "guess" correctly that a fellow passenger had died because the chance of dying was relatively great. Even when this possibility is taken into account, that still leaves cases of known deceased people not known to have died, in which normal explanations in some way fall short of accounting for all the facts. In this collection of confirmed NDEs, this situation is true particularly of Case 6.3, because the person involved had no reason to suspect that her aunt had died, and of Case 6.6, because Lucky had no reason to suspect that his beloved Big Gino had died. These two cases certainly point to the other cases of known deceased people not known to have died being attributable to more than mere chance. In other words, the NDErs appear to have actually had contact with someone who died.

In Case 6.1, as we mentioned, we also see a prediction that came true, which indicates that the person who died had paranormal foreknowledge or "precognition" with respect to events in the near future. This type of situation does not necessarily mean that the future is set in stone, but it does raise the notion that certain events are already "in the air" and are therefore more likely than others.

In a few unconfirmed NDEs described in the literature, we encountered a comparable form of "preview," although it occurred to patients *during* their NDEs. We even found a few NDEs that appeared to contain confirmed predictions. In his article "Sporen uit de toekomst" (Traces from the Future), Jim van der Heijden (2012) highlighted the predictions of NDErs Ned Dougherty (2002) and Dannion Brinkley (1994). Dougherty, for instance, made a prediction about a possible "major terrorist attack on New York City or Washington that would have a huge impact on the way of life in the U.S."

Economist Christophor (Bob) Coppes (2011), in his book *Messages from the Light*, reported the case of a woman who, in 2008, predicted a major worldwide crisis based, according to her, on what she had seen during her NDE in 1986. Coppes summarized this case for us as follows:

It was in March 2008 when I spoke with her. Bear Stearns, a large investment bank, had just been rescued by the Federal Reserve Bank of New York. The entire financial world breathed a sigh of relief and assumed that the crisis was over, stocks and commodities reached record highs. But she said then (in March 2008) that the real crisis was still coming, which ran totally counter to the consensus of the financial markets.

She said that it would be severe and impact many lives and everyone would be affected (which really is what happened). Only in September 2008 did things really go wrong, after the bankruptcy of Lehman Brothers (another American investment bank) and the near-bankruptcy of AIG (the largest insurance company in the world) and two of the largest mortgage banks in the U.S. (all three rescued by federal intervention and taxpayer money). The real height of the crisis was March 2009, although the crisis still isn't really over.

This wasn't just counter to my own expectations, but counter to the expectations of the whole financial world. This crisis has been the largest one since the Great Depression of the 1930s. So she predicted it perfectly; she had already seen it in 1986, but not comprehended it at that time because the information didn't contain any dates. She told me this in March 2008.

While cases of this type sometimes involve accurate predictions, they also sometimes appear to involve inaccurate ones (Ring, 1988). Even when the predictions are accurate, the question of whether they are the result of actual paranormal foreknowledge or instead might be attributable to pure chance seems difficult to answer. For these reasons, we decided not to include these cases in our collection. Obviously, our exclusion in this regard does not mean that we rule out that NDErs might, in fact, be able to obtain paranormal impressions of the (likely) future.

REFERENCES

Brinkley, D. (with Perry, P.). (1994). *Saved by the light: The true story of a man who died twice and the profound revelations he received.* New York, NY: Villard Books.

Coppes, C. (2010). *Messages from the light: True stories of near-death experiences and communication from the other side.* Wayne, NJ: Career Press / New Page Books.

Dougherty, N. (2002). *Fast lane to heaven: A life after death journey.* Charlottesville, VA: Hampton Roads.

Ohkado, M. (2013). On the term "Peak in Darien Experience." *Journal of Near-Death Studies, 31*(4), 203–211.

Ring, K. (1988). Prophetic visions in 1988: A critical reappraisal. *Journal of Near-Death Studies, 7*(1), 4–18.

van der Heijden, J. (2012). Sporen uit de toekomst [Traces from the future], *Terugkeer, 23*(1), 1–11.

CHAPTER 7

Observations of Out-of-Body NDErs by Others

*These phenomena prove, I think, that the soul exists, and that
it is endowed with faculties at present unknown.*
—Camille Flammarion, *The Unknown*

Surprisingly enough, authors have published not only confirmed cases in which, during near-death experiences (NDEs), experiencers (NDErs) observed known and unknown deceased persons but also confirmed cases in which NDErs made their presence known to others by appearing to them or through some other means. The evidential value of such cases is that both parties confirm each other's accounts. For example, the NDEr states that he or she visited a specific person at a particular moment, and before the two people have had the opportunity to communicate, the visited person also states that at that same moment he or she observed the NDEr as a kind of apparition or otherwise witnessed a remarkable phenomenon that signified the NDEr's presence and for which no commonsense explanation seems to exist.

CASE 7.1 The Open Front Door

The French astronomer and parapsychologist Camille Flammarion wrote in his book *L'inconnu et les problèmes psychiques* (The Unknown and Problems of the Psyche) the following case from the 19th century. Caroline Baeschly told Flammarion that when her father was 20 years old, he lived in a house in Brumath, in the French Alsace region, where he slept on the second floor. After midnight one night, he heard the front door open very noisily and was immediately awakened by the sound. His own father—Mrs. Baeschly's grandfather—was on the ground floor. He called down to ask whether his father was in his room or had gone outside and what on earth was making all that racket.

Camille Flammarion

Receiving no response, Baeschly's father ran downstairs and, without explanation and utterly bewildered, found the door ajar. Finally, father and son closed the door together, locked it, then went back to sleep in their respective rooms. A little while later, though, the door opened again, making all kinds of noise, and both men found themselves again standing in disbelief in front of the open front door. Again they carefully closed and locked the door and went back to bed. Nevertheless, it happened yet a third time, and so they bound the door shut with a thick rope. It stayed quiet the rest of the night.

Shortly after that night, they received a letter informing them of the death of Baeschly's grandfather's brother who had emigrated to the United States. The date of his death corresponded with the day on which the door had kept opening by itself. In addition, Mrs. Baeschly learned that as her great-uncle lay dying, he had apparently expired but then opened his eyes one last time and said, "I just went on a grand journey: I went to see my brother in Brumath."

In this case, no appearance of the NDEr was observed, but a not-so-trivial connection seems to have existed between his deathbed report of having left his body and visited his brother across the Atlantic and the inexplicable and noisy opening of the front door not once but three times where the surviving brother lived an ocean away.

SOURCE

Flammarion, C. (1900). *L'inconnu et les problèmes psychiques* [The unknown and problems of the psyche]. New York, NY: Harper & Brothers.

CASE 7.2 Mrs. Birkbeck

This case is exceptionally old but does contain convincing witness statements. In 1739, an English Quaker by the name of Mrs. Birkbeck was lying on her deathbed at the home of friends—evidently because she was in no condition to return to her own home.

After she had expressed the wish to see her three children again, she seemed to fall asleep. Ten minutes later, she claimed that she had gone home and seen the children. Birkbeck died soon after. At the same time, her children excitedly told the grownups who were looking after them that their mother had been to see them.

Both Birkbeck's claims and those of the children were confirmed shortly after the incidents.

SOURCES

Barrett, W. (1926). *Death-bed visions: The psychic experiences of the dying.* Wellingborough, Northampton, UK: Aquarian Press.

Ellwood, G. F. (2001). *The uttermost deep: The challenge of near-death experiences.* New York, NY: Lantern.

CASE 7.3 Olga Gearhardt

In his book *Parting Visions,* physician Melvin Morse described the case of 63-year-old Olga Gearhardt of San Diego, California. In 1988, a large part of Gearhardt's heart was attacked by a virus that impaired its function. Consequently, her name was placed on a heart transplant list, and at the beginning of 1989, a suitable heart became available. Her family, intensely concerned for her, filled the waiting room. However, one important person was missing: her son-in-law, who had nosocomephobia—a fear of hospitals. He remained at home, waiting for what he hoped would be a happy ending.

During the transplant, unexpected complications arose. At 2:15 a.m., the transplanted heart suddenly stopped beating altogether. Gearhardt was clinically dead for quite some time, and it took hours of resuscitation to get her new heart going steadily again.

The next morning, the medical staff told the family that the operation had gone exceptionally well; they were not told that Gearhardt had almost died. The wife of the son-in-law who had stayed at home called him to share the good news. He claimed that he already knew that his mother-in-law was doing well because he had heard it from her personally.

At 2:15 a.m. the previous night, he had witnessed the apparition of his mother-in-law standing at the foot of his bed. At first he had thought the operation simply had not taken place and had asked how she was. She had said, "I am fine, I'm going to be all right. There is nothing for any of you to worry about." After that, she had disappeared as suddenly as she had appeared.

Her son-in-law had not been afraid of the apparition, but he had immediately gotten up and written down what time he had seen her appear and what she had said.

When Gearhardt regained consciousness, her first words were, "Did you get the message?" She told her family that she had had a "strange dream" during the operation. In it, she had left her body and for a couple of minutes watched the doctors who were working on her. After that, she saw her family sitting in the waiting room. She tried to make contact with them but was unsuccessful. In frustration, she decided to go to her daughter's house some 30 miles away from the hospital and seek a connection with her son-in-law. When she got there, she had stood at the foot of his bed and told him that everything would be all right in the end.

Dr. Morse and his writing assistant, Paul Perry, interviewed a number of Gearhardt's family members and came to the conclusion that their stories were completely consistent with each other, without any discrepancies. They concluded that the experiences were explicable only by an actual out-of-body state plus an actual appearance.

SOURCES

Morse, M. (with Perry, P.). (1996). *Parting visions: Uses and meanings of pre-death, psychic, and spiritual experiences* (rev. ed.). New York, NY: HarperCollins.

Morse, M. L. (n.d.). *Are near death experiences real? (And if so, what are they good for?)*. Institute for the Scientific Study of Consciousness. Retrieved from http://spiritualscientific.com/yahoo_site_admin/assets/docs/Are_Near_Death_Experiences_Real.65201445.pdf

CASE 7.4 Mary Gosse

The case of Mrs. Mary Gosse stems from the late 17th century, making it the oldest case in this book. At that time, Puritan minister Thomas Tilson described the case in a letter to fellow preacher Richard Baxter, who included it in his 1691 book titled *The Certainty of the World of Spirits*. The case was finally rescued from oblivion by virtue of its inclusion in the famous 1886 work *Phantasms of the Living* by Edwin Gurney, Frederic W. H. Myers, and Frank Podmore. It was also addressed by Sir William Barrett in his 1926 book *Death-Bed Visions*. (This case was erroneously reported in the 19th-century literature as that of Mary Goffe due to a misreading of the typography of the original account.)

Pastor Tilson wrote:

Mary, the wife of John Gosse of Rochester, being afflicted with a long illness, removed to her father's house at West Mulling, which was about nine miles distant from her own; there she died, June 4th, 1691. The day before her departure she grew impatiently desirous to see her two children, whom she had left at home, to the care of a nurse. She prayed her husband to hire a horse, for she must go home to die with the children. . . .

Between one and two o'clock in the morning, she fell into a trance. One widow Turner, who watched with her that night, says that her eyes were open and fixed, and her jaw fallen; she put her hand on her mouth and nostrils, but could perceive no breath; she thought her to be in a fit, and doubted whether she were alive or dead.

The next day this dying woman told her mother that she had been at home with her children. "That is impossible," said the mother, "for you have been here in bed all the while." "Yes," replied the other, "but I was with them last night while I was asleep."

The nurse at Rochester, widow Alexander by name, affirms and says she will take her oath on it before a magistrate, and receive the sacrament upon it, that a little before two o'clock that morning she saw the likeness of the said Mary Gosse come out of the next chamber (where the elder child lay in a bed by itself, the door being left open), and stood by her bedside for about a quarter of an hour; the younger child was there lying by her; her eyes moved, and her mouth went, but she said nothing. The nurse, moreover, says that she was perfectly awake; it was then daylight, being one of the longest days in the year. She sat up in her bed, and looked steadfastly upon the apparition; in that time she heard the bridge clock strike two, and a while after said, "In the name of the Father, Son, and Holy Ghost, what art thou?" Thereupon the appearance removed and went away. . . .

At five o'clock she went to a neighbour's house and knocked at the door, but they would not rise; at six she went again, then they arose and let her in. She related to them all that had passed; they would persuade her she was mistaken, or dreamt; but she confidently affirmed, "If ever I saw her in all my life, I saw her this night." . . .

I fully discoursed the matter with the nurse and two neighbours, to whose house she went that morning.

Two days after, I had it from the mother, the minister that was with her in the evening, and the woman who sat up with her that last night. They all agree in the same story, and every one helps to strengthen the other's testimony.

They all appear to be sober, intelligent persons, far enough from designing to impose a cheat upon the world, or to manage a lie; and what temptation they should lie under for so doing I cannot conceive.

—Thomas Tilson

SOURCES

Barrett, W. (1926). *Death-bed visions: The psychic experiences of the dying.* Wellingborough, Northampton, UK: Aquarian Press.

Baxter, R. (1691). *The certainty of the world of spirits fully evinced by the unquestionable histories of apparitions and witchcrafts, operations, voices, &c. proving the immortality of souls, the malice and miseries of the devils, and the damned. And of the blessedness of the justified. Fully evinced by the unquestionable histories of apparitions, operations, witchcrafts, voices, &c. Written as an addition to many other treatises, for the conviction of sadduces and infidels.* Retrieved from https://archive.org/details/certaintyofworld00baxt

Gurney, E., Myers, F. W. H., & Podmore, F. (1886). *Phantasms of the living.* London, England: Rooms of the Society for Psychical Research/Trübner.

CASE 7.5 In Two Places at the Same Time

In addition to the cases from physician Laurin Bellg's book that we have already discussed in previous chapters, Dr. Bellg shared yet another relevant experience with an audience in her 2014 presentation at The Monroe Institute (TMI). Bellg described the case as follows during this TMI Professional Seminar:

There was a woman who was dying and we knew she was dying. And it was clearly her time; there was nothing that we could do to save her. But she was quite conscious.

And she had a son who had been quite naughty, and he had done some things that were just so unkind to his parents and alienated himself from his parents. He had spent some prison time for theft related to how he had really destroyed their financial lives. And so there's a lot of hate and animosity that existed between them. And her son wanted to come visit her on her deathbed and she said, "No. I don't want to see you."

And, of course, he's older, he's had more experiences—this is now 25 years after the fact—and he really wants to connect to his mom. He's sitting in a bar—we've got lots of them in Wisconsin—and he's experiencing deep sorrow, deep regret, deep remorse, wanting to connect with his mom before she crosses over. And she's refusing to see him, and he's wanting this so badly.

He looks up and he sees his mother coming into the bar, and he's so shocked and he's so elated, he's crying. He's excited, and he can't understand it because she's so sick. What is she doing there? And he gets up to go greet her and, as Wisconsin bars are always so crowded, there are people that obscure the view, and when they pass, she's no longer there.

His mother wakes up and says, "I had the strangest dream. I dreamed that I was in a bar and I saw my son sitting at a table crying, and he got up to start coming to me. And I got scared and I woke up."

Laurin Bellg, MD

And we were able to corroborate these stories and understand that her Higher Self...and this is how I see it. Because, unfortunately, before she passed, they were not able to make that physical connection—but I believe they made that soul connection.

And he was blown away. The family was blown away because they understood that something quite unusual had happened. And they were able to share the same data to confirm that this was true.

On February 8, 2016, Robert Mays interviewed Bellg about this case. Following are a few relevant excerpts from the recording of that interview:

RM: The woman who was dying of cancer was your patient, I guess?
LB: Correct.
RM: You knew some of the story from her?

LB: We knew some of the story from her and her family because she was pretty adamant. Sometimes when people come into the hospital they will actually say to us, "I want this person allowed into my hospital room. I don't want this person allowed into my hospital room." So there was still a lot of bitterness that had been harbored by the patient toward her son. So it was very evident that she did not want her son to come to her. He wanted to because he knew she was dying.

RM: Did you get a description of what she experienced from her?

LB: From her and from her daughter. It was her daughter who first brought it to my attention because she had maintained connection with her brother and she was kind of the go-between. A lot of it was verified and brought forth by the daughter who had said that the mother hadn't wanted to see him and the son really wanted to see her. And the son would talk to the daughter. The mother would talk to the daughter, but the son and mother would not talk to each other. So it was the son who had said to his sister about being in the bar and seeing his mother. And it was the patient who had said to her daughter, "I had the strangest dream that I saw my son crying in a bar." So I talked to the daughter and the patient about this.

RM: And they both repeated essentially what the daughter had told you?

LB: Right. And then I also talked to the son about what he had experienced.

RM: So the son described that he was in the bar, he was crying, he saw his mother . . .

LB: Starting to come toward him . . .

RM: And he got up?

LB: It was a crowded bar, and when the people moved away he no longer saw her.

RM: I thought the mother said he got up.

LB: He got up and started to move toward her, and then she was no longer there.

RM: And she reported that he was getting up?

LB: Getting up, starting to move toward her, and then she had this moment of panic and woke up.

RM: Is there any plausible, normal explanation for this case?

LB: I can't think of any because they're both describing the same situation in the same bar that's not too far from the hospital. I've never been to that bar but people who have been to that bar describe this bar and recognize that bar. The problem in Wisconsin is we have so many bars. They all look alike to me. I don't know. We don't go to bars. It's not a part of our culture but it's close enough to the hospital that people when they finish their shifts, sometimes, people who work at the hospital go to this bar, and they know this bar, so it's a bar that was able to be described. There is no plausible way because she couldn't get out of bed. She was dying. The thing that's so mysterious to me is for her to explain that she started walking toward her son, saw him crying, he got up and for him to say he saw his mom, got up, and started to go to her. That's pretty astonishing.

I was there the next day to hear it. What we *do* know is that the afternoon that it happened, the lady woke up and told her daughter and then the son that evening told his sister. She's the one who was able to put together that this had happened around the same time. She's told me because she was just so amazed that that happened.

RM: Is there any indication from the son how real his mother looked in the bar?

LB: Oh, he thought he saw her. There was indication from him that he thought his mother was actually there.

RM: So it looked like she was physically there then?

LB: It looked like she was physically there. It never occurred to him that this would be an apparition or a projection of some kind.

RM: So it happened in an afternoon, and the mother woke up and told the daughter, and then the son told his sister that evening?

LB: Correct.

RM: Can you say how many years ago this was?

LB: I would say this is probably five years ago.

RM: So 2011 maybe?

LB: Yeah.

SOURCE

Bellg, L. (2014). *Patient NDEs in the ICU.* Presentation at The Monroe Institute (TMI) Professional Seminar. Retrieved from https://www.youtube.com/watch?v=xdScjvc14xE starting at 31:08 in the video.

CASE 7.6 Stephen's Girlfriend

On the Near Death Experience Research Foundation website (nderf.org), run by radiation oncologist Jeffrey Long and his wife, attorney Jody Long, a man calling himself Stephen recounted an experience with his girlfriend. Following are the most significant passages from his account:

I had been seeing my girlfriend for a little over a year. We went on a camping trip that we had been planning for a while. But the camping trip wasn't fun the way we had planned. She was in a really bad mood—off and on not getting along with me—and complaining of feeling "off."

Anyway, we got back to her place, and an argument started, so I left and went home. What I didn't know was that my girlfriend was pregnant with twins, but it was an ectopic pregnancy. One of the babies was stuck in a fallopian tube. She got sicker soon after I left and had to be rushed to the hospital that same night. After a few tests and much pain and suffering, they began her surgery.

During the operation, she remembers that she saw me at my home, lying on my bed, and that she called out to me by name. Now—at this exact same moment, I was indeed lying on my bed, just dozing a little, when I was awakened, startled by someone shouting my name. I ventured out onto my stairway landing to see who was calling, but nobody was there. I went back to lying on the bed.

Over the next few days, I was able to speak to her and was brought up to date on all that had happened. A strongly surreal moment for me was when she said, "I saw you lying down on your bed, and I called to you." I exclaimed, "Oh my God, I heard you call! How can that be? You were 20 miles away!"

I have pondered this over the years, and it wasn't until I started reading about NDEs that it came to me that the only logical explanation for this would be that she did, indeed, leave her body and visit me. I did, absolutely, hear my name being called, clear as day! . . .

I very clearly heard my name and it was my girlfriend's voice! . . . Her voice rang out clearly and it startled me! . . . I felt confused as to who had called my name. It sounded so close that I was certain someone was right outside my door, on my landing, calling my name—but nobody was there! . . .

[Responding to the online question: *Did you observe or hear anything regarding people or events during your experience that could be verified later?*] Yes. She remembers calling my name, and I remember hearing it! . . . We do still talk about it to this day. And through our ups and downs over the years, it brings us peace to know that we are soul mates, and that this really happened! . . . The evidence is that she remembers saying it and I remember hearing it! We hadn't spoken yet, and it was one of the first things she said to me after I rang her to see what was happening. I had to sit down when she said, "I called your name." It was so real and loud, it awoke me, as it would you, if you had been dozing and someone in the room had shouted your name. . . . She needed me and came to get me. . . . It has kept us together when times are tough. The fact she came for me shows me how spiritual she is and how much she thinks of me.

SOURCE

Stephen. (2011, July 23). *Stephen's girlfriend's probable NDE*. Near Death Experience Research Foundation. Retrieved from http://nderf.org/NDERF/NDE_Experiences/stephen_gfriend_prob_nde.htm

CASE 7.7 Jed Archdeacon

The Australian television documentary series *The Extraordinary* (1993–1996) aired the case of a 10-year-old Australian boy named Jed Archdeacon who was living in the suburbs of Perth at the time. The show's hosts interviewed both Jed and his mother, Diana Archdeacon.

On August 27, 1990, during a game of "dodge" (similar to dodgeball) at school, Jed had an asthma attack that became fatal. Teachers tried to revive him, but when they failed, two of them brought him to the hospital as quickly as possible. There the emergency staff fought for his life. Resuscitation did not work at first, but he finally revived. His mother apparently knew that he would pull through, though, because she had had a reassuring experience earlier that morning.

That morning, Jed's mother was overcome by a strong feeling of love for him, and she also felt particularly drawn to a family photo, especially to his likeness in it. Still completely overwhelmed by these unusually intense feelings for Jed, she went out to work in the garden. Soon she had another strange feeling. She felt drawn to some alyssum flowers. They had planted the alyssum at Jed's request, because it bore his favorite flower, and Diana also liked it. Jed had selected the alyssum together with his mother and had helped plant it. She picked some of the tiny flowers from the bed, smelled them, and thought of her son. Again she was overcome by a remarkable, inexplicable feeling of peace. Regarding this experience, she said, "I'm unable to explain why. I was just suddenly thinking of Jed all the time. But I knew whatever it was, was something good."

Afterward, it turned out that Jed had had an NDE in which he had raced down a tunnel that looked like a mineshaft with different levels. He heard a beautiful kind of "humming" in the background and saw all different kinds of colored lights in the foreground, where he was going. Diana added that Jed said he felt fantastic and had the feeling he was surrounded by love. When he had almost reached the spiritual world, he stopped and was dragged back in the opposite direction, toward his body.

As he was lying in the hospital bed, Jed told his mother, "The funny thing was—I don't get it—I saw you in the garden smelling the flowers." Diana added, "Found out later that about the time I was smelling the flowers was about the time he was near to death, and he claims that he saw me in the garden smelling the flowers. And I really was there at that time."

Diana was convinced it was not a coincidence. Jed could not have known that she had been in the garden at that very moment. She believed that Jed had come to say good-bye.

SOURCE

Sutton, P., & Gershwin, N. (Executive producers). (1993). *The extraordinary: Episode 17* (11:28–21:13). Retrieved from https://www.youtube.com/watch?v=ZQwSO3_9lzI

Remarks

Parapsychological investigators such as Hornell Hart (1956) have often pointed out the extensive correlations between two types of paranormal experiences: those in which a living person perceives the apparition of another living person who is having an OBE and those in which the apparition is of a deceased person. In both types of cases, the apparition typically appears as an everyday person wearing clothing. This feature is characterized, for example, by Case 3.32, in which, as Jan Price lay in cardiac arrest, her husband, John, saw her leave her body "full-fleshed" in a green gown. (In a way, her NDE fits in this chapter, too, because she was having the OBE aspect of her NDE when her husband perceived her, even though she did not explicitly report that she saw her husband as well.) In a certain sense, the apparitions in this chapter can be considered a kind of "missing link" between the two categories, because they involve a living person perceiving the apparition of a person who is neither exactly living nor dead but who is having a near-death OBE—in essence, a person who is between life and death.

Further, we can ascertain a connection between the cases in this chapter and so-called crisis apparitions: ghosts of people who are in dire straits, particularly around the time they die. A frequent feature of crisis apparitions is that physical phenomena occur, such as in the Flammarion case involving the repeated opening of the front door.

In addition, the cases in this chapter remind us of the spontaneous telepathic after-death communications (ADCs) studied by former rational materialist and stockbroker Bill Guggenheim and his former wife, Judy Guggenheim (1995) and also by psychologist Erlendur Haraldsson (2012). Indeed, these are 2 of 35 studies of ADC published between the late 19th and early 21st centuries and recently systematically reviewed (Streit-Horn, 2011a, 2011b). The cases in this chapter might be considered akin to, or perhaps even a subset of, ADC, because they involve communication between someone living and someone not deceased but near death. We begin to see a continuum of telepathic communication between living people, between those living and those near death, and between the living and the deceased.

For the purpose of this book, however, this chapter documents confirmed cases in which individuals—one or more who are living and one near death— separated by considerable physical distance nevertheless each experienced that the person who was near-death visited and communicated "in spirit" with the living person(s), and each of the people later independently reported identical details of the visitation. Such occurrences add to the growing number of cases that seem to defy materialist explanations.

In the next chapter, we turn our attention to another category of confirmed paranormal phenomena that occur during NDEs: seemingly inexplicable healings.

REFERENCES

Guggenheim, W., & Guggenheim, J. A. (1995). *Hello from heaven: A new field of research—after-death communication—confirms that life and love are eternal.* New York, NY: Bantam Books.

Haraldsson, E. (2012). *The departed among the living: An investigative study of afterlife encounters.* Hove, England, UK: White Crow Books.

Hart, H. (1956). Six theories about apparitions. *Proceedings of the Society for Psychical Research, 50*(185), 153–239.

Streit-Horn, J. (2011a). A systematic review of research on after-death communi-
    cation (ADC) (Unpublished doctoral dissertation). University of North Texas,
    Denton, TX.
Streit-Horn, J. (2011b). *Fact sheet: After-death communication*. Retrieved from http://
    www.coe.unt.edu/sites/default/files/22/129/ADC.pdf

CHAPTER 8

Miraculous Healing

The bottom line is that miracles do happen, that is a
fact. How we interpret them is the issue.
—Winston Wu, "Debunking Common Skeptical Arguments Against
Paranormal and Psychic Phenomena" (www.victorzammit.com)

During some near-death experiences (NDEs), paranormal phenomena occur that seem to be an expression of psychokinesis: the influence of the psyche or mind on matter. As far as we know, the only confirmed cases of this kind that have been published involve the paranormal healing of serious diseases or disorders. Complete healing may take place during the NDE itself but, of course, will be noticed only after the patient has regained consciousness. Healing may occur either at once or in stages over time.

The following material concerns reported cases during which healing occurred completely unexpectedly. In these cases, a materialistic explanation involving a "spontaneous remission" of some kind—an entirely natural, spontaneous cure—seems utterly implausible, at least according to people medically qualified to determine such things.

A phenomenon seemingly related to this kind of healing is that near-death experiencers (NDErs) do not appear to sustain any serious, permanent brain damage despite cardiac arrests or other assaults on their brains. Sometimes this phenomenon crops up "secondarily" in reports about NDEs. For example, Michael Nahm discussed this phenomenon in *Wenn die Dunkelheit ein Ende findet* (When the Darkness Comes to an End), and Dr. Hans van Geel, a member of Merkawah's "Science Group," pointed it out when reading the original manuscript of our book. Case 3.11 and, as will be seen, Case 9.1 are obvious examples. It would be very intriguing to build a systematic medical assessment of the anomalous nature of this absence of neurological damage.

However, please note that as medical laymen, we certainly do not exclude the possibility that, especially in relatively short episodes of cardiac arrest, the absence of brain damage may be explained by entirely "normal" biological mechanisms.

Additional examples of this phenomenon include the Dean Braxton case (http://www.cbn.com/700club/features/amazing/SW141_Dean_Braxton.aspx). Dean Braxton was a patient whose body suddenly stopped functioning during an operation to remove a kidney stone at the St. Francis Hospital in Federal Way, Washington. He had an adverse reaction to antibiotics for a bacterial infection such that all his organs failed, and he eventually went into cardiac arrest, during which he experienced a distinctly Christian-flavored NDE. During intensive resuscitation efforts, his wife, Marilyn, prayed that he would be brought back to life. For an instant, it looked like the resuscitation was working, but then, 1¾ hours after the first arrest, Braxton had another—during which his NDE continued. It was only after this second episode that the medical team, led by Manuel Iregui, determined that the resuscitation had been a success. Braxton still had to undergo dialysis due to the original infection he had contracted, but Iregui considered Braxton's recovery "miraculous," particularly the fact that he was left with no permanent brain damage, considering everything the patient had been through. Dr. Iregui stated:

> It's a miracle that he's alive. There's no question about it. It is a miracle—that he's alive, that he is talking with no brain damage. But this is very exceptional, because he was really, really dead for a long time.

In this respect, this case is comparable to the Ruby Graupera-Cassimiro case in this chapter (Case 8.9). We did not include the Dean Braxton case among those involving a specific miraculous *healing*, because the paranormal aspect concerns the absence of damage and so is not healing in a strict sense.

CASE 8.1 The Claw Hand

In Chapter 1, Case 1.9, a patient of Welsh medical investigator Penny Sartori's, known in her prospective study as Patient 10, reported paranormal perceptions during his NDE that were later verified. However, his case also involved a congenital anomaly that was inexplicably healed following the patient's clinical death.

Since birth, the British patient had suffered from cerebral palsy with a right spastic hemiparesis, whereby his right hand was always contracted. The patient explained that his hand had been clawlike all his life; this assertion was supported by a witness statement from his sister.

After his NDE, the patient was suddenly able to open his hand—even though he did not report that the contents of the NDE explicitly involved or referenced healing.

Although no formal assessment or documentation of the extent of the contracture had been made by the medical staff at admission or at any time prior to the NDE, the patient's medical records documented that several years earlier, the hospital appliances department had made a splint for the patient's hand. The patient stated that the splint had not helped and that his hand had remained contracted. The medical and physiotherapy notes were checked to see whether any extensive physiotherapy had been performed on his hand; this was not the case. The notes prior to discharge did mention increased muscle tone in his contracted hand. This fact was discussed with the physiotherapist, who explained that the hand should not have been capable of opening without an operation to release the tendons that had been in a contracted position for more than 60 years.

Penny Sartori wrote:

> It remains unexplained how it is possible for the patient to be able now to open and use his previously contracted hand.
>
> There is no reason to disbelieve the patient's or his sister's statement regarding the extent of his contracture prior to his NDE. Indeed, the fact that his contracture had resolved was mentioned only when the patient misinterpreted one of the questions asked during the in-depth interview. Had he not misinterpreted the question, the fact that he is now able to open his hand may have gone unnoticed.

On a related note, the patient had also had a walking impediment since birth. After his NDE, his walking suddenly and markedly improved.

In a 2013 article in the *Journal of Near-Death Studies*, Michael J. Rush criticized this case. Concerning the claw hand, he asserted that it might be a case of spontaneous healing and that there is too little information to know what the state of the hand was before the NDE.

In the same journal issue, Sartori responded to this latter point:

Penny Sartori, PhD, RGN

It is correct that the hand had not been formally assessed immediately prior to the NDE. However, the hand had been assessed throughout the patient's life, as the medical diagnosis was documented in the medical notes: a right spastic hemiparesis of his right hand. This is a congenital abnormality that the patient had had for the 60 years of his life leading up to the time of his NDE. He also had a splint in his belongings that had been made several years earlier but the patient felt was ineffective. Such a splint would not have been constructed if such a contracture were not present.

The healed hand remains inexplicable as there is no known mechanism for how a hand that had permanently shortened tendons due to a spastic hemiparesis from birth has since been able to open fully. This development is something that should not be physiologically possible and something the patient stated he has not been able to do before. This entire matter was also supported by a signed statement from his sister.

SOURCES

Rush, M. J. (2013). Critique of "A prospectively studied near-death experience with corroborated out-of-body perceptions and unexplained healing." *Journal of Near-Death Studies, 32*(1), 3–14.

Sartori, P. (2008). *The near-death experiences of hospitalized intensive care patients: A five year clinical study.* Lewiston, UK: Edwin Mellen Press.

Sartori, P. (2013). Response to "Critique of 'A prospectively studied near-death experience with corroborated out-of-body perceptions and unexplained healing.'" *Journal of Near-Death Studies, 32*(1), 15–36.

Sartori, P., Badham, P., & Fenwick, P. (2006). A prospectively studied near-death experience with corroborated out-of-body perceptions and unexplained healing. *Journal of Near-Death Studies, 25*(2), 69–84.

CASE 8.2 The Broken Bone

In Sartori's book *The Near-Death Experiences of Hospitalized Intensive Care Patients* describing her prospective study, she reported the case of a man designated as

Patient 12 who had been involved in a traffic accident. He suffered serious injury to his chest, a torn liver, and a broken right shoulder.

Because the patient was hospitalized in critical condition, the orthopedic surgeon had to postpone surgery on the right shoulder until the patient was discharged from the intensive care unit. By that time, however, the surgeon was amazed to discover that the broken bone had already healed. This development was remarkable because the injury had involved a complex fracture.

The surgeon could not explain the healing, so he supposed that it was normal for patients with head injuries to heal quickly. Sartori pointed out, however, that this explanation was not relevant because the patient's injuries had not included head injury.

SOURCE

Sartori, P. (2008). *The near-death experiences of hospitalized intensive care patients: A five year clinical study.* Lewiston, UK: Edwin Mellen Press.

CASE 8.3 Ralph Duncan

In his book *Lessons from the Light*, social psychologist and NDE researcher Kenneth Ring reported a case of miraculous healing. The case derived from Professor Emeritus Howard Mickel of the religion department of Wichita State University in Kansas. Mickel investigated this case thoroughly and stood staunchly behind its authenticity.

In the 1970s, a leukemia patient named Ralph Duncan was dying. He had obviously been told that he only had a short time to live and had already prepared himself for his death. During his hospital admission, he had an NDE, during which he met a being of light. Duncan took this being for Jesus, even though the being did not look like traditional pictures of him. The being of light had eyes that were "shooting fire." Duncan and the being had telepathic contact with each other in the form of three brief sentences: "That's enough. It's dead. It's gone."

After he regained consciousness, these words were still echoing in his ears. He did not quite understand what was meant by "That's enough." But he associated "It's dead" with the disappearance of his leukemia.

The last time Ring had news of the man, in 1989, he was still doing well.

SOURCES

Ring, K., & Valarino, E. E. (1998). *Lessons from the Light: What we can learn from the near-death experience.* New York, NY: Insight Books.

Williams, K. (n.d.). *Scientific discoveries come from near-death experiences: Dr. Kenneth Ring*. Near-Death Experiences and the Afterlife. Retrieved from http://www.near-death.com/experiences/evidence07.html

CASE 8.4   Anita Moorjani

Anita Moorjani, of Indian heritage, was born in Singapore and grew up in Hong Kong. In April 2002, she was diagnosed with Hodgkin's lymphoma, a form

Anita Moorjani
Photo: Pamela Wallace Photography

of cancer of the lymph glands. After 4 years of being cared for at home, on February 2, 2006, she fell into a coma and was admitted to the intensive care ward of the local hospital. The attending oncologist told her husband, Danny, that her organs were shutting down and she would die soon—probably within 36 hours. He said, "Your wife's heart might still be beating, but she's not really in there. It's too late to save her." Moorjani's cancer had spread everywhere. Her hands, feet, and face were swollen, and she had open lesions on her skin. The medical team started a 3-week cycle of chemotherapy intravenously while giving her nourishment through a nasogastric tube and oxygen through another tube.

Moorjani later reported that during her coma, she had had a radical NDE. Although she was not aware of "leaving" her physical body, she was able to hear and see (extrasensorily) exactly what Danny and the doctors were discussing in the corridor almost 40 feet away from her room. In personal communication with NDE researcher Jan Holden (in person: Hong Kong, September, 2010; Arlington, VA, August, 2013), Danny confirmed this claim as well as Moorjani's extrasensory awareness that her brother was en route via airplane to be with her and her family. (Technically, because of these extrasensory perceptions, her case could be included in Chapter 2, but because the healing aspect of her case is such a predominant feature, we included her case in this chapter only.)

During her NDE, she was told that she could choose to stay in her physical life and be healed of her cancer. If she chose life, her organs would function normally again, but if she chose death, everything would happen as the doctors had foretold.

Under these circumstances, Moorjani chose life and then regained consciousness. The doctors told her that they had tremendous news for her: Her organs had recovered. They could not believe it. At this point, her oncologists insisted the chemotherapy—which she accepted despite her avowal that she did not need it—be continued. Her recovery was rapid. By mid-February, the outward signs of her cancer had disappeared, and she was eating normally. Moorjani had completed no more than her first cycle of only three chemotherapy drugs (instead of the originally planned seven drugs). Biopsies of lymph nodes in her neck and three ultrasound exams revealed no evidence of cancer. Nevertheless, oncologists insisted Moorjani undergo a second cycle of chemotherapy. Moorjani was finally allowed to go home after this cycle. She agreed to receive another six cycles of chemotherapy (a total of eight 3-week cycles were the planned treatment), but even the doctors were forced to cut the treatment short by two cycles because, despite numerous scans and tests, they could find no cancer. In spite of the fact that her recovery had progressed far more quickly than would normally be expected, some doctors tried to explain it by asserting that she had responded well to chemotherapy. However, each biopsy and scan since Moorjani had come out of coma had shown that she was no longer suffering from cancer. In addition, although doctors had predicted early on that she would need plastic surgery on her numerous, extensive skin lesions using skin grafts, the lesions simply healed by themselves in the first few weeks after she came out of her coma.

This case is particularly significant because U.S. oncologist Peter Ko became very curious about Moorjani and flew to Hong Kong to meet her. He copied all the relevant paperwork from her medical file and studied it closely. On the basis of available medical information, he concluded that Moorjani should simply have died. He sent his findings to cancer institutes all over the world, and they all responded that they had never encountered a case like Moorjani's before.

Dr. Ko appeared with Moorjani in the media and also assisted with a radio interview about the case. In addition, well-known NDE investigator and fellow oncologist Jeffrey Long had a long phone conversation with Ko about the case.

Another NDE investigator, Jerald Foster, met Ko personally to discuss the case. Moorjan's Internet home page includes a clip in which Ko (2006) tells his story.

In Moorjani's 2012 book, *Dying to Be Me*, there is also a fragment from the summary that Ko wrote after his study of all her medical files. Following is part of this report:

> When I came to HKG [Hong Kong] last month, my intention was to scrutinize her clinical history, and to either validate or invalidate her claims. . . .
>
> The evening of Feb 3, Anita awoke, sat up, and declared to her family she would be okay. She conversed with the oncologist, who was baffled by her ability to even recognize him.
>
> On Feb 4, Anita demanded to have her nasogastric tube removed, and promised her doctors she would eat what they brought her in order to gain some weight. . . .
>
> By that time [Feb 5], much of her neck and facial swelling had resolved; the massively enlarged lymph nodes began to soften, and she was able to turn her head for the first time. . . .
>
> Three ultrasound exams failed to reveal any obviously pathologic lymph nodes. On Feb 27, [the plastic surgeon] eventually biopsied one from her neck . . . and there was no evidence of cancer. The skin ulcers healed on their own without skin grafting.
>
> . . . [Eventually] she was given a clean bill of health, and they stopped 2 cycles short [of the planned complete chemotherapy regimen].
>
> Her recovery was certainly "remarkable." Based on my own experience and opinions of several colleagues, I am unable to attribute her dramatic recovery to her chemotherapy. Based on what we have learned about cancer cell behaviors, I speculate that something (non-physical . . . "information"?) either switched off the mutated genes from expressing, or signaled them to a programmed cell death. The exact mechanism is unknown to us, but not likely to be the result of cytotoxic drugs.

For the entire report and more details of other paranormal aspects of Moorjani's experience, see her book *Dying to Be Me*.

SOURCES

Ko, P. (2006). *Report: Dr. Peter Ko.* Retrieved from http://www.anitamoorjani.com/report-dr-peter-ko/

Moorjani, A. (2012). *Dying to be me: My journey from cancer to near death, to true heal-ing.* Carlsbad, CA: Hay House.

Moorjani, A. (n.d.). *Anita Moorjani: Remember your magnificence.* Retrieved from http://anitamoorjani.com/

Sartori, P. (2012, February 25). *Update on Anita Moorjani's case.* Retrieved from http://drpennysartori.wordpress.com/2012/02/25/update-on-anita-moorjanis-case/

CASE 8.5 Jennifer

This case appeared in a documentary on the Biography Channel. The segment has been posted online on YouTube without specific production information (Jennifer NDE, 2012).

Jennifer was the fourth of five girls who grew up in Vermont. She was the only one in the family who had a neurological disorder; it involved tics and epileptic seizures that would occur a dozen times a day. This condition was very problematic for her because it greatly limited her control over her body.

In June 1971, when Jennifer was 13 years old, she was home alone with her older sister Patti and Patti's boyfriend; the girls' parents had gone away for a few days, leaving Patti in charge. In documentary coverage, both Jennifer and her sister offered their stories of what transpired during a sudden thunderstorm, and these witness accounts confirm each other.

A big wind came up, rain started pelting down, and lightning flashed more and more frequently. The claps of thunder were coming closer. The girls' father had a ham radio tower that served as a kind of satellite receiver, located at the back of the house. From his location away from home, he became aware of the advancing storm and was concerned that the tower might act as a lightning rod that could cause a house fire. He telephoned the girls to ask them to lower the tower.

The girls ran outside, and Jennifer tried to lower the tower using its metal hand crank. As she did, lightning struck the tower. Jennifer felt a sharp pain and could not let go of the crank. Her whole body shook, and blood was coming out of her nose and ears. She felt her body become totally electrified, and it seemed as if all her insides were being destroyed by burning. She smelled the smell of frying meat. Patti asked her boyfriend to pull Jennifer off the crank, but when he tried, he himself received a huge electric shock.

During this time, Jennifer had an NDE in which she was surrounded by something like a cocoon of golden light. The light formed into the shape of a human without a face. The being came closer and closer in toward Jennifer until she was suddenly back in her body. She felt the electrical activity again and was thrown back onto the ground, screaming, with Patti's boyfriend holding her tightly from behind.

The three managed to get back inside the house. Because it was still storming badly and, as Patti observed, her boyfriend and Jennifer seemed to have fully recovered, the three decided not to go to the hospital right away. In Jennifer's words, "I knew that something had changed in my body, but I felt that everything was going to be OK because of the experience I had with the golden light and the being who came to me." The following week, Jennifer went to have a complete physical and some EEGs. To the doctors' amazement, something about the biochemistry of her brain had changed. Starting from the time of the incident, her seizures and tics had decreased. Two years later, she no longer needed any medications. Since then, she has had no neurological symptoms at all.

The miraculous aspect of this case is that healing effects are hardly to be expected from being struck by lightning. In fact, it is far more plausible to assume just the opposite. So it truly appears that this cure was not brought about because Jennifer was completely electrified but, as she claimed, because of her NDE: "The golden light had somehow cured me."

SOURCE

Jennifer NDE 2012. (2012, March 3). *The Biography Channel.* Retrieved from http:// www.youtube.com/watch?v=R8v6fw543OY

CASE 8.6 Will Barton

Sixteen-year-old Will Barton was out hunting for the perfect Christmas tree behind his mother's farm in the mountains of Idaho. His eye fell on a tall tree on a steep mountainside. He climbed it and tried to saw the top off of it, but the limb underneath him broke and, from a height of more than 40 feet, he crashed to the ground. As a result, he was instantly and totally paralyzed and could no longer feel anything. The family got Barton to the local hospital. In the documentary in which this case appears, *Unexplained Mysteries: Dead and Back Again* (Cook, Winkler, & Daniels, 2004), James F. Todd, the emergency room doctor involved, said that an X-ray made at the time showed that neck vertebrae were broken and dislocated. The only thing Barton was still able to do by himself was breathe. His condition worsened as he slipped in and out of consciousness, a development that did not improve his prospects.

Upon regaining consciousness, it became clear that Barton had become a prisoner of his own body. For this reason, he became suicidal, but he could not attempt suicide because he could not move. He had become so depressed that he asked his mother to help him escape life by smothering him with a pillow. She refused. Even though his family tried to cheer him up, they were not successful. Barton did not want to do any exercises to improve his condition, either.

Days later, physiotherapists raised the head of Barton's bed so he could sit up, but they did so too quickly. All the blood rapidly drained from his head, causing him to lose consciousness and suffer cardiac arrest.

He had an NDE that started out as a relatively gloomy and lonely experience but then transformed under the influence of a light that dispelled the darkness. His entire being was immersed in this light. The light told him that he was allowed to choose: Die, or go back to his body. Barton opted for life.

After his resuscitation, he was still paralyzed. His prospects were not any better medically, but he had changed mentally and emotionally. Quite unexpectedly, the NDE had had a very positive impact on him. Now he was suddenly willing to cooperate with a long-term, painful rehabilitation. One year later, against all expectation, he was able to walk again. Barton attributed his recovery not only to the support his family gave him and to their prayers but also to his NDE.

Dr. Todd claimed that, according to conventional medicine, Barton should have been a quadriplegic for the rest of his life. Todd therefore called the recovery a "miracle."

SOURCES

Cook, J. D., Winkler, H., & Daniels, A. (Executive producers). (2004, May 29). *Dead and back again*. Unexplained Mysteries, Season 1, Episode 26. Retrieved from https://www.youtube.com/watch?v=JBaBwMVg6dk

Viacom Productions. (Producer). (1999). *The most beautiful garden: The case of William (Will) Barton and his miraculous recovery after an NDE*. Beyond Chance with Melissa Etheridge. Retrieved from https://www.youtube.com/watch?v=hUqsRzBE2CM

CASE 8.7 Jake Finkbonner

Then 5-year-old Roman Catholic Jake Finkbonner, a member of the Lummi tribe in the state of Washington, cut his lip during a basketball game and contracted an infection involving a flesh-eating bacteria: necrotizing fasciitis. Within a day, his face was so swollen that he was unrecognizable. His condition quickly deteriorated to such an extent that he was expected to die soon. For 2 weeks, the doctors tried everything to stop the bacteria. During most of this time, Jake was kept in an artificial coma.

During his illness, Jake had an NDE. He had the feeling that his body was so light that he could "lift off," and then he had a vision in which he looked down on the hospital and saw his family. Then he went to his house, where he observed other family members. Finally, he ended up in "heaven," where he talked with God, who looked very big and sat in a tall chair, and he saw deceased family members and angels. Heaven was so much to his liking that he asked God if he could stay, but God said that his family and "all the others" needed him. Jake was then sent back.

His parents and doctors assumed that Jake could not survive his illness because the bacteria kept attacking more and more of his body, and treatments had not helped. Against all expectation and with no definable medical explanation, the infection suddenly stopped, and Jake healed from his gruesome illness.

Because Jake's face had been severely deformed by the illness, he underwent dozens of operations to resolve the deformity as much as possible. His recovery from these surgeries was also often remarkable.

Jake and his parents, Donny and Elsa Finkbonner, associate the miraculous healing from the bacterial infection with their worship of a 17th-century Native American woman, Kateri Tekakwitha, known as "Lily of the Mohawks." Family members and other believers had asked for her intercession, and one visitor, a nun coincidentally named Sister Kateri, had brought a Tekakwitha amulet, which was placed on Jake's hospital bed.

On the initiative of Jesuit priest Paolo Molinari, the Vatican initiated a rigorous official investigation of the healing. Molinari was able to review the boy's medical file, including the hospital records and photos that his doctors had made to document his condition. In addition, members of the archdiocese in Seattle questioned the doctors who had treated Jake. All the information was presented to the *Congregatio de Causis Sanctorum* (Congregation for the Causes of Saints), which concluded that, according to the current state of mainstream science, the healing was medically inexplicable. This finding contributed to the canonization of Kateri Tekakwitha, the first Native North American Catholic saint.

SOURCES

ABC News. (2011, August 3). *Jake Finkbonner among the angels.* ABC Primetime Nightline: *Beyond Belief.* Retrieved from http://abcnews.go.com/Nightline/video/jake-finkbonner-angels-flesh-eating-bacteria-eats-face-almost-kills-boy-talks-to-god-nightline-14227643

Hagerty, B. B. (2011, April 22). *A boy, an injury, a recovery, a miracle?* Northeast Public Radio/NPR. Retrieved from http://www.npr.org/2011/04/22/135121360/a-boy-an-injury-a-recovery-a-miracle

Mauser, E. W. (2012, October 20). Boy's recovery a Kateri miracle. *Canadian Catholic News.* Retrieved from http://www.catholicregister.org/features/item/15267-boy-s-recovery-a-kateri-miracle

CASE 8.8 Mellen-Thomas Benedict

P. M. H. Atwater investigated the case of Mellen-Thomas Benedict, a patient who in 1982 had terminal cancer in the form of an inoperable brain tumor. He

Mellen-Thomas Benedict

was expected to live no more than 6 to 8 months. Finally, Benedict had a cardiac arrest, after which he was clinically dead for 1½ hours. In this condition, he had an extensive NDE. He left his body and received images of the earth's past and humanity's future. In addition, he received insights with respect to the workings of biological systems. After his NDE, he apparently applied these insights to important, promising research and technology projects. For example, in one study at the University of North Texas, he underwent hypnosis to reexperience the omniscient—all-knowing—aspect of his NDE and generated accurate genetic information about a rare hereditary disease (Jan Holden, personal communication, April 20, 2016).

After Benedict regained consciousness following his NDE, his condition appeared to have changed. After 3 days, he began to feel more normal and lucid. Three months later, the tumor had disappeared of its own accord. The doctor treating him said that it was probably a "spontaneous remission," a healing that arises spontaneously without medical treatment coming into play.

P. M. H. Atwater stated:

I can attest that his case is genuine and his claims about the brain tumor and the conditions of his death are true. I have met his mother and step-father, been in his and their homes, and have followed his life since—his struggles and his accomplishments—as he sought to find a way to integrate his experience into his daily life while still honoring the mission he felt guided to fulfill.

On July 28, 2015, Atwater sent Rivas the following details:

As concerns Mellen-Thomas Benedict, I was with him several times after I discovered he was a near-death experiencer. The first was during the time when he was filming a conference I was attending in Kentucky. We met privately and I took notes. My husband and I later drove to Fayetteville, North Carolina, where he was living at the time, so I could spend more time with him. I spoke to his mother while there, and at length with his girl friend. His mother confirmed his brain tumor and that he was dying, that his hospice nurse felt he had died and his mother believed that to be true as well. Mellen-Thomas had been x-rayed about a week or so before he died, and then again shortly afterward. The doctors were stunned. The tumor had gone. Mellen-Thomas showed me his x-rays, before and after versions. In the before, you could see a brain tumor. In the after, the brain tumor was gone. When I was there, he was still having a challenge believing the tumor was really, truly gone, that it wouldn't come back, that he was safe. The x-rays, though, were plain enough for anyone to see, proof of a miracle. I asked him if I could keep the x-rays for him, to be certain nothing would ever happen to them. No, no, he said. They would be just fine. He wanted to keep them himself. After that time in Fayetteville, Mellen-Thomas moved multiple times, even across country to California.

Years later I asked him about the x-rays. He searched for them but could not find them. They were lost, perhaps during his various moves. He contacted the hospital where they were taken to get copies—but was told the hospital only keeps x-rays on hand for a relatively short period, then they are destroyed. His were destroyed. Neither one of us were able to contact the hospice nurse who once took care of him. I don't know about his doctor at the time. Mellen-Thomas said something about he was gone, too, moved away, or something like that. His mother could not be contacted for additional information as she died not too long after he moved away. Thus, in finding more evidence about the brain tumor of Mellen-Thomas Benedict, nothing exists today that might verify what I saw and learned while in Fayetteville. That makes my testimony all that's left in his case.

We see no reason to doubt Atwater's statement.

SOURCES

Atwater, P. M. H. (1994). *Beyond the light: The mysteries and revelations of near-death experiences.* New York, NY: Avon Books.

Benedict, M. T. (1996). Through the light and beyond. In L. W. Bailey & J. Yates (Eds.), *The near-death experience: A reader* (pp. 39–52). New York, NY: Routledge.

CASE 8.9 Ruby Graupera-Cassimiro

On September 23, 2014, doctors at the Boca Raton Regional Hospital in Boca Raton, Florida, were doing their very best to resuscitate a 40-year-old patient by applying electrical shocks and massage to her heart. The patient was Ruby Graupera-Cassimiro of Deerfield Beach, and the rescue efforts took some three hours, during which she did not have a pulse for 45 minutes. Ruby had just undergone a caesarian section to give birth to her baby daughter. Then she began exhibiting symptoms of a rare complication called amniotic fluid embolism, whereby amniotic fluid from the uterus ended up in her bloodstream, subsequently causing a dangerous clot in her heart. She had a cardiac arrest and lost consciousness.

When the resuscitation efforts appeared to be unproductive, the doctors asked her family to come in to say good-bye to Ruby. After some time, her family left the room so they could fervently pray for her. The doctors were at the point of pronouncing her dead, when suddenly they were again able to see a signal on her heart monitor. The attending nurse, Claire Hansen, made the connection to the prayers of Ruby's family members and encouraged them to continue.

A day later, the patient had recovered to such an extent that she could be disconnected from the equipment that had artificially kept her alive. Remarkably enough, she had suffered no brain damage or any injuries from the resuscitation, and soon she was once again the picture of health. This outcome was also true of her newborn daughter, Taily.

Many of the doctors and nurses involved considered this case to be one of the few true medical miracles that they had witnessed, and they attributed the patient's recovery to some kind of divine intervention.

A couple of hours after the resuscitation, Ruby spoke of having had a dream or vision in which she talked with a spiritual being whom she experienced as her deceased father. He let her know that her time had not yet come. She recalled a light behind her father and the presence of many other spiritual beings. She moved through this spiritual world not by walking but by "flowing." She said, "It was peaceful. There is nothing to be afraid of." At a certain point, she had the feeling that she was being held back by a kind of force; she could move up to a certain point but no further. "That's when I understood I was not going to stay there. (I'm) going to go back. It's not (my) time. I was chosen to be here."

SOURCES

Ally, R. (2014, November 11). "Miracle mom" talks about her near death experience. *CBS Miami.* Retrieved from http://miami.cbslocal.com/2014/11/11/miracle-mom-talks-about-her-near-death-experience/

Ellis, M. (2014, November 11). Miracle mom returns from the dead, saw glimpse of the afterlife. *Godreports.* Retrieved from http://blog.godreports.com/2014/11/moms-heart-stopped-for-45-minutes-after-childbirth-then-her-familys-prayers-were-answered

Phillip, A. (2014, November 10). Woman "spontaneously" revives after 45 minutes without a pulse. *The Washington Post.* Retrieved from http://www.washingtonpost.com/news/to-your-health/wp/2014/11/10/woman-spontaneously-revives-after-45-minutes-without-a-pulse/

CASE 8.10 Annabel Beam

Annabel Beam is a girl from Texas who, before her NDE, suffered from two serious, incurable gastrointestinal conditions: antral hypomotility disorder and pseudo-obstruction motility disorder. These disorders are forms of gastroparesis, which means that the muscles in her intestines were not functioning properly, causing her to suffer from severe, chronic pain and extreme bloating after eating. Her illness was so unbearable that she once told her mother that she would rather die and go to heaven.

In December 2011, when Annabel was 9 years old, she was playing outdoors with her sisters. She slipped off a branch and fell head first from a 30-foot tree. She landed in the hollow trunk of a cottonwood tree. She hit her head three times against the inside of the tree. Firemen rescued her from her plight and brought her to Cook Children's Hospital in Fort Worth. When she arrived, she turned out not to have incurred any serious injuries. Her mother, Christy Wilson Beam, said, "The ER doc told us the one thing we were not expecting to hear. He said, 'Other than a possible concussion and some superficial bumps and bruises, she doesn't appear to have been injured at all.'"

In the days that followed, Annabel started talking of an NDE. She recounted that she had visited heaven and had sat on Jesus's lap, and she described what Jesus had looked like. When she saw her dead grandmother, Mee Mee, she realized that she was in heaven. Annabel described the following episode:

> I started to wake up in the tree and I could hear the firemen's voices. And I saw an angel that looked very small, like a fairy. And the God winked at me through the body of the angel and what He was saying to me was, "I'm going to leave you now and everything is going to be okay." And then the angel stayed with me the entire time, shining a light so I could see. We didn't talk. We just sat together peacefully.

After the accident, Annabel was suddenly cured of her digestive disorders. She did not have any physical complaints afterward, and she also no longer used any medications. This outcome was confirmed to the *Star Telegram* by her doctor, Samuel Nurko, MD, affiliated with Boston's Children's Hospital and specializing in pediatric gastroenterology. Even though the doctors had no explanation for Annabel's cure, Dr. Nurko did not want to call it a miracle. He did say that Annabel "is completely asymptomatic, is leading a normal life, and is not requiring any therapies."

SOURCES

Beam, C. W. (2015). *Miracles from heaven: A little girl, her journey to heaven, and her amazing story of healing*. New York, NY: Hachette Books.

Garnar, C. (2015, April 14). Girl knocked out by 30-ft fall inside a hollow tree claims she went to heaven and met Jesus (who looks like Santa Claus) . . . then woke

up cured of a lifelong illness. *Daily Mail: Mail Online.* Retrieved from http://www
.dailymail.co.uk/femail/article-3038153/Girl-knocked-30ft-fall-inside-hollow
-tree-claims-went-heaven-met-Jesus-woke-cured-lifelong-illness.html

Martindale, D. (2015, April 10). "Miracle" in Burleson: Book tells girl's remarkable
story of healing. *Star Telegram.* Retrieved from http://www.star-telegram.com/
living/religion/article18229301.html

Sola, K. (2015, April 16). Girl fell from tree, visited Jesus in heaven and awoke
cured, mom claims in new book. *The Huffington Post.* Retrieved from http://www
.huffingtonpost.com/2015/04/16annabel-beam-tree-heaven_n_7072406.html

Remarks

All the cases in this chapter involve "medical miracles" for which there are no
standard medical explanations. Of course, the present authors are not medical professionals. Nevertheless, all the cases presented are supported by statements from doctors or investigators who had direct or indirect access to the
relevant medical files.

Evidently, one or more aspects of NDEs can awaken great psychokinetic
healing abilities that, from a materialistic perspective, cannot possibly exist.
This phenomenon may fit with other miraculous forms of recovery at the end of
life, such as terminal lucidity in patients with an advanced form of Alzheimer's
disease (Nahm & Greyson, 2009). Shortly before death, these patients suddenly regained their mental capacities, a recovery that, from a materialistic
perspective, should have been impossible because these patients' brains were
irreversibly damaged.

In this and previous chapters, we presented cases of paranormal phenomena that occurred during NDEs. We turn now to paranormal phenomena that
first occurred in the aftermath of an NDE.

REFERENCES

Nahm, M. (2012). *Wenn die Dunkelheit ein Ende findet* [When the darkness comes to
an end]. Amerang, Germany: Crotona Verlag.

Nahm, M., & Greyson, B. (2009). Terminal lucidity in patients with chronic
schizophrenia and dementia: A survey of the literature. *Journal of Nervous and
Mental Disease, 3*(12), 942–944.

CHAPTER 9

Paranormal Abilities After NDEs

Among near-death experiencers, psychic and psi-related experiences were
reported more frequently to have occurred after the NDE than before the NDE.
—Bruce Greyson, MD, "Increase in Psychic
Phenomena Following Near-Death Experiences"

As of 2006, scores of studies involving thousands of near-death experiencers yielded a consistent finding (Noyes, Fenwick, Holden, & Christian, 2009): After their near-death experience (NDE), experiencers (NDErs) received correct extrasensory—clairvoyant and telepathic—impressions more often than was the case prior to their NDE. Also, some are able to generate psychokinetic phenomena, varying from involuntary poltergeist-like effects to conscious control of physical processes. In this regard, an NDE might well awaken a slumbering ability that in principle is universally human but normally functions actively in only a few people.

As far as we know, hardly any researchers have focused on post-NDE impressions confirmed by third parties. In our study of the literature pertaining to this area of inquiry, we were able to find only the following four confirmed cases.

CASE 9.1 Denise

In the "Children and Near Death Experience" section of the Celestial Travelers portion of the Kuriakon00 website, a father from Utah described the consequences of his daughter Denise's NDE.

In the summer of 1999, when Denise was 10 years old, she fell into a diabetic coma that landed her in the hospital. Tests showed that she had also had a stroke that had destroyed two-thirds of the left side of her brain. All her organs were shutting down, and the doctors assumed that she would not survive. If she did, she would go through the remainder of her life in a vegetative state.

Three days after that prognosis, Denise surprisingly regained consciousness, and another 3 days after that she was even able to walk on her own. The doctors were amazed at her recovery. After being in the hospital for 25 days, she was able to go back home. Her parents had to administer daily insulin injections.

Back at home, her father tried to give her an insulin injection one day, but Denise adamantly refused. This argument went on for at least 45 minutes until her father let her know that he could not take her fighting him anymore. Then Denise yelled that he was angry and looked red, but rather than pointing directly at him, she pointed at something above his head. Her father explained to her that she might be seeing an energy field around his body. Denise told her father that she was able to see these kinds of things since she had awoken outside her body.

Her father wrote:

> Over the next month Denise displayed many gifts or abilities and told us many things. She not only could see the aura of a person; she knew what the color meant. . . . She is able to see "spirits" as we call them or people that have passed on (died). . . . She can tell what kind of person you are; she sees into your heart.

In the end, it turned out that Denise had had an NDE during her coma, which revolved around Christian religious imagery.

SOURCE
Doug. (n.d.). *Denise.* Celestial Travelers: Near Death Experiences. Retrieved from http://kuriakon00.com/celestial/child/denise.html

CASE 9.2 Enrique Vila López's Patient

In his book *Yo vi la luz* (I Saw the Light), the Spanish physician Enrique Vila López (2009) described how he himself had to deal with a psychic ability that a patient, Mrs. P. B. B., retained from her NDE. He wrote (authors' translation):

Enrique Vila López, MD

Whenever she sees somebody, she knows which part of his or her body is ill. . . . She personally foretold countless incidents to me and my wife, which later came about exactly as she had indicated. She knew, for example, that my wife was very nervous because of our dog and the kinds of problems that the extended visit of a particular person at our home would entail.

SOURCE

Vila López, E. (2009). *Yo vi la luz. Experiencias cercanas a la muerte en España* [I saw the light: Near-death experiences in Spain]. Madrid, Spain: Ediciones Absalon/Mentes Despiertas.

CASE 9.3 Cherylee Black

Canadian Cherylee Black, an artist and former Canadian Armed Forces music instructor, is an exceptional NDEr in a number of ways. Not only did she undergo no fewer than three NDEs, but she also developed extrasensory and psychokinetic abilities in their wake. The three NDEs in order of occurrence were when she fell down the stairs as a preschooler, when she had a ruptured appendix at age 10, and when she was in a car accident at age 29.

Her first NDE included seeing a lady whom she reported later recognizing in a photograph. The lady turned out to be her maternal grandmother who had died before Black's birth. At the time little Cherylee had her NDE, there were no photographs of this grandmother anywhere around because Cherylee's grandfather was so broken up over his wife's death that he could not bear to see pictures of her. Unfortunately, this experience can no longer be confirmed by immediate family, which is why it does not appear among related cases in Chapter 5 concerning ADCs with strangers.

Following that first NDE, Black received precognitive impressions of the future—likewise unconfirmed by third parties, unfortunately. She knew, for example, what presents Santa was going to bring her. She also experienced appearances of the same grandmother who had appeared in her first NDE; these appearances continued until her maternal grandfather died.

During her second NDE, she got to see what would happen should she remain in the other world or, instead, return to her earthly body. Psychologically speaking, this NDE was a lot weightier than her first, and afterward she was troubled by involuntary OBEs and nightmares.

Starting when she was 11 years old, recurrent spontaneous psychokinesis (RSPK), also known as poltergeist phenomena, was added to her NDE aftereffects. In RSPK, objects in a person's environment move seemingly on their own and seemingly in relationship to the person's emotional state. An example in Black's case derives from when she was doing poorly at school. A teacher apparently slapped her for inattention, and a book was lifted by an unseen force and thrown across the room, hitting the teacher.

Black became a pretty wild teenager. At that time, she started seeing colors around people, reminiscent of auras. She was also able to move objects with her mind.

During Black's third NDE, precipitated by a serious car accident that resulted in moderate to severe brain injury, she found herself with her dog, Cassie, in a gorgeous world. Following this NDE, Black experienced RSPK-like phenomena that were mechanical, electronic, and visual in nature. She also began hearing "taps" of 3 to 4 Hz and 40 to 50 decibels. "Luminous discharges" emitted from her left hand. She experienced the spatial movement of objects and disruptions in the operation of electronic equipment and appliances in her proximity—the latter being a well-established NDE aftereffect (Blalock, Holden, & Atwater, 2015; Greyson, Liester, Kinsey, Alsum, & Fox, 2015). She was also seeing auras around people.

In response to these phenomena, which she attributed to her NDE, Black decided to participate in scientific experiments. "None of the labs have been disappointed," she herself has noted—a claim that, indeed, we found not to be an exaggeration.

PSYCHOKINETIC ABILITIES

On August 3, 2015, NDE researcher Robert Mays wrote Titus Rivas the following regarding psychokinetic experiments in which Robert and his wife, fellow researcher Suzanne Mays, were personally involved:

> Suzanne and I worked with Cherylee primarily to understand physical interactions between the energetic field of a person and physical processes. So

with Cherylee we tried to understand what was happening with her PK influence on a pinwheel. We have come to understand that there is a kind of conditioning of an object or a region of space that occurs when there is an energetic interaction that results in PK. ([parapsychology investigator] Graham Watkins in the 1970s found the same thing—called the "linger effect"—with PK subject Felicia Parise.)

Cherylee reports that there are colors that she sees around and inside the equipment she works with. In this experiment video (from 2012), I used an induction coil (perhaps 30,000v) that seemed to nullify the "conditioning," and Cherylee had to build it up again (See: http://selfconsciousmind.com/SubjectSB-020612-Pinwheel2.mov).

In another set of experiments (in 2012 and 2014), John Kruth, Graham Watkins, Suzanne, and I worked with Cherylee in the Rhine Center Bioenergy Lab [Durham, North Carolina] using their photomultiplier tube (PMT) on fluorescent substances in a completely dark room. In a 2014 trial, Cherylee worked with a fluorescent powder (that apparently retains a certain small glow even when being in the dark for many days). She energized the powder so that the measured light jumped from the baseline (10 photons/half-second) to 57 photons/half-second for about 25 seconds and 70 photons/half-second for about 45 seconds, with an overall average of 23 photons/half-second.

During this trial, Cherylee reported interesting subjective perceptions and feelings that corresponded to the observed results (e.g., when it dropped down to about 4—below the baseline—Cherylee later reported that she "was out of it" until John remarked through the wall that "it's really dark now" and that "pulled her back.") These sessions are extremely exhausting, and emotionally draining as well, for Cherylee.

As far as future plans, we are developing a simple experiment using photographic paper in sealed, light-tight envelopes that will measure the energetic field with double-blind controls. The subject will try to send energy to the photographic paper, and then we will develop the paper and see what we get. . . .

All four of us—John Kruth, Graham Watkins, Suzanne, and I—as well as a number of other people who were present were all witnesses. On another occasion, Jim Carpenter was also a witness to Cherylee's PK in an informal environment.

In January 2016, parapsychology investigator John Kruth e-mailed us the following summary of the 2014 experiments to which Mays referred:

An Egely Wheel is a commercially produced instrument that consists of a small plastic wheel balanced on a pin. The wheel is contained in a plastic case that has a small light inside. When the wheel turns, it interrupts the light and a beeping sound is produced. This beeping sound indicates movement, and as the beeps increase in frequency, they indicate that the wheel is moving more quickly.

In four days of testing in multiple environments at the Rhine, Cherylee demonstrated a consistent ability to affect an Egely Wheel in a controlled environment with protections from air currents, heat, and static charges. She consistently caused the wheel to spin when she was within 20 cm of the wheel, but she was not able to cause movement in a wheel when it was further away, including testing of one to two meters away from her. Multiple tests were completed to determine if the wheel would turn as a result of air currents, heat, and static, but none of these factors affected the wheel in the control sessions.

She reported that moving the wheel was easier when she was electrically grounded or when the wheel was placed on a grounding plane. In addition, there seemed to be a rebound effect that lingered on the instrument after she had stopped focusing on the instrument. The wheel would continue to move in the same direction it was moving during a session even when the wheel was manually stopped. If the wheel was manually spun in the opposite direction, it would slowly come to a stop, reverse direction, and slowly spin in the direction consistent with its movement during the session. This effect seemed to last at least a few minutes after the session. Control sessions where the wheel was turned manually or using air currents did not elicit the rebound effect that was observed when Cherylee was focusing on the instrument.

Finally, after her sessions with the wheels, other people who had no success affecting the wheels in the past were able to cause the wheel to spin in a similar manner to Cherylee. This effect lasted for months after the sessions were completed, and many people—even people who were not familiar with the instrument or previous testing that was done—were able to cause the wheel to spin by putting their hand next to the instrument. In many cases, they did not even have to focus on the wheel, and the wheel would spin.

Other confirmations of Black's ability to turn a pinwheel came from L. Suzanne Gordon, associated with the Department of Communication at the

University of Maryland, as well as from well-known parapsychologist Dean Radin. In August 2015, Gordon e-mailed Rivas the following:

I know Cherylee from the [American Center for the Integration of Spiritually Transformative Experiences] ACISTE-sponsored online social networking site for experiencers of NDEs and NDE-like experiences. Then, a couple of years ago, I met her in person when she visited Maryland to participate in some telekinesis research being conducted by Dr. Norm Hansen. . . . What I observed directly, after the study, was how Cherylee could use her telekinetic ability to make a spinner inside a closed jar spin wildly at will. . . .

If you have seen these little spinner devices, I am not sure you would have asked that question [why it should be considered paranormal].

At about the same time, Radin e-mailed Rivas:

Over Skype I've watched Cherylee move an Egely wheel that was completely enclosed by a plastic CD disk case. When the Egely wheel is protected from air currents, as it appeared to be over the Skype video, it is exceptionally difficult to get it to move by ordinary means. So I'd say that based on what I saw that I find her apparent ability worthy of serious attention.

On September 9, 2015, Titus Rivas received an e-mail from Stephen Braude, another well-known U.S. researcher of paranormal phenomena, containing the following explanation:

I can only attest to what I saw on some of Cherylee's videos. These showed her sitting next to a glass-covered pinwheel, moving her hands around the container, trying to move, stop and reverse the direction of the pinwheel. I saw the pinwheel move both clockwise and counterclockwise, and I detected nothing suspicious. Indeed, I have no doubt that Cherylee was sincerely simply trying to explore the range and limits of what she could do psychokinetically.

On September 3, 2015, J. Norman Hansen, University of Maryland emeritus professor of biochemistry, sent Rivas a long e-mail with attachments regarding his experiences and thoughts about Black's psychokinetic skills in experiments involving a so-called torsion pendulum balance. He wrote the following:

My goal in working with Cherylee was to see if her purported psychokinetic abilities would be manifested by significant differences between her and the many ordinary subjects previously tested. Since I had performed hundreds of experiments with ordinary subjects, and was very familiar with the kinds of effects they exert; I was confident that if Cherylee exerted effects that were significantly different in any way, that I would notice it. . . .

There were some aspects that appeared to be unusual/different from what I had seen with ordinary subjects. As the experiments unfolded, I was consistently on the lookout to see if they occurred again. Unfortunately, they really didn't, so they cannot be considered to be reproducible effects.

As I said above, the variety of effects reported in the attachments occur consistently among ordinary subjects. The effects that Cherylee exerted were similar to those of ordinary subjects. However, for each effect, I would say that Cherylee's were stronger, more intense, and more consistently exerted than by ordinary subjects. Since some ordinary subjects also exert more intense effects than other subjects, it would be hard to argue that Cherylee's effects were evidence of her unique psychokinetic abilities. Perhaps psychokinetic abilities are common among the ordinary population.

My summary of the outcomes of my experiments with Cherylee is that her effects on the pendulum seem to be stronger than the typical ordinary subject, but some ordinary subjects rival the strength of her effects.

In any event, Hansen did acknowledge that Black scored well in his experiments, even if, as he claimed, his research participants had included "normal" test subjects—with no history of NDE—who had attained scores similar to Black's. Thus she appears to be exceptional—though not alone—in her PK ability.

Comparable PK experiments were conducted by neuroscience researcher Michael Persinger, the late psychologist and parapsychologist William Roll, and a few colleagues. Their interest differed significantly, however, from that of the previously mentioned investigators. Persinger believed that the unusual psychokinesis-poltergeist kinetics Black demonstrated (which he termed the "Ms. Black Effect," naming it after her) were not the result of one or more of her earlier NDEs but of the brain injury that she had incurred in the car accident. He consequently produced a neurologically oriented, materialistic, psychiatric explanation for many of Black's experiences.

Black herself wrote Rivas regarding this idea that the psychokinesis started only after her third NDE: "No. There was poltergeist activity after my second

NDE when I was a child. There were also various incidents of RSPK throughout my 20's, which was before the car accident."

Despite this controversy, even the investigators seeking to provide materialist explanations acknowledge that during the experiments several members of the team observed an anomalous effect in the form of the movement of a pinwheel.

EXTRASENSORY ABILITIES

Black was able to recommend to us several witnesses who could confirm her extrasensory abilities. We were interested in precognitive dreams as well as after-death communication (ADC) with unknown deceased persons who were later identified by third parties.

PRECOGNITIVE DREAMS

In August 2015, audio meditation specialist Karen Newell and dream investigator Doug D'Elia confirmed to us that they could testify to Black's reports on the contents of dreams that ended up accurately predicting future events. Black had this to say:

> As far as precognition goes, I have been doing an online precognitive dream group with some friends. My hit rate is about 40% (chance would be 25%). It hasn't been going long enough to have really significant statistics yet, but there have been some interesting hits. We use a double blind system of a target pool with four images. The target is chosen from the pool via RNG [random number generator] after everyone has recorded their dreams and ranked the four images based on dream content (it's basically the ganzfeld protocol using dreams). A few weeks ago the target image was of the mechanical shark from Jaws. I dreamt of Bruce Greyson holding a picture that looked something like a turtle in the water. Because I knew the mechanical shark from the movie was named "Bruce," it made perfect sense to connect my dream to that image from the target pool. If that would be an adequate example for you, I could ask the two individuals who have been running the dream group with me to confirm that example for you.

Doug D'Elia wrote Rivas:

> Yes, I can confirm that Cherylee has participated in the Dream Experiment group for the past six months (she founded it last February), and has one

of the highest hit rates among the members. During this time she has hit 9 targets in 20 trials (P(hit) = .25), for a combined probability of .0409 (odds = 23.4 to 1).

I should add that I don't know Cherylee personally. I only know her from messages and videos she's posted online over the years, and from private correspondence. I can state confidently, however, that nothing she's ever written or said has given me the slightest reason to doubt her truthfulness or sincerity. I believe wholeheartedly that she has the psychic gifts she claims.

He went on to explain to us the protocol of the dream experiments:

1. The experimenter (that has been me from the sixth week onwards) chooses a set of four images. Great care is taken to choose images that are as different from one another as possible, in terms of their prominent shapes, colors, settings, emotional content, and so on. It isn't always possible to find four images that differ in all these respects, but I do my best.
2. On Saturday, the dreamers record their dreams from Friday night (and optionally, from Thursday night as well).
3. At midnight (Eastern Time in North America) on Sunday morning, I post the four images for viewing by the dreamers.
4. On Sunday, the dreamers choose which of the four images best matches elements of their dreams. In addition, they list their reasons for choosing that image. They also confer with one another, noting similarities in their dreams and sometimes pointing out overlooked dream elements that match one of the images.
5. At midnight on Monday morning, I post the randomly chosen target image for viewing, and after viewing the dreamers' records, congratulate those who correctly chose the target image.

D'Elia sent us Black's various results, including the experiment with the image that she associated with a turtle, Sophia (or Sofia) the Turtle. As far as we have been able to determine, this is a well-known sea turtle. Below are Black's data for this dream, as sent by D'Elia. This material obviously was a "hit."

Dream 2

Title: Lunch with Sophia the Turtle.

Themes: more drama than I wanted there to be.

Emotions: bewilderment.

Major structural elements: outside in a street café, round tables, dipping dots ice cream, white dress with red dots, blue and red fluorescent lights, busy Las Vegas strip, cold air blasting from the buildings, but still very hot outside. Circles and dots. Minions.

Unexpected elements: Sophia wasn't a turtle anymore.

I was having lunch with Sophia, but it was too hot to eat, so I had ice cream instead. We were at an outdoor table with a round umbrella. There was a sort of outdoor air conditioning, but I was still too hot. I wanted to enjoy our time together, but Sophia kept going on about some guy who I was tired of hearing about. I hoped she would stay away from that loser. It looked like Las Vegas. There were Minions. Sophia was wearing a white dress with red polka dots.

IMAGE LIST

1. Mesa Verde
2. A-bomb test
3. Skiing
4. Shark Girl [A fashion photo of Rihanna who appears to be reclining in the maw of a shark]

DISCUSSION

Image 4 is my first choice. There is a woman who is not a turtle but she is in the water. The blue water with the interference pattern is pretty striking from my dream. Rhianna [Rihanna] has been in Vegas, and she used to date a loser.

Image 3 is my second choice because it has the three main colors from my dream, white, red and blue. It's also fun, lighthearted.

Image 2 is my third choice, because I dreamed of scientific tests and Vegas (which is in a state where such tests were done.) And circles. This is very close to image 3 in how I want to rank these images.

Image 1 is my last choice.

ADC WITH AN UNKNOWN DECEASED PERSON: BOB VAN DE CASTLE

As previously stated, Black reported that as a child she had contact with a deceased grandmother she had never seen before. However, the most extensive example of contact between Black and an unknown deceased person that is confirmed by third parties concerns communication with the late Robert Van de Castle during the period of January through December 2014 in the form of dreams and ghostly apparitions. Van de Castle was a psychologist and for over 25 years a pioneering dream researcher who remained active in his field even after his retirement from the University of Virginia Health System in 1993. During his career, he participated in research on dream telepathy, demonstrating his own abilities in that regard. In late January 2014, he died without warning at age 86.

Black first had a lucid dream of someone who called himself Bob, who mentioned details that made it possible to identify him as Bob Van de Castle. Later, other dreams followed and Bob also allowed himself to be seen during the day. He would ask Black to convey his regards to particular people with whom he had been associated during his life.

Karen Newell, cofounder of Sacred Acoustics, confirmed to Rivas in August 2015 that Black shared these experiences with her:

> I'm happy to share my part of the story, I also find it fascinating, especially as it was unfolding back in January 2014. I have written up the events in the enclosed attachment. It includes the exact email exchanges that occurred over the several days of the original encounter. Cherylee continued to email me her encounters with Bob over many months, and even her most recent communication in the past week. . . .
>
> I do not believe Cherylee would have heard of Bob's passing in a normal way. To my knowledge, she did not know who he was prior to me telling her about him. She reported her first dream about him on our test site prior to Eben [Alexander] receiving the email that he had passed. To know he had passed prior to that, she would have had to be a family member or very close friend.
>
> Bob's [partner] confirmed the difficulty with sleeping (among other things) in the following article, the writing of which is discussed in the attached email correspondence (["Celebrating the Life and Afterlife of Bob Van de Castle"] http://dreamtalk.hypermart.net/pdc2014/presentations/pdc2014-pimm-black.pdf).
>
> In my correspondence with Cherylee, it was very clear that Bob has played (and I believe continues to play) a huge role in Cherylee's processing of all her "beyond normal" abilities. She has struggled with accepting such abilities her entire life. It seems Bob's counseling mode has continued beyond the grave.

Following is the e-mail attachment Newell provided:

Dr. Eben Alexander and I were invited to a meeting of the Department of Perceptual Studies [DOPS] at University of Virginia on January 28, 2014, to present information on the sound technology developed by Sacred Acoustics, designed to enhance altered states of awareness. I spent most of that meeting explaining the history of how I came to be involved with developing such technology, results we had witnessed and some of our future development goals.

One of the DOPS team, Ross Dunseath, offered to refer me to an individual with psychokinetic abilities, Cherylee Black, who had reported to him her abilities were enhanced when listening to a recording on our website. We briefly discussed possibilities of creating sounds specific to enhancing such abilities. Later that day, he sent me her email so we could have direct contact.

Directly following the meeting, Dr. Alexander had a brief conversation with Bob Van de Castle who was in attendance during the presentation. One of our stated development goals was to create tones specific to dream enhancement and we were actively in the process of having people listen to these tones. Bob offered to assist with this development since he is a long-time dream researcher and they agreed to be in touch.

The next morning, I sent an email to Cherylee, introducing myself and invited her to listen to more of our tones in order to identify the most effective for psychokinetic enhancement. She rapidly agreed and that same day she registered on our private testing website in order to access our test files and report the results. She began to listen to our back files and posted feedback immediately.

Rather than paraphrasing the next sequence of events, I have included all email correspondence related to the event.

January 31, 2014—Feedback from Cherylee
posted on Sacred Acoustics test site

In addition to what I posted earlier, I found that after listening to this recording late last night, I had a very clear, realer-than-real lucid dream. I had the most remarkable dream in which I was communicating with a man named Bob who had just passed away. He wasn't using words to talk, it was more like ideas, feelings and images. We had a lot in common, because I'm an NDEr and we've had some similar experiences. It was a remarkable dream. I didn't know Bob when he was alive, but I wish I had.

January 31, 2014—Email from Karen to Cherylee

Dear Cherylee . . .

I can see your feedback on our sound files will be very useful. I am especially intrigued with your mention of Bob. We know someone named Bob who died recently. Do you have more details? Let's compare.

January 31, 2014—Email from Cherylee to Karen

Hi Karen,

There was this guy named Bob in the dream who had just passed away. We didn't talk using words, but I understood him very clearly. We talked about what it was like to "die" (although I guess people don't really die). He had wanted to come back, but he explained to me why he didn't. It wasn't because he was blissed out on the light and couldn't imagine leaving it (which was why I wanted to stay dead when I had my last NDE). I thought that would have been enough of a reason, and he admitted that the light was pretty awesome, but he said that he considered both futures and this one was better for his family because he couldn't come back and be OK. There would have been more strokes and he wouldn't have been him anymore. He did feel badly that there wasn't a better option, but he said that things were really for the best even if it didn't always seem that way.

I talked to him about a bunch of things (although we didn't actually "talk"). I don't know why I had that dream, since I've never met Bob before. It was really comforting though. He encouraged me to keep working on the PK stuff. Nice man. I felt a lot better after that.

He told me that his partner was having difficulty sleeping. She (I'm guessing it was a she, I'm not sure about that) would know to find him that way, but he said she would sleep better when things had settled down a bit. He seemed quite confident that she knew he was OK and that he loved her. I guess this wasn't something anyone expected to happen. He sort of had a feeling something was going to happen, but not like this. He was doing what he loved and things were great . . . then he was gone. No Pain. He said he could probably get more work done now.

I'm very sorry for your loss, Karen. If that was your Bob, he is a very nice person.

best wishes,
Cherylee

February 1, 2014—Email from Karen to Cherylee

Hi Cherylee,

. . .

For your validation, here is some information regarding Bob. I am not close with Bob, but we are acquaintances. I first met Bob during the same week I first met Kevin, who is our audio engineer and co-founder with me of Sacred Acoustics. I assume Ross told you that I work closely with Eben Alexander. Eben knows Bob better, but like me, they are not real close. As it happens, we have seen Bob 3 times in the last year. Once was last January during our first workshop we taught together, the first time I presented Sacred Acoustics technology to the public. Next, we saw him in the summer at a Dream Conference, where I sat next to Bob while Eben presented. The third time was this past Tuesday, when we presented the Sacred Acoustics technology to the DOPS group, where Ross told me about you. Bob greeted Eben happily that day and offered to help with getting our sound technology out to the world. The next day (Wednesday) we learned quite surprisingly that he had died. I believe this was the same night you had your lucid dream so it was a very fresh encounter. He died of a stroke, clearly sudden since he looked fine on Tuesday.

Bob has a [partner], but I'm not sure if she has trouble sleeping. [Authors' note: As we already mentioned, Bob Van de Castle's partner's insomnia was later confirmed.] They are both very progressive in their spiritual concepts, so I am sure she knows he is OK. He is the author of Our Dreaming Mind (Robert van de Castle) so it is no surprise you encountered him in a lucid dream. And yes, he is a very, very sweet soul.

That wasn't part of our testing per se, but we are delighted that you encountered Bob. We are sad for his physical passing, but are quite sure he will continue to be involved from the other side. . . .

Kind regards,
Karen

June 11, 2014 [E-mail from Cherylee to Karen]

I saw Bob again.

I had been having a really bad dream on Saturday night after falling asleep in front of my computer. I'm probably the only person I know who has lucid nightmares. Sometimes it's something precognitive, but more often it's something that's happened to someone else that I can't change (because it's their reality, not mine). I usually try to wake myself up, hopefully without waking up screaming and scaring everyone within earshot. I was trying to wake myself up when Bob showed up, but wasn't having much luck.

Bob helped me with the nightmare and made it OK for me. He sort of talked me through and out of it. Then he asked me to wake up and give a message to Larry Burk. It wasn't a complicated message, I was just supposed to say "yes, Bob has been hanging around you for the past few days." I wasn't keen on doing that, but I did owe Bob for helping me on a number of occasions. I said I'd try.

I was worried I'd forget about the message when I woke up, but Bob said that he would give me a reminder. I woke up, and I could still see him. He wasn't able to talk to me after I woke up, but he was still very reassuring somehow. I knew it was more than a dream.

So I sent Larry the message on Facebook, wrote a note in my log, and then went to bed and kind of forgot about it all.

On Tuesday I heard from Larry. He had just returned from a conference on dreams.

July 10, 2014 [E-mail from Cherylee to Karen]

I recently got in touch with Bobbie Ann Pimm, Bob Van de Castle's [partner], about my experiences of seeing Bob. I was reluctant to contact her, but Larry Burk has been pushing me to do so for a while, and I finally did. She's a very nice lady. We [were] talking for over an hour on the phone. What was really great was that she explained all sorts of stuff that I had experienced in regards to Bob, and told me what it meant and why it was significant to the two of them.

She asked me to write an article about those experiences for a conference. [Authors' note: Pimm and Black did eventually write this article together.]

July 30, 2014 [E-mail from Cherylee to Karen]

I guess Bob has been pretty good about connecting me with people who have gone through, and are going through similar things.

In the article that she wrote with Black, Pimm explained:

This [message from Cherylee] in particular really "hit" me:

"He had considered both futures and this one was better for his family. He couldn't come back and be OK. There would have been more
strokes and he wouldn't have been himself anymore. He did feel
badly that there wasn't a better option, but he said that things were
really for the best even if it didn't always seem that way."

Bob always said he wouldn't want to come back if he was going to be a
burden on his family.

[This message was] followed by [another that stood out]:

"Bob told me that his partner was having difficulty sleeping. He said
she would know how to find him that way, but Bob said she would
sleep better when things had settled down a bit. He seemed quite
confident that she knew he was OK and that he loved her."

I was definitely having trouble sleeping and was disappointed that Bob
hadn't visited me in a dream yet. I knew it was because I wasn't sleeping
well—and I did know that he was OK and that he loved me, even if I didn't
have "proof" of it myself.

"I guess this wasn't something anyone expected to happen. Bob sort
of had a feeling something was going to happen, but not like this. He
was doing what he loved and things were great . . . then he was gone.
No pain. He said he could probably get more work done now."

This describes exactly how he passed. He was on a real high that evening of the 28th. He was feeling great that afternoon and went to the DOPS
meeting without me, which he normally wouldn't do. That evening, we just
finished going over the results of the psi testing that we did with the Guna
children in Panama earlier in the month. The results were pretty astounding and he was really excited. We were talking about accepting the Guna
chief's offer of returning to Panama in February to attend and talk at their
Independence Day celebration. He got up from the table, walked into his
office and within minutes he had a massive stroke in the brain stem. Quick,
no pain and without warning, other than Bob's own premonitions that he
wasn't going to go to another Dream Ball—and his dream in December telling him that he wouldn't be returning to Panama. I also recall mentioning

to someone soon afterward that I thought that Bob would probably be able to get more work done now. . . .

There is not a doubt in my mind that "her" Bob is "our" Bob and this confirmation that he is continuing to do what he loved to do is very comforting to me.

On September 3, 2015, neurosurgeon Eben Alexander sent Rivas the following statement, as dictated to his assistant:

Bob had become a close friend and was quite helpful with early versions of my book, *Proof of Heaven*, I felt a strong connection to him. The day before Bob died, I saw him at the regular Tuesday meeting at the Division of Perceptual Studies at University of Virginia in Charlottesville, VA. I had seen him only two other instances over the previous year. As I recall, he and I warmly greeted each other and we had a discussion about recent activities. I specifically told him that we had recently made some Sacred Acoustics tones that were working towards something of value for dream work, especially an interest in lucid dreaming tones. Bob was very enthusiastic about collaborating on developing the tones by listening to the test files and giving feedback. He seemed to be doing well at the time, although he did say something about not feeling so well lately, but seemed bright and energized. Because of the brightness and interaction of that encounter, I was especially shocked to receive the email a day or so later that he had passed over. In retrospect, I felt grateful for the opportunity to see him one last time before his departure from the physical plane.

After receiving the email with the news of Bob's passing, I forwarded it to Karen Newell, who had also been at the same meeting. She immediately shared with me the report Cherylee had provided on her first feedback after listening to Sacred Acoustics test files regarding a dream about someone named Bob. Karen and I thought to ask Cherylee for further information to see if it could possibly be Bob Van de Castle, we were very cautious not to frontload Cherylee with any specific information about him. Karen kept me apprised of further email reports from Cherylee. I was quite amazed by Cherylee's information that seemed strongly to be directly about Bob, even though she had not met him.

ADC WITH AN UNKNOWN DECEASED PERSON: ARI WEISSMANN

A second, less extensive case of contact with someone who had died concerns physicist George Weissmann's deceased son, Ariel (Ari) Weissmann, which

Black e-mailed Rivas about in August 2015. She felt this contact was especially strong because she did not even know that Weissmann had a son. In addition, there was no information about his son's death on the Internet at the time of the contact.

In an interview with investigator Robert Mays at the end of September 2015, George Weissmann stated that he was convinced of Black's psychokinetic abilities which, in his experience, are influenced by her convictions and beliefs. During a Skype conversation with her, he connected strange quirks of his computer screen with a moment of embarrassment she was experiencing. Against this backdrop, Weissmann stated:

> Somewhere in late 2011 we were talking about PK on Skype and so on, and then she suddenly said there is someone standing behind you with medical scrubs. It's a young man and his name is Ari. She then proceeded to have contact with him. He was helping her with difficulties [surrounding her]. I just go by her word and have no reason to doubt it. She mediated a medium session once. I communicated with my son, which was very wonderful. But she was uncomfortable doing that. She doesn't like to be a medium and we didn't do it again after that.

SOURCES

Black, C. (2014, August 29). *My NDEs, aftereffects and what I'm doing about them now.* Presentation at the 2014 International Association for Near-Death Studies (IANDS) Conference, Newport Beach, CA. Retrieved from https://www.youtube.com/watch?v=MZpBV3BZ1lc

Blalock, S., Holden, J. M., & Atwater, P. M. H. (2015). Electromagnetic and other environmental effects following near-death experiences: A primer. *Journal of Near-Death Studies, 33*(4), 181–211.

Greyson, B., Liester, M. B., Kinsey, L., Alum, S., & Fox, G. (2015). Electromagnetic phenomena reported by near-death experiencers. *Journal of Near-Death Studies, 33*(4), 213–243.

Hansen, J. N. (2013). Use of a torsion pendulum balance to detect and characterize what may be a human bioenergy field. *Journal of Scientific Exploration, 27*(2), 205–225.

Mays, R. G., & Mays, S. B. (2012). *Subject SB pinwheel psychokinesis and induction coil effect (February 6, 2012).* Retrieved from http://selfconsciousmind.com/SubjectSB-020612-Pinwheel2.mov

Persinger, M. A. (2015). Neuroscientific investigation of anomalous cognition. In
    E. C. May & S. B. Marwaha (Eds.), *Extrasensory perception: Support, skepticism, and
    science.* Santa Barbara, CA: Praeger/ABC-CLIO.

Pimm, B. A., & Black, C. (2014). *Celebrating the life and afterlife of Bob Van de Castle.*
    Presentation at the 2014 International Association for the Study of Dreams
    (IASD) PsiberDreaming Conference. Retrieved from http://dreamtalk.hyper
    mart.net/pdc2014/presentations/pdc2014-pimm-black.pdf

Roll, W. G., Saroka, K. S., Mulligan, B. P., Hunter, M. D., Dotta, B. T., Gang, N.,
    . . . Persinger, M. A. (2012). Case report: A prototypical experience of "polter-
    geist" activity, conspicuous quantitative electroencephalographic patterns,
    and sLORETA profiles—suggestions for intervention. *Neurocase, 18*(6), 1–10.

CASE 9.4 Thomas (Tom) Sawyer

NDE researcher Robert Mays brought to our attention the case of the U.S. com-
petitive cyclist Tom Sawyer of Rochester, New York. On May 23, 1978, Sawyer
had an NDE while he was clinically dead for 15 minutes after the pickup truck
he was working on fell on him, crushing his chest. Following his NDE, Sawyer
became acquainted with a number of NDE investigators, including Kenneth
Ring and Bruce Greyson. Rather than discuss the NDE itself here, we would like
to focus on its aftereffects, because it is these hallmarks of the case that make
it suitable for this chapter.

In October 1983, Sawyer made a noteworthy prediction about a plane
crash that later occurred in August 1985 involving a Lockheed L-1011 Tri-
Star. In an interview with Sidney Farr, Sawyer described how this prediction
came about:

> It was in the middle of October, 1983, when I had this precognition. We now
> know the event took place on August 2, 1985. It was a time over a year and
> a half in duration [between precognition and event].
>
> I was in a round-table discussion at the Near-Death Hotel in Connecti-
> cut [nickname for NDE researcher Kenneth Ring's home, where he hosted
> NDErs whom he was interviewing for his research]. . . .
>
> There happened to be near me a group of four women who were talking
> about a movie or a book. The title, as best as I can recall, was *The Ghost of
> Flight 401.* It is about the ghostly apparition of the pilot of a plane that had
> crashed in the Everglades four or five years before.

Now, even though I'm talking very intently with another person, if anyone within my hearing range says a non-truth, I have to correct him. I mean it lovingly when I do. . . .

They were discussing the ending of the book or the ending of the movie, how the ghostly apparition of the pilot of that plane appeared to one of the stewardesses and said there will never be another crash of an L10-11 [sic]. Well, the misconception by the general population was that there will never be another crash in that type of plane.

My understanding, from hearing them say that, was that first of all they didn't understand what the ghostly apparition meant by that. What he meant was in *his* time there will never be another crash of one of *his* planes. He's personally involved, he's spiritually involved, and he's on the other side. He's dead. But he's earthbound, if you will, and while he's in this condition, he will do whatever's necessary to assist and protect *his* airplanes, meaning Lockheed L10-11 Tri-Stars. I don't know if there's been any writing or anything about this, but I'm telling you this from information that I have. . . .

The statement was that there will never be another crash of an L10-11. I stopped and turned toward them and blurted out, with a great deal of emotion, "That's not true!" Then I realized what I'd said. Right away I knew that in order for me to say that, I have to know that there *will be* another crash of an L10-11. That just shut my throat right off and I put my head down and started to cry. I didn't like the emotion and sensationalism involved in that.

They were now silent, looking at me. Ken [Kenneth Ring], in his psychology voice said, "Well, Tom, obviously what you've said is—"

I looked at him and said, "Ken, knock off the psychology talk; this is just me." I got up from the table and walked out onto the balcony for a few minutes.

When I came back, Ken very lovingly and carefully said, "Tom, is there anything that you wish to add to what you've said? I would like to ask you a couple of questions: is this something that you actually know about or is it a precognition that has not taken place yet?" . . .

I said, "Well, there will be" (and I had to cover my face because I was crying), "there will be. . . ." Time delay and some emotions and then I said, "But some of it is so confusing to me." I swore and I was damning myself because, among other things, I was saying, "Why do I have to know this? I know so much about the details of the crash, but yet I'm contradicting myself and saying these half-sentences out loud." . . .

"Why can't I identify this white building that's very important to me?" And I said white building. I didn't say gas tank or object, or white round disk, or any of those things, I said white building. That technically was a mistake. It wasn't a building. It turned out to be a water tank.

I also said, "How can I know it's exactly 103 degrees and yet not know where it is?" The frustration was summed up in two main questions: when and exactly where? By that time it was about 3:30 in the morning. I looked at Ken and I said, "Ken, I know *all the people* on the plane!" That was about the worst part of it. I knew those people personally, privately, intimately, and I must be able to deal with the fact that 90 percent of them would die.

"How could you know them?" Ken asked.

"Ken, I can read you off their first names!" Some other details were that it was a Lockheed L10-11 Tri-Star. I said, "They're so beautiful. Do you know how many people they carry?" Which of course swelled up the emotions again because I was then thinking of the people. There were several other statements about details. . . .

I also knew there would be a man killed in the crash who did not belong. I knew details about him; who he was and where he was going. I told Ken later that night that the man was not on the plane. Ken, I'm sure, thought that he was a stowaway or something like that. But I was aware that he was in a car; he was also a mechanic. He was a really nice guy. I said I could identify more with him than the businessmen on the airplane.

I met with Ken privately a month or so later and he brought the subject up. He asked some specific, detailed questions which I answered very accurately. "Tom, if you can see the airport, is it an airport that you've been to before?"

"What I'm about to say isn't right, but of the airports that I've been to it looks most like either Philadelphia or Pittsburgh, but I'm not sure which. It's the one with the water alongside of it; there are ships there."

Ken said, "Tom, you also said something very specifically; you said it several times; 103 degrees. What do you mean by that?"

"Well, it's very hot; it's never that hot in Rochester, New York. Also, that tells you that it has to be—" . . .

On the morning of August 2 [1985], I opened the door to leave for work, the newspaper that had been wedged there fell at my feet. A feeling spread through my body. It was as if I could see the headline *that would be there* tomorrow! And it had to be a day after the event for it to be in the newspaper. Maybe it was just the timing which brought up the subconscious awareness that this wasn't going to be a good day for me. So I said out loud, "Oh God! This is the day." . . .

I called the University of Connecticut Hospital and asked for Dr. Bruce Grayson [*sic*], a very good friend of mine, who also just happens to be a psychiatrist.

On the very day of the crash, August 2, 1985, about 6 or 7 hours before it happened, Sawyer told psychiatrist and NDE researcher Bruce Greyson that his prediction (of a Lockheed L-1011 Tri-Star plane crash) would come to pass that day. According to Dr. Greyson (personal communication, April 2016), the veridical elements of Sawyer's prediction, in addition to the type of aircraft and the day and time frame, encompass the following points as well.

- The plane was to go down in a thunderstorm as a result of wind shear as it approached an airport.

The thunderstorm in question was one in Dallas, Texas. In an e-mail to Titus Rivas, researcher Robert Mays made the following comment about this fact:

Tom's prediction of the cause of this accident—flying into a storm with severe microburst-induced wind shear—is very notable because this was not something that was able to be detected in aircraft at the time (I remember this crash and the subsequent focus on detecting microburst wind shear and avoiding severe wind shear).

Because evidence of microburst-induced wind shear was not something forensic specialists could look for at the time, other, often human, causes were considered, such as pilot error.

- The crash was to occur in the United States and the temperature would be 103° F, so it was probably going to happen in the southern United States.

The crash occurred at the Dallas-Fort Worth Airport in the late summer, where the temperature was 103° F that day.

Greyson confirmed to Mays that Sawyer had most likely not had any paranormal abilities prior to his NDE. Greyson e-mailed, "As far as I know, Tom had no psychic abilities before his NDE, as from my knowledge of him as a person, I would suspect that prior to his NDE, he would have ridiculed anyone who claimed such abilities." In his interview with Sidney Farr, Sawyer himself says that his 1978 NDE is responsible for his enhanced abilities:

> There is a characteristic with me, and I know of other people who have had a near-death experience, or a spontaneous spiritual awakening[,] where their psychic ability has been greatly enhanced. . . . From 1978 to 1985 I experienced many psychic things.

The remarkable prediction was not the only indication of Sawyer's psychic ability. In addition, he demonstrated the ability to find lost objects through clairvoyance, and he succeeded in locating a child lost in the woods. Sawyer also made another prediction that was verified by Greyson.

SOURCE
Farr, S. S. (1993). *What Tom Sawyer learned from dying.* Norfolk, VA: Hampton Roads.

Remarks

As we have said, we were able to find only four cases of verified paranormal experiences following NDEs, which by no means signifies that they seldom occur. On July 22, 2015, Greyson e-mailed Rivas on this topic: "I know of a great many near-death experiencers who report an increase in paranormal abilities after their NDEs. However, I cannot think of a single case in which those abilities have been confirmed by an independent objective investigation."

These kinds of cases should be distinguished from cases in which any abilities clearly existed before the NDE. The NDE would then not have induced the abilities but would only have strengthened them, perhaps by breaking through the NDEr's inhibiting (unconscious) convictions about them. An example of such a case can be found in the American psychic Joseph (Joe) McMoneagle (1993), who became known for his involvement in experiments on remote viewing—clairvoyance at a distance—particularly in the U.S. Army unit known as the Stargate Project, which was set up to investigate the potential for psychic phenomena in military and domestic applications.

Another example is Pam Reynolds (see Chapter 3, Case 3.29). Only in 2014, after her death, did it become clear that she had shown paranormal abilities after her NDE. It was journalist Judy Bachrach who made this discovery during a conversation with Reynolds's daughter, Michelle. As Bachrach described in her 2014 book *Glimpsing Heaven:*

[Pam] knew, for instance . . . where Michelle's school friend had left a purse— and there was no empirical way for Pam to know this, because that purse was at the bottom of yet another girl's hall closet under some coats. She knew—it is Pam's best friend who tells me this story—that a teenage boy who was in a coma in the ICU of the Phoenix hospital where both were patients would, in fact, recover. It was Pam who walked up to the still body on the bed, whispering in the boy's ear: "I don't know about you, but I want to call the pizza dude and get some slices, because I hate this food here." And the boy woke up and smiled.

She knew that still another young boy (this one having drowned, then having been resuscitated—but not before breathing in a lot of chlorinated water that burned his lungs) would also recover. It was her cousin Joe Smith who asked Pam to go to the Savannah hospital where the child was. "I saw his mother," Smith recalls, "I said, 'Would it be OK, if you don't mind, my cousin has come in to see him because she might be able to do something for him.'

"And Pam held his hand, and she told him to wake up. And he did. The boy woke up 15 minutes after we left. He is fine. He is healed."

However, Reynolds's husband, Butch Lowery, told Bachrach that she already seemed to show paranormal gifts prior to the NDE. One example occurred long before Reynolds became ill, according to Lowery. The two of them had been waiting in line, and Pam knew that a totally unknown woman standing in front of them had not long ago witnessed a poignant death. The woman in question confirmed this fact to him.

When paranormal abilities are verified as accurate, whether they begin or are "merely" enhanced following an NDE, they represent a unique source of data regarding NDE-related phenomena that defy materialist explanation. As Black's experimental results regarding dream precognition show, such abilities are not infallible. However, the empirical evidence for the existence of psychic phenomena rests not on research subjects' absolute infallibility but on their ability to produce verified phenomena at a rate significantly above chance accuracy (Radin, 1997). It is for future researchers to assess whether NDErs have average accuracy levels above those of gifted people who have not had an NDE.

REFERENCES

Bachrach, J. (2014). *Glimpsing heaven: The stories and science of life after death*. Washington, DC: National Geographic Society.

Greyson, B. (1983). Increase in psychic phenomena following near-death experiences. *Theta, 11*(2), 26–29.

McMoneagle, J. (1993). *Mind trek: Exploring consciousness, time, and space through remote viewing*. Charlottesville, VA: Hampton Roads.

Noyes, R., Fenwick, P., Holden, J. M., & Christian, S. R. (2009). Aftereffects of pleasurable Western adult near-death experiences. In J. M. Holden, B. Greyson, & D. James (Eds.), *The handbook of near-death experiences: Thirty years of investigation* (pp. 41–62). Santa Barbara, CA: Praeger/ABC-CLIO.

Radin, D. (1997). *The conscious universe: The scientific truth of psychic phenomena*. New York, NY: HarperOne.

CHAPTER 10

General Remarks

The reports of these cases may be rare, but their numbers are not insignificant.
—Emily Williams Cook, Bruce Greyson, and Ian Stevenson,
"Do Any Near-Death Experiences Provide Evidence
for the Survival of Human Personality After Death?"

This suggests the mind and brain can separate.
—Peter Fenwick, during a panel discussion at
the New York Academy of Sciences

*Scientists have discovered that there is no credible
evidence for the existence of the soul.*
—Julien Musolino, *The Soul Fallacy*

In this book, we discussed a total of 104 cases of near-death experiences (NDEs) with paranormal aspects that were confirmed by doctors, nurses, family members, friends, or medical records. We limited ourselves to cases in which we believe the reported phenomena cannot or can hardly be explained by standard factors such as chance, foreknowledge, or unnoticed (residual) activity in the physical senses and the nervous system. In addition, we included in the book only those cases whose sources, investigators, and witnesses we could categorize as sufficiently reliable. Also, we excluded cases of confirmed clinical death that lacked sufficient information to conclude that the associated NDE actually occurred during cardiac arrest. In this chapter we review the evidence from those cases and summarize the conclusion to which that evidence points. We then present arguments that various authors have put forth to invalidate that conclusion, and we finally refute those arguments by drawing from additional evidence and from logical deduction.

Our hope is that readers will judge each case separately on its own merits. We do not expect that every reader will find every case equally convincing. We believe it is unfounded to assert, as some materialistic skeptics (or pseudo-skeptics) do, that the "core" cases in this book should be limited to only a few cases or even that they should not be taken seriously at all. We therefore do not address unreasonable arguments such as these. In our view, unreasonable arguments include the following:

- "It can't be true because materialism was incontrovertibly proven long ago."
- "All the investigators of these cases are either unscrupulous cheaters or utterly incompetent."
- "Only evidence that has been obtained under strictly controlled (quasi-) experimental circumstances may be called scientific. The rest has to be ignored, by definition, as nothing more than unreliable anecdotes."
- "It would be *so* amazing if these things were true that I just *can't* believe they are. We live in a grim, tragic reality, and these kinds of things don't fit in."
- "Well-documented cases are valid as scientific evidence, but the reported phenomena have to be 100%, not just 90%, materialistically inexplicable. The patient's eyes have to have been taped shut when the NDE occurred, and the ears have to have been completely blocked, too, by being plugged with wax, for instance." (Although we can imagine that others want evidence that is even more convincing, this desire cannot be an excuse for setting absurd conditions for such evidence.)
- "Cases in which the subjectively perceived situation doesn't correspond with reality have also been documented. This indicates that all NDEs must be based on dream images and so have nothing to do with paranormal phenomena."

Regarding this last point: in 2009, past International Association for Near-Death Studies (IANDS) president and longtime NDE veridical perception researcher Jan Holden (2009) reported her analysis of as many credible published cases of apparently nonphysical veridical perception as she could locate. Holden found that discrepancies of any kind between experiencers' reports and later fact-checking occurred in about 10% of cases, with major discrepancies in only about 2% of cases. We consider it bizarre to conclude from a smattering of inaccurate perceptions that there are no such things as NDEs with paranormal aspects. This conclusion is just as unreasonable as denying that sensory perception exists because people sometimes have hallucinations or illusions or make occasional errors in sensory interpretation.

Paranormal Phenomena

From this collection, we think the conclusion can be drawn that at least the following phenomena can and do occur during NDEs:

- clairvoyance with respect to the immediate vicinity
- clairvoyance with respect to affairs or incidents beyond the range of the physical senses, including when there is low vision or blindness on the physical level
- telepathy
- a complex form of human consciousness that is not supported by neurological activity
- actual contact with those who are deceased (including deceased pets, see Case 3.32)
- paranormal manifestations of the near-death experiencer (NDEr) during an out-of-body experience (OBE)
- shared paranormal experiences during an NDE

The following phenomena at least seem to occur as a result of NDEs:

- awakening of ESP abilities
- "miraculous" healing of physical impairments
- psychokinetic abilities
- unintentional poltergeist-like influences (on electricity, for instance)

For some of these phenomena, we were able to find a relatively large number of confirmed cases, whereas for other phenomena, we found only a limited number. Obviously, it is useful to collect as many confirmed cases as possible, although in principle one well-documented case should be sufficient to establish the existence of a particular phenomenon. This is related to the crow (or raven) paradox in the philosophy of science, in which the existence of one white crow is enough to contradict the assertion that all crows are black. A variation on this metaphor for falsifiability or testability is that one black swan is enough to contradict the assertion that all swans are white.

Readers may be interested to know that our sleuthing did not uncover confirmed cases of all the paranormal phenomena mentioned in NDE literature. These phenomena include

- healing abilities as a result of an NDE
- specific, verifiable recollections of a previous life during or after an NDE
- precognitive impressions of the (likely) future during an NDE
- intentional psychokinetic influence on objects during an NDE itself (notwithstanding Case 7.1, because the NDEr did not explicitly state that he opened the distant front door but only that he visited his brother at that location)

We hope that readers will now agree with us that confirmed cases—the "core" of the evidence for paranormal phenomena during NDEs—deserve further attention. We therefore invite readers to share with us specific cases of this kind that they believe should appear in the next edition of this book. Qualifying cases would be those in which follow-up investigation confirmed the paranormal phenomena involved.

CASES WITHOUT CONFIRMATION BY THIRD PARTIES

Considering the body of cases presented in this book, it does not make much sense to continue doubting the existence of the paranormal aspects of NDEs. This conclusion does not mean that we have to accept "hook, line, and sinker" that every story about NDEs is true. As we already mentioned in the introduction, a few authors have published accounts that were later revealed to be utterly fictitious.

Nevertheless, in addition to the confirmed cases of NDE-related paranormal phenomena presented in this book, the professional literature is replete with examples of similar cases unconfirmed by third parties. The evidential value of confirmed cases lends credibility to many unconfirmed cases. Numerous examples of unconfirmed cases with possible paranormal aspects can be found on the Near Death Experience Research Foundation (NDERF) website (www.nderf .org), for example. Following are a few examples from the professional literature:

- Extrasensory perceptions during Stefan von Jankovich's NDE (Cook, Greyson, & Stevenson, 1998, pp. 395–398). Von Jankovich had a car accident in Switzerland in 1964 while travelling from Zurich to Lugano. His sports car collided with an oncoming truck. He suffered a cardiac arrest, during which he had an NDE. Among other things, he saw a woman (with a red car and a young daughter) praying for him, and he claimed to have tracked her down after his recovery. It had become impossible to verify this incident in 1992 when Ian Stevenson approached him about his experience.
- Visual perception despite congenital physical blindness in Vickie Umipeg (Ring & Cooper, 1999, pp. 22–28).
- Paranormal contact with an unknown deceased person in the "Lynn From Michigan" case in P. M. H. Atwater's (2003) book *The New Children and Near-Death Experiences* (pp. 72–76).
- Various shared NDEs and shared-death experiences of the kind discussed by Raymond Moody (2010) in *Glimpses of Eternity*.
- All the cases not included in this book from paranormal case review articles by Janice Holden, Emily Williams Cook (now Emily Williams Kelly), Bruce Greyson, and Ian Stevenson.
- An after-death communication, with a known person not known to have died, that Pam Reynolds (Case 3.29) had concerning the death of one of her aunts, which she described in the last interview she gave prior to her death.

And the list goes on.

Brain and Mind

Based on the cases in this book, we may also draw the following general conclusion regarding the relationship between the brain and the mind: *During NDEs, people can apparently have not only conscious experiences but also paranormal experiences—those that cannot be explained in terms of current mainstream understanding of physical–sensory, brain–functioning. Therefore, people's conscious experiences and mental abilities evidently do not depend ultimately on the functioning of their brains. Although during life, the mind typically functions in conjunction with the brain, it has the ability to function independent of the brain; thus, it is essentially a phenomenon that is independent of the brain.*

Of course, evidence for this conclusion also comes from extensive research on paranormal phenomena that occur outside the domain of NDEs. Yet there is still something going on in NDEs that promotes the occurrence of paranormal phenomena in people who, for the most part, have had no previous paranormal experiences. Thus NDEs provide an extensive source of evidence regarding the question of the relationship between mind and brain.

Theorists have proposed possible dynamics involved in a mind that is essentially independent of the brain. One such proposal is the "transmission" or "filter" theory. According to this theory, the brain does not produce consciousness but rather, under normal circumstances, limits consciousness—precisely by focusing primarily on sensory information. This explanation is associated with the fact that, for whatever reason, people live in a physical reality and therefore must be able to cope with that material reality. Particular brain diseases, in which the mind is restricted in cognitive processes such as thinking, speaking, and remembering, could perhaps be conceived of as the "filtering" of a malfunctioning brain to the detriment of the mind's functioning. NDEs may be one relatively reliable circumstance in which people's minds are freed from their restrictive relationships with their brains and with an exclusive focus on material phenomena, enabling them to perceive and act in previously unrealized ways.

Under normal circumstances, the contents of human consciousness do not consist exclusively of what is immediately perceivable by the senses. This fact is obviously revealed by typical human abilities such as fantasizing, being creative, and abstract thinking. Furthermore, as we mentioned, there are also many, many situations that have nothing to do with NDEs in which people report having paranormal experiences, and there are even so-called paragnosts (psychics), shamans, and mediums who appear to have some control over their extrasensory perceptions.

Perhaps more than any other source of evidence, confirmed cases of paranormal phenomena during NDEs support the theory that mind is separate from brain, even though mind and brain interact during physical life. It is then only a further step to consider that, as most NDErs claim, the mind survives the death of the brain. In this respect, NDEs enable us humans to see the greater freedom that we likely will have as spiritual beings without a body after we die. Based on NDErs' descriptions and assertions—and the evidence we have for those assertions, as presented in this book—we will, among other things, have access to more information than we typically have here on Earth, will be able to move ourselves more freely, and will communicate telepathically with the living and the dead.

Many people consider NDEs to be experiences in which the experiencer is actually making contact with the hereafter. Critics point out that NDErs have not really been dead, so there is no guarantee that they caught a glimpse of a spiritual world where people supposedly end up after they die. On the face of it, this seems like a significant argument, but it does not stand up to scrutiny, as we will explain below.

In confirmed NDEs, we see at least two lines of evidence for personal survival after physical death: (a) evidence for personal survival from consciousness during cardiac arrest (Chapter 3) and (b) evidence for personal survival from apparent contact with deceased persons (Chapters 5 and 6). In the balance of this chapter, we will explore these two lines of evidence.

Evidence for Personal Survival From Consciousness During Cardiac Arrest (Chapter 3)

Remarkably enough, a large number of the confirmed NDEs in this book are cases of consciousness during cardiac arrest—some combined with extrasensory perceptions. Simply the sheer number of cases provides reason to acknowledge the reality of this phenomenon.

The cases in Chapter 3, involving NDEs during an acute cardiac arrest, constitute an enormous anomaly for the materialistic worldview. According to that worldview, complex human consciousness is a product of brain activity. However, after an average of about 15 seconds of cardiac arrest, the victim shows a flat EEG, indicating no measurable brain activity. As we argued, recent evidence has not refuted this central fact. Thus after only 10–20 seconds of cardiac arrest, there should be too little cortical activity to enable complex consciousness, yet NDErs appear to demonstrate exactly that: complex consciousness during the absence of measurable brain activity.

From a materialistic perspective, NDEs during an acute cardiac arrest simply *cannot* exist because they would indicate that personal consciousness in the ultimate sense does not depend on activity in the cerebral cortex. Even if, in a portion of the cases, external CPR—heart massage plus ventilation—*did* provide enough blood circulation to the cortex, the remaining cases occurred in the absence of resuscitation and, therefore, the absence of sufficient circulation to support complex consciousness. The latter condition was present in cases such as "The

Man with the Dentures" (Case 3.7), "Lloyd W. Rudy's Patient" (Case 3.11), "Tom Aufderheide's Patient" (Case 3.13, also Case 4.2), "Richard Mansfield's Patient" (Case 3.16), and "The Jacket and the Tie" (Case 3.24). The hypothesis of temporary circulation in the cerebral cortex through external CPR falls short because it cannot explain these cases in which no circulation apparently occurred. Skeptical claims that the NDE consciousness could still be explained by low-level, unmeasured processing in the cortex causing primary, relatively simple forms of consciousness, such as pain during a coma, do not take away from this fact.

During an interview with Alex Tsakiris of Skeptiko.com, radiation oncologist Jeffrey Long made the following remarkable statement regarding this point, based on his own investigations into NDEs:

> The substantial majority of people that have a near-death experience associated with cardiac arrest are actually seeing their physical body well prior to the time that CPR is initiated. Once CPR is initiated, you don't see any alteration in the flow of the near-death experience, suggesting that blood flow to the brain isn't affecting the content in any way. (See http://www.skeptiko .com/jeffrey_long_takes_on_critics_of_evidence_of_the_afterlife/)

Although the cases in Long's collection generally do not meet the criteria for inclusion in this book, it is certainly remarkable that many NDErs evidently claim to have observed their bodies prior to the start of resuscitation.

Another hypothesis that some materialists have offered is that although the cortex may be disabled, in the absence of cortical viability, other, subcortical parts of the brain may assume the function of producing complex consciousness. However, once again, such an assumption of functions would have to happen within no more than about 20 seconds. Furthermore, according to materialism, mental functions are strictly coupled with certain areas of the brain. Even if, through long-term, intensive neuropsychological training—such as in cognitive rehabilitation after brain damage following an accident—a victim can learn to access other areas of the brain to assume functions previously associated with now-damaged areas, such extensive retraining is absent in the acute condition of cardiac arrest: The assumption of critical processes by parts of the brain other than the cortex cannot suddenly occur as if by magic. The execution of critical "computational" processes by non-cortical parts of the brain might occur in the rare individual whose cortical activity already played no significant role in complex mental functions long before the NDE, but we actually know of no such case, and that process clearly is not at play in the vast majority of NDErs. Hence the materialist hypothesis—that in cardiac arrest, subcortical structures would spring into action to assume other mental functions—fails. Even in such individuals, there is no sudden assumption of functions by other parts of the brain prior to the NDE—only a different, unusual organization of existing functions within the brain.

The fact that no standard medical explanation is possible for consciousness during cardiac arrest is very relevant to the question of whether there is personal survival after death. If conscious mental functioning continues while the part of the brain that, according to materialists, "produces" this mental activity has shut down, it is reasonable to conclude that consciousness is not a product of the brain. Consciousness does not issue from the brain but is simply in interaction with the brain. Even when (the relevant part of) the brain shuts down, consciousness survives.

We should acknowledge here that for the question of personal survival, irreversible death is the *functional* equivalent of clinical death. Sam Parnia stated that NDEs during an acute cardiac arrest are in fact "actual-death experiences" (ADEs) because in clinical death, a patient is, from a biological and medical perspective, already dead. Also, in both cases, *the same relevant brain functions—that are considered essential to support consciousness*—shut down, even though these functions are generally regained after clinical death but, obviously, not after irreversible death. Only if other relevant circumstances are different in the two situations should one be cautious to extrapolate survival during clinical death to survival after irreversible death. Could this be the case? In what respects are there relevant differences between clinical death and final, physical death in this context?

We can see two hypothetical, relevant differences in this context between clinical death and irreversible death:

- unknown bodily factors (aside from the brain) that do keep consciousness going during clinical death but not after irreversible death
- unknown "supernatural" (nonbodily) factors, such as gods, demons, or whatever these might be, that "tolerate" personal, conscious survival during clinical death but mercilessly guarantee definitive destruction after final physical death

In practical terms, one need not take either type of factor into account, considering there is absolutely no indication of either one, and their existence is not plausible in the least, as far as we can see at this time. David Rousseau, for instance, has argued—in an overview of arguments for and against the conclusion that NDEs indicate survival—that consciousness might, in theory, depend on the body as a whole (even though he is not a proponent of this notion). But a long-standing conclusion from empirical research is that within the body, only the brain is *directly* involved in consciousness. All other organs are only *indirectly* involved in consciousness via the brain. Thus in principle, all the other bodily organs are secondary and, therefore, ultimately unnecessary with regard to consciousness; only the brain is central to the question of consciousness.

In theory, a brain could survive completely apart from a whole biological body if it were hooked up to artificial systems that kept it alive. Assuming that the conscious mind that is linked to that brain can also survive circumstances like this (and from a materialistic standpoint, that would certainly be expected), there is no longer any reason to claim that consciousness might inherently depend on the body as a whole rather than on the brain alone. The thought that the whole body is directly involved in consciousness seems to be based more on a naïve interpretation of a possible subjective experience rather than on relevant, scientific data.

Then some scholars mention the possibility that reported consciousness during a flat EEG is based on "retrocognitive" perceptions right before the patient regains consciousness. In this scenario, the patient would receive impressions of incidents that took place during the cardiac arrest, not during the arrest itself but only after the fact via retrocognition or postcognition (extrasensory perception with respect to the past), after the brain had become sufficiently active again. This process cannot hold true for some of the cases in Chapter 3, because the patient regained consciousness so quickly after the cardiac arrest that investigators have concluded that the NDEs must have actually happened during clinical death.

Some authors claim that instead of retrocognition, there is a form of precognition—extrasensory perception with respect to the future—at play: that the NDE may occur in the seconds or milliseconds *before* cardiac arrest and may include precognitive information about what will happen during cardiac arrest. But this argument is applicable a priori only to NDEs during which the patient was already unconscious for a long enough period of time to have been capable of having an NDE during that phase. Therefore, such precognition cannot be applied to cases during which the patient was normally conscious before the cardiac arrest.

In any event, we cannot call on such hypotheses to come to the rescue of materialism, because neither retrocognition nor precognition fit into the materialistic model.

Michael Martin and Keith Augustine wrote in their book *The Myth of an Afterlife*:

> Dualists are thus forced to make a difficult choice: either retain a belief in personal survival at the expense of ignoring or dismissing the implications of our best evidence, or accept those implications at the expense of acknowledging that the prospects for personal survival are extremely dim.

We find this claim to be untenable because there is absolutely no evidence that would unequivocally and convincingly confirm the materialistic worldview. *All the neurological and medical evidence* that materialists such as Martin and Augustine have presented—demonstrating that the mind totally depends on the brain—can easily fit into a dualistic (or more broadly: nonmaterialistic) worldview. This point even applies to cases of extreme dysfunction in mental processes due to neurological disorders, diseases, or lesions (Beauregard, 2007; James, 1898). Within a dualistic-interactionistic worldview, mind and brain interact. This dynamic means that the brain happens to exercise an undeniable influence on the mind and vice versa without meaning that the mind is suddenly reducible to the brain or the other way around. This influence can occasionally also have very negative consequences, as we see, for instance, in an illness like dementia.

Sometimes the influence of the brain on the mind is particularly bizarre, as demonstrated not only in experiments with so-called "split-brain" patients but also in the consequences of alcohol or narcotics use. Still, not a single case involving the influence of the brain on the mind "therefore," necessarily, proves that that mind, as such, is the product of the brain or that that mind must be completely dependent on the brain (Rivas, 2004). *Similarly, there is no proof that the influence of consciousness on brain processes means that no brain processes exist that are not paired with consciousness.* Mutual interaction is just not the same thing as complete dependence.

This representation of matters is not the ad hoc solution of desperate dualists who do not dare confront certain facts but, rather, is an integral component of the dualistic-interactionistic worldview. As philosopher of science and survivalist Neal Grossman stated in an excellent 2008 letter to the editor in the *Journal of Near-Death Studies*:

William James (1898) showed, more than a hundred years ago, that (1) the most that the facts of neurology can establish is a correlation between mental states and brain states and (2) correlation is not causation. The data of neuroscience will always be neutral with respect to the hypotheses of (1) causation or materialism and (2) what James called "transmission," the hypothesis that the brain merely transmits an already existing consciousness.

Whereas the "proofs" of materialism can be excellently placed within dualistic interactionism, the evidence that we have presented in this book is without a doubt incompatible with a materialistic theory. For this reason, materialists rationalize away or negate this evidence as much as possible. Examples of this tendency can be seen in the recent arguments by Gerald Woerlee in his 2013 book, *Illusory Souls*, and in the 2013 article, "Occam's Chainsaw" by Jason Braithwaite and Hayley Dewe.

From a more general perspective, alternative, non-survivalist parapsychological hypotheses such as retrocognition or precognition (instead of consciousness occurring during cardiac arrest itself) need to be taken seriously only if there is a mechanism or psychological motive that could explain why the presumed retrocognition or precognition occurs. A possible hypothetical motive could be that the patient wants to (unconsciously) reassure himself or herself that he or she was still mentally there during clinical death. But a motive such as that is conceivable only if the NDEr is convinced, prior to clinical death, that a cardiac arrest might take place. However, this conviction is not an option for people who completely unexpectedly, without preparation, experience an acute cardiac arrest; likewise for children who are not aware of the gravity of their condition. And it also cannot play a role for infants and toddlers who, prior to their NDEs, do not even have a clear picture of what it means to physically die, as in Case 3.28 in this book, the Mark Botts case. Rousseau recognized the great value of such cases.

We therefore conclude that extrapolation from an NDE during a clinical death to personal survival after death is completely justifiable. In other words, *the presence of personal consciousness during a cardiac arrest implies that humans can expect personal survival after irreversible death.* This is not irrational, utterly arbitrary wishful thinking but, rather, a rational conclusion from the type of cases that we presented in Chapter 3.

HARD-WIRED MECHANISM VERSUS PERSONAL MOTIVE

Opponents of the survival hypothesis might argue that the veridical impressions of events that apparently occur in real time could in fact be based on retrocognition or precognition (ESP relating to the past or the future, respectively) *without being driven by any psychological motive*. The retrocognitive or precognitive ESP would simply be part of an inborn "hard-wired" mechanism. Such a hypothetical mechanism would have arisen as the result of a random mutation and then evolutionarily selected because it was beneficial for the dispersion of the underlying genes that are ostensibly responsible for the mechanism. Close or distant family members with—in this respect—the same genetic predisposition would thereby overcome their fear of death more easily, which would affect their genetic success.

What makes this hypothesis so improbable is that until recently, people usually did not survive cardiac arrest, so that such hypothetical genes would hardly ever have been able to express themselves during an NDE in such a way as to be able to influence others with whom the experience would later be shared. Nowadays, patients regularly survive cardiac arrest thanks to modern means of resuscitation. So it is difficult to understand how genes that hardly ever expressed themselves before, and thus could almost never have had an impact, should have dispersed themselves so widely.

A last resort for opponents might be to suppose that the mechanism is only one of the effects produced by genes that had already been successful for many thousands of years in *other* respects. However, this hypothesis would appear to us to be a classic example of an implausible ad hoc speculation without any empirical foundation.

COLLECTIVE UNCONSCIOUS VERSUS PERSONAL SELF

Another approach, which Michael Sudduth has mentioned to us (in personal communication), could be that the motive is not part of one's personal motivation but rather inspired by a hypothetical Jungian collective unconscious (or subconscious). This hypothetical entity could generate paranormal phenomena that always seem to indicate personal survival, even if the NDEr in question has no (subconscious) need for such reassurance. The collective unconscious is supposed to be "intelligent," and due to its paranormal abilities, it is also supposed to be perfectly up-to-date on the strictest theoretical criteria for scientific evidence. Its supposed purpose would be to reconcile people with their mortality.

We reject this hypothesis because we already know with absolute certainty that we are persons who are not reducible to our bodies, and we do not know with any comparable degree of certainty whether the hypothetical collective unconscious actually exists.

REQUIRING ABSOLUTE CERTAINTY

There are, however, several scholars who challenge this positive conclusion. They usually assert that other theories cannot be ruled out 100%, so humanity will never know with absolute certainty. We emphasize (Rivas, 2003, 2010), though, as do others (for example, Carter, 2010, 2012; Gauld, 1983; Grossman, 2002, 2008; Kelly et al., 2000; Lund, 1985, 2005) that from a rational perspective, it is sufficient to be able to conclude that the theory of personal survival (within the current state of scientific knowledge) is *far more persuasive and plausible* than other theories. Absolute certainty in empirical science is, strictly speaking, never attainable. Empirical science is always about plausibility, making sense, and probability. Not being able to rule out other theories 100% is very different from adhering to a theory that is utterly arbitrary and unfounded. As Grossman remarked, "The debunker wants us to refute mere logical possibilities before we can legitimately make the inference from the data to survival."

Some authors claim that in this context, assessing the plausibility of a theory is always arbitrary, whereas we are emphasizing that plausibility relates to more general knowledge and specific information from relevant fields, such as, in this context, neurology and psychology. The fact that people do not agree with a particular assessment of the degree of plausibility is irrelevant until they indicate *why* the assessment is unfounded. Proceeding in this way would demonstrate a rational process based not in arbitrariness but in discussion involving evidence and argumentation, as well as implicit and explicit assumptions.

For examples of some of the more farfetched theories, see the accompanying intermezzo.

Intermezzo

There are authors, for instance, who claim that paranormal NDEs in young children could in theory be telepathically induced by their parents. The parents, with the help of retrocognition, would apparently manage to have their child obtain paranormal information about what happened during the period of time that the child was clinically dead. The NDE would not occur during the cardiac arrest itself but be artificially and unconsciously induced in the child by the parents via telepathy after the cardiac arrest was over. The parents would apparently do this completely unconsciously because they long for proof of life after death. Hypotheses like this may, from a purely technical perspective, be conceivable but are so farfetched that we honestly do not know why we should not simply ignore them. Most parents, for example, are not even aware of the strict criteria for experiences that might imply survival. Also, parents are often just as surprised by the cardiac arrest of their child as the child is.

Moreover, such a hypothetical form of unconscious telepathic influence is quite far removed from the experiences of telepathy between parents and children that parapsychologists have collected, so it certainly would not be defensible to justify a speculative form of telepathy simply by making reference to the known form that is qualitatively quite different. Telepathy between parents and children under other circumstances would involve experiences or thoughts that parents receive from children, or vice versa. If the child is the "receiver," the child's own interests play an important role in whether or not the parents' telepathic signals come through into the child's consciousness.

Michael Sudduth (2016) reasoned that maybe someday, new theories that do not include survival may be formulated that would preemptively address counterarguments. Therefore, according to his argument, certain aspects, such as concrete motives for having retrocognitive impressions during an NDE, say, right after a cardiac arrest, may be overlooked for the time being. It would therefore—as we understand him—be sufficient that there *can* be a motive, in theory, no matter how hard it would be to imagine one at the current time. This seems, in our opinion, suspiciously like a dishonest way of always being right from the start, without ever having to tailor one's own hypothesis to incorporate actual evidence.

We think this is such an ad hoc rationalization that we cannot take it seriously. It seems to come down to "who knows, the human mind may work totally differently from the way we thought it did until now"—so one should not dare to draw even tentative conclusions based on a substantial amount of evidence already in existence. Who knows. . . . But simply *making suppositions* just to be able to reject all the evidence for survival (considering that, purely hypothetically, so-called living-agent psi [LAP; Braude, 2003, 2009; Sudduth, 2009, 2016], a variant of the super-psi hypothesis, could still explain all the evidence for survival without survival) does not impress us. We have no reason to believe that people, unconsciously, simply go after something without some kind of a comprehensible psychological motive. According to us, there is not a single piece of evidence for such an idea, not even in cases of dissociation. (We note, though, that we are talking about psychological dynamics, not about the consequences of mental illness.)

Rousseau agreed with us in this respect, when, on page 52 of his 2012 article "The Implications of Near-Death Experiences for Research into the Survival of Consciousness," he wrote:

In my view there is another way to challenge the super-psi hypothesis [the hypothesis that paranormal phenomena arise from the mind of someone (a "living agent") who is not dead or clinically dead], by identifying cases that challenge its premises or ontological parsimony. The super-psi hypothesis is grounded in the conjunction of two very specific claims, namely, that super-psi is motivated by deep-seated needs or intense emotions, and that it operates to produce compensatory or mitigating outcomes. This suggests that at least in principle it may be possible to find cases where psychological motivations needed to mediate super-psi are clearly absent, or where the outcomes are contrary to how things would be if super-psi were involved (e.g., the psychological stresses are not mitigated, and may even be enhanced). Note that such a counterexample would not count against the existence of super-psi, but only against it being the source of the survival-suggesting evidence in that given case. However, for these cases it may be impossible to develop explanations that maintain the super-psi hypothesis's neutrality about the existence of souls.

As long as there are no acceptable underpinnings for the possible presence of motives that we might have overlooked until now, it does not make sense to us to seriously take such theories into account. Therefore, we argue that, from a psychological perspective, certain general suppositions about the human mind are clearly more plausible than others.

As we have understood Sudduth, he argued that the survival hypothesis would require extra so-called "auxiliary hypotheses" in order to be at all viable. However, he failed to note that these "auxiliary hypotheses" would be entirely *compatible* with what is already (empirically) known about the mind and psychology. Assuming that personal survival after death is real does not imply one needs to adjust any basic theories about motivation, cognition, and so on. Most dualists would not even need to adapt their theory about brain-mind relations.

In contrast, the kind of "auxiliary hypotheses" that the so-called LAP hypothesis would need would be incompatible with what is known about psychology. For instance, regarding NDEs with paranormal aspects, LAP would make it necessary to postulate that, outside a psychopathological context, people do far-reaching things for absolutely no intelligible (conscious or subconscious) reason. Therefore, unlike the hypothesis or theory of personal survival after death, LAP would be forced to go against what is already known—that people are *motivated* to do the things they do rather than doing them for absolutely no reason—regarding a considerable number of NDEs. Given this important difference, it does not make sense to speak of a "draw" between the two hypotheses. We conclude that Sudduth is mistaken in his analysis of the field.

Empirical knowledge is always provisional, and with the current state of science, it certainly makes (far) more sense that NDEs point to survival after death than that they do not. In practicing science, investigators do not wait to draw provisional conclusions until it is absolutely certain that they are correct. The highest degree of certainty is associated with mathematics, logic, and analytical philosophy, not with the formulation of empirical theories. It is also not reasonable to require such a high degree of certainty first, before someone can even make any justified statements.

If, in the context of NDEs, someone has trouble with the conclusion that the evidence points to survival, then the only way to defend such a position is to *plausibly* undermine all the various indications substantiating life after death. In our opinion, no one has yet accomplished this goal successfully. All the formulated alternatives are more contrived and more complex. Some scholars find this situation to be an advantage, however, as if from the outset, they have greater confidence in theories that are more complex. This predilection for complexity may be related to a more general expectation that from a scientific perspective, reality has very little to do with human projections or desires. As if, for this reason alone, people should expect that everything is far less simple (and less positive) than humans would think or want. As if it had in fact been established that from a human perspective, reality is essentially very cold, bizarre, and *inhuman*. (Incidentally, only a few scholars appear to be aware that this expectation—that reality ultimately will not much appeal to us humans—usually relates directly to a materialistic worldview [Tart, 2009].) Be that as it may, from a theoretical standpoint, such expectations carry absolutely no weight. In our view, they should not lead people to avoid rational conclusions.

We should be aware that the alternatives that have been formulated thus far are quite farfetched. If anyone comes up with new alternative hypotheses—*that would imply* that there is no survival after death—we can only assume that they will be even more farfetched than the alternatives that have already been thought up. This will literally be the case anyway, because in the search for new alternatives, people will have to look *farther* than they have until now.

Grossman wrote in his 2008 letter to the editor:

There is a big difference between a hypothesis that is merely logically possible (that is, a hypothesis that is not self-contradictory) and a hypothesis that is really possible (that is, a hypothesis for which there are empirical reasons to believe it might be true). Of course, any real possibility must also be a logical possibility, but the converse is not true. The fact that a given hypothesis is logically possible, that is, is not self-contradictory, is not a reason to believe that it is a real possibility, that is, that it might be true. Science is concerned only with real possibilities, not with merely logical possibilities.

We know of Grossman's work mainly thanks to the work of author Chris Carter. Carter himself made the following relevant statement in this context in an online interview with Jime Sayaka in 2013:

Chris Carter

Materialism *as a scientific hypothesis* makes two bold and admirable predictions: psychic abilities such as telepathy do not exist; and we will find no convincing evidence that the mind can operate without a properly functioning brain. But both of these predictions have been violated again and again, by evidence that stands up to the most severe critical scrutiny. Hence, it is unscientific to continue to believe in materialism. Those who do so are either ignorant of the evidence, or have ideological motivations.

Naturally, people should at all times remain tolerant of those who think differently. This principle applies to us just as much as it does to our intellectual opponents.[2] But we do not have to accept it when arguments for survival are intentionally misrepresented to make it seem as if the proponents are driven primarily by irrational motives, such as a fear of death, rather than by thoughtful, rational argumentation.

MORTALITY AS THE BASIS OF A MEANINGFUL LIFE?

Some opponents of the theory of survival after the death of the body go even a step further in their challenge. They argue that a spiritual survival of death cannot even be termed a positive concept because the value of human life, according

---

2. Respect for those who think differently, or pluralism, can be distinguished from relativism. A relativist considers all views to be equal, whereas a pluralist can persist in believing in the truth or superiority of the pluralist's own theory. Pluralistic respect is based on a belief in the equality of people and their intellectual freedom, not on an assumed equality of theories. This is why a pluralist can intellectually attack a theory without denying opponents the right to continue adhering to that theory.

to them, depends on its mortality. This thought is popular among materialistic humanists because it appears to offer comfort in the face of death and in fact seems to turn the terrifying notion of a final demise into something meaningful. From a dispassionate perspective, this theory is just as implausible as the idea that the value of peace can exist only if war also continues to exist, or that love is worthwhile only if people simultaneously continue to hate others.

In reality, existence is precisely the basis for everything that is valuable and worthwhile in someone's life. If existence were to be truly and finally ended, that would mean that death is coupled with the destruction of all that is valuable and worthwhile (in that life; only a legacy would continue to exist in the lives of others). The value of someone's life, as such, thus depends on the continuance of life and not at all on its destruction.

The mistake that materialists make in their thinking in this context is what is called a *category error,* meaning that they confuse the *conceptual* relationships between opposing concepts (existence and nonexistence) with a *factual* dependence of phenomena on their opposite.

PERSONAL SURVIVAL

Assuming survival after death, is it then plausible to conclude that it will be *personal* survival? We get the impression that some authors are unnecessarily uncertain on this point. The (possibly enhanced) consciousness during cardiac arrest with a flat EEG is by definition a *personal* consciousness, considering that the person who is undergoing the conscious experiences is the same one who undergoes everyday waking consciousness. Actually, it is also hard to grasp purely logically how anyone could have conscious experiences that would not immediately be his or her own personal, conscious experiences. In this context, there is no need for the concept of a "higher self," for instance, considering that the individual (the self) who undergoes the NDE is the same person who experiences earthly consciousness. In this sense, NDEs are not "transpersonal" experiences—in the sense of positing a transcendent, higher "Self"—but rather fully *personal* experiences.[3] Unless, that is, the concept of "person" is per se materialistically defined or defined in an "Aristotelian" manner as an inseparable unity of body and mind. But then, such definitions are precisely the topic of discussion here. The person is clearly a psychic unity that may or may not be coupled to a physical body (incarnated). NDEs do transcend the physical (they

---

3. We are aware of other meanings of the term "transpersonal," for instance as it is used within "transpersonal psychology," but here we are using it only in this specific, limited sense.

are "transphysical," if you will) but do not transcend the personal, considering they are always the experiences of a person.

We have just referred to a person as being a psychic unity, so it is pertinent here to remind readers that the root of the term "psychology" is "psyche," meaning the breath of life or life force, the soul, the intangible self—and that psychology originally meant the study of that force or motivator in individual thought and behavior, and in conscious and unconscious processes. The psyche is therefore basically the personal mind in its broadest sense.

In a wider context, *all* the paranormal phenomena in this book already point to a personal consciousness or psyche that possesses characteristics that do not stem from the physical body. In that respect, the psychic functioning of the personal mind exceeds the boundaries of the brain, and this characteristic makes it convincing from the start that that mind will survive brain death at least as far as these aspects are concerned.

Evidence for Personal Survival From Apparent Contact With Deceased Persons (Chapters 5 and 6)

In the previous major section, we considered the evidence for personal survival from consciousness during cardiac arrest (Chapter 3). Here we consider evidence for personal survival from apparent contact with deceased persons (Chapters 5 and 6). Obviously, evidence for communication with somebody who has already died is implicitly evidence for personal survival in a spiritual world. After all, someone can only really be communicated with directly if that person still exists.

In some spiritual circles, people occasionally come up with alternative models for this kind of phenomenon. They do not doubt the paranormal nature of such experiences and consider them, as we do, strong indications against the materialistic view of human life. However, these individuals do not assume personal survival after death, so there cannot be any real communication with deceased persons. Instead, they propose a kind of universal field of consciousness—that may or may not be divine—into which all conscious beings are taken up immediately after their death and into which they completely dissolve. This universal field is supposed to contain all possible information about reality, including all the thoughts, feelings, and desires each human being has. Based on this notion, the field supposedly triggers images of people who have died whom individuals would like to see again, thus satisfying each person's personal expectations. We see something akin to this conceptualization in the

1997 science fiction film *Contact*, starring Jodie Foster, in which an extraterrestrial being takes on the form of her character's beloved late father.

In principle, a theory of universal consciousness that would create chimeras to fulfill human expectations might explain a number of experiences. However, this reasoning definitely does not apply to the veridical cases in Chapters 5 and 6. Why not? Chapter 5 is not about NDErs longing to see a specific person who died, because the NDErs never knew the deceased to begin with. Regarding the NDErs who encounter a known person not known to have died from Chapter 6, there is no question of wish fulfillment because the NDErs were not aware of the death of the person who appeared to them. We can certainly argue, regarding Case 6.1, that chance is sufficiently ruled out.

We can imagine that a postulated universal field of consciousness meets people's wishes to be put at ease. However, in our view, to assume that such a field would intentionally create chimeras that do not even correspond with the wishes or expectations of the NDEr is going too far. This rationale is why we do not consider this alternative explanation to be a serious contestant for the theory that people actually can communicate with deceased persons during their NDEs.

Some investigators then claim that the NDEr might have caught telepathic messages from dying loved ones *prior* to their death without realizing this on a conscious level. The NDEr would subsequently have unconsciously processed these messages in the form of images of those loved ones after their loved ones died. The assumed motive of NDErs to see images of loved ones during their NDEs would depend on assuming unconscious telepathic contact prior to the deaths of the persons involved.

The following point can be brought to bear against this argument. Telepathic contact with a dying person must involve the process of dying and the medical circumstances that can lead to death. There are, in fact—beyond the context of paranormal NDEs—known cases of telepathy involving a death that contain only information about the process of dying. It is even conceivable that a person might telepathically catch this information unconsciously at first, and only after some delay, receive it on a conscious level if the deceased died in the meantime. Encounters with a known person not known to have died, however, do not involve (information about) someone else's *process of dying* but are specifically about the fact that that other person was *already dead* when he or she was perceived. The images are consequently often positive and loving—not awful, as can be the case with images of the process of dying. This situation is therefore not comparable. A more complicated hypothesis would be required, namely, that the NDEr unconsciously catches on to the fact that someone is dying and unconsciously processes this fact in a kind of hallucination of the deceased during the NDE in order to be reassured that that deceased person is still there. We find this hypothesis just plain too complex to really take seriously as an explanation for cases involving encounters with a known person not known to have died.

In our view, this kind of complex alternative hypothesis would become important only if the proposition that living persons can communicate with the dead had been precluded. As far as this point goes, a clear parallel can be drawn with the explanation for indications of paranormal perceptions in general. Materialistic skeptics will *always* prefer extremely complex normal explanations to, say, true telepathy and clairvoyance, because in their worldview, there simply is not any room for actual extrasensory perception. These complex, farfetched, standard explanations are important only if we first share the skeptics' conviction that it is all but certain that extrasensory perception does not exist. If it *does* exist, then there is no reason to take these farfetched, complex, standard explanations seriously, either. Nor is there any reason to dwell on farfetched hypotheses that do not assume survival of or communication with individuals who have died, unless of course the existence of these phenomena is already considered to have been virtually precluded.

In fact, scholars who take paranormal phenomena seriously due to the lack of plausible materialistic explanations for the evidence, but who do not accept that there are indications for survival after death, should explain this point, too, either by clarifying why an explanation of relevant concrete evidence that does not assume survival is plausible, or by clarifying why the very existence of (particular manifestations of) survival itself should practically be precluded.

In our opinion, opponents should guard against circular thinking. They run the risk of rejecting, out of hand, strong indications of a phenomenon that does not fit into their worldview, because they assume in advance that such indications do not exist. We believe this matter is not only about a clash between basically comparable theories. We are genuinely convinced that NDEs actually point to the reality of personal survival and contact with people who have died and that alternative hypotheses are not sufficiently plausible. So we think that an agnostic position, according to which scholars and others are at some sort of impasse because all theories are equally convincing in and of themselves, has no merit.

The theory of personal survival after death can be further developed and refined using evidence involving NDEs and related fields of investigation, such as spontaneous recollections of previous lifetimes in young children, preexistence memories of a spiritual world, deathbed visions, or communication (outside of an NDE) with those who have died. Cardiologist and researcher Pim van Lommel (2010) has referred to this accumulation of data from related fields as a convergence of evidence pointing to the survival of consciousness after death (Carman & Carman, 2013; Rawat & Rivas, 2007; Rivas, 2010).

Then there are some scholars who consider the theory of personal survival to be utterly "unfalsifiable" (irrefutable). This line of reasoning is misleading. The theory happens to be based on the falsification of the hypothesis put forward by materialists and some parapsychologists that there is no such thing as personal survival. Once that hypothesis has been convincingly disproved by the evidence, the theory that there *is* such a thing as personal survival can no longer be falsified by putative evidence for the thesis that the brain produces the mind. (Complex alternative hypotheses to replace personal survival, as proposed by Michael Sudduth, are only relevant in this context if those hypotheses themselves are refutable. So we are assuming that they are, in fact, and moreover that they have already been refuted convincingly enough.) This is not to say that the theory of survival is therefore unfalsifiable by evidence in all respects. The theory has to be further developed and concretized using falsifiable hypotheses, such as hypotheses about contact after death and the way that contact takes place, for instance.

RELIGIOUS ELEMENTS IN NDES

Some critics argue that NDEs certainly cannot be a glimpse of the hereafter because they contradict one another too much for that to be the case. For example, people with different religious or spiritual backgrounds may see images that differ radically from one another. A conservative Christian may have a vision of a traditional hell where everybody goes who does not accept Jesus Christ as their Lord and Savior. An orthodox Jew may get to see a reality in which the consequences of *mitzvot* (religious precepts) largely determine the degree of happiness after death. Asian NDEs may contain encounters with gods and other spiritual beings from Hindu or Buddhist belief systems.

This problem arises, however, only if all the impressions of the hereafter from every NDE are viewed as objective characteristics of that hereafter. As religious studies professor Lewis Stafford Betty (2006) suggested (largely following Bruce Greyson's lead), this interpretation is not the only possible one. According to him, NDEs consist of an interaction between actual contact with a spiritual world and elements from the patient's own unconscious mind. These elements may be used by the spiritual world in the way in which it manifests itself, but they may also lead to (sometimes serious) aberrations in perception. This process might be compared to combining paranormal impressions with content from the personal unconscious in telepathic dreams. The religious elements may be a component of the experience after death (and be "objective" in the sense that after death, people can really have experiences like that), but the religious elements do not necessarily reveal the objective organization of the spiritual world.

IMPLICATIONS FOR THE EXISTENCE OF AN IRREDUCIBLE PSYCHE

NDEs during clinical death indicate more generally that the patient's personal mind is not limited to his or her conscious experiences but also includes such aspects as memory and personality. In other words, these NDEs point to the existence of a nonphysical psyche or soul that does not coincide with neural patterns of activity in the brain. In this sense, such NDEs lead to conclusions that dovetail with *substance dualism*, or substantialist dualism, in the philosophy of mind.[4] Proponents of this form of dualism argue not only that there are conscious experiences that are irreducible to the physical brain but also that there is a completely personal "inner" domain, a personal soul or psyche, that is sharply distinct (and ultimately separate) from the brain. This psyche contains all possible impressions, thoughts, feelings, and desires, as well as a memory in which recollections can be stored—even while the brain shows no neurological activity.[5]

Philosophers of mind are familiar with what is called the *binding problem*. How is it possible that experiences involving different parts of the brain get

---

4. Within the worldview of ontological idealists, who reject the existence of physical reality, there is obviously also room for a personal soul.

5. Materialists like Gerald Woerlee tend to argue that an NDE can be remembered only if someone's cortex was still sufficiently active during that NDE. Otherwise the memory, in the brain, would not be up to registering NDEs, so nobody would be able to remember such an NDE during a flat EEG. This argument becomes interesting only if the existence of the psyche's memory, not "embodied" in the brain, were to be ruled out on purely logical grounds beforehand. Based on the evidence in this book, the theory of a neurological memory, in which experiences are literally stored in the brain, itself has to be reconsidered. Probably only neurophysiological patterns are registered in the brain, and when somebody remembers something, the activation of those patterns interacts with the psyche's actual memory.

integrated into human consciousness? Materialists these days usually look for an answer in a functional integration of neuronal patterns but without any anatomical counterpart. This answer cannot stand up in light of the evidence for consciousness in the clinically dead patients in Chapter 3.

In the opening chapter, the authors of the book *Beyond Physicalism* stated, in Edward Kelly's words:

> Indeed, contemporary physicalism has crystallized neurophysiologically in the form of a family of "global neuronal workspace" theories, all of which make the central claim that conscious experience occurs specifically—and only—in conjunction with large-scale patterns of oscillatory neuroelectric activity capable of linking widely separated areas of the brain at frequencies extending into the gamma band. . . .
>
> The neurophysiological global workspace, however, cannot be the whole story, because a large body of recent research on "near-death experiences" (NDEs) demonstrates that elaborate, vivid, and life-transforming conscious experience sometimes occurs under extreme physiological conditions—including conditions such as deep general anesthesia, cardiac arrest, and coma—that *preclude* normal workspace operation (Kelly, 2015, pp. 21–22).

In other words, the unity of personal consciousness cannot result from a functional integration by the brain. It must be an inherent quality of the irreducible psyche itself.

Moreover, such experiences show that this psyche not only is irreducible to neurological processes but also can function mentally. This ability means that during physical life the psyche is not merely a powerless "epiphenomenon" (side effect) of the brain but plays an active, generative role in human consciousness. Once again, authors such as Mario Beauregard (2012) have brought to bear a convergence of evidence from not only NDEs but also a variety of other phenomena in support of this conclusion.

We obviously realize that the idea of an irreducible psyche, independent in the ultimate sense, is contrary to the worldview of many contemporary Western intellectuals. This conclusion on our part certainly does not mean, though, that we want to turn our backs on reason or empirical science. It is precisely within the context of rational thought that the materialistic worldview should be abandoned, based on the kind of cases that are addressed in this book (as well as other parapsychological evidence and, obviously, analytical, philosophical argumentation). The materialistic worldview should be replaced by a coherent worldview that is consistent with all the ascertained facts. In a new theoretical framework, there would be more leeway for investigating all kinds of aspects of psychology that are hardly, if at all, addressed in the current paradigm. We would then finally arrive at a fruitful science of the psyche or personal soul that deviates in crucial respects from current, mainstream psychology (Mays & Mays, 2008; Rivas, 2006; Rivas & van Dongen, 2003).

In Conclusion

NDEs are, as a rule, dismissed by materialists as nothing more than the last spasms of a dying brain. Skeptics are open to almost all the dimensions and aspects of NDEs and, bizarrely enough, can even consider them to be the ultimate source of creativity, mythology, and spirituality. Some of them think NDEs are "gripping," "beautiful," and "fascinating" and pretend to utterly respect, from the outset, the NDEr's personal experience.

There is only one aspect that skeptics do not want to acknowledge—namely, the (actual) paranormal experiences that can arise in connection with NDEs. Obviously, skeptics are ready to accept that people *think* they have really gone through a paranormal experience, but skeptics then zealously attempt to demonstrate that the NDEr is always and without exception mistaken about this experience. For these skeptics, this "domino" may not fall, because then the game is up with the credibility of materialism as a thought context.

In our view, the collection of cases we present in this book demonstrates that skeptics are very mistaken on precisely this point. What is more, from our point of view, paranormal experiences are precisely what make NDEs so important. Without the parapsychological aspects, NDEs, no matter how moving, would only be remarkable subjective experiences during an altered state of consciousness. With paranormal aspects, they have far-reaching implications for humanity's self-image and worldview and therefore also for the way we feel about and face life. Accepting such paranormal aspects does not constitute a return to dogmatic religions but, instead, frees us mentally, on rational grounds, not only from any disadvantages of a materialistic worldview but also from being bound by religious or philosophical presumptions and intolerance.

Moreover, other aspects of NDEs, such as spiritual experiences and altered insights with respect to norms and values, also become more interesting as soon as NDEs are accepted as more than some kind of ultimate dream. Paranormal phenomena during NDEs thus provide a key to possible implications of these experiences for our philosophy of the world.

References

Atwater, P. M. H. (2003). *The new children and near-death experiences.* Rochester, VT: Bear.

Beauregard, M. (2007). Mind does really matter: Evidence from neuroimaging studies of emotional self-regulation, psychotherapy, and placebo effect. *Progress in Neurobiology, 81*(4), 218–236.

Beauregard, M. (2012). *Brain wars: The scientific battle over the existence of the human mind and the proof that will change the way we live our lives.* New York, NY: HarperCollins.

Betty, L. S. (2006). Are they hallucinations or are they real? The spirituality of deathbed and near-death visions. *Omega, 53*(1–2), 37–49.

Braithwaite, J. J., & Dewe, H. (2013). Occam's chainsaw: Neuroscientific nails in the coffin of dualist notions of the near-death experience (NDE). *The Skeptic [UK magazine], 25*(2), 24–30. Retrieved from http://www.academia.edu/10060970/Occams_Chainsaw_Neuroscientific_Nails_in_the_coffin_of_dualist_notions_of_the_Near-death_experience_NDE_

Braude, S. E. (2003). *Immortal remains: The evidence for life after death.* Lanham, MD: Rowman & Littlefield.

Braude, S. E. (2009). Perspectival awareness and postmortem survival. *Journal of Scientific Exploration, 23*(2), 195–210.

Carman, E. M., & Carman, N. J. (2013). *Cosmic cradle: Spiritual dimensions of life before birth.* Berkeley, CA: North Atlantic Books.

Carter, C. (2010). *Science and the near-death experience: How consciousness survives death.* Rochester, VT: Inner Traditions.

Carter, C. (2012). *Science and the afterlife experience: Evidence for the immortality of consciousness.* Rochester, VT: Inner Traditions.

Cook, E. W., Greyson, B., & Stevenson, I. (1998). Do any near-death experiences provide evidence of the survival of human personality after death? Relevant features and illustrative case reports. *Journal of Scientific Exploration, 12*(3), 377–406.

Gauld, A. (1983). *Mediumship and survival: A century of investigations.* London, England: Paladin Books.

Grossman, N. (2002). Who's afraid of life after death? [Guest editorial]. *Journal of Near-Death Studies, 21*(1), 5–24.

Grossman, N. (2008). Letter to the editor: Four errors commonly made by professional debunkers. *Journal of Near-Death Studies, 26*(3), 227–235.

Holden, J. M. (2009). Veridical perception in near-death experiences. In J. M. Holden, B. Greyson, & D. James (Eds.), *The handbook of near-death experiences: Thirty years of investigation* (pp. 185–212). Santa Barbara, CA: Praeger/ABC-CLIO.

James, W. (1898). *Human immortality: Two supposed objections to the doctrine.* Ingersoll Lecture, 1897. Cambridge, MA: Riverside Press.

Kelly, E. F. (2015). Empirical challenges to theory construction. In E. F. Kelly, A. Crabtree, & P. Marshall (Eds.), *Beyond physicalism: Toward reconciliation of science and spirituality* (pp. 3–38). Lanham, MD: Rowman & Littlefield.

Kelly, E. W., Greyson, B., & Stevenson, I. (2000). Can experiences near death furnish evidence of life after death? *OMEGA-Journal of Death and Dying, 40*(4), 513–519.

Lund, D. H. (1985). *Death and Consciousness.* Jefferson, NC: McFarland.

Lund, D. H. (2009). *Persons, souls, and death: A philosophical investigation of an afterlife.* Jefferson, NC: McFarland.

Martin, M., & Augustine, K. (Eds.). (2015). *The myth of an afterlife: The case against life after death.* Lanham, MD: Rowman & Littlefield.

Mays, R. G., & Mays, S. B. (2008). The phenomenology of the self-conscious mind. *Journal of Near-Death Studies, 27*(1), 5–45.

Moody, R. A., Jr. (with Perry, P.). (2010). *Glimpses of eternity: An investigation into shared death experiences.* New York, NY: Guideposts.

Musolino, J. (2015). *The soul fallacy: What science shows we gain from letting go of our soul beliefs.* Amherst, NY: Prometheus Books.

Rawat, K. S., & Rivas, T. (2007). *Reincarnation: The evidence is building.* Vancouver, BC: Writers Publisher.

Ring, K., & Cooper, S. (1999). *Mindsight: Near-death and out-of-body experiences in the blind.* Palo Alto, CA: William James Center for Consciousness Studies at the Institute of Transpersonal Psychology (2008; 2nd ed.). Bloomington, IN: iUniverse.

Rivas, T. (2003). The survivalist interpretation of recent studies into the near-death experience. *Journal of Religion and Psychical Research, 26*(1), 27–31.

Rivas, T. (2004). *Neuropsychology and personalist dualism: A few remarks.* New Dualism Archive, September/October 2004. Retrieved from http://www.new dualism.org/papers/T.Rivas/Dualismlives.htm

Rivas, T. (2006). Metasubjective cognition beyond the brain: Subjective awareness and the location of concepts of consciousness. *Journal of Non-Locality and Remote Mental Interactions, IV*(1). Retrieved from http://txtxs.nl/artikel.asp?artid=645

Rivas, T. (2010). Is it rational to extrapolate from the presence of consciousness during a flat EEG to survival of consciousness after death? *Journal of Near-Death Studies, 29*(2), 355–361.

Rivas, T., & van Dongen, H. (2003). Exit epiphenomenalism: The demolition of a refuge. *Journal of Non-Locality and Remote Mental Interactions, II*(1). Retrieved from http://txtxs.nl/artikel.asp?artid=624

Rousseau, D. (2012). The implications of near-death experiences for research into the survival of consciousness. *Journal of Scientific Exploration, 26*(1), 43–80.

Sudduth, M. (2009). Super-psi and the survivalist interpretation of mediumship. *Journal of Scientific Exploration, 23*(2), 167–193.

Sudduth, M. (2016). *A philosophical critique of empirical arguments for postmortem survival*. New York, NY: Palgrave Macmillan.

Tart, C. T. (2009). *The end of materialism: How evidence of the paranormal is bringing science and spirit together*. Oakland, CA: New Harbinger.

van Lommel, P. (2010). *Consciousness beyond life: The science of near-death experiences*. New York, NY: HarperCollins.

Woerlee, G. M. (2013a). *Illusory souls* [Kindle ed.]. Amazon Digital Services: Author.

CHAPTER 11

How Skeptics Attempt to Explain Away Near-Death Experiences . . . and Fail

Rudolf H. Smit

I fully expect to see the pragmatist view of truth run through the classic stages
of a theory's career. First, you know, a new theory is attacked as absurd; then
it is admitted to be true, but obvious and insignificant; finally it is seen to be
so important that its adversaries claim that they themselves discovered it.
—William James, *Pragmatism: A New Name*
for Some Old Ways of Thinking

In the preceding chapters, we have responded a number of times to arguments that skeptics have put forward to explain near-death experience (NDE) phenomena—or rather *to explain them away*. To conclude this book, we will closely consider a number of their arguments.

Although we welcome a healthy and sound skepticism, we find it unfortunate to conclude that in the skeptical movement we have found a tendency toward an approach based foremost on ideology—namely, the monistic materialistic paradigm—rather than following the evidence to wherever it may lead. Quite often it has been obvious to us that those critics appeared incorrectly informed about NDE phenomena and also that they seemed unwilling to inform themselves better—which we find inexcusable for people who purport to be seeking truth. It also is sad to note that such critics have tended to resort to disrespectful treatment of NDErs as well as NDE researchers. For example, following is the message prominent Dutch skeptic (and CSICOP Fellow) Jan Willem Nienhuys (PhD in mathematics) posted on February 7, 2011, to a blog of the Dutch Skepsis organization:

> I find it quite understandable that people who have experienced an NDE after or during a very serious illness are impressed by it, but that has little to

do with religion. I can better identify with Einstein who, after he had been outside and contemplated the cosmos, was overwhelmed with awe, than with people who attach so much value to something that ultimately does not differ from dreams and chemical hallucinations, *and hence who have a loose screw in their head.* [emphasis added]

A more recent 2016 statement about NDEs, posted by an anonymous participant to a Dutch blog, was just as clearly dismissive: "Het is doodgewoon doorgedraaide fantasie over hallucinaties" (It is nothing but a worn out fantasy about hallucinations.)

Indeed, William James's (1907, p. 198) description of the three stages through which truth passes on its journey to widespread social acceptance is as valid today as when he offered it more than a century ago. The current tone of debate regarding acceptance of the validity of NDEs points clearly to the conclusion that society is now in the first stage: The more prominent NDEs become as a serious object of scientific study, the more intently they are disparaged by those who wish to maintain the status quo of philosophical materialism. The contents that follow in this chapter will amply support this conclusion.

Negativity in any field does a great disservice to the individuals, the discoveries, and the research involved. Nevertheless, we feel it is important to provide readers with a better sense of the emotionally charged atmosphere to which NDE research and researchers are exposed, and we could think of no better and more positive illustration than by devoting a few pages to the very controversial case of neurosurgeon Eben Alexander. When we wrote the Dutch version of this book, we did not include his case because it contained few independently verified observations confirming the phenomena he had presented. That situation has now changed due to the good work of Robert and Suzanne Mays, who have since received information that corroborates certain statements that Dr. Alexander made. Because the material in this chapter includes some technical medical terms, we have included a glossary of many of those terms at the end of the book.

Eben Alexander's Controversial Book *Proof of Heaven*

Toward the end of 2012, a book appeared on the American market that quickly rose to the top of the *New York Times* bestsellers list (Alexander, 2012). At the same time, it provoked strong negative reactions among the mainstream scientific

Eben Alexander III, MD
Photo: Deborah Feingold

community. That reaction is not surprising in view of the title: *Proof of Heaven*. The author, Eben Alexander III, MD, is a brain surgeon whose background boasts the experience of many years in the operating room. Not only was he educated at Harvard Medical School, but he has taught prospective surgeons at that same institution. Further, he is a scientist in his own right, with an outstanding research record and a truly impressive list of scientific publications that he has authored or coauthored. It is an understatement to say that he is not just an ordinary but rather an outstanding authority in his rarified field.

He acknowledged in *Proof of Heaven* that as a physician he had heard of near-death experiences, but based on the way he had been taught, he had never paid much attention to them. He said he would not have made much fuss if a patient had told him about having had such an experience; instead, he would have given the patient a friendly pat on the shoulder, quickly moving on to the next patient.

But something happened to him that completely overturned his views on NDEs and changed his life forever.

ALEXANDER'S BACTERIAL MENINGITIS

One morning in the fall of 2008, Alexander woke up with a terrible headache, which quickly got worse—much worse. His wife and sons became extremely worried and wanted him to go straight to the hospital. He refused, hoping his headache would go away. But it did not go away, and finally he was rushed to the emergency room. By the time he arrived, he appeared to have lapsed into a coma; his doctors' diagnosis was bacterial meningitis. This was terrible news for his wife and sons, because that disease is fatal in 9 out of 10 cases. In the rare event that a bacterial meningitis patient does survive, he or she usually recovers only partially, "even with proper treatment, with long-term disabilities, including deafness, seizures, paralysis, blindness or loss of limbs" (Martinez-Alier, 2010). Alexander's prospects were bleak indeed.

As the days passed, Alexander's situation only got worse, with not a trace of improvement. His coma remained deep. After six days, the doctors presented his family with a horrible choice: whether or not to pull the plug. Then something happened that can only be viewed as a medical miracle: He suddenly awoke and looked quite attentively at the people at his bedside.

His awakening caused an enormous shock. His family and the hospital staff crowded in to see for themselves that Alexander had regained consciousness. They could also see that he was hampered by something. The doctor in charge saw the problem and removed the respiration tube from the patient's mouth. For just a moment, Alexander gasped for breath. Then he said, loudly and clearly, "All is well," and then, "Don't worry . . . all is well." And finally, he asked a question aimed at all around him, "What are you doing here?" Whereupon one of them riposted, "What are *you* doing here?"

In the days that followed, Alexander recovered quickly, to the great joy of his family and his doctors. Yet not everything went smoothly. There were moments of confusion, hallucinations, weird behavior, and a not-surprising loss of memory of the days just before his illness struck. Those symptoms were diagnosed as indications of intensive care psychosis—not uncommon in such circumstances.

Despite those symptoms, he recovered completely, and by examining the CT scans of his own brain and other medical data relevant to his case, he was made aware of the very unusual trial he had endured. The scans showed that the spaces between his brain and his cranium, and also the spaces around the folds of his brain, had completely filled with pus caused by his meningitis. It remains an enigma how he survived at all.

Yet what was more significant to him than his medical condition was the very profound experience he had undergone during his coma, the memories of which dawned on him bit by bit. It was a near-death experience of a clarity and beauty that he, like so many NDErs, could hardly describe. His son advised him to write down every detail he could recall before he started to read external sources about the NDE phenomenon. One idea dominated: the fact that his miraculous experience in deep coma was "ultrareal," exceptionally real, or as so many of those who have described their NDEs have expressed it, "realer than real."

ALEXANDER'S NDE

As he recovered more access to his experience, he remembered finding himself surrounded in darkness—a visible, murky, but translucent sort of darkness. He was aware of himself as a person, as someone with consciousness, but without memory or self-identity, as in a dream when you know what is happening around you, yet have no idea who or what you are. He just *was*, without a physical body—although initially he was not aware of that.

Then there was a great change: From the darkness above, a spinning, white-gold light approached, and slowly the thick darkness around him shattered and dispersed. He noticed that the monotonous drone that had surrounded him until then was gradually replaced by the most beautiful music one could ever experience. In the center of that light, an opening appeared, growing into a passage to another world; without hesitation, he moved into it—through the passage and into the most wonderful, most beautiful world he had ever seen. It was as if he had been born again into this glorious world—or rather, not born again, but simply *born*.

Spread out below him lay a beautiful landscape, luxuriantly, verdantly green. It was Earth, yet it was somewhere else. He glided over trees and fields, over streams and rivers and waterfalls, and here and there he saw men, women, and happily playing children. It was an indescribably wonderful world, as if in a magnificent dream. Except . . . it was not a dream. He realized that this world he had entered so suddenly was real—the real world, truly real.

All of a sudden he noticed that he was not alone; he was flying on one wing of a huge butterfly, and on the other wing perched a beautiful young woman. She spoke to him, but without using words: *Here you are loved and cherished forever. You have nothing to fear. There is nothing that you can do wrong. We will show you many things, but eventually, you will go back.*

And indeed, he did return—but with his worldview turned upside down by his "realer than real" experience.

That recollection of his revelation was followed by a time of deep doubt, when he struggled with his feelings and everything he had learned about the human body and about death. As he himself told readers in *Proof of Heaven*:

> Remember who is talking to you right now. I'm not a soft-headed senti-mentalist. I know what death looks like. I know what it feels like to have a living person, whom you spoke to and joked with in better days, become a lifeless object on an operating table after you have struggled for hours to keep the machine of their body working. I know what suffering looks like, and the answerless grief on the faces of loved ones who have lost someone they never dreamed they could lose. I know my biology, and while I am not a physicist, I am no slouch at that, either. I know the difference between fantasy and reality, and I know that the experience I am struggling to give

you the vaguest, most completely unsatisfactory picture of, was the single most real experience of my life. (p. 41)

INTELLECTUAL STRUGGLE

Now his distinguished background as a physician and scientist was his greatest obstacle. For months he struggled with the question of what could have been the medical cause of his experience. He thoroughly studied all the medical facts of his case, discussing them at great length with the specialists who had treated him, and he read everything he could find about the NDE phenomenon—literature he never had found reason to consult before his experience. In short, he had developed no a priori beliefs about NDEs before he had one. More and more he found himself forced to lean toward considering his experience too real to be merely the rich hallucination of a dying brain. In contrast to what his fellow professionals maintained, he could argue based on the medical data of his case that his brain had "fully shut down." Therefore, he could conclude only that this particular experience of consciousness had been theoretically impossible.

He did not explain to his readers the medical technicalities of "how" and "why" it should not have happened, because such a discussion would have involved a technical analysis incomprehensible to most of them. But one medical fact he did emphasize was the minute amount of glucose that had been measured in his cerebral fluid: "The amount of glucose in my cerebral fluid, which normally should be 60–80 milligrams per 100 milliliters and in the case of severe meningitis 20, had dropped down to 1 milligram per 100 milliliters." This datum is crucially important simply because brains run on glucose; in fact, it is their only source of energy. Glucose, also called dextrose, is the most important energy source for the entire body. This fact, plus the information that his meningitis had progressed to such an extremely advanced stage, led him to say, "I cannot tell you how close to death I have been, because of the damage to my entire neo-cortex." (See the schematic diagram of the brain, Note 1.)

In short, it was as clear as it could be that in such a condition no brain could function properly.

But then, where did that hyperrealistic, thoroughly coherent experience come from? Was it indeed a totally transcendent phenomenon, an out-of-body experience of the kind so many NDErs want humanity to believe in? Or was it a hallucination, however vivid and peculiar? He was far from sure about how he should understand it.

The certainty he sought was provided to him in a very unexpected way by the very woman who had accompanied him during his trip through that celestial realm.

ALEXANDER'S CONNECTION WITH HIS BIOLOGICAL RELATIVES

Delving into Alexander's personal history reveals that he became an adoptee at 4 months of age. Throughout most of his life, all he knew of his birth parents was that they were very young and unmarried when they gave him away. It was something Alexander thought about very little until the year 2000, when his youngest son participated in a genealogical project about his family, which involved Alexander willy-nilly in the search for his biological roots. He discovered that his birth parents had married and had another three children: two girls and a boy. Via an intermediary, he learned from his oldest biological sister that their youngest sister had died in 1998. His birth parents were still in deep mourning and did not want Alexander to contact them. Alexander experienced this rebuff as a strong rejection that continued to rankle him in the years that followed.

In 2007, he again sought contact, and this time his eldest biological sister responded positively. At last in October of that year, and just about a year before his nearly fatal meningitis, Alexander met with his birth parents and his siblings Kathy and David. He received a warm reception. They also told him the name of his biological sister who had died in 1998: Betsy. Sister Kathy promised to send him a picture of Betsy, which she actually did 4 months after Alexander had been released from the hospital.

When he thoroughly examined Betsy's picture, recognition came like a bolt from the blue: The young woman who had accompanied him through the celestial realm on the wings of a giant butterfly was the exact likeness of Betsy, the biological sister he had never known, whose image he had never seen until a few months after his illness.

THAT SETTLED IT

To him, that settled the matter. His experience had been "realer than real": He had been "in the beyond," period. As he wrote in *Proof of Heaven*:

Eben Alexander's sister Betsy

I know there will be people who will seek to invalidate my experience anyhow, and many who will discount it out of court because of a refusal to believe that what I underwent could possibly be "scientific"—could possibly be anything more than a crazy, feverish dream. (p. 170)

How true this prophecy would turn out to be.

But Alexander was now completely convinced; in that sense he had made a U-turn. From his prior philosophical position as a materialist skeptical denier of life after death, he had now found reason for absolute certainty that personal consciousness does not vanish when the body dies but rather continues its existence while departing into a different dimension . . . call it heaven. That conviction caused him to change his life. Now he travels all over the world, delivering one lecture after the other, appearing on television—all to spread the unambiguous message that life does not end when the body dies. He succinctly summarized his opinion about neuroscience in the title of the lecture he delivered at the 2011 Conference of the International Association for Near-Death Studies (IANDS), "Childhood's End," whereby he compared his previous extensive knowledge of neuroscience—which, prior to his NDE, seemed like the totality of information on the topic of the brain and mind—to a naïve childhood from which, thanks to his NDE, he had now grown up.

Up to that time he had been ignored by his fellow neurosurgeons, neurologists, and neurobiologists—and by mainstream science in general. That situation changed in the fall of 2012, shortly after *Proof of Heaven* was published, when *Newsweek* magazine devoted the cover story of its October 15 issue to Alexander and his proof of heaven (Alexander, 2012, October 15). Pandemonium broke out, and a swarm of skeptics drew their knives and began slashing away at Alexander's contentions.

A BARRAGE OF INTEMPERATE CRITICISM

Although Alexander's comatose NDE had occurred in the fourth quarter of 2008, it was only years later that he shared his story publicly. Though he told his story in 2011 in the TV series *Through the Wormhole* (Freeman & Andreae,

2011), it was hardly a breakthrough into the major media. Then, a few months before the book was published, media interest began to build, leading up to the cover story in *Newsweek*. The *Newsweek* coverage brought huge publicity and positive responses from thousands of people who perceived in his story a message of hope—but it also incurred the wrath of skeptics whose criticism knew no bounds. Take Steven Novella, a neuroscientist and enthusiastic blogger, as well as a member of the board of the Committee for Skeptical Inquiry (CSI, formerly the notorious CSICOP). Following is his commentary from his October 11, 2012, blog:

> Alexander, in my opinion, has failed to be true to the scientist he claims that he is. He did not step back from his powerful experience and ask dispassionate questions. Instead he concluded that his experience was unique, that it is proof of heaven, and that it defies any possible scientific explanation. He then goes on to give a hand-waving quantum mechanics, the universe is all unity, explanation for the supernatural. This is a failure of scientific and critical thinking. Addressing his one major unstated premise, that the experience occurred while his cortex was inactive, demolishes his claims and his interpretation of his experience. The Harvard neurosurgeon presents an absolute claim—scientifically impossible—and makes it sound as if science supports it. I suspect this will become the irrefutable evidence that many people make the central piece of their belief for an afterlife, and therefore the supernatural. It would be bad for it to go unchallenged.

Although Novella expressed himself with some restraint, it is his claims that have no ground in reality. Alexander had employed all his professional skills to gain a grasp of the medical hows and whys of his experience in his quest for a rational, scientific, materialist explanation for it. Novella would have been satisfied only by Alexander's admission that his entire experience had been "nothing but" an extensive hallucination evoked by his dying brain, presumably to spare him from a terrible agony. But Alexander remained faithful to his experience; it was impossible to belie himself, no matter how much he might have wanted to do so, if only to avoid the scorn of his fellow physicians and neuroscientists. That implicit blackmail did not shake his conviction or his determination to share his revelation.

Next it was the well-known neuroscientist and arch-skeptic Sam Harris, atheist, materialist, and author of books such as *The Moral Landscape*, who issued a very long and devastating attack on Alexander's article in *Newsweek*, as seen in this brief excerpt from his blog entry of October 12, 2012:

Everything—absolutely everything—in Alexander's account rests on repeated assertions that his visions of heaven occurred while his cerebral cortex was "shut down," "inactivated," "completely shut down," "totally offline," and "stunned to complete inactivity." The evidence he provides for this claim is not only inadequate—it suggests that he doesn't know anything about the relevant brain science. . . .

Let me suggest that, whether or not heaven exists, Alexander sounds precisely how a scientist should not sound when he doesn't know what he is talking about. And his article is not the sort of thing that the editors of a once-important magazine should publish if they hope to reclaim some measure of respect for their battered brand.

Harris also gave neuroscientist Mark Cohen space to add this remark:

As is obvious to you, this is truth by authority. Neurosurgeons, however, are rarely well-trained in brain function. Dr. Alexander cuts brains; he does not appear to study them.

On October 13, scientist and philosopher Bernardo Kastrup offered this succinct rejoinder in his comment on the above:

Now pause for a moment and read this quote again. The notion here is that Alexander, a practicing neurosurgeon and Professor at Harvard Medical School, does not understand what part of the brain does what, while he is hacking at people's brains every day. He supposedly does not understand what parts of the brain are correlated to confabulation, dreams, feelings, etc., yet he has a license to slice your brain if you so need. Maybe neurosurgeons are not doing research at the leading-edge of functional mapping, but *Alexander is most certainly well qualified to understand what parts of the brain should correlate to what kinds of experience. It is ludicrous to suggest otherwise.*

The bottom line is this: *Alexander not only has the scientific credentials required to interpret his experience properly, he also has the unique perspective of having had the experience himself, something Harris didn't.* It is Alexander that is in the best position to judge the situation, both from an empirical and from an academic background perspective.

Kastrup's response was criticized by philosopher Michael Sudduth in a blog entry titled "In Defense of Sam Harris on Near-Death Experiences" (Sudduth, 2015, December 21). Sudduth concluded that Kastrup misrepresented the position that Harris had adopted. According to Sudduth, Harris did not claim that Alexander's own nonmaterialist interpretation of his NDE was false but simply that, to date, Alexander had not provided sufficient evidence to substantiate this "extrasomatic" interpretation. Sudduth believed that Harris was correct on this point. In Sudduth's view, Alexander either should have published data from CT scans or neurological examinations or should at least have made his reasoning about cortical activity during his NDE more explicit.

Our own commentary on this matter is as follows. Maybe Sudduth has a point. Indeed, it would have been better if Alexander had written a thorough scientific paper about his experience, including all the data Sudduth referred to. But that omission on Alexander's part does not alter Harris's shameful claim that a neurosurgeon would not understand neuroscience. This claim is like asserting that a car mechanic has no real knowledge of cars simply because he has not designed them. This reasoning is reminiscent of the situation cardiologist Pim van Lommel, certainly Europe's leading NDE researcher, found himself in when he was reproached by his opponents for "knowing nothing of neuroscience"—as if after having mastered one branch of medical science (in this case, cardiology), it would be improper for him to want to know more about the human body (in this case, the brain). In fact, any physician has a general knowledge of the human body that far outdistances that of most laypersons.

With another skeptic, there is also little nuance:

My hypothesis is that [Eben Alexander] was a struggling neurosurgeon with alcohol and family-related troubles who contracted a rare disease and saw a way to make a lot of money by making up a story about an NDE. Much like Todd Burpo fabricated the book "Heaven is for Real" and became a millionaire. ("Weedar" on mind-energy.net, November 7, 2012)

Skeptics will continue to denounce the book for offering "false hope" and continue to bombard Alexander with attacks the viciousness of which borders on pure character assassination. Following is such a character assassination:

Quite honestly I think of [Eben Alexander] as someone of the worst kind. Purposefully preying on people who trust him, make them a prey of false hope and benefiting from it. For me he is a thief, or worse, who is preying on the most vulnerable. There is not much [in] this world which I think is worse than that. The only mitigating circumstance I can forward is the possibility that he is mentally ill, or mentally instable due to advanced age, or due to a sickness of his brain. (Holly S. Kennedy on Novella's blog, posted December 12, 2012)

Then there are those who have attributed to him a "narcissistic personality." Why? Among other things, because he always wears a bowtie.

A VICIOUS ARTICLE ABOUT ALEXANDER BY AN AWARD-WINNING JOURNALIST

These feeble but nonetheless mean attempts to damage Alexander's reputation were surpassed by a long and harshly critical article in *Esquire* magazine by Luke Dittrich (July 2, 2013).

Dittrich is the recipient of important journalism awards, suggesting that he is a fine journalist. Yet it seems that with this article he was doing his best to throw his reputation as an objective writer out the window. What happened?

After the publication of Alexander's article in *Newsweek* stirred up enormous controversy, Dittrich decided to find out all he could about the case, apparently with the aim to expose Alexander as a fraud. It is hard to surmise otherwise after having read the article that resulted from his "research," because the facts were so clearly concealed, distorted, or misrepresented. Robert Mays, NDE researcher and IANDS board member, scrutinized Dittrich's article and showed in a long rebuttal that Dittrich strayed off the right path, either deliberately or due to sheer sloppiness (Mays, 2013).

What now follows is a brief summary of Dittrich's distortions, provided for this book by Mays.

Intermezzo 1 (Summary From Robert Mays)

EBEN ALEXANDER AND *ESQUIRE* MAGAZINE

Luke Dittrich's long article "The Prophet" appeared in the July 2, 2013, issue of *Esquire*. In it, Dittrich tried to show that Eben Alexander's account of his near-death experience was full of embellishments and fabrications, pointing out three critical details of the story with serious factual errors. Dittrich also pointed to Alexander's record as a neurosurgeon with numerous malpractice lawsuits—including a case of altering a patient's records to cover a medical error—and being forced out of multiple jobs in neurosurgery.

Dittrich further pointed out that even His Holiness the Dalai Lama had seen through Alexander's fabrications and declared him a liar. So Dittrich concluded that Alexander's *Proof of Heaven*—featuring a beautiful girl on a butterfly wing—was fabricated out of hallucinations produced by a drug-induced coma to enable Alexander to elevate himself from a failed neurosurgeon to the new "Prophet of Heaven."

Dittrich's article presented a well-crafted case, one that *Esquire*'s editor-in-chief called "great journalism." The trouble is that we found it was full of holes, with its own serious distortions, even to the point of being ludicrous. Two of the critical details Dittrich "exposed" in the story as false turned out to be true and were supported by multiple direct witnesses. Dittrich easily could have checked with these witnesses but chose not to.

The third critical detail was that Alexander's coma (and thus his entire experience) was not caused by a serious illness but was medically induced. This "fact" was based on ER physician Laura Potter's statement that Alexander's state would be considered "conscious but delirious." Dittrich did *not* check with Dr. Potter about the accuracy of his interpretation of her statement. Indeed, after the *Esquire* article appeared, Potter was extremely distressed that Dittrich had led her to say certain things and had twisted her remarks. Potter issued a statement that **the article had taken her statements out of context, had misrepresented them, and did not accurately portray Alexander's condition.**

So Dittrich's major contention—that Alexander's experience was a drug-induced hallucination—is completely baseless, founded on Dittrich's apparently deliberate twisting of Potter's statements, and also in complete contradiction to the ample evidence presented in the book that Alexander's coma was due to a very severe case of bacterial meningitis.

Another of Dittrich's contentions has proven to be ludicrous: that even His Holiness the Dalai Lama had declared Alexander's story unreliable and Alexander a liar. The Dalai Lama invited Alexander to address the students at his college in Oregon and had commented that Alexander's experience is of the sort whereby one must do a thorough investigation to insure the person is reliable and not lying. Dittrich interpreted His Holiness's comments as a judgment that Alexander's story is indeed unreliable and that, in the Dalai Lama's judgment, Alexander is a liar.

In fact, a careful listen to the Dalai Lama's comments (available on YouTube) reveals that **the Dalai Lama was saying exactly the opposite: that Alexander's story is "amazing" and that in Alexander's particular case there is no reason to lie, and, therefore, one can take his testimony to be credible.**

It is laughable that Dittrich (and his editors) would think that the Dalai Lama would invite Alexander to be his honored guest at his college, only to turn around and call him unreliable and a liar.

Less laughable are the other allegations insinuated or leveled at Alexander: that he was a failed neurosurgeon who had been sued numerous times for malpractice, was forced out of multiple jobs in neurosurgery in Massachusetts, and was dogged with further lawsuits when he practiced in Virginia. Alexander deserves to have his side of these cases heard as well.

In the most serious of the malpractice cases—that Alexander altered medical records in a case of wrong-level spine surgery—Dittrich again distorted the truth, according to Alexander. Wrong-level spine surgery is a relatively common error in neurosurgery, and this was the only instance of wrong-level surgery in Alexander's 25-year career that included over 4,000 surgeries. The patient in question had excellent relief of his symptoms after the surgery, delaying Alexander's discovery that surgery had been performed at an unintended level. Alexander corrected the record to reflect the newly learned facts of the case and disclosed the surgical error to all parties after follow-up revealed a genuine surgical benefit. After a full investigation by three state medical boards and the American Board of Neurological Surgeons, Alexander continued to practice medicine without restriction, with his board certification intact.

Rather than "great journalism," we consider the Dittrich article to be shoddy and irresponsible—shoddy due to Dittrich's and his editors' failure to check sources, witnesses, medical experts, and especially their main witness, Potter. Dittrich acted unethically in twisting and distorting Potter's statements to imply something different from what she meant, and then he repeated that tactic by distorting the Dalai Lama's statements. The *Esquire* article is undeniably irresponsible because of the real harm it has caused Alexander, whose reputation has been severely damaged by Dittrich's distortions and erroneous pronouncements.

The suggestion that Alexander's experience was a hallucination raises the question whether it was a genuine NDE. Yes, it definitely was. Researchers gauge whether an experience can be considered an NDE based on the elements of the experience and their intensity. Alexander's experience included a transition to a higher place, being in a heavenly place, meeting a deceased loved one, being transported to a place of pure Love and Wisdom, being in the presence of a high spiritual being, and being told that he must go back, all of which unequivocally determine that it was an NDE.

In addition, **there are 3 corroborating "time anchors" in Alexander's experience that strongly suggest that the experience occurred during his**

coma. During 3 separate parts of his experience, Alexander observed a murmuring around him—a great throng of beings, people, who were praying for him. Each time, he later recognized some of the faces of the people involved. It happens that those specific people were in fact praying for him on 3 separate days during his coma, in the days just prior to his recovery. Two of the people, Page Sullivan and Susan Reintjes (friends of the family), were not present in the hospital when they were praying. In fact, Reintjes was some 120 miles away during her meditative prayer. The final person Alexander saw, he later recognized was his son, Bond, who was pleading with his father to wake up, just prior to Alexander's return to consciousness.

So Alexander's *Proof of Heaven*—rather than a story concocted out of the hallucinations of a sick brain under sedation and embellished with fanciful stories— turns out to be an honestly portrayed true account of a dangerously close brush with death, a genuine near-death experience of love, spiritual healing, and heavenly revelation, and a miraculous physical healing.

(Mays's entire critique of the *Esquire* article
is available at this link: http://iands.org/esquire)

In the end, these attacks cannot sway at all the feelings of the thousands of people who are very much in favor of Alexander's book. Why? It is our contention that the book offers hope to all those people who experience their existence as miserable, distressful, senseless. And what about responses to *Proof of Heaven* from the general public? As of this writing the Amazon.com web page devoted to the book includes well over 500 of the lowest-possible one-star reviews, many written in language that is far from polite. The good news is that the highest-possible five-star reviews of the book on Amazon. com outnumber them by 10 to 1—well over 5,000.

The Remarkable Argument of Dr. Woerlee

Skeptics come in various stripes. Of course, there are good skeptics—the people who thoroughly consider the evidence while trying to be as unbiased as possible in order to come to a verdict that may even shatter their own previously held beliefs. Perhaps aware that there is no absolute knowledge, they remain friendly and respectful at all times toward their opponents. With that kind of skeptic, we can get along very well. We and they can even become friends.

Gerald M. Woerlee, MD

A different sort are those whose behavior we have already hinted at in the beginning of this chapter: the hard cynic, the arrogant debunker, the perpetual denier . . . in other words, those whose minds are made up and who do not want to be confused by the facts. The hard skeptic is even harder when also a militant atheist and materialist. An attempt to have a decent scientific discussion with such people almost invariably turns into a shouting match, resulting in frustration or even helpless anger on the part of anyone who tries to generate a fruitful exchange of ideas.

For several years, the authors of this book struggled to exchange ideas with Dr. Gerald M. Woerlee (pronounced "WOOR-lay"), a Dutch-Australian anesthesiologist who lives and works in the Netherlands. After all that time, we can only conclude that Dr. Woerlee is a skeptic of the second kind. He is a passionate materialist who fosters a remarkably militant atheism along with the outspoken wish that the whole world would be converted to the rational humanism that forms the basis of hard materialism: There is only the material domain, and consciousness is nothing but an emergent property of the material brain—or, to paraphrase the prominent Dutch neurobiologist Professor Dick Swaab, "Just as the kidneys produce urine, the brain produces consciousness." Hence, according to both Swaab and Woerlee, when the brain dies, consciousness dies with it.

WOERLEE'S "EXPLANATIONS" OF THE DENTURES MAN CASE (CASE 3.7)

In what follows, we will delve deeper into the Dentures Man case, and after that we will elaborate on the case of Pam Reynolds (Case 3.29), which is also well known to those interested in NDEs. To conclude, we will return to the Eben Alexander case, this time including Woerlee's views.

In contrast to many of his colleagues and other physicians, Woerlee has more than an average interest in NDE phenomena. He has written much about the topic and has devoted an entire website to it, claiming that his site is the only truly reliable source of knowledge about NDEs. Yet in the view of most people who have actually had an NDE, Woerlee's ideas are quite disrespectful. The few statements he has made that NDEs can be beautiful, life-changing experiences have hardly appeared to be sincere, because everywhere else in his argumentation his sole aim seems to have been to reduce to zero the import of NDEs and the phenomenon itself to nothing but the consequence of chemical processes in a dying brain. For cases that absolutely are not correlated with a dying brain—here we are not referring to veridical cases—he has presented "explanations" that seemed ingenious but have not held up under closer scrutiny.

In all his contentions against any alternative to the materialist vision of reality, Woerlee has somehow managed to involve NDE phenomena. We believe this strategy is due to Woerlee's conviction that NDEs, as powerful mystical experiences that indicate what van Lommel terms "nonlocal consciousness," are at the root of all the great religions. As Woerlee states in his preface to *Illusory Souls*, his reason for writing and self-publishing the book was to provide "freedom for all whose minds and bodies groan under the oppressive weight of philosophical systems and religions." Since he has considered all religions to be downright evil (Woerlee, 2007), he naturally has considered NDEs to be as well—evil, despite their often wonderful nature (as discussed at the end of this chapter).

Thus we have found that a well-substantiated discussion with him about NDE phenomena has proven virtually impossible. No matter if the proof supporting nonlocal consciousness has accumulated sky high; even then, he has stuck to his position—by accusing his opponents of a total lack of medical knowledge or just a lack of common sense, among other insults. The fanatical way Woerlee has dealt with the case of the man whose upper denture was removed during his resuscitation is quite illustrative, as the following paragraphs will show.

Woerlee first became involved in what has become known as the Man with the Dentures or the Dentures Man case when it was briefly mentioned in the famous article about the Dutch NDE study published in 2001 in *The Lancet*, the leading British medical science journal (van Lommel et al., 2001). Some years later, Woerlee (2004) published an article in the *Journal of Near-Death Studies* wherein he advanced what he considered a sound medical explanation for the case. One of the major flaws in his article is that he did not attempt to seek contact in any way with members of the Merkawah Foundation—the Netherlands branch of IANDS—who had interviewed the prime witness, a nurse who had resuscitated the patient now known as the Dentures Man. In short, Woerlee bluntly alleged that the whole case must have happened in such and such a way, but without having ascertained the facts of the case.

Meanwhile, thanks to a suggestion from Ruud van Wees, a former Merkawah board member and coauthor of the famous *Lancet* article, I (RHS) located a full report in the Merkawah Archives from its then-staff-member Ap Addink, who in 1994 had interviewed the nurse. Careful scrutiny of this report revealed that Woerlee was simply wrong in his assertions about the Dentures Man.

After much searching, I finally made contact with the man who had brought the Dentures Man case back to life again: cardiac nurse TG (initials only, as he wishes to remain anonymous). He was pleasantly surprised that after so many years there was still interest in this case, which at the time had made such a deep impression on him. He told me that he remembered every detail as if it had happened yesterday.

I then asked Titus Rivas to visit Nurse TG with the specific aim of interviewing him in depth about the Dentures Man case. This interview would be the basis for a publication in *Terugkeer* (Return), the quarterly journal of the Dutch branch of IANDS, of which I was then editor. That very extensive article was indeed published in the fall 2008 issue of *Terugkeer* (Rivas, 2008b).

I then made what in hindsight seems to have been a mistake: I invited Gerald Woerlee to write a rejoinder to the aforementioned article. Why? Because, as a former journalist, I consider it only correct to publish various opinions on particular subjects, including opposing views; the public is entitled to know the various positions on an issue, particularly when the subject at hand is of a somewhat controversial nature. Besides, I believed that Woerlee could not deny the facts—namely, that it was a veridical NDE with verifiable components. How wrong I was to assume that he could be persuaded so easily by what I and my like-minded researchers considered common sense.

To be sure, Woerlee began by saying that the report of the exchange between Rivas and TG was of an excellent quality. Then, to my astonishment, he gave it an entirely different twist that put the whole matter into a patently narrow view. Issues he did not like were simply ignored or, worse, twisted in such a way that plain truths were violated.

POINT AND COUNTERPOINT IN THE DENTURES MAN CASE

Now let us concentrate on the moment when the Dentures Man (also referred to by TG as Mr. B) was brought into the cardiology ward. It was then that the

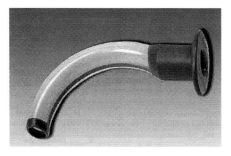

Mayo tube

crucial event took place that made this case so famous, as extensively described in Case 3.7 in this book.

To reiterate, upon the patient's entry into the resuscitation room, he did not show any signs of life. He was extremely cold, with no discernable respiration or heartbeat, and his pupils did not contract when his closed eyes were opened and a bright light was shone into them. He even showed postmortem lividity—the bluish discoloration of the skin of a cadaver where blood has pooled. In the past, he would have been declared dead without wasting words, or, as Dr. Sam Parnia said it in his book *Erasing Death* (2013), "In such a case you are not almost dead, but simply dead."

As soon as the patient was brought in, TG and his team made preparations for the resuscitation procedure. One step is the insertion of the Mayo oropharyngeal airway tube—an oral airway (see picture)—into the throat of the patient with the aim to thus secure access to the patient's windpipe. During this insertion, TG discovered that the patient still had an upper denture stuck in his mouth. Consequently, TG removed the denture and placed it on a small wooden shelf that was part of the so-called crash cart on which all sorts of resuscitation appliances lay ready for use. TG then intubated the man, at which point the patient was finally ready for the actual resuscitation procedure. That procedure was promptly started by activating the Thumper, a device that presses on the patient's chest with great power and regularity, thus providing external heart massage.

It seems perhaps miraculous that afterward, the aforementioned procedure was quite precisely described by the patient himself. He had "seen" everything from a position near the ceiling of the room—what TG had done, including when TG removed the denture from his mouth and placed it on the wooden shelf of the crash cart—all while he lay essentially dead on the resuscitation table.

It is at this point that Woerlee gave his own twist to the story and thus intentionally overlooked the statements of cardiac nurse TG, who was actually on the scene. First of all, Woerlee asserted that the patient was only slightly suffering from hypothermia. This assertion is in complete contrast to TG's report, which made clear that, in fact, the patient was clinically dead:

extremely cold, with lividity stains and no respiration or heartbeat, hence no blood pressure whatsoever. Again, according to Parnia's criterion, he was not near death but dead.

Woerlee also claimed that during the ambulance ride from the spot where the patient was found to the hospital, sufficient resuscitation had taken place, thanks to which the patient had been conscious. One wonders how Woerlee could have known that; was he there at the time? No, he worked in a UK hospital, and he only became aware of the case many years later, after having read the article in the *Lancet*. Indeed, the ambulance staff did carry out resuscitation attempts during that transport to the hospital, as confirmed by TG. But the report makes it abundantly clear that the ambulance staff did not succeed at all in restoring Mr. B to consciousness.

Readers are invited also to see Appendix A, attached to this chapter, in which cardiologist Pim van Lommel elucidated why the ambulance staff could not be successful with their resuscitation attempts. He summarized it thus:

> We know that proper resuscitation, with adequate external heart massage and mouth-to-mouth respiration or respiration via a mask, will produce minimal blood flow ("low-flow") to the brain, which increases the chances of recovery of brain function after the cardiac arrest has been successfully treated with defibrillation. By this minimal cerebral blood flow the no-longer-functioning neurons will be able to survive for a longer period of time in the minimal energy state ("pilot light state"), also called "hibernation" or "ischemic penumbra" of the brain (Coimbra, 1999), because it prolongs the period of reversibility (viability) before neuronal cell death and brain death occur (Appendix A).

Beyond the challenge of providing resuscitation in the ambulance, another challenge to even providing consistent resuscitation upon arrival at the hospital involved the relative locations of the emergency room entrance and the resuscitation room. As TG explained in the 2008 *Terugkeer* article (authors' translation):

> At arrival in the [CCU] department [the patient had] widely dilated pupils, signs of serious oxygen deprivation in the brain, no heart rhythm capable of maintaining the pump function, but instead ventricular fibrillation. The transport of the patient from the moment of his arrival at the hospital up to the moment of

[his] arrival at the [CCU] took more than five minutes. During that period the ambulance nurse could only run beside the gurney; hence resuscitation was hardly possible. It was only possible to maintain some ventilation. In the old Canisius Hospital the distance between First Aid where patients arrived and the CCU was considerable. One even had to take an elevator to the third floor as it was there where the CCU was located. So, much precious time was lost to reach the CCU and next resume the resuscitation procedure. Between the lifting of the patient from the gurney onto the bed, the installation of the heart massage pump, and the factual resumption of the resuscitation, much time was lost, certainly more than a minute. In that period no resuscitation took place and there was definitely no blood circulation. *The denture—and I say this with strong emphasis—was removed from the mouth before the heart massage machine was switched on. So it was impossible that Mr. B would have been conscious and could physically have done the observations of his surroundings as Woerlee alleges he [Mr. B.] had done.* Besides, as far as I know nobody has ever been conscious when his pupils did not react to light. (TG, 2008)

We invite readers to closely inspect the italicized line: *The denture—and I say this with strong emphasis—was removed from the mouth before the heart massage machine was switched on.* We highlight this line because in the interview with Titus Rivas, TG had said, and we translate:

RIVAS: Naturally, the insertion of the Mayo [airway] tube occurred, at least so it seems to me, within a context when there was still no evidence of a heart rhythm?

TG: Yes, there was none at the time. No heart rhythm.

RIVAS: So no blood circulation and therefore also no brain activity?

TG: Yes!

RIVAS: Am I going too fast or is that correct?

TG: No, uh, you could roughly say this. The patient is placed under the pump, the pump starts pumping, it could be that you then get some circulation going. I go to inspect the man's mouth, I remove the denture, insert the Mayo tube. . . .

Apparently, Woerlee focused entirely on TG's last comment, which Woerlee interpreted to indicate a different sequence of events than TG had previously described: that the Thumper (heart massage pump) had first been started and—*in a very short time*—had already restored blood circulation sufficiently for the patient to become conscious so that he had "felt" his upper denture being removed from his mouth and next had "heard" how the denture had been placed on the shelf of the crash cart. Woerlee persisted in claiming this sequence, despite the following facts:

1. TG most emphatically corrected himself in his rejoinder to Woerlee: *The denture—and I say this with strong emphasis—was removed from the mouth before the heart massage machine was switched on.* As we wrote in the treatment of this case:

   > TG never meant to say that he first turned on the CPR device; rather, his intention had been to account for all the procedures that had been employed during the resuscitation, which he had listed in a random order. Without the sequence of events TG adamantly contended took place—that he first took the dentures out and *only then* turned on the device—it would be hard to understand why he would still be so impressed by this case decades after it had occurred.

   Another way to understand TG's remark was that he first responded to the interviewer's question, and then, to emphasize his point, launched into a reiteration of the entire sequence of events *from the beginning.*

2. This correction ought to have been sufficient, but to be certain that we were understanding the sequence correctly, we consulted two cardiologists with more than 30 years of experience between them. They each independently confirmed the sequence TG had clarified: first Mayo airway tube insertion, next oxygen mask, and only after that switching on the heart massage machine (Thumper). Indeed, it would be a hard task to insert a Mayo tube when the body is shaking under the violent pressure of the Thumper. (We were told by the two cardiologists that the Thumper is only rarely used nowadays.) In addition, it does not make sense to begin circulation—the purpose of which is to bring oxygen to the body—if no oxygen can enter the body due to a blocked airway.

3. Woerlee can claim what he wants, but of all people, he, as an anesthesiologist, should know that the return of lucid consciousness is not a matter of seconds—which would have been the case here if things had happened the way he claimed. As neuropsychiatrist Peter Fenwick (2005) made clear in his Bruce Greyson Lecture at the 2004 Annual IANDS Conference,

"coming to" is a slow and confused process during which there is no lucid consciousness whatsoever for at least several minutes.

"CURIOUS"

All the same, Woerlee continued to hammer on TG's first statement; he even called TG's correction "curious." It is quite understandable that this term caused TG deep indignation. He was so frustrated at being so fundamentally misunderstood and misinterpreted that he greatly regretted ever having brought the case into the open and wanted nothing more to do with it. Consequently, further investigation into this case has unfortunately ceased—due primarily to Woerlee's casting aspersion on TG for TG's comment, which Woerlee appears to have interpreted literally rather than contextually.

Testimony by TG and corroborating expert cardiologists indicates clearly that the crucial event happened just in the brief time between the patient's entry into the resuscitation room and the moment the Thumper was switched on. The patient consciously observed everything looking down from above so that afterward he could precisely describe all that had happened. He had seen how the denture had been removed from his mouth and placed on the small wooden pull-out shelf. He also described the entire room, including the sink that was hidden behind a curtain from the vantage point of the patient's physical body. Note that he "saw" everything from *above* and that from the position of his body, laid out on the resuscitation bed, it would have been impossible for him to observe the sink because it was located behind a closed curtain.

But these facts presented no problem for Woerlee. He claimed with dogmatic certainty that the patient, although clinically dead on the table, had heard everything and had, based on the sounds around him, correctly visualized the resuscitation room—including the sink hidden by the curtain. This is the part of Woerlee's argument that we found most surprising. To reveal its errors, we return to TG's translated account (taken from Smit & Rivas, 2010):

That Mr. B could have made observations during resuscitation when I opened his eyelids seems very farfetched to me. Every time when I checked the pupil reflex and size it appeared that the pupils remained fully dilated while not responding to the light.

The description of the room Mr. B gave was from a point of view located in the upper left corner in the resuscitation room and, therefore, could not possibly have been due to my opening of his eyelids to check the pupil reflexes.

The details he described could only be given if indeed he actually had had an OBE and thus saw himself and the resuscitation team from a totally different perspective than from the bed onto which he had been laid. (TG, 2008, p. 8)

To this testimony we would like to add the following. Woerlee said that the patient could see during the very brief moments when his pupil reflexes were checked. First of all, there were no reflexes; the patient's pupils did not respond to the *intense* light that was shone into his eyes, so in actuality they—and he— did not see. Second, if indeed there could have been a response to the beam of intense light, then this situation would have resulted in a large purple blotch blocking the view; anyone who has had a flashlight shone in his or her eyes can imagine how the afterimage would obscure what could be seen. Once again, with such a retinal afterimage, the patient would have had no chance of seeing anything—and certainly not in detail. Third, the range of view would have been so limited as to make it impossible to get the overall view of the resuscitation room that the patient later described. This point alone makes Woerlee's claim untenable.

Another of Woerlee's assertions was that blind people can construct an accu- rate mental picture of their surroundings simply by listening to the ambient sounds. We do not question this possibility when it concerns people who have been blind all their lives or at least for a very long time—time enough to develop the considerable skill involved in developing such an ability. Perhaps *some* of those people are able to build the aforementioned accurate mental picture, but certainly not all of them—and most certainly not someone who had no experi- ence with such a sophisticated perceptual process.

Smit recalls an acquaintance of his, now deceased, who became totally blind 35 years ago; despite more than three decades of experience, this man never developed the capability to orient himself on the basis of sounds alone, let alone the capability to describe the properties of objects about which no one had given him a clue. It is reasonable to assume that most people who are not blind—let alone a person lying on a resuscitation bed and not even on the verge of consciousness—would hardly be capable of accomplishing such a remarkable feat as to accurately describe in detail a scene as unfamiliar as a resuscitation procedure.

Fortunately, Woerlee's bold claim can be easily tested. We have challenged him several times via e-mail to set up a simple experiment. Just ask 10 subjects chosen at random to sit together in a room and let someone else carry out a few tasks behind a screen. Let that person make some sounds with objects and so on. Then ask those 10 subjects to make a mental picture of what happened there and describe it. Every experimental psychologist will confirm that the outcome is likely to be 10 different descriptions—and none of them accurate.

Yet Woerlee has apparently retained the sincere belief that the patient, despite having been in a very dire situation—on the verge of actual death and hardly, if at all, conscious—did accomplish a feat of which any fully conscious professional mentalist would be proud. But whatever Woerlee may think and assert, given the fact that the patient was most certainly not conscious (not in the usual sense—that is, not from a materialist point of view) at the time when his denture was removed from his mouth, one central observation remains inexplicable: his observation of what was, in fact, a custom-built crash cart and its wooden pull-out shelf, upon which the denture was laid. We do not need an experiment to establish that Mr. B's report indicates that he saw this cart in detail—which, given the situation he was in, would have been physically impossible.

But it gets stranger still. A bit further into the interview that Rivas conducted with Nurse TG, they discussed the fact that the resuscitation of the patient was quite a laborious affair. From the discussions TG had afterward with the patient, it appeared that his departed consciousness had sensed the doubt that was emerging within the people treating him—their doubt that the entire resuscitation procedure could succeed. There was still no heartbeat, and the pupils in his eyes remained rigid: The patient was still very (physically) unconscious. For the sake of clarity, the pertinent part of the interview with Rivas follows (authors' translation).

PAIN UNDER THE THUMPER

RIVAS: Now I have what I consider a very important question. At one point, the patient told you he experienced severe pain on that bed [during the resuscitation]. I suppose that was at a moment when he had no circulation.

TG: That was during the resuscitation. During resuscitation you get some circulation, but that is an artificial circulation. That is the aim of the resuscitation: It does not come from the heart itself; instead you generate circulation from the outside. That is what you do with cardiac resuscitation: You generate circulation. And in most cases circulation only occurs between thorax and head. So only the "small circulation" works. This is also the most important circulation, because if it does not occur, there is a major risk of brain damage. In fact, the only thing that happens is circulation to major organs. The brain is relatively close to the heart and is part of the "small circulation."

RIVAS: Is it conceivable that this small artificial circulation, as you call it, is in principle sufficient to cause [permit] sensations of pain?

TG: Yes it is. I had the experience in the case of another patient who was under the heart massage pump and was even more afraid than B. He even woke up and we quickly turned the pump off, after which he lost consciousness again. Therefore, he did not have sufficient circulation of his own. It is possible that you resuscitate so efficiently that sufficient oxygen is transported to the brain for the patient to regain consciousness.[6]

RIVAS: If I connect that back to one of my initial questions, that is, at what point during the whole resuscitation process would you say: B may have had enough circulation, as the skeptical anesthesiologist Gerald Woerlee also asserts, to explain any form of consciousness?

TG: He may have had that after we had been resuscitating for some time. At the moment of removal of the denture from his mouth—at that moment he had no circulation and no heartbeat, so at that moment he could not have seen it. We had to start the resuscitation at that time. Removal [of the denture] was in preparation for continuation of resuscitation after the patient was transferred to us by the ambulance staff.

RIVAS: That is clear. And the moment at which he could have felt pain, about how long after removing the denture from his mouth was that? Are we talking about minutes or perhaps a quarter of an hour?

TG: Theoretically, if we look at his pupil reactions throughout the resuscitation, that occurred much later, because his pupils were nonreactive, as we say; they did not respond to light until much later. They began to react somewhat to light only after more than 15 minutes after we had begun resuscitation—just as his pulse and heart rhythm began later, after about 20 minutes.

RIVAS: But do I understand properly what you are saying: "The pain is actually inexplicable by current standards"?

6. In reference to the statement made by cardiology unit nurse TG—that is, that it is possible for someone to regain consciousness during mechanized external heart massage—it should be pointed out that such consciousness, which is very brief and superficial, is extremely rare. It is a result of the function of a heart massage machine such as the Thumper to sustain rudimentary circulation. This phenomenon has not been scientifically objectivized or confirmed.

TG: From what I know, and from what I saw with this man, I cannot explain how he could have felt anything at that moment.

RIVAS: No, okay. By the way, did he report that he could see anything at the same time as he felt pain? Was there a combination. . . .

TG: He saw himself lying under the heart massage pump, and that was incredibly painful. And in between he also saw me busy with him. . . .

RIVAS: And he felt pain at the same time. So there is some sort of input from two sides, from his physical body, and from a position outside his body.

TG: Yes.

ABSURD BEHAVIOR

It is an enigma how someone could have insufficient circulation and, at the same time, feel considerable pain. And on this point, Woerlee reacted in a rather absurd manner. First, he had rebuffed Nurse TG by not taking seriously TG's rectifying remark; now he was making gratuitous use of previous statements from TG by saying, in effect, "See, I told you so! TG says so himself. With a heart massage machine one can get blood circulation going again, to the extent that the patient 'comes to'! And that is precisely what happened after the patient was brought in." He reproached us in an Amazon.com blog post (on February 7, 2012, 2:48:17 PM PST):

> Smit and his associates ignored all medical facts, totally destroying any credibility in their explanation of the Dentures Man case. I even had to translate the report for them, so that others could read the truth of the case for themselves. And they still have not realized how foolish their arguments were.

This is plain slander; there is no other word for it. It is clear from the preceding paragraphs the extent to which we devoted time and effort to the medical aspects of this case, even consulting experts. And as of the 2012 blog date, we had already translated all relevant passages for our 2008 and 2010 *Journal of Near-Death Studies* articles. But apparently those actions did not satisfy Woerlee. He even insinuated that we deliberately did not translate various texts so as to keep readers from the real data. This is downright nonsense, of course. Yet Woerlee then translated the entire text for himself. True, he did this within a day or two while maintaining his normal workload, an impressive feat for which we were quite grateful. However, it did not help him much, because now readers of English could judge Woerlee's arguments for themselves—quite extraordinary arguments, to say the least.

Returning to the theme that the patient's out-of-body consciousness apparently began to feel pain later in the resuscitation process, we deem it possible that this pain was of a psychogenic nature, evoked by the patient's fear of what he saw via extrasensory perception.

But Woerlee's contention that the pain was "normal" does not explain away the fact that the patient's out-of-body experience already had begun shortly after the patient was brought into the resuscitation room and before the Thumper was switched on. Nurse TG was adamant in this regard, and we are quite prepared to accept his explanations. After all, *he* was there, and it was *he* who almost single-handedly conducted the entire resuscitation activity. Woerlee was *not* there, and *he* only became acquainted with the case a few decades after these events occurred. Surely it is more sensible to privilege the explanations of this case given by Nurse TG over those given by someone who was not in any way involved. (See also Appendix B, in which Pim van Lommel explained that such regaining of consciousness is extremely rare.)

Woerlee's tunnel vision is reminiscent of the moon hoaxer who confronted Buzz Aldrin, the second man on the moon, and demanded that Aldrin admit on the Bible that he had never been on the Moon and that the whole Moon-caboodle was nothing but a hoax. (A moon hoaxer is a person who is convinced that the moon landings in 1969 and thereafter have been nothing but an expensive TV show presented as a hoax—a first-order absurdity, in our view.) Aldrin, who had heard many such silly allegations, had finally had enough and gave the poor man a pretty tough response. (The YouTube films of this encounter have been removed for copyright reasons.)

WOERLEE AND THE PAM REYNOLDS CASE

We are not yet finished with Woerlee. Another hobbyhorse he has been riding for years is the well-known Pam Reynolds case (Case 3.29 in this book). He wrote in his Amazon.com blog post (February 7, 2012, 2:48:17 PM PST): "As for Pam Reynolds, I have been expounding the real medical facts since 2004. And most people [including Rudolf Smit] still believe in fairy tales."

Woerlee has firm explanations for this case, which, we must acknowledge, are mainly based on his own considerable expertise and experience as an anesthesiologist. There is nothing wrong with that basis were it not that Woerlee has been led first and foremost by his own materialist presumptions about reality and that those presumptions led him to ignore relevant facts that did not fit into this worldview or to twist facts in such a way that they *did* fit his views; thus he has completely misrepresented the case.

This misrepresentation began with Woerlee's failure to contact Reynolds, even though he had had plenty of opportunities to do so. Does it not seem crucial to contact anyone who can help one know what is what? As Titus Rivas can testify, Reynolds was quite approachable from the time his extensive e-mail exchange with her began in 2003 until her death in May of 2010. Also, for years Woerlee failed to contact Reynolds's surgeon, Robert Spetzler. Given the fact that Rivas and Smit had little trouble receiving speedy and adequate responses to their questions, we wonder why it was so difficult for a colleague physician to ask such questions and then receive useful responses.

Nevertheless, Woerlee has claimed to have all the answers, despite another argument that works against him: He was never there—never participated in Reynolds's surgical procedure. So he has based his judgments on what he believed should have happened—in accordance with his knowledge of anesthesiology—and not on what actually did happen.

Robert F. Spetzler, MD

Of course, Woerlee has brushed aside the argument of not having been there; he claimed that the operation report and some articles gave him enough to go on. Dr. Spetzler has testified about this case, but the anesthesiologist who assisted with Reynolds's operation never spoke or wrote about it. We may safely assume that for him, just as for the surgeon, Spetzler, the miraculous happenings around this operation are a grand enigma. If he had known what the true cause had been of Reynolds's OBE/NDE, then no doubt Spetzler would have urged him to speak out to share his informed opinion. After all, it is known that Spetzler was not at all happy about being in the dark concerning the case. He, like any scientist, would have preferred a sound explanation. (More about this point in Intermezzo 4, below.)

In any event, the core of Woerlee's opinion has been that Reynolds awoke during the operation and hence that the anesthesiology had failed—partly awoke, that is, because due to certain chemicals that had been administered, she was paralyzed and could not say anything. But she could have heard everything, Woerlee has claimed, and based on what she heard, she could have formed an image in her mind of what happened in the operating room. (Seeing with her eyes was impossible, because they were taped shut.) This phenomenon of awakening during surgery is known as "anesthesia awareness," something every anesthesiologist fears with horror. Patients who awaken during surgery but cannot signal their awareness can experience excruciating pain caused by surgical incisions. In short, during such awareness, they go through hell. Obviously, this situation can lead to deep trauma for the patient. In addition, the anesthesiologist responsible would bear the guilt and the blame for apparently incorrectly administering the anesthetics. Such an occurrence is considered a blemish on an anesthesiologist's professional record.

However, in a small number of anesthesia awareness cases, the patient does not feel pain, and apparently Woerlee has concluded that this was the case with Reynolds. After all, in the many interviews she gave, she never spoke about pain but only about her beautiful experience. Nor did she mention the extremely loud clicks caused by the small loudspeakers in the earbuds stuffed into her ears—a very crucial matter (more about that later).

In our Chapter 3 discussion of Case 3.29, we conveyed enough information about Woerlee's various other claims. From here on, we will concentrate on Woerlee's contention that Reynolds simply was awake and could have heard everything that happened in the operating room.

WAS PAM REYNOLDS TRULY AWAKE?

First of all, Woerlee has ignored completely Spetzler's forceful testimony that Reynolds could not have heard anything, let alone have "seen" what happened in the operating room. In the excellent BBC documentary *The Day I Died* (Broome, 2002), Reynolds's case was discussed at length. Reynolds herself spoke extensively about her experience, along with cardiologist Michael Sabom and Spetzler, who addressed the matter in no uncertain terms:

> I don't think that the observations she made were based on what she experienced as she went into the operating room. They were just not available to

her. For example, the drill and so on, those things are all covered up. They're not visible. They were inside their packages. You really don't begin to open them up until the patient is completely asleep so that you maintain a sterile environment.

Following is an excerpt from Smit's letter to the editor of the *Journal of Near-Death Studies* (Smit, 2008c):

Regarding Reynolds' hearing the conversation between Spetzler and the cardiac surgeon, he [Spetzler] said:

> At that stage of the operation nobody can observe or hear in that state. I find it inconceivable that your normal senses such as hearing, let alone the fact that she had clicking modules in each ear, that there was any way for her to hear those through the normal auditory pathways.

In summarizing this case, Spetzler declared:

> I don't have an explanation for it. I don't know how it is possible for it to happen considering the physiological state she was in. At the same time, I have seen so many things that I cannot explain, that I won't be so arrogant to say that there is no way that it can happen.

Spetzler, who performed the operation, showed his greatness of mind by admitting that he did not know. Woerlee and [Keith] Augustine [of Secular Web and Internet Infidels, a staunch supporter of Woerlee's ideas], however, who were not there when the surgery was performed, were indeed so arrogant as to forward a mere speculation as truth. When I told this to Woerlee he retorted that Spetzler, as a surgeon, would not have known about the phenomenon of "awareness during anesthesia." Now it is my turn to find that inconceivable, that a pioneering neurosurgeon such as Robert Spetzler would not have known of this phenomenon that is taught to all surgeons and surgery assistants.

To ascertain what Spetzler thought of all this, we contacted him by e-mail on April 5, 2013. His response was quick and stated in no uncertain terms: "*Pam was under EEG burst suppression, and that is incompatible with anesthetic awareness.*" (our emphasis; see Note 2).

A few weeks later, on April 15, 2013, blogger and correspondent Stephen Woodhead (writing under the pseudonym Tim Tobias) asked Spetzler the following question:

> Sir, I wonder if you would mind answering a question that is troubling me. I would be very grateful. In the famous Pam Reynolds aneurysm case, when she overheard the conversation about her femoral arteries being too small (and you, Sir, said "Try the other side") . . . at that point in the operation, were her brainwaves effectively flat? And is that why you have said that you don't have an explanation for it?

Spetzler's straightforward and unequivocal response came the same day: "*Yes—RFS.*"

Readers should note that the question posed to Spetzler was "Were her brainwaves *effectively* flat?" The brainwaves are indeed *effectively* flat during "burst suppression" in anesthesia (see Note 2) but this situation is not to be confused with "flat line" brain waves which occur during cardiac arrest. At the point in the operation in question, Reynolds was under anesthesia but not yet in hypothermic cardiac arrest.

Woerlee was not at all impressed by the above arguments and responses from Spetzler. He even insinuated that Spetzler's statements *could not* be correct. Never mind that Spetzler is a first-class neurosurgeon who performed and led this operation. But Woerlee, who was never there, shouted from the rooftops that he knew better than Spetzler.

Readers should note that at this stage Woerlee did finally try to contact Spetzler via e-mail. He never received a reply. No wonder: Woerlee had claimed so many times on various blogs and articles on the Internet that Spetzler had been wrong, thus actually insinuating incompetence, that Spetzler had undoubtedly become aware of these communications and consequently felt no inclination to respond.

Woerlee went to great lengths, even absurd lengths, to justify his claim that Pam was awake and she heard everything, period. From the perspective of his materialist worldview, there is actually no way to falsify this claim. The following discussion illustrates his attempts to prove this claim. Here we concentrate on the clicking modules—the little speakers inserted into Reynolds's ears.

WOERLEE: PAM REYNOLDS IGNORED THE NOISE OF 95–100 DECIBELS

The clicking modules used in Reynolds's surgical procedure were set into plugs that were malleable so that when they were inserted into the ears, they could be molded to fit tightly inside the ear canals. The purpose of this tight fit was to greatly reduce the outside noise intruding into the ears, thus isolating the clicking sounds produced by the modules. The clicks were produced 11 times per second by the little speakers at a very loud volume: between 95 and 100 decibels (decibels being the international norm of sound volume). That sound volume is comparable to the very loud "rat-tat-tat" of a hydraulic jackhammer breaking up concrete pavement about five feet away. That is loud enough to cause severe hearing damage if applied long enough—which is why road workers wear sound-dampening ear plugs. In other words, the clicks in Reynolds's ears constitute an utterly irritating noise that would be impossible to ignore, as any audiologist can testify (see the table in Appendix C).

The purpose of applying that level of noise to Reynolds's ears was to monitor her brain function. As long as her brain was functioning normally, it would detect each click, which, in turn, would appear as a "blip" on the electroencephalogram (EEG) recording, therefore yielding a continuous pattern of blips. The clicks were used primarily to determine whether her brainstem—the most basic part of the brain—was adversely affected by the surgery. Then, the clicks had the *added* benefit of readily showing on the EEG if anesthesia was no longer effective. In other words, the clicks helped prevent the deeply feared anesthesia awareness described previously, which is exactly what this monitoring system was designed to do. If Reynolds's brain was not fully under anesthesia, it would detect the clicks and register continuous blips on the EEG readout. Only when the EEG showed the burst suppression pattern—a repeated sequence of a brief "burst" of blips followed by a "suppression" or complete absence of blips (see Note 2)—that characterizes complete anesthesia, could the surgeon be certain that Reynolds's conscious awareness had come to a full stop so that it was safe to start the interventional parts of the operation.

During a surgical procedure, the anesthetist continuously monitors the EEG to ascertain that the patient continues to be fully "under" the anesthesia. The loud clicks provide an additional level of assurance that the patient remains unconscious. (See Appendix E for more information on the monitoring procedures used in Reynolds's type of surgery.)

Nevertheless, suppose that Mrs. Reynolds had indeed been "awake" as Woerlee contended. Recall that she was an active, professional musician. There can be no doubt that she would have heard those deafening clicks and, above all, that her brain would have reported them via the EEG. Again, with emphasis: She was a *musician*. Such a person devotes much of her life to listening to sound, especially *meaningful* sound. Very loud white noise (in one ear) and click sounds (in the other, alternating from time to time at 95–100 decibels) could hardly be ignored by such a person. If she had become aware of that terrible noise in her ears, it would have been torture while she was on the operating table.

But what are the facts? In none of the several interviews Reynolds gave, all of which are available via the Internet, did she ever speak about those deafening clicks. This fact points strongly to the conclusion that her "hearing" of the verbal exchange between the two surgeons was extrasensory (detected by her out-of-body consciousness) rather than sensory (detected by her ears).

Intermezzo 2

At the time this chapter was being translated into English (early May 2015), an in-depth interview with Reynolds conducted by *Coast to Coast AM* radio host Art Bell on December 6, 2001, was posted on the show's "Somewhere in Time" archives (Bell, 2001). In this interview, in which Reynolds demonstrated her ready mind and her familiarity at that point with the entire procedure of the operation, she said the following:

REYNOLDS (01:01:55 TIME CODE): As I exited through the top of my head, I had this incredibly clear vision, and my hearing was enhanced.

ART BELL (01:06:12): Did you feel conscious in the way you feel conscious right now?

REYNOLDS: It was a heightened consciousness, Art, it was very heightened. I have never experienced anything before or since like that . . . It was absolute, total, and complete focus. My eyesight was clearer, my hearing was more acute . . . I was just . . .

BELL: In pain?

REYNOLDS: None! Oh no, the feeling was incredible!

BELL (01:47:42): In an attempt to explain what you're talking about now, a lot of neurosurgeons have said . . . Oh . . . well . . . you know . . . The brain dies from the outside moving inwards, so this pinpoint of light is the very center of the brain, the last place where the neurons are firing, et cetera, et cetera . . .

REYNOLDS: *That's really hard to do when you don't have any brainwaves . . . !* So, the very last bastion for the brainwave theory is that they don't believe the technology—the equipment we have—is sensitive enough to pick up the minute brainwave activity that may have been occurring. But I am told et cetera, et cetera that this kind of hallucination would definitely have been recorded [on the EEG]; we would have seen something [spikes on the EEG printouts] . . . And the whole theory that I heard—what was going on in the operating room—and then built a picture . . . They put speakers in my ears that made a loud clicking noise, I'm told. *Even if I was fully conscious, I couldn't have heard a thing!*

She then explained the purpose of the clicks and stated that both her upper and lower brain were at complete flat line.

From reading the intermezzo, it is clear that Reynolds did not hear—and could not have heard—outside sounds via her physical auditory pathways. How can Woerlee, *who was never there* and who has never had a similar experience, deny or ignore her testimony?

NO PROBLEM FOR WOERLEE

Again, Woerlee was not impressed. He thought he could deliver the proof via a simple test. In the *Journal of Near-Death Studies*, Woerlee (2011) provided instructions for downloading and utilizing software that produces sounds of variable volumes and frequencies. The software could be tuned to 11 clicks per second and to any volume, even 100 decibels. Next, the experimenter could don over-the-ear headphones or insert earbuds that nestle more tightly into the ear canals and thus test whether surrounding sounds such as speech between persons could be heard with ease, with some difficulty, or not at all.

Rudolf Smit downloaded the software and installed it in accordance with Woerlee's instructions and gives the following account:

I used hi-fi headphones with ear pads that fit snugly over my ears. And yes—I must be honest—amid the incredible din of the 100-decibel clicks, I could hear sounds around me. But . . . was the din tolerable? Not at all! After only a few seconds, it was so strong that it caused pain to my eardrums, and I had to remove the headphones.

I repeated the test—quite grudgingly, I must admit—except this time I pressed the ear pads as close as possible to my skull in an attempt to simulate as closely as possible Reynolds's inserted earbuds. As could be anticipated, the surrounding sounds became muffled. With these 100-decibel clicks in the foreground, I had much more difficulty discerning talk in the room.

The test was repeated three more times, with three different subjects: the American writer Michael Prescott and two Amazon Forum participants, Kris Key and Theresa. All three were in consensus: The clicks were extremely irritating and could in no way be ignored. Conversation among people was hard to discern. In sum, the "proof" that Woerlee had announced was not at all convincing.

When I conveyed these results to Woerlee, referring also to a list I had found of decibels and their related sound sources [see Appendix C], again he was not impressed—not even by the fact that the list indicated that sounds exceeding 90 decibels are so loud that even a brief exposure can cause hearing damage. Consequently, Reynolds, if she had been conscious and hearing through normal sensory pathways, could be expected to have heard these clicks and, after surgery, to have reported what she heard. Woerlee reacted with what I took as a surly remark that I had come with "poor evidence" and next referred to all kinds of sources that dealt with chemical aspects connected to anesthesia, which really were irrelevant considering that this entire matter was not about chemicals but about *sound and the hearing of all sorts of sounds.*

When I told Woerlee that I had sent a letter about this matter for publication in the *Journal of Near-Death Studies,* he advised me to withdraw my letter immediately, because otherwise I would make an absolute fool of myself. Why? Woerlee had found a new argument, which in his mind was decisive.

Woerlee's first argument was that Reynolds had simply "neurologically" filtered out the terrible noise of those clicks. His second argument was that, according to various studies, musicians are much better than other people in distinguishing various sounds; thus, she would have filtered out the clicks and focused on the dialog between the surgeons. This argument demonstrated that Woerlee had no understanding of music (which he implicitly admitted elsewhere) or of musicians.

Certainly, musicians who play in an orchestra are trained to distinguish the individual sounds and tones the orchestra is playing, and certainly that ability applies to the conductor, who immediately singles out unwanted dissonance. But does that imply that they can ignore—that is, "neurologically filter out"—additional sounds, as Woerlee claimed? Most likely, as musicians they must remain highly attuned to external sounds, if only to ensure that they are playing with their fellow musicians even while concentrating on their own instruments.

Many orchestra musicians suffer from tinnitus, an occupational disease that causes a ringing in the ears. This hearing damage results from the sound volume produced by a full-sized unamplified symphony orchestra. Sound levels of 100 to 110 decibels are not uncommon. Pam Reynolds played music that was usually amplified. No wonder that many professional musicians develop serious hearing problems after years of exposure to such high levels of sound.

Given professional musicians' desire to hear well running up against an inability to do so that may increase over time, one can safely assume that Woerlee's contention that Reynolds must have been able to neurologically filter out unwanted sounds while picking up voices at some distance is far-fetched. In Intermezzo 2, Reynolds emphatically explained that despite her heightened hearing and vision, she had not heard those clicks. We still have no reason to disbelieve her.

SUMMARY OF WOERLEE'S CONTENTIONS ABOUT PAM REYNOLDS

First of all, Woerlee's hypothesis that, due to anesthesia awareness, Reynolds was awake during the operation has insufficient evidence. See Spetzler's position that Reynolds was under EEG burst suppression, which is incompatible with anesthesia awareness. Second, even if Reynolds had been awake, it would have been impossible for her to hear clearly with her ear canals packed and closed; see again Spetzler's forceful denial that she could have heard anything in that situation, confirmed by Reynolds herself in the December 6, 2001, interview. And third, the modules inserted in her ears produced exceptionally loud and very irritating clicks that hindered entry of outside sounds. Woerlee's claim that Reynolds neurologically filtered out those terrible clicks and thus could have listened "quietly" to what was happening in the OR we find baseless. Apparently, Woerlee has been hell-bent on defending at all costs his materialist worldview, which dictates that what happened to Reynolds and others who have experienced NDEs must be explained entirely in medical terms, even if that defense requires that the truth be corrupted.

This conclusion gains even more support when Woerlee's views on other matters pertaining to NDE phenomena are considered. But first we offer the following intermezzo.

Intermezzo 3

brillation, again at approximately 18-
mained in ventricular fibrillation as
t esophageal temperature of 27 degrees,
irdioversion with 100 joules and conver
1e sinus rhythm stabilized and accelera
irther and eventually was able to be ta
/pass when she had reached a warm enoug
egrees with normal cardiac rhythm and o

t this point the heparinization that ha
/pass, was reversed using Protamine and
irried out in the intracranial operativ

Excerpt from Pam Reynolds's medical report

Blogger Stephen Woodhead ("Tim Tobias"), who located the December 6, 2001, interview with Reynolds, found two other items of great interest. The first was in another *filmed* interview that is quite telling, posted online without complete credits (MSNBC, 2001).

Reynolds reported being aware during both defibrillations when her body temperature was 27° C, as shown in the operation report (at the end of the third line of the image). This discovery was surprising because it was previously assumed, also by Woerlee, that her body temperature at that time was 32° C.

The second item was found in a medical article describing the states of a body at various low temperatures (Weinberg, 1993):

TABLE: KEY FINDINGS AT DIFFERENT DEGREES OF HYPOTHERMIA

TEMPERATURE (C)	CLINICAL FINDINGS
37	Normal oral temperature
36	Increased metabolic rate
35	Maximum shivering seen; impaired judgment
33	Severe clouding of consciousness
32	Most shivering ceases and pupils dilate
31	Blood pressure may no longer be obtainable
28–30	Severe slowing of pulse and respiration
	—Increased muscle rigidity
	—Loss of consciousness
	—Ventricular fibrillation
27	Loss of deep tendon, skin, and capillary reflexes
	—Patients appear clinically dead
	—Complete cardiac arrest

According to these clinical findings, at 27° C, Reynolds was at best in deep coma and, during defibrillation, was effectively dead. Physically waking up in this state is therefore out of the question. Normally, one does not regain consciousness at 27° C. Woodhead informed Woerlee about this fact, after which Woerlee admitted that Reynolds was indeed defibrillated when her body temperature was only 27° C. On his website, Woerlee acknowledged this point, but asserted that Reynolds could have been awake *during her defibrillation* and *only later* heard "Hotel California" (song by the Eagles, a U.S. rock band). Actually, consciousness is not possible when the heart is in ventricular fibrillation. Furthermore, Reynolds reported hearing the music *prior* to the first electric shock, when the body temperature was still at 27° C—a condition at which, according to Weinberg (1993), "physical consciousness" is completely absent.

WOERLEE'S CLAIMS ABOUT NDERS' ENCOUNTERS WITH DECEASED PERSONS, KNOWN AND UNKNOWN

One of the most extraordinary phenomena associated with NDEs is encounters with deceased persons—most often relatives such as grandparents, parents, siblings, uncles, and aunts. Sometimes these encounters involve relatives who were totally unknown to the NDEr but who could be identified afterward. We addressed cases of after-death communication (ADC) with strangers in Chapter 5 and such communication with familiar people in Chapter 6. Many people consider the ADC aspect of NDEs to be perhaps the most miraculous—and those with a materialist view consider it to be perhaps the most difficult to accept. As a rule, skeptics reject this phenomenon outright. Either they consider ADCs to be outright lies, generated by NDErs seeking to attract attention, or they shrug off ADCs as nothing more than accessories to entertaining anecdotes.

Woerlee has delved deeply into the ADC phenomenon, although we have not been satisfied by his explanations. So far, he has avoided cases that do not entirely fit within his explanatory model. In addition, he has totally ignored the fact of the exceptional "coincidence" that during such a "hallucination," someone emerges who happens to be a deceased relative or, an even more exceptional confluence, an *unknown* relative who afterward could be identified as such. Woerlee produced a series of possible explanations (Woerlee, 2012a). To be clear, he has referenced the single case of a hospitalized man who had an NDE involving his sister and then discovered that his sister had died at the same time he was having his NDE. She had been admitted to the same hospital, suffering from advanced diabetes:

> What did the person reporting such an NDE know about the illness of the relative seen during the NDE? Or did he know that the relative was likely to be exposed to danger such as an explorer, a player of dangerous sports, a soldier, or someone living in an area of violence such as riots, revolution, or war? In other words, what was the likelihood that such a relative would have died? (Woerlee, 2012a)

We consider this line of argument legitimate, but only partly so, because to see a deceased loved one in a near-death encounter when her demise came unexpectedly is potentially more powerful than when the loved one is known to be constantly exposed to danger. Nevertheless, it is rare to the point of being miraculous when such a deceased loved one appears during an NDE and even makes it known that he or she is "elsewhere." In our view, to dismiss this feature as the simple coincidence of a mere hallucination occurring in parallel with a verifiable truth is going too far.

> Did the family know of the demise of the relative, but not directly communicate it to the sick person, who then reported seeing the deceased relative during an NDE? Communication can be direct, or indirect by nonverbal behavior. So the person reporting the NDE may have suspected the death of the family member by clues provided by the behavior of healthy visitors. Alternatively, the family may have told the person, and both simply could have forgotten. These are all possible sources of prior knowledge (Woerlee, 2012a).

We read this argument quite often. Theoretically, it could be possible, but in the cases that have been published, this possibility was hardly ever discussed. More often there are descriptions of relatives who sat with the seriously ill patient, trying their very best not to show the patient that another relative was not doing well, or even had just passed. After all, such an announcement can put a heavy emotional burden on the patient and negatively influence the recovery process.

If the patient had regained physical consciousness, then in theory the patient could have deduced something from the body language of the visitors, but then it would be likely that the worried facial expressions would be interpreted as pertaining to the patient rather than to some other relative who has not been mentioned. In most such ADCs, visitors are quite surprised to hear the NDEr claim shortly after he or she regains consciousness (and the ability to speak), that he or she "saw" and "spoke with" Uncle Peter, especially if Uncle Peter died so recently that the patient could not have known. The possibility that the NDEr was told of the death of a loved one and then forgot about it does exist in theory, but whether this is a common phenomenon is a big question that so far has received no answer. In any event, we have never heard or read of such cases.

> What was the exact timing of the demise of the relative, and the occurrence of the vision of that relative in the reported NDE? (Woerlee, 2012a)

Of course, this point is important. But in every case we have studied, the timing was known. (See the examples provided in Chapter 6.)

> How accurate was the reporting of the content of the NDE?

This point, on the other hand, is not important at all. It is actually a non sequitur. The accuracy of ADC with a deceased person not known to have died is relevant only with regard to two points: Was the observed deceased individual truly dead when the NDEr saw him or her, and was the NDEr unaware of the death? The next two cases illustrate these points.

"CHERRY PICKING"

It should be obvious that Dr. Woerlee has been engaging in "cherry picking": choosing only those cases that fit his theories. He has avoided exploring the cases that are medically and psychologically the hardest to explain. For example, he has not commented on the next two highly interesting cases cited by investigators Brad Steiger and Sherry Hansen Steiger (1995) and psychiatrist Bruce Greyson (2010) (Case 6.4 in this book).

> Physician K. M. Dale related the case of 9-year-old Eddie Cuomo, whose fever finally broke after nearly 36 hours of anxious vigil on the part of his parents and hospital staff. As soon as he opened his eyes, at 3:00 in the morning, Eddie urgently told his parents that he had been to heaven, where

he saw his deceased Grandpa Cuomo, Auntie Rosa, and Uncle Lorenzo. His father was embarrassed that Dr. Dale was overhearing Eddie's story and tried to dismiss it as feverish delirium. Then Eddie added that he also saw his 19-year-old sister Teresa, who told him he had to go back. His father then became agitated, because he had spoken just two nights ago with Teresa, who was attending college in Vermont; he asked Dr. Dale to sedate Eddie. Later that morning, when Eddie's parents telephoned the college, they learned that Teresa had been killed in an automobile accident just after midnight and that college officials had tried unsuccessfully to reach the Cuomos at their home to inform them of the tragic news. (Steiger & Steiger, 1995)

This case occurred in the early 1990s, before the widespread availability of mobile phones. Nineteen-year-old sister Theresa was killed just after midnight, hence only about three hours before Eddie woke up! Obviously, the parents (and the physician) could not have been aware of her tragic demise prior to Eddie's "heavenly" encounter with her. So all of Woerlee's possible explanations do not hold water in this case.

The second case may be even more difficult to explain away:

John Myers related the case of a woman who, in an NDE, perceived herself leaving her body and viewing the hospital room, and saw her distraught husband and the doctor shaking his head. She reported that she went to heaven and saw an angel and a familiar young man. She exclaimed: "Why, Tom, I didn't know you were up here," to which Tom responded that he had just arrived. The angel then told the woman that she would be returning to earth, and she found herself back in the hospital bed with the doctor looking over her. Later that night, her husband got a call informing him that their friend Tom had died in an auto accident. (Myers, 1968, pp. 55–56)

Out of many cases that could be cited, these two provide circumstances in which Woerlee's (2012a) arguments do not hold true at all. These cases have been available since 2010 (and even earlier, from their original sources), but Woerlee has not mentioned them, despite his passion for NDEs. Perhaps Woerlee's commitment to the materialist ideology continues to prevent a balanced perspective on these cases.

GENETIC RECOGNIZABILITY

Another approach Woerlee has taken in his effort to discredit the validity of ADC during NDEs is that deceased relatives are "easily recognizable" because of their genetic similarities to the NDEr. He has attempted to demonstrate this point on his website by showing a picture of himself with his son on one side and his father on the other. And yes, there is a close resemblance. But how convincing is that fact for the entire issue in question?

First, Woerlee's claims in this matter are weak; everyone knows that not all relatives resemble each other, not even within a single family. For example, if we compare Rudolf Smit to his brother or sister, there is no striking resemblance. Among his wife's relatives are two nephews who are brothers. One has a round, rosy face, whereas his brother has an angular, pale face. It would be next to impossible to guess that they were sons of the same parents. And there are many other examples, of course.

Ironically, in advancing the recognizability argument, Woerlee has implicitly acknowledged that an NDE sometimes does feature encounters with deceased relatives, even as he has maintained that these encounters are nothing more than hallucinations. It is very coincidental, then, that such hyperrealistic hallucinations have shown (a) relatives of whose death the NDEr was completely unaware or (b) an unknown person or persons who afterward could be identified only by way of old, often forgotten photographs—as in the earlier case in this chapter of Eben Alexander's heavenly guide, later recognized to be his deceased sister.

WHAT WOERLEE HAS SAID OF THE EBEN ALEXANDER CASE

Although we could guess beforehand how Woerlee would react to the now world-famous case of neurosurgeon Eben Alexander, we were nevertheless quite curious and looked forward to what he had to say, and we have not been disappointed. Woerlee has attempted to debunk Alexander and has lashed out at him with a vengeance, in the same ways other critics had.

First, Woerlee has written that Alexander's NDE could not have been an NDE, because in contrast to other NDErs, he did not know his own identity during his NDE. Later, however, after he had consulted the items in Bruce Greyson's NDE Scale, which is used to assess the presence and depth of an NDE, Woerlee conceded that Alexander's NDE did satisfy those criteria. Then it indeed became an NDE or, rather, an NDE hallucination—wording that demonstrates how, to skeptics, including Woerlee, no NDE can be anything more than a hallucination. Also, if details are incomplete or they do not meet his criteria, Woerlee will likely dismiss a case. Woerlee apparently has not grasped, as NDE researchers have, that there is great variation among NDEs and that NDErs are often not aware of their own identities during their NDE but are again aware of who they are after returning to their bodies.

Another example of being distracted by incomplete or simplistic detail is Woerlee's response to the description in Alexander's book of the removal of a tracheal tube. In a blog post (March 25, 2013) on Amazon.com, Woerlee wrote:

> After reading the book "Proof of Heaven," I can only conclude that even you may have done a better write-up than the ghostwriter used. Just look at this howler:
>
> > "... *Dr. Wade immediately understood what it was: the breathing tube that was still in my throat. The tube I no longer needed, because my brain, along with the rest of my body, had just kicked back to life. He reached over, cut the securing tape, and carefully extracted it.*"

Next, Woerlee wrote:

> Try that method of removing an endotracheal tube in any advanced Dutch, English or USA hospital intensive care unit and you'll find yourself facing a disciplinary committee before you can say "nasi goreng." However, this was apparently a neurologist who did this, so I am not all that surprised. This description is theater. *Most intensivists would be incontinent with laughter on hearing this description.* . . . [emphasis added]

With this, Woerlee demonstrated that he understood little of the category into which Alexander's book falls. A little further, he even exclaimed, *"Is this science?!"* Of course it is *not* science. Alexander's book was never meant to be scientific in the first place. On the contrary, it is a report of a very peculiar experience, specifically written for a mass audience, not just for physicians. If the editor of this book had come across a very detailed medical explanation describing the removal of a breathing tube, then no doubt the editor would have deleted or simplified the passage. The public at large is generally not interested in all the details of medical procedures.

Woerlee then addressed Alexander's encounter with his biological sister Betsy on "the other side." In Woerlee's eyes, everything Alexander had said about this encounter was nothing more than "New Age fodder." That this encounter turned Alexander's entire life upside down, both intellectually and emotionally, did not affect Woerlee at all. To him, it was just "silly." In all his books, articles, and Internet blogs, it is quite evident to us that Woerlee has no empathic feelings whatsoever regarding NDEs and the people who have undergone these very peculiar, mystical, often life-altering phenomena.

All Woerlee has been willing to concede is, "Yes, the NDE is a wonderful experience." However, he has made that concession only to break it down in subsequent paragraphs. Like other skeptics, he has shown no profound wonder about the life-altering and character-changing effects of the experience. Woerlee's statements regarding Alexander's testimony have provided yet more proof of his objectionable treatment of people with the courage to share these transformative experiences.

Skeptics Who Go Too Far

As we have indicated previously, "hard" skeptics tend to go too far with assumptions about the cases they question. They often employ a tactic called "moving the goal posts." This analogy means that if their original demands are met, they come up with additional requirements and keep doing so ad nauseam. There comes a time, however, when professionalism requires that a debater either yield to the arguments or admit openly that doing so is an emotional impossibility. Regrettably, some skeptics do not engage in that level of professionalism. Following are some examples, drawing from the Reynolds case.

On an American blog (Mind-Energynet, first quarter 2013), that case was brought up for the umpteenth time, this time focusing on the question of whether Reynolds had received a "pre-op briefing" during which many details about the forthcoming operation would have been shared with her. It is true that Reynolds did receive a briefing. However, because she had "seen" so many things during her NDE, such as the operating room, the surgical instruments, and actions that had been performed on her body, skeptics wondered whether the instruments had been shown to her during the pre-op briefing or whether she might even have been shown around the operating room.

From the very start, this idea is completely off base: No surgical team would allow any such thing. A briefing is limited to general information, and it certainly does not include giving the patient a tour of the operating room, for the obvious reason that the room and everything in it must remain as sterile as possible. Fortunately, Rivas had the foresight to e-mail Pam Reynolds to ask her some very relevant questions in this regard. She responded quickly. Some of his comments and questions and her equally relevant responses follow.

EXCHANGE BETWEEN PAM REYNOLDS AND TITUS RIVAS

RIVAS: I've been in touch through e-mail with the brain surgeon in question, Dr. Spetzler, who referred me to the account given of the case in Michael B. Sabom's book *Light and Death*, adding that Pam's account was "remarkably accurate" [posted August 7, 2003, on JREF forum].

RIVAS: Yesterday (August 13, 2003), I sent a message to Pam Reynolds, who can be reached through her website. [No longer, since she died in May of 2010.] Though I had asked her some questions twice before, she was kind enough to answer a few additional ones only a few hours later. About any pre-op briefing she might have had, she answers me:

REYNOLDS: I saw Dr. Spetzler in the afternoon. I was examined and informed that the surgery would involve stopping my heart. My mother, brother and husband were present at all times. I was not given a tour, nor was I "walked thru the process." My examination took 20 minutes and we left immediately as we had a tee time [for golf].

RIVAS: [Asks about normal sources of information]

REYNOLDS: The surgery was new and was certainly not publicized enough to warrant media coverage.

RIVAS: [Asks about the procedure on her arteries]

REYNOLDS: Yes, they did access my arteries post mortem. At the time, my eyes were taped shut and my ears were plugged [with the clicking earphone modules].

RIVAS: Pam Reynolds has sent me a fourth reply. First, she states that she had never read any article or book about NDEs before her operation. She even remained skeptical about her own NDE until Dr. Sabom's investigation.

RIVAS: [Again asks about pre-op briefing]

REYNOLDS: Dr. Karl Greene was in charge of that part. He's no longer at Barrows [Barrow Neurological Institute]. I suppose you could ask virtually anyone about pre-op procedure. I have, and they all find it laughable to suggest that any patient would be led to the O.R. or shown the instruments. I would have chickened out.

The full exchange between Rivas and Reynolds was quite extensive; therefore, only the relevant lines have been cited. Nevertheless, it is clear from those lines that Reynolds knew very little about the operating procedure, she was not shown around the operating room, and she was not shown the surgical instruments, such as the special bone saw. Did these definitive responses end the matter? Hardly.

The moving of the goal posts began immediately. The skeptics did not say that Reynolds was lying but suggested bluntly that she might have read about similar operations, then forgotten, or that she had seen TV programs showing operating rooms and the surgical instruments her doctors used, or photos in magazines, and so on. Certainly these are theoretical possibilities, but when one begins to indicate mistrust for the central figure in this drama, then one has exceeded the credible basis for one's skepticism. Here the skeptics are not dealing with someone accused of a horrible crime who should be exposed at all costs. Such unwillingness to assume the sincerity of the patient and her surgical team is downright disrespectful if not contemptuous and therefore cannot be taken seriously.

Intermezzo 4

Karl A. Greene, MD

Karl Greene, MD, mentioned previously, was one of the neurosurgeons who assisted Robert Spetzler with this operation and who was very much involved in Reynolds's aftercare. Although he is now an independent neurosurgeon and no longer works at the Barrow Neurological Institute, where Reynolds's surgery took place, Rivas and Smit were able to track him down and found him to be quite forthcoming in answering the questions that were sent to him. The full text of his response can be found in Appendix D.

Essentially, Greene's response was this: Reynolds's entire conscious experience during her operation can be considered anomalous. Her account of what happened in the operating room during her operation was remarkably accurate, even though there can be no doubt that she was under full anesthesia and could not have had any anesthesia awareness whatsoever. This point is certain because the clicks in her ears, registering between 95 and 100 decibels, were continuous during the entire procedure and would have registered on her EEG if she had possessed even a trace of awareness. But there was no sign of the clicks on her EEG. This comment by Dr. Greene (in Appendix D) supports this finding:

> EEG activity is continuously monitored throughout any neurosurgical procedure for which any method of intraoperative monitoring is utilized. To ignore ongoing electrophysiological activity during monitoring for neurosurgical procedures, as inferred, and overlooking seizure activity in a surgical patient places a provider in the United States of America at risk for medical malpractice!

In addition, a recent e-mail message from Michael Sabom, the cardiologist who was the first to thoroughly investigate this case, confirmed that not one of the operating personnel considered the possibility of anesthesia awareness. Instead, Greene said (in Appendix D),

> The vast majority of the medical providers at Barrow Neurological Institute that were involved in Pam's case or recollect her case take a more traditional/conventional approach to Mrs. Reynold[s]'s experience. Some have even stated to me that "she was crazy."

In a separate message (not included in Appendix D), Greene also confirmed that the song "Hotel California" by the Eagles was played only once in the operating room while the operation was steadily progressing, as Reynolds later reported having heard when she reentered her body. Greene was in the operating room while the song was playing.

As far as we are concerned, this last point ends the discussion. The above statements by Greene, a neurosurgeon directly involved with the Reynolds case, conclude this discussion of that case and confirm our hypothesis that

NDEs can and do occur during confirmed cardiac arrest, and that they indicate that the mind exceeds brain function.

Summing Up

We have paid much attention to Gerald Woerlee's critiques and explanations, singling him out to represent all the "hard" skeptics simply because he has been the one most vocal on the subject of NDEs. There are other skeptics who have had no qualms about spreading opinions about NDE cases that are hardly worth printing, such as the commentary from "Internet Infidel" Keith Augustine, or from Robert Todd Carroll in his *Skeptical Dictionary*. Woerlee not only is the most vocal; he also is the most medically knowledgeable—far more than any other skeptic. He did and does delve into the subject, which, we repeat, is commendable—but unfortunately it is from a parochial and often zealous materialist viewpoint. This is clearly illustrated by some statements he posted on a *Skeptiko* blog under the nickname of Swiferobi (which Smit repeated on the Amazon.com blog, mentioned previously):

> As regards the NDE and OBE as a basis for religion, most of the well-known NDE researchers consider it just that. Just think of Moody, Rawlings, Sabom, etc. There are even fundamentalist Christians touring and teaching in the USA this very day, who teach that the NDE is either the work of the devil, and therefore proof of God, or that the NDE is a glimpse of the afterlife. The same is true of fundamentalist Islam where the "night journey" or "miraj" of Mohammed where he visited heaven and hell as well as the farthest mosque in one evening is also a classic NDE/OBE. (January 27, 2011)

> As regards my attitude towards religion, my opinions are very simple. Some might criticize this, but this website and the book reveal that the basis of most religious beliefs is NDEs, OBEs, and other apparently paranormal phenomena. Combine this with interpretations from these illogical and very evil holy books, and you have religions. This is the basis of the book *The Unholy Legacy of Abraham*. This book explains the physiology behind all these phenomena. (January 26, 2011)

> As I said on *Skeptiko*, I have already written two books detailing the physiology of near-death experiences [one of them being *The Unholy Legacy of*

Abraham mentioned above]. Please note that this book is not specifically about NDEs or OBEs and the paranormal, but explains that these are the basis for belief in other irrational paranormal phenomena such as religions. Moreover, it is designed to reveal the iniquities and madness contained in the Bible and Koran. (April 19, 2010)

In response to these entries, Rudolf Smit commented via this same Amazon. com blog:

From these three statements above one can deduce that Woerlee is not primarily motivated by science—i.e. the unbiased desire to know—but at least equally so by his revulsion against religions which, as he sees it, are the source of all evil in this world and thus, ideally, should be made to disappear. And then, quite logically, it follows that NDEs are the cause of these evils. Consequently, Woerlee is not primarily interested in the real nature of the NDE; no, he uses his own brand of science to explain the NDE away, even if he has to twist the facts to achieve that goal.

Since, according to Woerlee, NDEs are at the source of all evil in this world, then it follows that all NDE researchers should be considered with suspicion, particularly when they do not adhere to Woerlee's brand of science: hard materialism. Thus, in his eyes NDE researchers Greyson, Sabom, Ring, Fenwick, van Lommel, Morse, Moody, Long, and of course Carter are, at best, misled and foolish, or, at worst, frauds.

Given the gist of his website, his true motives, and the lengths to which he goes to explain away the facts . . . how can any reasonable person believe that here is a true, unbiased scientist at work?

No Criticism Allowed?

One might get the impression from those comments that no criticism of NDE cases is allowed. Not so: We believe firmly that a critical approach to NDE phenomena is essential at all times, because someone could indeed present an NDE that is no more than a fantasy or even something dreamed up to make things "interesting." Consequently, NDE researchers are quite keen to investigate only authentic NDE reports and have learned to separate the wheat from the chaff. Extensive stories told with great exuberance about journeys to higher spheres populated by miraculous divine beings do not come across as authentic and thus have much less evidential power than brief and soberly written accounts. Reports supported by veridical and verifiable details have the greatest evidential power.

Such is true about the cases reviewed in this book—cases for which "normal explanations," invoking causes limited to the physical world, do not seem to exist. After all, anomalous phenomena that can be part of NDEs are not only mentioned by NDErs themselves but sometimes also corroborated by third parties. Admittedly, it is not at all forbidden to deny that such phenomena can possibly happen simply because they cannot be explained based on materialist principles. However, such denials seem futile, inspired by the emotional need to defend at all costs the materialist worldview, even if doing so forces the defender to deny every reasonable interpretation of the facts. But to deny even the *possibility* of NDE phenomena solely because those facts do not fit with one's ideological presumptions is simply unscientific.

THE ESSENTIALS OF SOUND SKEPTICISM

Once, a friend made two statements that we think can be regarded as the essentials of sound skepticism:

1. *Criticism is the lifeblood of science*, meaning that criticism is welcome if only because it is often the only way to get to whatever truth is out there.
2. *Science is a tough business*, meaning that one should do one's best to overcome the inevitable hurdles and potholes on the path to the truth, including vehement resistance from certain parties and sources when newly revealed facts require a new view of reality. This principle also means that one has to be both critical and skeptical of one's own ideas and findings—and even tougher on them than on the work of others.

Seemingly the very opposite of this sound skepticism is an attitude we have seen among certain self-appointed skeptics. It goes something like this: "I have made up my mind; don't confuse me with the facts—especially new ones."

To adhere to the essentials of sound skepticism makes it morally compulsory to go wherever the evidence leads, irrespective of ideology, prejudices, beliefs, or objections to how things seem to be turning out. If the evidence is clear and the implications of that evidence are sound, then the conscientious scientist has to accept it, period.

We have singled out pseudoskeptics for going to extremes in proposing explanations even more incredible than the phenomena they are meant to explain away in order to demonstrate that we have made an honest effort to adhere to the essentials of sound skepticism as we have considered the remarkable phenomena entailed in the cases we have presented.

Having presented in this book over 100 cases of NDEs involving confirmed paranormal aspects, and having demonstrated the inadequacy of arguments that pseudoskeptics have proffered in an attempt to discredit paranormal NDEs, we are left with the conclusion that mind and brain are essentially independent, though closely associated during physical existence, and that consciousness continues when the brain and body have ceased to function.

Notes

1 The Neocortex

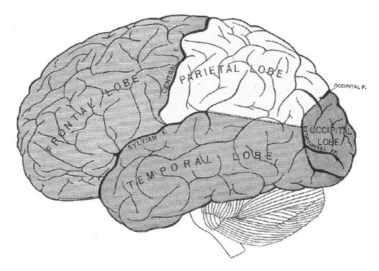

Human neocortex, showing the main lobes of the cortex

The neocortex is a part of the brains of mammals, including humans. It consists of the upper layer (2–4 mm thick) of the two hemispheres. The neocortex is part of the cerebral cortex and is involved with higher functions, such as sensory observations; conscious movements; and, in people, reasoning, abstract thinking, and language. The gray matter consists of cellular bodies of neurons and glial cells, the white matter of axons, which are covered with a layer of myelin.

2 **EEG Burst Suppression**

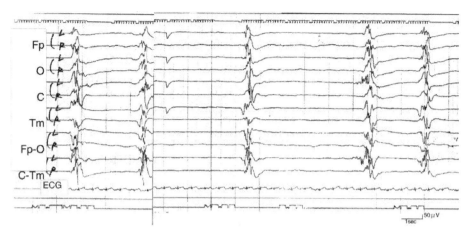

Electroencephalogram of typical burst suppression electrical activity

The electroencephalogram shows a typical pattern. Rather than the continuous generation of brain waves that typically characterizes brain function, in burst suppression, the EEG shows a "burst" of brain waves represented as "blips" followed by a "suppression" (absence) of brain waves represented by a flat line, and that sequence of burst and suppression is repeated over and over. This pattern is characteristic of a nonactive brain and is usually observed in association with deep levels of anesthesia, hyperthermia, and coma.

References

Alexander, E. (2012). *Proof of heaven: A neurosurgeon's journey into the afterlife*. New York, NY: Simon & Schuster.

Alexander, E. (2012, October 15). Proof of heaven: A doctor's experience with the afterlife. *Newsweek*. Retrieved from http://www.newsweek.com/proof-heaven-doctors-experience-afterlife-65327

Bell, A. (2001, December 6). REPLAY of Pam Reynolds 12/06. [Coast to Coast AM show archive, interview with Pam Reynolds]. Retrieved from http://www.coast tocoastam.com/guest/reynolds-pam/5854

Broome, K. (Producer). (2002). *The day I died: The mind, the brain, and near-death experiences*. [Motion picture]. Glasgow, Scotland: British Broadcasting Corporation. Retrieved from http://topdocumentaryfilms.com/day-i-died/ (17:40–32:00 minutes)

Coimbra, C. G. (1999). Implications of ischemic penumbra for the diagnosis of brain death. *Brazilian Journal of Medical and Biological Research, 32*(12), 1479–1487.

Dittrich, L. (2013, July 2). The prophet: An investigation into Eben Alexander, author of the blockbuster *Proof of Heaven. Esquire,* June/July 2013, 88–95. Retrieved from http://www.esquire.com/entertainment/interviews/a23248/the-prophet/

Fenwick, P. (2005). Science and spirituality: A challenge for the 21st century [The Bruce Greyson Lecture from the International Association for Near-Death Studies 2004 Annual Conference]. *Journal of Near-Death Studies, 23*(3), 131–157.

Freeman, M., & Andreae, L. (Executive producers). (2011, June 8). *Is there life after death?* Through the Wormhole, Season 2, Episode 1. Retrieved from https://www.youtube.com/watch?v=YukKDzSzxEI

Greyson, B. (2010). Seeing dead people not known to have died: "Peak in Darien" experiences. *Anthropology and Humanism, 35*(2), 159–171.

James, W. (1907). *Pragmatism: A new name for some old ways of thinking.* London, UK: Longmans, Green.

Martinez-Alier, N. (2010, March 26). *Clinical review–bacterial meningitis.* Retrieved from http://www.gponline.com/clinical-review-bacterial-meningitis/article/991614

Mays, R. G. (2013). Esquire *article on Eben Alexander distorts the facts.* Retrieved from http://iands.org/esquire

MSNBC (Producer). (2001, April 11). *Back from the dead* [interview with Pam Reynolds]. Retrieved from https://www.youtube.com/watch?v=YO8UVebuA0g

Myers, J. G. (Ed.). (1968/2012). *Voices from the edge of eternity.* New Kensington, PA: Whittaker House.

Parnia, S. (with Young, J.). (2013). *Erasing death: The science that is rewriting the boundaries between life and death.* New York, NY: HarperCollins.

Rivas, T. (2008b). Een gesprek met TG over de man met het gebit [A conversation with TG about the man with the dentures]. *Terugkeer, 19*(3), 12–20.

Smit, R. H. (2008c). Letter to the editor: Further commentary on Pam Reynolds's NDE. *Journal of Near-Death Studies, 26*(4), 308–309.

Smit, R. H. (2012). Letter to the editor: Failed test of the possibility that Pam Reynolds heard normally during her NDE. *Journal of Near-Death Studies, 30*(3), 188–192.

Smit, R. H., & Rivas, T. (2010). Rejoinder to "Response to 'Corroboration of the dentures anecdote involving veridical perception in a near-death experience.'" *Journal of Near-Death Studies, 28*(4), 193–205.

Steiger, B., & Steiger, S. H. (1995). *Children of the light: The startling and inspiring truth about children's near-death experiences and how they illumine the beyond.* New York, NY: Signet.

Sudduth, M. (2015, December 21). *In defense of Sam Harris on near-death experiences.* Retrieved from http://michaelsudduth.com/in-defense-of-sam -harris-on-near-death-experiences/

TG. (2008). Commentaar op Woerlee door A-verpleegkundige TG [Comments on Woerlee by registered nurse TG]. *Terugkeer, 19*(4), 8.

van Lommel, P., van Wees, R., Meyers, V., & Elfferich, I. (2001). Near-death experience in survivors of cardiac arrest: A prospective study in the Netherlands. *The Lancet, 358*(9298), 2039–2045.

Weinberg, A. D. (1993). Hypothermia. *Annals of Emergency Medicine, 22*(2), 370–377. Retrieved from http://www.hypothermia.org/weinberg.htm

Woerlee, G. M. (2004). Cardiac arrest and near-death experiences. *Journal of Near-Death Studies, 22*(4), 235–249.

Woerlee, G. M. (2007). *The unholy legacy of Abraham.* Leicester, UK: Troubador

Woerlee, G. M. (2011). Could Pam Reynolds hear? A new investigation into the possibility of hearing during this famous near-death experience. *Journal of Near-Death Studies, 30*(1), 3–25.

Woerlee, G. M. (2012a). Seeing family members during NDEs: "Peak in Darien" experiences & NDEs. Retrieved from http://neardth.com/seeing-family-during -nde.php

Acknowledgments

My special thanks for their invaluable help at composing this chapter go to Titus Rivas, Pim van Lommel, Stephen Woodhead (UK), Robert Mays (U.S.), Karl Greene (U.S.), and James van Pelt (U.S.).

From an article by Pim van Lommel (2013, pp. 26–27), reprinted with his permission:

No Blood Flow to the Brain

If the absence of blood flow to the brain ("no-flow") prevents the supply of glucose and oxygen, a neuron's first symptom will be the inability to maintain its membrane potential, resulting in the loss of neuronal function (Van Dijk, 2004). The acute loss of electrical and synaptic activity in neurons can be seen as the cell's inbuilt defense and energy-saving response and is called a "pilot light state." When the electrical functions of neurons cease, the remaining energy sources can be deployed very briefly for the cell's survival. In the case of short-term oxygen deficiency, dysfunction can be temporary and recovery is still possible because the neurons will remain viable for a few more minutes. During cardiac arrest the entire brain is deprived of oxygen, resulting in the loss of consciousness, of all body and brainstem reflexes, and of respiration. This period of "clinical death" is usually reversible, i.e., temporary, if cardiopulmonary resuscitation (CPR) is initiated within five to ten minutes. Within seconds, cardiac arrest will result in a total loss of oxygen supply and a build-up of carbon dioxide (CO_2) in the brain. This situation cannot be remedied during the resuscitation procedure itself, but only after the cardiac rhythm has been re-established through defibrillation (an electric shock). A delay in starting adequate resuscitation may result in the death of a great many brain cells and thus in brain death, and most patients will ultimately die. A study carried out at a coronary care unit has shown that patients whose resuscitation was started within one minute had a 33% chance of survival, compared to only 14% for those who, due to circumstances, were only resuscitated after more than a minute since the onset of unconsciousness (Herlitz et al., 2002).

Low Blood Flow to the Brain in Effective CPR
Prolongs the Viability of the Brain

Research has shown that external heart massage during CPR cannot pump enough blood to the brain to restore brain function. Nobody has ever regained consciousness during external resuscitation of the heart. This always requires defibrillation to re-establish the cardiac rhythm. Without restoration of normal blood pressure and the resumption of cardiac output, which only can be achieved by successful defibrillation, a long duration of CPR is considered an indication of poor outcome and high mortality because CPR alone cannot ultimately prevent the irreversible damage of brain cells (Peberdy et al., 2003). During CPR, blood supply to the brain is 5–10% of its normal value (White et al., 1983), and during external heart massage the systolic pressure will usually reach approximately 50 mmHg, with an average of 20 mmHg because of the low diastolic pressure. The maximum average blood pressure during proper resuscitation is 30–40 mmHg (Paradis et al., 1989), which is still far too low for the blood to deliver enough oxygen and glucose to the brain. The administration of certain medication during resuscitation can increase blood pressure a little (Paradis et al., 1991), but it will remain well below normal. Furthermore, in the absence of a normal blood supply, the brain cells are likely to swell (edema), which results in increased pressure in the brain (intracranial pressure), and also an increase of cerebral vascular resistance occurs. This is why it was found in animal studies that it actually requires a higher than normal blood pressure to maintain adequate cerebral perfusion and to supply the brain with sufficiently oxygenated blood and to enable the removal of carbon dioxide (Fisher and Hossman, 1996). During resuscitation, blood gases (O_2 and CO_2) are sometimes measured to determine the severity of the oxygen deficiency in the blood. However, normal levels of oxygen and carbon dioxide do not guarantee that enough arterial blood, and thus enough oxygen, will reach the brain during resuscitation.

To summarize: we know that proper resuscitation, with adequate external heart massage and mouth-to-mouth respiration or respiration via a mask, will produce minimal blood flow ("low-flow") to the brain, which increases the chances of recovery of brain function after the cardiac arrest has been successfully treated with defibrillation. By this minimal cerebral blood flow the no-longer-functioning neurons will be able to survive for a longer period of time in the minimal energy state ("pilot light state"), also called "hibernation" or "ischemic penumbra" of the brain (Coimbra, 1999), because it prolongs the period of reversibility (viability) before neuronal cell death and brain death occur.

References

Coimbra, C. G. (1999). Implications of ischemic penumbra for the diagnosis of brain death. *Brazilian Journal of Medical and Biological Research, 32*(12), 1479–1487.

Fischer, M., & Hossmann, K. A. (1996). Volume expansion during cardiopulmonary resuscitation reduces cerebral no-reflow. *Resuscitation, 32*(3), 227–240.

Herlitz, J., Bång, A., Alsén, B., & Aune, S. (2002). Characteristics and outcome among patients suffering from in hospital cardiac arrest in relation to the interval between collapse and start of CPR. *Resuscitation, 53*(1), 21–27.

Paradis, N. A., Martin, G. B., Goetting, M. G., Rosenberg, J. M., Rivers, E. P., Appleton, T. J., & Nowak, R. M. (1989). Simultaneous aortic, jugular bulb, and right atrial pressures during cardiopulmonary resuscitation in humans. Insights into mechanisms. *Circulation, 80*(2), 361–368.

Paradis, N. A., Martin, G. B., Rosenberg, J., Rivers, E. P., Goetting, M. G., Appleton, T. J., . . . & Nowak, R. M. (1991). The effect of standard-and high-dose epinephrine on coronary perfusion pressure during prolonged cardiopulmonary resuscitation. *Journal of the American Medical Association, 265*(9), 1139–1144.

Peberdy, M. A., Kaye, W., Ornato, J. P., Larkin, G. L., Nadkarni, V., Mancini, M. E., . . . NRCPR Investigators. (2003). Cardiopulmonary resuscitation of adults in the hospital: A report of 14 720 cardiac arrests from the National Registry of Cardiopulmonary Resuscitation. *Resuscitation, 58*(3), 297–308.

van Dijk, G. W. (2004). Hoofdstuk 3: Bewustzijn [Chapter 3: Consciousness]. In B. T. J. Meursing & R. G. van Kesteren (Eds.), *Handboek reanimatie: Tweede herziene druk* [Resuscitation handbook: 2nd rev. ed.] (pp. 21–25). Utrecht, Netherlands: Wetenschappelijke Uitgeverij Bunge.

van Lommel, P. (2013). Non-local consciousness: A concept based on scientific research on near-death experiences during cardiac arrest. *Journal of Consciousness Studies, 20*(1–2), 7–48.

White, B. C., Winegar, C. D., Jackson, R. E., Joyce, K. M., Vigor, D. N., Hoehner, T. J., . . . & Wilson, R. F. (1983). Cerebral cortical perfusion during and following resuscitation from cardiac arrest in dogs. *American Journal of Emergency Medicine, 1*(2), 128–138.

Appendix B

In accordance with good scientific practice, in his writings, anesthesiologist Gerald Woerlee (2010) referred to a great number of articles. Three of them in particular seem to support his assertion that external heart massage can lead to a return to consciousness. However, as cardiologist Pim van Lommel made clear in an extensive letter to Titus Rivas and Rudolf Smit in October 2009, Woerlee did not tell the whole story.

WOERLEE WROTE:

> Human research demonstrates that manual external cardiac massage is less effective in generating a flow of blood around the body than is external machine cardiac massage with a "Thumper," which in turn is less effective than internal cardiac massage (AHA, 2005). Reports of experiences with these three forms of cardiac massage applied to cardiac arrest patients show that some people do regain [!!] consciousness during cardiac massage for cardiac arrest applied by hand (Bihari & Rajajee, 2008) or by means of a "Thumper" (Lewinter et al., 1989), as well as by internal cardiac massage (Miller et al., 1961).

VAN LOMMEL RESPONDED with regard Woerlee's reference to Bihari and Rajajee, 2008:

> This is the only article ever published in the medical literature reporting that a patient suffering cardiac arrest resulting from complications during a medical procedure received immediate external chest massage due to the fact that physicians and nurses were present during this procedure. This patient did not lose his consciousness. This patient suffered an asystole, and not ventricular fibrillation (VF). This is of course quite different from the situation of a patient suffering VF who regains consciousness during cardiopulmonary resuscitation (CPR). In the case of patients suffering cardiac arrest due to an acute myocardial infarction, CPR is usually initiated in the intensive care

unit (ICU) or coronary care unit (CCU) from thirty to 120 seconds after the onset of VF, or sometimes even much later in a general ward or in an out-of-hospital cardiac arrest. Woerlee quotes this article, entitled "Prolonged awareness during CPR for asystolic arrest", but he quotes it wrongly, because the patient described in this article had asystole and not VF, and he **did not regain consciousness, but had a prolonged period of awareness enabled by external chest massage** by means of a thumper (Lewinter et al., 1989).

VAN LOMMEL RESPONDED with regard to Woerlee's reference to Lewinter et al.:

This is the only article ever published in the medical literature in which a single patient with a **"wide-complex rhythm without measurable output"** became conscious during cardiopulmonary resuscitation (CPR), but this patient died because the CPR was not effective to restore normal heart rhythm and blood pressure. The type of cardiac rhythm described in reference to this patient is totally different from ventricular fibrillation (VF).

VAN LOMMEL RESPONDED with regard to Woerlee's reference to Miller et al., 1961:

This is the only article (from 1961!) where a patient is described who regained consciousness during **open-heart massage**, a procedure in which the heart is massaged directly following an emergency opening of the patient's chest by a surgeon. This patient suffered cardiac arrest as a complication of surgery elsewhere in her body. She was under general anesthesia, but due to the restoration of her blood pressure and normal heart rhythm she regained con-sciousness after the administration of anesthesia was halted following her open-heart massage. It is important to mention that in 1960 neither external nor internal defibrillation was technically available as a treatment option.

References

AHA (2005). 2005 American Heart Association guidelines for cardiopulmonary resuscitation and emergency cardiovascular care, part 6: CPR techniques and devices. *Circulation, 112,* IV-47–IV-50.

Bihari, S., & Rajajee, V. (2008). Prolonged retention of awareness during cardio-pulmonary resuscitation for asystolic cardiac arrest. *Neurocritical Care, 9*(3), 382–386.

Lewinter, J. R., Carden, D. L., Nowak, R. M., Enriquez, E., & Martin, G. B. (1989). CPR-dependent consciousness: Evidence for cardiac compression causing forward flow. *Annals of Emergency Medicine, 18*(10), 1111–1115.

Miller, J. B., Davie, R. D. M., & Douglas, D. M. (1961). The efficiency of cardiac massage in ventricular fibrillation: Description of an instance of recovery of consciousness without spontaneous heart beat. *British Journal of Anaesthesia, 33*(1), 22–23.

Woerlee, G. M. (2010). Response to "Corroboration of the dentures anecdote involving veridical perception in a near-death experience." *Journal of Near-Death Studies, 28*(4), 181–191.

Appendix C

TABLE OF ENVIRONMENTAL NOISES IN DECIBELS AND HOW THEY ARE EXPERIENCED

SOURCE OF SOUND	SOUND PRESSURE LEVEL (IN DECIBELS)
Jet engine at 1 meter (3 feet)	150
Threshold of aural pain	130–140
Loudest human voice at 1 inch	135
Trumpet at 0.5 meters (1.5 feet)	130
Stadium horn at 1 meter (3 feet)	120
Risk of instantaneous noise-induced hearing loss	120
Jet engine at 100 meters (300 feet)	110–140
Gas-powered chainsaw at 1 meter (3 feet)	110
Jackhammer at 1 meter (3 feet)	100
Traffic on a busy roadway at 10 meters (30 feet)	80–90
Hearing damage (long-term exposure; need not be continuous)	85
Passenger car at 10 meters (30 feet)	60–80
EPA-identified maximum to protect against hearing loss and other disruptive effects from noise, such as sleep disturbance, stress, learning detriment, etc.	70
Handheld electric mixer	65
TV (set at home level) at 1 meter (3 feet)	60
Washing machine, dishwasher	42–53
Normal conversation at 1 meter (3 feet)	40–60
Very calm room	20–30
Light leaf rustling, calm breathing	10
Auditory threshold at 1 kHz	0

Note: The shaded area is where the sound is so loud that it begins to become unbearable even after a short while, and hearing damage may occur. It is within this range, at 95–100 decibels, that, in the Reynolds case (see Case 3.29 and Chapter 11), the earbud loudspeakers produced 11 clicks per second in Reynolds's ears. Gerald Woerlee's claim that this sound could be "neurologically filtered out," is highly unlikely in our estimation.
Source: Courtesy Wikipedia

The following is excerpted from an e-mail to Titus Rivas, dated July 7, 2015, from neurosurgeon Karl Greene, who assisted neurosurgeon Robert Spetzler during the surgery on Pam Reynolds (see Case 3.29).

Below are responses to your questions referred to me in a correspondence dated June 8, 2015, from Nijmegen [Holland] regarding a former patient, Pamela Reynolds. In response to your questions, I will first provide you with the question asked of me, followed by my response. As a side note, please forgive my delayed response.

1. **Are there any aspects in Pam's account that you consider anomalous, in the sense that they normally could not be reconciled with the physiological state she was in at the time?**

   From a practical standpoint, Mrs. Reynolds' entire conscious experience could be considered anomalous, in that such conscious experience as described by Mrs. Reynolds does not typically occur in our consensus reality while under the influence of doses of barbiturates that markedly suppress brain electrophysiological activity (burst-suppression on electroencephalogram); profound hypothermia (loss of spontaneous electroencephalographic activity, somatosensory evoked potential responses, and brain stem auditory evoked potential responses), and circulatory arrest (complete loss of all electrophysiological activity). Mrs. Reynolds' well-informed account of a conscious experience during profound alteration and suppression of central nervous system activity could all be considered anomalous in this setting.

2. **Was there sufficient blood circulation in her brain to explain her NDE-consciousness during the** *first phase* **of Pam's NDE involving perception of the bone saw, etc.?**

   While it is possible that Mrs. Reynolds briefly visualized an instrument used to perform craniotomy bone flap procedures as she was brought into the operating room just prior to surgery, her knowledge of its use and her recollection of its tone and pitch while being used, make Mrs. Reynolds' "NDE-consciousness" experience unique. The aspect of the surgical proce-dure involving the use of a bone saw for craniotomy takes place during cooling of the body for hypothermia combined with infusions of barbiturates at substantial doses. Following aneurysm exposure, extracorpor[e]al circula-tion utilizing cardiopulmonary bypass is initiated and this is usually when the patient's core temperature reaches 32 degrees centigrade. Circulatory arrest occurs between 18 degrees centigrade and 22 degrees centigrade, with the cardiac arrest time being as limited as possible in an effort to satisfacto-rily clip-obliterate the brain aneurysm and to prevent untoward complica-tions of prolonged cardiopulmonary arrest.

Depending on one's interpretation of satisfactory or sufficient cerebral blood flow to explain Mrs. Reynolds' NDE-consciousness during the first phase involving the bone saw, electrophysiological activity in the central nervous system was more likely than not to have been so profoundly sup-pressed that Mrs. Reynolds would not have had such a well-formed con-scious experience of the use of a bone saw and its sequelae.

3. Was there significant blood circulation in Pam's brain to support her NDE-consciousness during the *second phase* involving seeing her body jump and hearing the song "Hotel California"?

As described above with regard to technical aspects of basi-lar artery aneurysm surgery managed with circulatory arrest, hypo-thermia, and barbiturates for cerebral protection, there was no blood flow at the time that Pam recalled seeing her body jump, as her body moved as a result of electrocardioversion to restart her heart and, therefore, initiate recirculation of blood to her entire body, including her brain. Her recollection of the song "Hotel California" in its detail (you can check out any time you like, but you can never leave . . .) is an unlikely event from a physiological standpoint, including cerebral blood flow levels.

4. What is your opinion about the hypothetical possibilities that these experiences could still be explained by as yet unknown residual activity in her brain—say, in subcortical areas?

While I am aware of theories regarding low-level residual brain activ-ity being associated with well-formed experiences of consciousness, the relationship between low-level residual brain activity and consciousness remains theoretical. In the absolute [sense] however, I supposed this hypothetical possibility could not entirely be ruled out with our present knowledge and technological capabilities.

5. Could some of her perceptions be explained away by lucky guessing?
No.

6. What is your opinion about the attempts by so-called skeptics to explain Pam's NDE away?

Until the day arrives that human beings have a clear understanding of consciousness and those factors that impact our perception of consciousness, I suppose there will always be a debate with regard to the subjective experiences of individuals who encounter unique experiences of consciousness that do not easily reside within the realm of consensus reality.

7. Have there been similar cases of consciousness/NDEs involving the standstill procedure?

As I do not routinely utilize circulatory arrest, hypothermia, and barbiturate cerebral protection for cerebral aneurysm management in my clinical practice, I do not consider myself an expert in the field. The answer to your inquiry may be better suited for those surgeons who routinely utilize circulatory arrest with hypothermia with or without barbiturate cerebral protection in their practices (cardiothoracic surgeons, neurovascular surgeons, and neuropsychologists with an interest in consciousness).

It is my hope that this information is useful to you during your endeavor to translate your coauthored book on near-death experiences. Below I have included four references on the use of cardiopulmonary bypass, hypothermic circulatory arrest, and barbiturate cerebral protection for cerebral aneurysm management for your future reference.

Sincerely, Karl A. Greene, MD, PhD, FACS, FAANS

As often happens when many questions are answered, the responses generate new or clarifying questions. The following is excerpted from a second e-mail to Rivas from neurosurgeon Karl Greene, dated August 1, 2015:

Was there anyone involved in the surgery who stuck to a mainstream conventional interpretation of the case?

The vast majority of the medical providers at Barrow Neurological Institute that were involved in Pam's case or recollect her case take a more traditional/conventional approach to Mrs. Reynold[s]'s experience. Some have even stated to me that "she was crazy." As you are probably aware, I do not concur with such opinions.

Do you think the song "Hotel California" was playing at the very moment Pam was being resuscitated?

I have no way of accurately responding to this inquiry, as the discrete details of human memory tend to fade over the course of more than two decades. I am merely being honest. [However, in an additional e-mail, Dr. Greene stated that the song was played only once, in the operating room, and that he was there when it was played (also Bachrach, 2014).]

When Pam was connected up to the bypass machine to cool her down, is it the case that a significant quantity of her blood (up to 3 units) was removed for storage (to be returned later for good clotting) and replaced with saline? And that her remaining blood would have been diluted significantly with saline as it flowed in and out of the heat exchanger?

The details of Barrow's protocol can be found in the citations referenced in the previous responses forwarded to you. I am unable to comment any further.

When you and the other doctors became aware of Pam's very unusual observations, are we correct in assuming that the EEG charts were checked for spikes and none were found?

EEG activity is continuously monitored throughout any neurosurgical procedure for which any method of intraoperative monitoring is utilized. To ignore ongoing electrophysiological activity during monitoring for neurosurgical procedures, as inferred, and overlooking seizure activity in a surgical patient places a provider in the United States of America at risk for medical malpractice!

Does Pam's anesthetist concur with your opinion? (That is, does he reject Dr. Woerlee's anesthetic awareness conjecture?)

I have not recently or remotely discussed Pam's case with her treating anesthesiologist, and I therefore cannot address this question. However, my life experience tells me that many people that are living the conscious experience moment by moment, day by day, do not concur with Franklin Merrell-Wolff's Philosophy of Consciousness Without an Object.

Were the click modules in Pam's ears continuously switched on or switched off when she was completely under?

The auditory "clicks" of BAER monitoring are continuously monitored throughout the entire neurosurgical procedure, as outlined in the citations referenced in the previous responses forwarded to you.

My hope is that the above responses are helpful to you.

Sincerely, Karl A. Greene, MD, PhD, FACS, FAANS

References

Bachrach, J. (2014). *Glimpsing heaven: The stories and science of life after death.* Washington, DC: National Geographic.

Greene, K. A., Marciano, F. F., Hamilton, M. G., Herman, J. M., Rekate, H. L., & Spetzler, R. F. (1994). Cardiopulmonary bypass, hypothermic circulatory arrest and barbiturate cerebral protection for the treatment of giant vertebrobasilar aneurysms in children. *Pediatric Neurosurgery, 21*(2), 124–133.

Lawton, M. T., Raudzens, P. A., Zabramski, J. M., & Spetzler, R. F. (1998). Hypothermic circulatory arrest in neurovascular surgery: Evolving indications and predictors of patient outcome. *Neurosurgery, 43*(1), 10–20.

Merrell-Wolff, F. F. (1973). *The philosophy of consciousness without an object: Reflections on the nature of transcendental consciousness.* New York, NY: Julian Press.

Silverberg, G. D., Reitz, B. A., & Ream, A. K. (1981). Hypothermia and cardiac arrest in the treatment of giant aneurysms of the cerebral circulation and hemangioblastoma of the medulla. *Journal of Neurosurgery, 55*(3), 337–346.

Spetzler, R. F., Hadley, M. N., Rigamonti, D., Carter, L. P., Raudzens, P. A., Shedd, S. A., & Wilkinson, E. (1988). Aneurysms of the basilar artery treated with circulatory arrest, hypothermia, and barbiturate cerebral protection. *Journal of Neurosurgery, 68*(6), 868–879.

Monitoring Procedures Used in Hypothermic Circulatory Arrest Surgery

There are three monitoring procedures used in this specialized surgical procedure (Spetzler et al., 1988, pp. 868–869), which Pamela Reynolds underwent in 1991 (see Case 3.29):

1. Electroencephalography (EEG) measures generalized cortical electrical activity and is used to monitor anesthesia dosage during an operation and to detect adverse changes in cortical responses postoperatively. Shortly after the anesthetic agent is administered, the patient becomes unconscious and the EEG activity goes into burst suppression (see Chapter 11, Note 2). During the cooling phase when the patient's temperature drops below 25° C, EEG activity goes to a flat line.

2. Somatosensory evoked potentials (SSEPs) measure electrical activity in bodily sensory pathways by applying electrical stimulation to the skin. The SSEPs persist even during anesthesia burst suppression but are not felt by the patient. They are used to monitor sensory pathway conduction during an operation and to detect adverse changes in thalamocortical pathways postoperatively. SSEPs persist to around 18–20° C during the cooling phase, a lower temperature than when EEG activity ceases.

3. Brainstem auditory evoked potentials (BAEPs; also BAERs, brainstem auditory evoked responses) measure electrical activity in auditory brainstem pathways by applying very loud clicks in both ears. They are used to monitor auditory pathway conduction during an operation and to detect adverse changes in the brainstem postoperatively. The BAEPs persist until interrupted by circulatory arrest and so are an indication that

circulatory arrest has occurred. They are recorded if brainstem structures are threatened, as was the case with Pam Reynolds. If, following circulatory arrest, there are no response changes, then brainstem function has not been affected by the surgical procedure.

EEG, BAEPs, and SSEPs are all monitored simultaneously during hypothermic circulatory arrest surgery. The EEG is used to monitor the level of anesthesia via the presence of burst suppression. All three procedures are used to monitor the progress of hypothermic cooling and to detect adverse changes in brain structures postoperatively. Because BAEPs and SSEPs persist well below EEG activity (the burst suppression state is lost below 25° C), they are better than EEG as an indication of circulatory arrest.

Reference

Spetzler, R. F., Hadley, M. N., Rigamonti, D., Carter, L. P., Raudzens, P. A., Shedd, S. A., & Wilkinson, E. (1988). Aneurysms of the basilar artery treated with circulatory arrest, hypothermia, and barbiturate cerebral protection. *Journal of Neurosurgery, 68*(6), 868–879.

Glossary of Terms

After-death communication (ADC) is an experience in which a living person has a feeling or sense of direct contact with a deceased person (Streit-Horn, 2011a, p. 1).

After-death communication with persons not known to have died is an experience in which a living person has a feeling or sense of direct contact with a deceased person who, at the time of the experience, is either known or not known to the experiencer but whose death is not known to the experiencer.

Apparently nonphysical veridical perception (AVP) is a perception (visual, auditory, kinesthetic, and so on) occurring during a near-death experience that is later verified as accurate—that is, it is *veridical*—that apparently could not have resulted from normal sensory processes or logical inference, either before, during or after the NDE (Holden, 2009, p. 186).

Apparition is the paranormal vision of a living or deceased person or animal, or an object, that is not visible by normal sight.

Asystole: see Cardiac arrest.

Automated external defibrillator (AED) is a portable electronic device that automatically diagnoses cardiac arrest arrhythmias, such as ventricular fibrillation, and is able to apply electric shock defibrillation to the patient to reestablish an effective heart rhythm.

Brain perfusion: see Cerebral perfusion pressure.

Brainstem auditory evoked potential (BAEP): Electrical activity in brainstem auditory pathways that are measured and recorded by applying loud clicks in both ears. BAEPs are used to monitor brainstem auditory pathway conduction during brain surgery.

Burst suppression: Characteristic electrical activity in the brain during anesthesia and other states of unconsciousness, seen in EEG as brief bursts of electrical activity alternating with long periods of suppressed electrical activity (flat line). (See also Chapter 11, Note 2.)

Carbon dioxide (CO_2): A gas that is exhaled by animals and that dissolves in the blood. Excess dissolved CO_2 results in increased acidity in the blood. A test that measures CO_2 in the blood can provide information about the blood's acid level, or pH. This blood test can indicate whether there is an oxygen/carbon dioxide imbalance, or pH imbalance, in the blood. Such imbalances may be a sign of a kidney, respiratory, or other metabolic disorder. CO_2 levels in the blood are affected by cardiac, lung, and kidney function and dysfunction.

Cardiac arrest is the sudden stop in effective blood circulation due to the failure of the heart to contract effectively or at all. A cardiac arrest is different from, but may be caused by, a **heart attack** (myocardial infarction), in which blood flow to the heart muscle is impaired but blood circulation continues. In a cardiac arrest, the heart may be in the condition of **ventricular fibrillation (VF)**—that is, quivering and not contracting properly, or the heart may be in **asystole**—that is, completely stopped. A heart in ventricular fibrillation may be defibrillated (electrically shocked) back to normal heart contractions, whereas a heart in asystole will not respond to electric shock and must be treated with CPR and intravenous drugs.

Cardiopulmonary resuscitation (CPR) is an emergency procedure for a person in cardiac arrest that combines chest compression often with artificial ventilation in order manually to effect sufficient circulation of oxygenated blood to preserve brain viability, until further measures can restore spontaneous blood circulation and breathing.

Cerebral perfusion pressure is the pressure causing cerebral blood flow to the brain (**brain perfusion**). It must be maintained within narrow limits because too little perfusion pressure could cause brain tissue to become ischemic (having inadequate blood flow), and too much could raise intracranial pressure, possibly causing brain damage, stroke, or brain hemorrhage. Physiologically, increased intracranial pressure, as in patients with traumatic or anoxic (oxygen-deprived) brain injury, causes decreased blood perfusion of the brain.

Clairvoyance is the extrasensory ability to see persons or events outside normal physical sight or to see aspects of reality that are not visible by normal sight, such as auras or apparitions.

Defibrillation: The administration of an electric shock to the chest of a cardiac arrest patient (with ventricular fibrillation) during resuscitation in an attempt to restore normal heart rhythm and blood pressure.

Diastolic blood pressure: The lesser of the two numbers of a blood pressure reading, indicating the pressure in the arteries when the heart is at rest between beats. A normal diastolic blood pressure reading is generally considered to be 80 mmHg or less.

Dualism is the philosophical belief that there are two kinds of phenomena— physical phenomena and nonphysical (mental) phenomena. One form of dualism holds that the nonphysical phenomena interact with physical phenomena, such as the physical body (**interactionism**), and that there is a substantial nonphysical being (soul, mind, psyche, consciousness) that can still exist after the death of the physical body (**substantialism**).

Electrocardiogram (EKG) is the graphical record of the electrical activity of the heart over a period of time, measured using electrodes placed on the skin. EKG is a very common cardiology test.

Electroencephalography (EEG): Measurement and recording of generalized electrical activity in the brain by multiple electrodes placed on the scalp. In surgery, EEG is used to monitor the level of anesthesia in the patient.

Extrasensory perception (ESP) is the reception of information not gained through the recognized physical senses or through logical deduction, but apprehended through the mind. ESP includes several modalities of perception such as clairvoyance (paranormal sight), clairaudience (paranormal hearing), telepathy (paranormal transmission of information), precognition (paranormal knowing of future events) and retrocognition (paranormal knowing of the past).

Flat line is an electrical time sequence measurement that shows no activity in some physiological process and therefore, when represented, shows a flat line instead of a varying one. Flat line can refer to a flat electrocardiogram (EKG) or a flat electroencephalogram (EEG). In a flat line EEG, the brain shows no electrical activity as measured from the surface of the scalp.

Heart attack: see Cardiac arrest.

Interactionism: see Dualism.

Living-agent psi (LAP) is a hypothesized process similar to super-psi, whereby a person *subconsciously* obtains information from a living person using a form of extrasensory perception or clairvoyance. (See also Super-psi.)

Materialism is the philosophical belief that matter is the fundamental substance in nature and that all phenomena, including mental phenomena and consciousness, are results of material interactions. **Physicalism** is closely related to materialism but constitutes the broader view that physicality includes forces, energies, and other properties that are more fundamental than physical matter and from which physical matter arises. Both materialism and physicalism are **monistic** philosophies, that is, recognizing only a single fundamental substance of reality—namely, physical matter or physical forces, respectively.

Membrane potential: The electrical voltage on the membrane encapsulating the cell. By means of changes in the membrane potential, nerve cells (neurons) are capable of communicating with each other.

mmHg: Millimeters of mercury. Blood pressure is measured in millimeters of mercury (mmHg) within the blood pressure testing apparatus.

Monism: see Materialism.

Naturalism is the philosophical position that only natural (as opposed to supernatural or spiritual) laws and forces operate in the world. Materialism and physicalism are forms of naturalism.

Near-death experience (NDE) is a profound psychological experience typically occurring to persons who are close to death or are in intense physical danger or emotional distress. NDEs include a number of possible elements such as feelings of peace, a sense of being out-of-body, meeting spiritual beings or deceased human beings, experiencing a bright light or a "being of light," having a life review, reaching a border or being told to go back, and returning to the physical body. It also is followed by characteristic aftereffects such as loss of fear of death and greater concern for other people's well-being.

Neocortex is the largest part of the cerebral cortex, covering the two hemispheres of the brain. The neocortex is involved with the higher cognitive functions, such as sensation, motor movement, reasoning, abstract thinking, and language. (See also Chapter 11, Note 1.)

Out-of-body experience (OBE) is the experience that one's "self" or center of awareness is located and functioning outside of the physical body. An OBE may include sensations of floating, traveling to distant locations, and observing the physical body from a distance.

Parapsychology, or psychical research, is the discipline that investigates the existence and causes of psychic abilities, as well as the possibility of life after death, using scientific methods. Parapsychological phenomena refer to paranormal phenomena caused or experienced by living beings that cannot fully be explained by known natural laws or natural forces. Parapsychology includes the study of clairvoyance, telepathy, psychokinesis, precognition, near-death experiences, and after-death communication.

Peak-in-Darien experience: see After-death communication with persons not known to have died. See also Chapter 6 for the derivation of this term.

Physicalism: see Materialism.

Poltergeist phenomenon: see Recurrent spontaneous psychokinesis.

Precognition is the extrasensory ability to see or know events that will occur in the future. A closely related ability is **retrocognition**, the ability to see or know events from the past without using known sensory channels or logical deduction.

Psyche is the totality of the human mind, which is experienced as a completely personal "inner" domain containing all impressions, thoughts, feelings, and desires, as well as a memory from which recollections can be recalled. The unity of personal consciousness and the sense of selfhood are inherent qualities of the irreducible psyche itself. The nonphysical psyche is sharply distinct (and ultimately separate) from the brain. (See also Self.)

Psychokinesis (PK) is the paranormal ability to influence a physical system without using physical interaction.

Recurrent spontaneous psychokinesis (RSPK) is a repeating paranormal occurrence involving physical disturbances, such as loud knocking with no apparent source and objects being moved or destroyed by apparent levitation. RSPK is frequently associated with the presence of a particular individual, the RSPK agent.

Retrocognition: see Precognition.

Self is the subject of one's own experience of perceptions, emotions, thoughts and memories. The self is the intrinsic, interior dimension of one's own personal, conscious experiences. The self is the first-person view of a person's nonphysical, irreducible psyche and, as such, may or may not be coupled to a physical body (incarnated). (See also Psyche.)

Shared-death experience (SDE) is the experience of a healthy, awake person who is in the presence of a dying person. An SDE may include a number of elements similar to an NDE. In an SDE the shape of the room may appear to change; a mystical light may be seen, or beautiful music heard, that have no apparent source; a mist or cloud may appear to rise from the dying person's body. The shared-death experiencer may experience being out-of-body along with the spirit of the dying person and may share the life review of the person. When the experience is over, the dying person has died (Moody, 2010).

Shared near-death experience (SNDE) is the experience of a person psychologically accompanying another person in the other person's NDE, after which the NDEr survives.

Somatosensory evoked potential (SSEP): Electrical activity in bodily sensory pathways in the brain that are measured and recorded by applying electrical stimulation on the skin. SSEPs are used to monitor sensory pathway conduction during brain surgery.

Substantialism: see Dualism.

Systolic blood pressure: The greater of the two numbers of a blood pressure reading, indicating the pressure in the arteries when the heart muscle contracts and pushes the blood through the veins and arteries. A normal systolic blood pressure reading is generally considered to be 120 mmHg or less.

Telepathy is the extrasensory ability to send and receive information from one person to another without using known sensory channels or known forms of physical interaction.

Terminal lucidity (TL) is the unexpected return of mental clarity and memory shortly before the death of patients suffering from dementia or severe mental disorders (Nahm & Greyson, 2009).

Super-psi is a hypothesized process whereby a person *subconsciously* obtains information, usually from a deceased person, using a form of extrasensory perception or clairvoyance. Super-psi is also hypothesized to subconsciously produce physical phenomena using a form of psychokinesis. "Super" refers to the unusually powerful extrasensory abilities the person needs to use subconsciously.

Ventricular fibrillation (VF): see Cardiac arrest.

Veridical (adjective): True. Pertaining to an experience, perception, or interpretation that accurately represents reality. A perception is considered veridical if it has been verified as accurate.

References

An online version of this list is available at http://iands.org/theself-references.

ABC News. (2011, August 3). *Jake Finkbonner among the angels.* ABC Primetime Nightline: Beyond Belief. Retrieved from http://abcnews.go.com/Nightline/video/jake-finkbonner-angels-flesh-eating-bacteria-eats-face-almost-kills-boy-talks-to-god-nightline-14227643 (Case 8.7).

AHA (2005). 2005 American Heart Association Guidelines for Cardiopulmonary Resuscitation and Emergency Cardiovascular Care, Part 6: CPR Techniques and Devices. *Circulation, 112,* IV-47-IV-50. (Referenced in Appendix B).

Alexander, E. (2012). *Proof of heaven: A neurosurgeon's journey into the afterlife.* New York, NY: Simon & Schuster. (Referenced in Chapter 11).

Alexander, E. (2012, October 15). Proof of heaven: A doctor's experience with the afterlife. *Newsweek.* Retrieved from http://www.newsweek.com/proof-heaven-doctors-experience-afterlife-65327 (Referenced in Chapter 11).

Ally, R. (2014, November 11). "Miracle mom" talks about her near death experience. *CBS Miami.* Retrieved from http://miami.cbslocal.com/2014/11/11/miracle-mom-talks-about-her-near-death-experience/ (Case 8.9).

American Academy for Oral Systemic Health. (2011, June 24–25). *Dr. Lloyd Rudy, famous cardiac surgeon, talks about the importance of oral systemic health* [2-part interview]. Retrieved from http://oralsystemiclink.pro/heart-attack-stroke/1st-scientific-session-of-the-academy-for-oral-systemic-health/ (Case 3.11).

Astorga, J. V. (2014, November 9). Miguel Ángel Pertierra: "No entusiasmo a la profesión médica de forma oficial pero sí individualmente" [Miguel Ángel Pertierra: "No enthusiasm from the medical establishment, just individuals"]. *Diario Sur–Málaga.* Retrieved from http://www.diariosur.es/malaga/201411/04/miguel-pertierra-entusiasmo-profesion-20141104221417.html (Case 1.13).

Atwater, P. M. H. (1994). *Beyond the light: The mysteries and revelations of near-death experiences.* New York, NY: Avon Books. (Case 8.8).

Atwater, P. M. H. (2003). *The new children and near-death experiences.* Rochester, VT: Bear. (Referenced in Chapter 10).

Atwater, P. M. H. (2009). *Beyond the light: What isn't being said about near death experience: From visions of heaven to glimpses of hell.* Kill Devil Hills, NC: Transpersonal. (original work published 1994). (Case 4.3).

Augustine, K. (2007). Does paranormal perception occur in near-death experiences? *Journal of Near-Death Studies, 25*(4), 203–236. (Case 2.3).

Bachrach, J. (2014). *Glimpsing heaven: The stories and science of life after death.* Washington, DC: National Geographic. (Case 3.29, Chapter 9).

Bale Doneen Method. (2012, May 1). *Making headlines: News & Press: In memoriam—Dr. Lloyd Rudy, Jr.* Retrieved from http://www.baledoneen.com/announcements/in-memoriam-dr-lloyd-rudy-jr (Case 3.11).

Barkallah, S. (Producer & Director). (2015). *Untimely departure* [motion picture, English translation]. Berre l'Etang, France: S17.TV 2015. Retrieved from https://www.s17.tv/documentaires/faux-depart.html (Case 3.1).

Barrett, W. (1926). *Death-bed visions: The psychic experiences of the dying.* Wellingborough, Northhampton, UK: Aquarian Press. (Cases 7.2, 7.4).

Barrington, M. R. (1999). *What is proof? The assessment of past events.* Retrieved from http://parapsychologie.ac.at/programm/ss1999/barringt/proof_txt.htm (Referenced in the Introduction).

Baxter, R. (1691). *The certainty of the world of spirits fully evinced by the unquestionable histories of apparitions and witchcrafts, operations, voices, &c. proving the immortality of souls, the malice and miseries of the devils, and the damned. And of the blessedness of the justified. Fully evinced by the unquestionable histories of apparitions, operations, witchcrafts, voices, &c. Written as an addition to many other treatises, for the conviction of sadduces and infidels.* Retrieved from https://archive.org/details/certaintyofworld00baxt (Case 7.4).

Beam, C. W. (2015). *Miracles from heaven: A little girl, her journey to heaven, and her amazing story of healing.* New York, NY: Hachette Books. (Case 8.10).

Beauregard, M. (2007). Mind does really matter: Evidence from neuroimaging studies of emotional self-regulation, psychotherapy, and placebo effect. *Progress in Neurobiology, 81*(4), 218–236. (Referenced in Chapter 10).

Beauregard, M. (2012). *Brain wars: The scientific battle over the existence of the human mind and the proof that will change the way we live our lives.* New York, NY: HarperCollins. (Referenced in Chapter 10).

Beauregard, M., St-Pierre, É. L., Rayburn, G., & and Demers, P. (2012). Conscious mental activity during a deep hypothermic cardiocirculatory arrest? *Resuscitation, 83*(1), e19. (Case 1.10).

Believe it or Not! #3. (2014). *NDE Kristle Merzlock near death experience of 7 year old girl.* Retrieved from https://youtu.be/RaUN_KcX78o (Case 3.31).

Bell, A. (2001, December 6). REPLAY of Pam Reynolds 12/06. [Coast to Coast AM show archive, interview with Pam Reynolds]. Retrieved from http://www.coast tocoastam.com/guest/reynolds-pam/5854 (Referenced in Chapter 11).

Bellg, L. (2014). *Patient NDEs in the ICU.* Presentation at The Monroe Institute (TMI) Professional Seminar. Retrieved from https://www.youtube.com/watch?v=xdScjvc14xE starting at 31:08. (Case 7.5).

Bellg, L. (2015). *Near death in the ICU: Stories from patients near death and why we should listen to them.* Appleton, WI: Sloan Press. (Cases 1.11, 1.12, 2.15, 2.16, 2.17, 2.18, 3.33).

Benedict, M. T. (1996). Through the light and beyond. In L. W. Bailey & J. Yates (Eds.), *The near-death experience: A reader* (pp. 39–52). New York, NY: Routledge. (Case 8.8).

Betty, L. S. (2006). Are they hallucinations or are they real? The spirituality of death-bed and near-death visions. *Omega, 53*(1–2), 37–49. (Referenced in Chapter 10).

Bihari, S., & Rajajee, V. (2008). Prolonged retention of awareness during cardiopulmonary resuscitation for asystolic cardiac arrest. *Neurocritical care, 9*(3), 382–386. (Referenced in Appendix B).

Black, C. (2014, August 29). *My NDEs, aftereffects and what I'm doing about them now.* Presentation at the 2014 International Association for Near-Death Studies (IANDS) Conference, Newport Beach, CA. Retrieved from https://www.youtube .com/watch?v=MZpBV3BZ1lc (Case 9.3).

Blackmore, S. J. (1993). *Dying to live: Near-death experiences.* Amherst, NY: Prometheus Books. (Referenced in the Introduction and Chapter 3).

Blalock, S., Holden, J. M., & Atwater, P. M. H. (2015). Electromagnetic and other environmental effects following near-death experiences: A primer. *Journal of Near-Death Studies, 33*(4), 181–211. (Case 9.3).

Borjigin, J., Lee, U., Liu, T., Pal, D., Huff, S., Klarr, D., . . . Mashour, G. A. (2013). Surge of neurophysiological coherence and connectivity in the dying brain. *Proceedings of the National Academy of Sciences, 110*(35), 14432–14437. (Referenced in Chapter 3).

Braithwaite, J. J., & Dewe, H. (2013). Occam's chainsaw: Neuroscientific nails in the coffin of dualist notions of the near-death experience (NDE). *The Skeptic* [UK magazine], *25*(2), 24–30. Retrieved from http://www.academia.edu/10060970/Occams_Chainsaw_Neuroscientific_Nails_in_the_coffin_of_dualist_notions_of_the_Near-death_experience_NDE_ (Referenced in Chapter 10).

Braude, S. E. (2003). *Immortal remains: The evidence for life after death.* Lanham, MD: Rowman & Littlefield. (Referenced in Chapter 10).

Braude, S. E. (2009). Perspectival awareness and postmortem survival. *Journal of Scientific Exploration, 23*(2), 195–210. (Referenced in Chapter 10).

Brinkley, D. (with Perry, P.). (1994). *Saved by the light: The true story of a man who died twice and the profound revelations he received.* New York, NY: Villard Books. (Referenced in Chapter 6).

Broome, K. (Producer). (2002). *The day I died: The mind, the brain, and near-death experiences.* [Motion picture]. Glasgow, Scotland: British Broadcasting Corporation. Retrieved from http://topdocumentaryfilms.com/day-i-died/ (17:40–32:00 minutes) (Case 3.29, Chapter 11).

Burpo, T., & Vincent, L. (2010). *Heaven is for real: A little boy's astounding story of his trip to heaven and back.* Nashville, TN: Thomas Nelson. (Case 5.2).

Carman, E. M., & Carman, N. J. (2013). *Cosmic cradle: Spiritual dimensions of life before birth.* Berkeley, CA: North Atlantic Books. (Referenced in Chapter 10).

Carter, C. (2010). *Science and the near-death experience: How consciousness survives death.* Rochester, VT: Inner Traditions. (Referenced in Chapter 10).

Carter, C. (2011). Response to "Could Pam Reynolds Hear?" *Journal of Near-Death Studies, 30*(1), 29–53. (Case 3.29).

Carter, C. (2012). *Science and the afterlife experience: Evidence for the immortality of consciousness.* Rochester, VT: Inner Traditions. (Referenced in Chapter 10).

Celestial Travelers. (2016). *Children and the near death experience: Kristle Merzlock.* From *Reader's Digest,* February 2006; Crossing into another realm. Retrieved from http://kuriakon00.com/celestial/child/kristle_merzlock.html (Case 3.31).

Chawla, L. S. (2011, May). *Surges of electroencephalogram activity at the time of death: A case series.* Conference: Science of Consciousness: Brain, Mind, Reality. Stockholm, May 3–7, 2011. (Referenced in Chapter 3).

Chawla, L. S., Akst, S., Junker, C., Jacobs, B., & Seneff, M. G. (2009). Surges of electroencephalogram activity at the time of death: A case series. *Journal of Palliative Medicine, 12*(12), 1095–1100. (Referenced in Chapter 3).

Coimbra, C. G. (1999). Implications of ischemic penumbra for the diagnosis of brain death. *Brazilian Journal of Medical and Biological Research, 32*(12), 1479–1487. (Referenced in Appendix A).

Cook, E. W., Greyson, B., & Stevenson, I. (1998). Do any near-death experiences provide evidence for the survival of human personality after death? Relevant features and illustrative case reports. *Journal of Scientific Exploration, 12*(3), 377–406. (Case 1.5, Chapter 10).

Cook, J. D., Winkler, H., & Daniels, A. (Executive producers). (2004, May 29). *Dead and back again.* Unexplained Mysteries, Season 1, Episode 26. Retrieved from https://www.youtube.com/watch?v=JBaBwMVg6dk (Case 8.6).

Coppes, C. (2010). *Messages from the light: True stories of near-death experiences and communication from the other side.* Wayne, NJ: Career Press / New Page Books. (Referenced in Chapter 6).

Dittrich, L. (2013, July 2). The prophet: An investigation into Eben Alexander, author of the blockbuster *Proof of Heaven. Esquire,* June/July 2013, 88–95. Retrieved from http://www.esquire.com/entertainment/interviews/a23248/the-prophet/ (Referenced in Chapter 11).

Doug. (n.d.). *Denise.* Celestial Travelers: Near Death Experiences. Retrieved from http://kuriakon00.com/celestial/child/denise.html (Case 9.1).

Dougherty, N. (2002). *Fast lane to heaven: A life after death journey.* Charlottesville, VA: Hampton Roads. (Referenced in Chapter 6).

Dreyfus, H. L. (1978). *What computers can't do: The limits of artificial intelligence.* New York, NY: HarperCollins. (Referenced in the Introduction).

Ellis, M. (2014, November 11). Miracle mom returns from the dead, saw glimpse of the afterlife. *Godreports.* Retrieved from http://blog.godreports.com/2014/11/ moms-heart-stopped-for-45-minutes-after-childbirth-then-her-familys -prayers-were-answered (Case 8.9).

Ellwood, G. F. (2001). *The uttermost deep: The challenge of near-death experiences.* New York, NY: Lantern. (Case 7.2).

Ewald, G. (2007). *Nahtoderfahrungen: Hinweise auf ein Leben nach dem Tod?* [Near-death experiences: Indications of life after death?]. Kevelaer, Germany: Topos. (Case 6.3).

Farr, S. S. (1993). *What Tom Sawyer learned from dying.* Norfolk, VA: Hampton Roads. (Case 9.4).

Fenwick, P. (2005). Science and spirituality: A challenge for the 21st century [The Bruce Greyson Lecture from the International Association for Near-Death Studies 2004 Annual Conference]. *Journal of Near-Death Studies, 23*(3), 131–157. (Referenced in Chapter 11).

Fenwick, P., & Fenwick, E. (1995). *The truth in the light: An investigation of over 300 near-death experiences.* London, UK: Headline (2012, reprint). Hove, UK: White Crow Books. (Case 2.7).

Fischer, M., & Hossmann, K. A. (1996). Volume expansion during cardiopulmonary resuscitation reduces cerebral no-reflow. *Resuscitation, 32*(3), 227–240. (Referenced in Appendix A).

Flammarion, C. (1900). *L'inconnu et les problèmes psychiques* [The unknown and problems of the psyche]. New York, NY: Harper & Brothers. (Case 7.1).

Frank. (2010–2013). *Out of body.* Retrieved from http://www.emergencymedical paramedic.com/out-of-body/ (Case 3.12).

Freeman, M., & Andreae, L. (Executive producers). (2011, June 8). *Is there life after death?* Through the Wormhole, Season 2, Episode 1. Retrieved from https://www.youtube.com/watch?v=YukKDzSzxEI (Referenced in Chapter 11).

Garnar, C. (2015, April 14). Girl knocked out by 30-ft fall inside a hollow tree claims she went to heaven and met Jesus (who looks like Santa Claus) . . . then woke up cured of a lifelong illness. *Daily Mail: Mail Online.* Retrieved from http://www.dailymail.co.uk/femail/article-3038153/Girl-knocked-30ft-fall-inside-hollow-tree-claims-went-heaven-met-Jesus-woke-cured-lifelong-illness.html (Case 8.10).

Gauld, A. (1983). *Mediumship and survival: A century of investigations.* London, UK: Paladin Books. (Referenced in Chapter 10).

Greene, K. A., Marciano, F. F., Hamilton, M. G., Herman, J. M., Rekate, H. L., & Spetzler, R. F. (1994). Cardiopulmonary bypass, hypothermic circulatory arrest and barbiturate cerebral protection for the treatment of giant vertebrobasilar aneurysms in children. *Pediatric neurosurgery, 21*(2), 124–133. (Referenced in Appendix D).

Greyson, B. (1983). Increase in psychic phenomena following near-death experiences. *Theta, 11*(2), 26–29. (Referenced in Chapter 9).

Greyson, B. (2010). Seeing dead people not known to have died: "Peak in Darien" experiences. *Anthropology and Humanism, 35*(2), 159–171. (Referenced in Chapter 11).

Greyson, B., Liester, M. B., Kinsey, L., Alum, S., & Fox, G. (2015). Electromagnetic phenomena reported by near-death experiencers. *Journal of Near-Death Studies, 33*(4), 213–243. (Case 9.3).

Grossman, N. (2002). Who's afraid of life after death? [Guest editorial]. *Journal of Near-Death Studies, 21*(1), 5–24. (Referenced in Chapter 10).

Grossman, N. (2008). Letter to the editor: Four errors commonly made by professional debunkers. *Journal of Near-Death Studies, 26*(3), 227–235. (Referenced in Chapter 10).

Guggenheim, W., & Guggenheim, J. A. (1995). *Hello from heaven: A new field of research—after-death communication—confirms that life and love are eternal.* New York, NY: Bantam Books. (Referenced in Chapter 7).

Gurney, E., Myers, F. W. H., & Podmore, F. (1886). *Phantasms of the living.* London, UK: Rooms of the Society for Psychical Research/Trübner. (Case 7.4).

Habermas, G. R., & Moreland, J. P. (2004). *Beyond death: Exploring the evidence for immortality.* Eugene, OR: Wipf & Stock. (Case 3.30).

Hagerty, B. B. (2011, April 22). *A boy, an injury, a recovery, a miracle?* Northeast Public Radio/NPR. Retrieved from http://www.npr.org/2011/04/22/135121360/a-boy-an-injury-a-recovery-a-miracle (Case 8.7).

Hamilton, A. J. (2009). *The scalpel and the soul: Encounters with surgery, the super-natural, and the healing power of hope.* New York: NY: Jeremy P. Tarcher/Penguin. (Referenced in the Introduction).

Hansen, J. N. (2013). Use of a torsion pendulum balance to detect and character-ize what may be a human bioenergy field. *Journal of Scientific Exploration, 27*(2), 205–225. (Case 9.3).

Haraldsson, E. (2012). *The departed among the living: An investigative study of afterlife encounters.* Hove, UK: White Crow Books. (Referenced in Chapter 7).

Hart, H. (1956). Six theories about apparitions. *Proceedings of the Society for Psychical Research, 50*(185), 153–239. (Referenced in Chapter 7).

Heritage Funeral Home & Crematory. (2012). *Lloyd William Rudy, Jr. | 1934–2012 | Obituary.* Retrieved from http://www.meaningfulfunerals.net/fh/obituaries/obituary.cfm?o_id=1464561&fh_id=11479 (Case 3.11).

Herlitz, J., Bång, A., Alsén, B., & Aune, S. (2002). Characteristics and outcome among patients suffering from in hospital cardiac arrest in relation to the inter-val between collapse and start of CPR. *Resuscitation, 53*(1), 21–27. (Referenced in Appendix A).

Holden, J. M. (2009). Veridical perception in near-death experiences. In J. M. Holden, B. Greyson, & D. James (Eds.), *The handbook of near-death experiences: Thirty years of investigation* (pp. 185–212). Santa Barbara, CA: Praeger/ABC-CLIO. (Referenced in the Foreword and Chapters 1 and 10).

Jakoby, B. (2006). *Begegnungen mit dem Jenseits* [Encounters with the beyond]. Hamburg, Germany: Rowohlt Taschenbuch Verlag. (Case 4.4).

James. (2015). *James grandfather's NDE.* Retrieved from http://www.nderf.org/NDERF/NDE_Experiences/james_gpa_nde.htm (Case 3.17).

James, W. (1907). *Pragmatism: A new name for some old ways of thinking.* London, UK: Longmans, Green. (Referenced in Chapter 11).

James, W. (1898). *Human immortality: Two supposed objections to the doctrine.* Inger-soll Lecture, 1897. Cambridge, MA: The Riverside Press. (Referenced in Chapter 10).

Jennifer NDE 2012. (2012, March 3). *The Biography Channel.* Retrieved from http://www.youtube.com/watch?v=R8v6fw543OY (Case 8.5).

Kelly, E. F. (2015). Empirical challenges to theory construction. In E. F. Kelly, A. Crabtree, & P. Marshall (Eds.), *Beyond physicalism: Toward reconciliation of sci-ence and spirituality* (pp. 3–38). Lanham, MD: Rowman & Littlefield. (Referenced in Chapter 10).

Kelly, E. F., Kelly, E. W., Crabtree, A., Gauld, A., Grosso, M., & Greyson, B. (2007). *Irreducible mind: Toward a psychology for the 21st century.* Lanham, MD: Rowman & Littlefield. (Case 3.29).

Kelly, E. W., Greyson, B., & Stevenson, I. (2000). Can experiences near death furnish evidence of life after death? *OMEGA-Journal of Death and Dying, 40*(4), 513–519. (Referenced in Chapter 10).

Ko, P. (2006). *Report: Dr. Peter Ko.* Retrieved from http://www.anitamoorjani.com/report-dr-peter-ko/ (Case 8.4).

Kübler-Ross, E. (1983). *On children and death: How children and their parents can and do cope with death.* New York, NY: Simon & Schuster. (Case 6.5).

Lawton, M. T., Raudzens, P. A., Zabramski, J. M., & Spetzler, R. F. (1998). Hypothermic circulatory arrest in neurovascular surgery: Evolving indications and predictors of patient outcome. *Neurosurgery, 43*(1), 10–20. (Referenced in Appendix D).

Lerma, J. (2007). *Into the light: Real life stories about angelic visits, visions of the afterlife, and other pre-death experiences.* Wayne, NJ: Career Press / New Page Books. (Case 2.6).

Lewinter, J. R., Carden, D. L., Nowak, R. M., Enriquez, E., & Martin, G. B. (1989). CPR-dependent consciousness: Evidence for cardiac compression causing forward flow. *Annals of emergency medicine, 18*(10), 1111–1115. (Referenced in Appendix B).

Long, J. (with Perry, P.). (2011). *Evidence of the afterlife: The science of near-death experiences.* New York, NY: HarperCollins. (Referenced in the Introduction).

Losasso, T. J., Muzzi, D. A., Meyer, F. B., & Sharbrough, F. W. (1992). Electroencephalographic monitoring of cerebral function during asystole and successful cardiopulmonary resuscitation. *Anesthesia & Analgesia, 75*(6), 1021–1024. (Referenced in Chapter 3).

Lund, D. H. (1985). *Death and Consciousness.* Jefferson, NC: McFarland. (Referenced in Chapter 10).

Lund, D. H. (2009). *Persons, souls, and death: A philosophical investigation of an afterlife.* Jefferson, NC: McFarland. (Referenced in Chapter 10).

Malarkey, K. (2011). *The boy who came back from heaven: A remarkable account of miracles, angels, and life beyond this world.* Carol Stream, IL: Tyndale Momentum. (Referenced in the Introduction).

Marney S. (n.d.). *Marney S's daughter's NDE.* Retrieved from http://www.nderf.org/NDERF/NDE_Experiences/marney_s_daughter_nde.htm (Case 3.5).

Martin, M., & Augustine, K. (Eds.). (2015). *The myth of an afterlife: The case against life after death.* Lanham, MD: Rowman & Littlefield. (Referenced in Chapter 10).

Martindale, D. (2015, April 10). "Miracle" in Burleson: Book tells girl's remarkable story of healing. *Star Telegram.* Retrieved from http://www.star-telegram.com/living/religion/article18229301.html (Case 8.10).

Martinez-Alier, N. (2010, March 26). *Clinical review—bacterial meningitis.* Retrieved from http://www.gponline.com/clinical-review-bacterial-meningitis/article/ 991614 (Referenced in Chapter 11).

Mauser, E. W. (2012, October 20). Boy's recovery a Kateri miracle. *Canadian Catholic News.* Retrieved from http://www.catholicregister.org/features/item/15267-boy -s-recovery-a-kateri-miracle (Case 8.7).

Mays, R. G. (2013). Esquire *article on Eben Alexander distorts the facts.* Retrieved from http://iands.org/esquire (Referenced in Chapter 11).

Mays, R. G., & Mays, S. B. (2008). The phenomenology of the self-conscious mind. *Journal of Near-Death Studies, 27*(1), 5–45. (Referenced in Chapter 10).

Mays, R. G., & Mays, S. B. (2010). *Investigation of George Ritchie's NDE OBE.* Retrieved from http://selfconsciousmind.com/ritchie/ (Referenced in Chapter 2).

Mays, R. G., & Mays, S. B. (2012). *Subject SB pinwheel psychokinesis and induction coil effect (February 6, 2012).* Retrieved from http://selfconsciousmind.com/ SubjectSB-020612-Pinwheel2.mov (Case 9.3).

McMoneagle, J. (1993). *Mind trek: Exploring consciousness, time, and space through remote viewing.* Charlottesville, VA: Hampton Roads. (Referenced in Chapter 9).

Merrell-Wolff, F. F. (1973). *The philosophy of consciousness without an object: Reflections on the nature of transcendental consciousness.* New York, NY: Julian Press. (Referenced in Appendix D).

Miller, J. B., Davie, R. D. M., & Douglas, D. M. (1961). The Efficiency of Cardiac Massage in Ventricular Fibrillation: Description of an instance of recovery of consciousness without spontaneous heart beat. *British journal of anaesthesia, 33*(1), 22–23. (Referenced in Appendix B).

Mitchell-Yellin, B., & Fischer, J. M. (2014). The near-death experience argument against physicalism: A critique. *Journal of Consciousness Studies, 21*(7–8), 158– 183. (Referenced in the Foreword).

Moody, R. A., Jr. (1975). *Life after life.* Atlanta, GA: Mockingbird Press. (Referenced in the Foreword).

Moody, R. A., Jr. (1996). The light beyond: The experience of almost dying. In L. W. Bailey & J. Yates (Eds.), *The near-death experience: A reader* (pp. 25–38). New York, NY: Routledge. (Case 2.10).

Moody, R. A., Jr. (with Perry, P.). (1988). *The light beyond.* New York, NY: Bantam Books. (Cases 3.15, 4.1, 5.5, 6.2).

Moody, R. A., Jr. (with Perry, P.). (2010). *Glimpses of eternity: An investigation into shared death experiences.* New York, NY: Guideposts. (Referenced in the Foreword, Chapter 4, and Chapter 10).

Moorjani, A. (2012). *Dying to be me: My journey from cancer to near death, to true healing*. Carlsbad, CA: Hay House. (Case 8.4).

Moorjani, A. (n.d.). *Anita Moorjani: Remember your magnificence*. Retrieved from http://anitamoorjani.com/ (Case 8.4).

Morris, L. L., & Knafl, K. A. (2003). The nature and meaning of the near-death experience for patients and critical care nurses. *Journal of Near-Death Studies, 21*(3), 139–167. (Cases 1.3, 2.2).

Morse, M. L. (n.d.). *Are near death experiences real? (And if so, what are they good for?)*. Institute for the Scientific Study of Consciousness. Retrieved from http://spiritualscientific.com/yahoo_site_admin/assets/docs/Are_Near_Death _Experiences_Real.65201445.pdf (Case 7.3).

Morse, M. L. (with Perry, P.). (1990). *Closer to the light: Learning from the near-death experiences of children*. New York, NY: Villard Books. (Cases 3.28, 3.30, 3.31).

Morse, M. L. (with Perry, P.). (1996). *Parting visions: Uses and meanings of pre-death, psychic, and spiritual experiences* (rev. ed.). New York, NY: HarperCollins. (Cases 3.14, 7.3).

MSNBC (Producer). (2001, April 11). *Back from the dead* [interview with Pam Reynolds]. Retrieved from https://www.youtube.com/watch?v=YO8UVebuA0g (Case 3.29, Chapter 11).

Musolino, J. (2015). *The soul fallacy: What science shows we gain from letting go of our soul beliefs*. Amherst, NY: Prometheus Books. (Referenced in Chapter 10).

Myers, F. W. H. (1903/2005). *Human personality and its survival of bodily death*. London, UK: Longmans, Green; Mineola, NY: Dover Publications. (Case 1.7).

Myers, J. G. (Ed.). (1968/2012). *Voices from the edge of eternity*. New Kensington, PA: Whittaker House. (Referenced in Chapter 11).

Nahm, M. (2012). *Wenn die Dunkelheit ein Ende findet* [When the darkness comes to an end]. Amerang, Germany: Crotona Verlag. (Referenced in Chapter 8).

Nahm, M., & Greyson, B. (2009). Terminal lucidity in patients with chronic schizophrenia and dementia: A survey of the literature. *Journal of Nervous and Mental Disease, 3*(12), 942–944. (Referenced in Chapter 8).

NBC (Producer). (1989). *Near death experience of 7 year old girl—Dr. Melvin Morse*. Unsolved Mysteries, Season 1, Episode 17. Retrieved from https://www.youtube .com/watch?v=H319Mg5PfyQ (Case 3.31).

NDEAccounts. (2014). *Michaela's—NDE—Meeting with her future family*. Retrieved from https://www.youtube.com/watch?v=EydWO5vqT80 (Case 2.14).

NDEAccounts. (n.d.). *Al Sullivan's—NDE—Confirmation of out of body experience*. Retrieved from https://www.youtube.com/watch?v=J5_x8U7SROI (Case 1.5).

Nelson, K. (2011). *The spiritual doorway in the brain: A neurologist's search for the god experience*. New York, NY: Dutton. (Referenced in the Introduction).

NHNE Near-Death Experience Network. (2012). *Beyond the light* [Motion picture]. Retrieved from http://nhneneardeath.ning.com/video/beyond-the-light (Case 2.5).

Nicholls, G. (2013). *Verified out-of-body experience—with author Graham Nicholls*. Retrieved from https://www.youtube.com/user/shahmainetwork; part 1 at https://www.youtube.com/watch?v=bCEivV6RhEI; and part 2 at https://www.youtube.com/watch?v=F-qjAVBIk4g (Referenced in Chapter 2).

Nikolay, J. (2015, September 7). Attachment to e-mail to Wilfried Kuhn, forwarded to Titus Rivas on September 10, 2015. (Case 3.34).

Noyes, R., Fenwick, P., Holden, J. M., & Christian, S. R. (2009). Aftereffects of pleasurable Western adult near-death experiences. In J. M. Holden, B. Greyson, & D. James (Eds.), *The handbook of near-death experiences: Thirty years of investigation* (pp. 41–62). Santa Barbara, CA: Praeger/ABC-CLIO. (Referenced in Chapter 9).

Ohkado, M. (2013). On the term "Peak in Darien Experience." *Journal of Near-Death Studies, 31*(4), 203–211. (Referenced in Chapter 6).

Ojeda-Vera, R. (n.d.). Roseann's DBV: Report by Ricardo Ojeda-Vera. *Near Death Experience Research Foundation*. Retrieved from http://www.nderf.org/NDERF/NDE_Experiences/roseann_dbv.htm (Case 2.1).

Paradis, N. A., Martin, G. B., Goetting, M. G., Rosenberg, J. M., Rivers, E. P., Appleton, T. J., & Nowak, R. M. (1989). Simultaneous aortic, jugular bulb, and right atrial pressures during cardiopulmonary resuscitation in humans. Insights into mechanisms. *Circulation, 80*(2), 361–368. (Referenced in Appendix A).

Paradis, N. A., Martin, G. B., Rosenberg, J., Rivers, E. P., Goetting, M. G., Appleton, T. J., . . . & Nowak, R. M. (1991). The effect of standard-and high-dose epinephrine on coronary perfusion pressure during prolonged cardiopulmonary resuscitation. *Jama, 265*(9), 1139–1144. (Referenced in Appendix A).

Parnia, S. (2006). *What happens when we die: A groundbreaking study into the nature of life and death*. Carlsbad, CA: Hay House. (Cases 1.2, 2.13, 3.2, 3.16, 5.3).

Parnia, S., Spearpoint, K., de Vos, G., Fenwick, P., Goldberg, D., Yang, J., . . . & Schoenfeld, E. R. (2014). AWARE—AWAreness during REsuscitation—A prospective study. *Resuscitation, 85*(12), 1799–1805. (Case 3.21 and the Introduction).

Parnia, S. (with Young, J.). (2013). *Erasing death: The science that is rewriting the boundaries between life and death*. New York, NY: HarperCollins. (Cases 3.13, 3.21, 4.2, the Introduction and Chapter 11).

Peberdy, M. A., Kaye, W., Ornato, J. P., Larkin, G. L., Nadkarni, V., Mancini, M. E., . . . & NRCPR Investigators. (2003). Cardiopulmonary resuscitation of adults in the hospital: A report of 14 720 cardiac arrests from the National Registry of Cardiopulmonary Resuscitation. *Resuscitation, 58*(3), 297–308. (Referenced in Appendix A).

Persinger, M. A. (2015). Neuroscientific investigation of anomalous cognition. In E. C. May & S. B. Marwaha (Eds.), *Extrasensory perception: Support, skepticism, and science*. Santa Barbara, CA: Praeger/ABC-CLIO. (Case 9.3).

Pertierra, M. Á. (2014). *La última puerta. Experiencias cercanas a la muerte* [The last door: Near-death experiences]. Madrid, Spain: Ediciones Oberón. (Cases 1.13, 1.14, 3.18, 3.35).

Phillip, A. (2014, November 10). Woman "spontaneously" revives after 45 minutes without a pulse. *The Washington Post*. Retrieved from http://www.washington post.com/news/to-your-health/wp/2014/11/10/woman-spontaneously-revives -after-45-minutes-without-a-pulse/ (Case 8.9).

Pimm, B. A., & Black, C. (2014). *Celebrating the life and afterlife of Bob Van de Castle*. Presentation at the 2014 International Association for the Study of Dreams (IASD) PsiberDreaming Conference. Retrieved from http://dreamtalk.hypermart .net/pdc2014/presentations/pdc2014-pimm-black.pdf (Case 9.3).

Pinto, L. F. S., & Raimundo, J. (2011). *Menina ressuscitada em hospital reconhece médico que a salvou* [Resuscitated girl in hospital recognizes doctor who saved her]. Retrieved from http://g1/globo.com/globo-reporter/noticia/2011/09/ menina-ressuscitada-em-hospital-reconhece-medico-que-salvou.html (Case 3.27).

Price, J. (1996). *The other side of death*. New York, NY: Ballantine Books. (Case 3.32).

Radin, D. (1997). *The conscious universe: The scientific truth of psychic phenomena*. New York, NY: HarperOne. (Referenced in Chapter 9).

Rawat, K. S., & Rivas, T. (2007). *Reincarnation: The evidence is building*. Vancouver, BC: Writers Publisher. (Referenced in Chapter 10).

Rawlings, M. (1991). *Beyond death's door*. New York, NY: Bantam Books. (Cases 3.24, 3.25, 3.26).

Ring, K. (1988). Prophetic visions in 1988: A critical reappraisal. *Journal of Near-Death Studies, 7*(1), 4–18. (Referenced in Chapter 6).

Ring, K., & Cooper, S. (1999). *Mindsight: Near-death and out-of-body experiences in the blind*. Palo Alto, CA: William James Center for Consciousness Studies at the Institute of Transpersonal Psychology; (2008; 2nd ed.). Bloomington, IN: iUniverse. (Case 1.8, the Introduction, and Chapter 10).

Ring, K., & Lawrence, M. (1993). Further evidence for veridical perception during near-death experiences. *Journal of Near-Death Studies, 11*(4), 223–229. (Cases 2.4, 2.11, 3.6).

Ring, K., & Valarino, E. E. (1998). *Lessons from the light: What we can learn from the near-death experience.* New York, NY: Insight Books. (Cases 2.3, 3.28, 8.3).

Ritchie, G. G. (with Sherrill, E.). (1978/2007). *Return from tomorrow.* Grand Rapids, MI: Chosen Books. (Referenced in the Foreword and Chapter 2).

Rivas, T. (2003). The survivalist interpretation of recent studies into the near-death experience. *Journal of Religion and Psychical Research, 26*(1), 27–31. (Referenced in Chapter 10).

Rivas, T. (2004). *Neuropsychology and personalist dualism: A few remarks.* New Dualism Archive, September/October 2004. Retrieved from http://www.new dualism.org/papers/T.Rivas/Dualismlives.htm (Referenced in Chapter 10).

Rivas, T. (2006). Metasubjective cognition beyond the brain: Subjective awareness and the location of concepts of consciousness. *Journal of Non-Locality and Remote Mental Interactions, IV*(1). Retrieved from http://txtxs.nl/artikel.asp?artid=645 (Referenced in Chapter 10).

Rivas, T. (2008a). Artikelen uit het zomernummer 25(4) van het *Journal of Near-Death Studies* van 2007 [Articles from the summer issue *25*(4) of the *Journal of Near-Death Studies* of 2007]. *Terugkeer, 19*(1), 24–28. (Case 2.3).

Rivas, T. (2008b). Een gesprek met TG over de man met het gebit [A conversation with TG about the man with the dentures]. *Terugkeer, 19*(3), 12–20. (Referenced in Chapter 11).

Rivas, T. (2008c). Enkele reacties op het stuk van Gerald Woerlee [A few comments on the paper by Gerald Woerlee]. *Terugkeer, 19*(4), 9. (Case 3.7).

Rivas, T. (2009a). *The scalpel and the soul: Encounters with surgery, the supernatural, and the healing power of hope,* by Allan J. Hamilton (Book review). *Journal of Near-Death Studies, 27*(4), 255–259. (Referenced in the Introduction).

Rivas, T. (2009b). *Uitspraken van Hiroyoshi Takata over de casus van Al Sullivan* [Statements made by Hiroyoshi Takata about the Al Sullivan case]. *Terugkeer, 20*(3), 22. (Case 1.5).

Rivas, T. (2010). Is it rational to extrapolate from the presence of consciousness during a flat EEG to survival of consciousness after death? *Journal of Near-Death Studies, 29*(2), 355–361. (Referenced in Chapter 10).

Rivas, T., & Dirven, A. (2009). Twee bijna-doodervaringen gemeld naar aanleiding van een oproep in De Gelderlander over "de man met het gebit." [Two near-death experiences reported in response to an announcement in *De Gelderlander* about "The Man with the Dentures"]. *Terugkeer, 20*(3), 9. (Case 3.10).

Rivas, T., & Dirven, A. (2010a). *Van en naar het Licht* [From and to the Light]. Leeuwarden, Netherlands: Uitgeverij Elikser. (Cases 1.1, 1.5, 3.7, 3.29, 6.1, the Introduction and Chapter 2).

Rivas, T., & Dirven, A. (2010b). De bijna-doodervaring van Huriye Kacar [Huriye Kacar's near-death experience]. *Terugkeer, 21*(3), 6–7. (Case 6.1).

Rivas, T., & Smit, R. H. (2013). Brief report: A near-death experience with veridical perception described by a famous heart surgeon and confirmed by his assistant surgeon. *Journal of Near-Death Studies, 31*(3), 179–186. (Case 3.11).

Rivas, T., & van Dongen, H. (2003). Exit epiphenomenalism: The demolition of a refuge. *Journal of Non-Locality and Remote Mental Interactions, II*(1). Retrieved from http://txtxs.nl/artikel.asp?artid=624 (Referenced in Chapter 10).

Roll, W. G., Saroka, K. S., Mulligan, B. P., Hunter, M. D., Dotta, B. T., Gang, N., Scott, M. A., St-Pierre, L. S., & Persinger, M. A. (2012). Case report: A prototypical experience of "poltergeist" activity, conspicuous quantitative electroencephalographic patterns, and sLORETA profiles—suggestions for intervention. *Neurocase, 18*(6), 1–10. (Case 9.3).

Rommer, B. R. (2000). *Blessing in disguise: Another side of the near death experience*. St. Paul, MN: Llewellyn. (Case 2.12).

Rousseau, D. (2012). The implications of near-death experiences for research into the survival of consciousness. *Journal of Scientific Exploration, 26*(1), 43–80. (Referenced in Chapter 10).

Rush, M. J. (2013). Critique of "A prospectively studied near-death experience with corroborated out-of-body perceptions and unexplained healing." *Journal of Near-Death Studies, 32*(1), 3–14. (Case 8.1).

Sabom, M. B. (1982). *Recollections of death: A medical investigation*. New York, NY: Harper & Row. (Cases 1.4, 1.6, 2.9, 3.19, 3.20, 3.23).

Sabom, M. B. (1998). *Light and death: One doctor's fascinating account of near-death experiences*. Grand Rapids, MI: Zondervan. (Case 3.29).

Salter, J. (2008, September 18). Scientists study "out of body experiences." *The Telegraph*. Retrieved from http://www.telegraph.co.uk/news/uknews/2980578/Scientists-study-out-of-body-experiences.html#dsq-content (Case 3.8).

Sartori, P. (2008). *The near-death experiences of hospitalized intensive care patients: A five year clinical study*. Lewiston, UK: Edwin Mellen Press. (Cases 1.4, 1.9, 3.3, 3.4, 8.1, 8.2).

Sartori, P. (2012, February 25). *Update on Anita Moorjani's case*. Retrieved from http://drpennysartori.wordpress.com/2012/02/25/update-on-anita-moorjanis-case/ (Case 8.4).

Sartori, P. (2013). Response to "Critique of 'A prospectively studied near-death experience with corroborated out-of-body perceptions and unexplained healing.'" *Journal of Near-Death Studies, 32*(1), 15–36. (Case 8.1).

Sartori, P., Badham, P., & Fenwick, P. (2006). A prospectively studied near-death experience with corroborated out-of-body perceptions and unexplained healing. *Journal of Near-Death Studies, 25*(2), 69–84. (Cases 1.9, 8.1).

Seara Espírita. (2012). *Cirurgião cardíaco fala sobre experiência de quase morte* [Cardiac surgeon speaks about a near-death experience; interview in Brazilian Portuguese with Leonardo Miana]. Retrieved from http://youtu.be/zpUh5sI2Keg (Case 3.27).

Sharp, K. C. (1995). *After the light: What I discovered on the other side of life that can change your world.* New York, NY: William Morrow; (2003; 2nd ed.) Lincoln, NE: iUniverse. (Case 2.3).

Sharp, K. C. (2007). The other shoe drops: Commentary on "Does paranormal perception occur in NDEs?" *Journal of Near-Death Studies, 25*(4), 245–250. (Case 2.3).

Sherry. (n.d.). *My son's drowning NDE.* Retrieved from http://www.angelsghosts .com/my-son-s-nde. (Case 5.4).

Sherry, C. (2008, January 25). *Neurosurgeon and his story of survival after death.* Retrieved from http://mysterial.org.uk/cgi-bin/index.cgi?action=viewnews&id=444 (Case 3.29).

Shockey, P. (Director). (1992). *Life after life: Official documentary with Dr. Raymond Moody.* Cascom International. Retrieved from https://vimeo.com/85524391 (Case 5.5).

Shockey, P. (1999). *Reflections of heaven: A millennial odyssey of miracles, angels, and afterlife.* New York, NY: Doubleday. (Case 5.5).

Shockey, P. (Director). (2013). *Viola Horton's NDE–light at the end of the tunnel* (NDE Accounts excerpt from documentary *Life After Life*). Retrieved from https://www .youtube.com/watch?v=ihaKOubzcKg (Case 5.5).

Shockey, P., & Shockey, S. D. (2014). *Miracles, angels & afterlife: Signposts to heaven.* New York, NY: Open Road. (Case 5.5).

Silverberg, G. D., Reitz, B. A., & Ream, A. K. (1981). Hypothermia and cardiac arrest in the treatment of giant aneurysms of the cerebral circulation and hemangioblastoma of the medulla. *Journal of neurosurgery, 55*(3), 337–346. (Referenced in Appendix D).

Smit, R. H. (2008a). Corroboration of the dentures anecdote involving veridical perception in a near-death experience. *Journal of Near-Death Studies, 27*(1), 47–61. (Case 3.7).

Smit, R. H. (2008b). De Geleerde en de Last van het Geleerde [The scholar and the burden of what has been learned]. *Terugkeer, 19*(4), 1–2. (Case 3.7).

Smit, R. H. (2008c). Letter to the editor: Further commentary on Pam Reynolds's NDE. *Journal of Near-Death Studies, 26*(4), 308–309. (Referenced in Chapter 11).

Smit, R. H. (2012). Letter to the editor: Failed test of the possibility that Pam Reynolds heard normally during her NDE. *Journal of Near-Death Studies, 30*(3), 188–192. (Case 3.29, Chapter 11).

Smit, R. H., & Rivas, T. (2010). Rejoinder to "Response to 'Corroboration of the dentures anecdote involving veridical perception in a near-death experience.'" *Journal of Near-Death Studies, 28*(4), 193–205. (Case 3.7, Chapter 11).

Smit, R. H. (with van Lommel, P.). (2003). De unieke BDE van Pamela Reynolds (Uit de BBC-documentaire "The Day I Died") [Pam Reynolds' unique NDE (from the BBC documentary *The Day I Died*)]. *Terugkeer, 14*(2), 6–10. (Case 3.29).

Sola, K. (2015, April 16). Girl fell from tree, visited Jesus in heaven and awoke cured, mom claims in new book. *The Huffington Post*. Retrieved from http://www.huffingtonpost.com/2015/04/16annabel-beam-tree-heaven_n_7072406.html (Case 8.10).

Speer, C. (2007, December). Sterbebettvisionen [Deathbed visions]. *NTE-Report: Informationsbrief des Netzwerk Nahtoderfahrung, 5*(3), 4–5. Retrieved from http://www.netzwerk-nahtoderfahrung.org/images/Bilder/Dokumente/newsletter/oeffentlich/NTE-Report3-07.pdf (Case 2.1).

Spetzler, R. F., Hadley, M. N., Rigamonti, D., Carter, L. P., Raudzens, P. A., Shedd, S. A., & Wilkinson, E. (1988). Aneurysms of the basilar artery treated with circulatory arrest, hypothermia, and barbiturate cerebral protection. *Journal of neurosurgery, 68*(6), 868–879. (Referenced in Appendices D and E).

Steiger, B., & Steiger, S. H. (1995). *Children of the light: The startling and inspiring truth about children's near-death experiences and how they illumine the beyond.* New York, NY: Signet. (Case 6.4, Chapter 11).

Stephen. (2011, July 23). *Stephen's girlfriend's probable NDE.* Near Death Experience Research Foundation. Retrieved from http://nderf.org/NDERF/NDE_Experiences/stephen_gfriend_prob_nde.htm (Case 7.6).

Streit-Horn, J. (2011a). A systematic review of research on after-death communication (ADC) (Unpublished doctoral dissertation). University of North Texas, Denton, TX. (Referenced in Chapters 5 and 7).

Streit-Horn, J. (2011b). *Fact sheet: After-death communication.* Retrieved from http://www.coe.unt.edu/sites/default/files/22/129/ADC.pdf (Referenced in Chapters 5 and 7).

Sudduth, M. (2009). Super-psi and the survivalist interpretation of mediumship. *Journal of Scientific Exploration, 23*(2), 167–193. (Referenced in Chapter 10).

Sudduth, M. (2015, December 21). *In defense of Sam Harris on near-death experiences.* Retrieved from http://michaelsudduth.com/in-defense-of-sam-harris-on-near -death-experiences/ (Referenced in Chapter 11).

Sudduth, M. (2016). *A philosophical critique of empirical arguments for postmortem survival.* New York, NY: Palgrave Macmillan. (Referenced in Chapter 10).

Surel, D. (2010). [Untitled entry]. Retrieved from members-only section at https:// www.scientificexploration.org/ (Case 3.22).

Sutton, P., & Gershwin, N. (Executive producers). (1993). *The extraordinary: Episode 17* (11:28–21:13). Retrieved from https://www.youtube.com/watch?v=ZQwSO3_9lzI (Case 7.7).

Targ, R., & Puthoff, H. E. (1978). *Mind-reach: Scientists look at psychic abilities.* New York, NY: Delacorte. (Referenced in Chapter 2).

Tart, C. T. (2009). *The end of materialism: How evidence of the paranormal is bringing science and spirit together.* Oakland: New Harbinger. (Referenced in Chapter 10).

TG. (2008). Commentaar op Woerlee door A-verpleegkundige TG [Comments on Woerlee by registered nurse TG]. *Terugkeer, 19*(4), 8. (Case 3.7, Chapter 11).

Tiegel, E. (1983, March 30). His "deaths" transformed the course of his life. *Los Angeles Times.* (Case 2.8).

University of California, Riverside. (n.d.). *The science, philosophy, and theology of immortality.* Retrieved from http://www.sptimmortalityproject.com/ (Referenced in the Foreword).

van der Heijden, J. (2008). Wat écht is voelt gewoon échter aan dan wat niet écht is [What is *real* simply feels more *real* than what is not *real*]. *Terugkeer, 19* (4), 13. (Case 3.7).

van der Heijden, J. (2012). Sporen uit de toekomst [Traces from the future], *Terugkeer, 23* (1), 1–11. (Referenced in Chapter 6).

van Dijk, G. W. (2004). Hoofdstuk 3: Bewustzijn. In B. T. J. Meursing & R. G. van Kesteren (Eds.), *Handboek reanimatie: Tweede herziene druk* (pp. 21–25). Utrecht, Netherlands: Wetenschappelijke Uitgeverij Bunge. [Chapter 3: Consciousness. In *Handbook resuscitation: 2nd revised edition.*] (Referenced in Appendix A).

van Lommel, P. (2008). Reactie op "de man met het gebit" naar aanleiding van het artikel "Een gesprek met TG over de Man met het gebit" door Titus Rivas [Response to the "Man with the Dentures" on occasion of the article "Een gesprek met TG over de Man met het gebit" by Titus Rivas]. *Terugkeer, 19*(4), 10–12. (Case 3.7).

van Lommel, P. (2010). *Consciousness beyond life: The science of the near-death experience.* New York, NY: HarperCollins. (Case 3.7, the Introduction and Chapter 10).

van Lommel, P. (2013). Non-local consciousness: A concept based on scientific research on near-death experiences during cardiac arrest. *Journal of Consciousness Studies, 20*(1–2), 7–48. (Referenced in the Foreword and Appendix A).

van Lommel, P., van Wees, R., Meyers, V., & Elfferich, I. (2001). Near-death experience in survivors of cardiac arrest: A prospective study in the Netherlands. *The Lancet, 358*(9298), 2039–2045. (Case 3.7, Chapter 11).

Viacom Productions. (Producer). (1999). *The most beautiful garden: The case of William (Will) Barton and his miraculous recovery after an NDE.* Beyond Chance with Melissa Etheridge. Retrieved from https://www.youtube.com/watch?v=hUqsRzBE2CM (Case 8.6).

Viacom Productions. (Producer). (1999, December 19). *Matters of life and death.* Beyond Chance with Melissa Etheridge [Video posted online by NDEAccounts. (2015). *Shared near-death experience—Pet spirit guides.*]. Retrieved from https://www.youtube.com/watch?v=lLIYZ_SLuHQ (Case 3.32).

Viacom Productions. (Producer). (2000). *Medical miracle.* Beyond Chance with Melissa Etheridge. Retrieved from https://www.youtube.com/watch?v=lKxBnUzAke8 (Case 6.6).

Vila López, E. (2009). *Yo vi la luz. Experiencias cercanas a la muerte en España* [I saw the light: Near-death experiences in Spain]. Madrid, Spain: Ediciones Absalon/ Mentes Despiertas. (Case 9.2).

von Wilmowsky, A. (2012). *Segelfalter* [Sail swallowtail; e-book]. Amazon Digital Services. (Case 3.9).

Weinberg, A. D. (1993). Hypothermia. *Annals of Emergency Medicine, 22*(2), 370–377. Retrieved from http://www.hypothermia.org/weinberg.htm (Referenced in Chapter 11).

White, B. C., Winegar, C. D., Jackson, R. E., Joyce, K. M., Vigor, D. N., Hoehner, T. J., . . . & Wilson, R. F. (1983). Cerebral cortical perfusion during and following resuscitation from cardiac arrest in dogs. *The American journal of emergency medicine, 1*(2), 128–138. (Referenced in Appendix A).

Williams, K. (2014). *Jan Price's near-death experience with her pet dog.* Retrieved from http://www.near-death.com/experiences/with-pets/jan-price.html (Case 3.32).

Williams, K. (n.d.). *Scientific discoveries come from near-death experiences: Dr. Kenneth Ring.* Near-Death Experiences and the Afterlife. Retrieved from http://www.near-death.com/experiences/evidence07.html (Case 8.3).

Williams-Murphy, M. (2013, January 21). *"I died and you brought me back to life": How one patient's near death experience changed my life.* Retrieved from http://www.oktodie.com/blog/i-died-and-you-brought-me-back-to-life-how-one-patients-near-death-experience-changed-my-life/#sthash.8S8WG4cs.dpuf (Case 3.36).

Williams-Murphy, M., & Murphy, K. (2011). *It's okay to die* [Kindle ed.]. Amazon Digital Services: The authors and MKN, LLC. (Case 3.36).

Wilson, I. (1997). *Life after death: The evidence.* London, UK: Sidgwick & Jackson. (Case 5.1).

Winfrey, O. (Producer). (2011). *Oprah children's near death experiences Dr. Morse presents.* Retrieved from https://www.youtube.com/watch?v=Cz6mqa1s21s (Case 3.31).

Woerlee, G. M. (2004). Cardiac arrest and near-death experiences. *Journal of Near-Death Studies, 22*(4), 235–249. (Referenced in Chapter 11).

Woerlee, G. M. (2005). *Mortal minds: The biology of near-death experiences.* Amherst, NY: Prometheus Books. (Referenced in the Introduction).

Woerlee, G. M. (2007). *The unholy legacy of Abraham.* Leicester, UK: Troubador. (Referenced in Chapter 11).

Woerlee, G. M. (2010). Response to "Corroboration of the dentures anecdote involving veridical perception in a near-death experience." *Journal of Near-Death Studies, 28*(4), 181–191. (Case 3.7, Appendix B).

Woerlee, G. M. (2011). Could Pam Reynolds hear? A new investigation into the possibility of hearing during this famous near-death experience. *Journal of Near-Death Studies, 30*(1), 3–25. (Case 3.29, Chapter 11).

Woerlee, G. M. (2012a). Seeing family members during NDEs: "Peak in Darien" experiences & NDEs. Retrieved from http://neardth.com/seeing-family-during -nde.php (Referenced in Chapter 11).

Woerlee, G. M. (2012b). Setting the Record Straight: Commentary on an Article by Pim van Lommel "The Failure of Expert Authority." Online article at Near Death Experiences. Retrieved from http://www.neardth.com/setting-the-record -straight.php (Referenced in Chapter 3).

Woerlee, G. M. (2013a). *Illusory souls* [Kindle ed.]. Amazon Digital Services: Author. (Referenced in the Introduction and Chapter 10).

Woerlee, G. M. (2013b). *Successful test of the possibility that Pam Reynolds heard normally during her NDE.* Retrieved from http://www.neardth.com/failed-hearing -test.php (Case 3.29).

Woerlee, G. M. (2014a). *Pam Reynolds near death experience.* Retrieved from http:// www.neardth.com/pam-reynolds-near-death-experience.php (Case 3.29).

Woerlee, G. M. (2014b). *Rivas and Smit & a near-death experience reported by Lloyd Rudy.* Retrieved from http://www.neardth.com/lazarus.php (Case 3.11).

Index

About the Authors

Titus Rivas (born 1964) wears many hats: theoretical psychologist, philosopher, parapsychological researcher, and writer of books and articles (in both Dutch and English). Published highlights include *Parapsychologisch onderzoek naar reïncarnatie en leven na de dood* (Parapsychological Research on Reincarnation and Life after Death); *Onrechtvaardig diergebruik* (Unjust Animal Use); *Geesten met of zonder lichaam* (Spirits With or Without Bodies); *Encyclopedie van de Parapsychologie* (Encyclopedia of Parapsychology). Coauthored works include *Reincarnation* with Kirti Swaroop Rawat; *Gek Genoeg Gewoon* (It's Really Rather Normal) with Tilly Gerritsma; and *Van en naar het Licht* (From and to the Light) with Anny Dirven. Co-founder of Athanasia Foundation, a nonprofit to investigate survival after death, reincarnation and spiritual evolution, Rivas continues to pursue his interests in

Titus Rivas with his dog, Moortje

parapsychology and philosophy also by instructing home-study courses for the National Business Academy in Panningen, Netherlands. Rivas happily shares his life in Nijmegen with his four-footed companions, (cat) Pipi and (dog) Moortje. Work on this book accompanied the final days of dear friend and coauthor Anny Dirven, and two beloved feline friends, Cica and Guusje, making this most recent project all the more meaningful.

Anny Dirven (1935–2016), who was paranormally gifted, was active for years as a general assistant and researcher affiliated with the Athanasia Foundation, often working together with Titus Rivas. Dirven

Anny Dirven

came to know Rivas by way of the parapsychology course he teaches for the National Business Academy. Together, Dirven and Rivas produced many parapsychological and philosophical articles and books, some of which she coauthored. They were particularly proud of *Vincent, Karim en Danny* (Vincent, Karim, and Danny) at Lulu.com, and *Van en naar het Licht* (From and to the Light), published by Elikser. In 2007, an in-depth interview with Anny Dirven appeared in *Spiritualiteit, vrijheid en engagement* (Spirituality, Freedom, and Engagement), edited by Titus Rivas and Bert Stoop, with assistance from Dirven. Dirven was a mother, grandmother, and great-grandmother, as well as the widow of Wim Stevens. She spent most of her life in Budel, Netherlands.

Rudolf H. Smit

Rudolf H. Smit (born 1942) is the author of books and articles in both English and Dutch on subjects ranging from photography to near-death experiences to computer programming. Former editor of the Dutch photographic monthly *Foto* and the British Astrological Association's scientific journal *Correlation*, Smit is the current editor of the Dutch quarterly *Terugkeer* published by the Network for Near-Death Experiences (Netwerk NDE), the Dutch affiliate of IANDS. Interested in promoting critical research in the field of astrology, Smit also runs the internationally acclaimed *Astrology and Science* website. When not writing, he enjoys retired life with his wife, Miny, in the Netherlands.

Relevant Addresses and Websites

Eben Alexander, MD
Eternea
Website: http://www.eternea.org
Personal website: http://www.ebenalexander.com/

American Society for Psychical Research (ASPR)
5 West 73rd Street
New York, New York 10023
United States
P: +1 212.799.5050
Fax: +1 212.496.2497
E-mail: aspr@aspr.com
Website: http://www.aspr.com

Evelyn Elsaesser-Valarino
10, Pré de la Croix
CH-1279 Chavannes de Bogis
Switzerland
E-mail: evelyn@elsaesser-valarino.com
Website: http://www.elsaesser-valarino.com

Horizon Research Foundation
Mailpoint 810
Level F, Southampton General Hospital
Tremona Road
Southampton
Hampshire SO16 6YD
United Kingdom
P: +44 (0)238.000.1016
Website: http://www.horizonresearch.org

IANDS Flanders / Limen VZW
E-mail: vze.limen@yahoo.com
Website: http://www.bijnadoodervaring.be

IANDS France
Website: http://iands-france.org.pagesperso-orange.fr

International Association for Near-Death Studies (IANDS)
2741 Campus Walk Avenue, Building 500
Durham, NC 27705-8878
United States
P: +1 919.383.7940
E-mail: services@iands.org
Website: http://www.iands.org

Bernard Jakoby
Sterbeforschung.de / Leben nach dem Tod—Die Erforschung einer Unerk-
    lärlichen Erfahrung (Life after Death—Investigation of an Unexplained
    Experience)
Website: http://sterbeforschung.de/de

Robert and Suzanne Mays / The Self-Conscious Mind
E-mail: mays@ieee.org
Website: http://selfconsciousmind.com

Near Death Experience Research Foundation (NDERF)
Jeffrey and Jody Long
Website: http://www.nderf.org

Near-Death Experiences and the Afterlife
Kevin Williams
Website: http://www.near-death.com

Netwerk Nabij-de-dood Ervaringen (Netwerk NDE)—formerly Stichting
  Merkawah / IANDS Netherlands
Administration
Zilverschoon 33
8265 HD Kampen
Netherlands
P: +31 (0)63.015.0554
E-mail: info@netwerkNDE.nl
Website: http://netwerknde.nl
English section: http://netwerknde.nl/534-2/

Netzwerk Nahtoderfahrung / Near-Death Experience Network
Borheeserweg 90
46446 Emmerich a. R.
Germany
P: +49 (0)2.822.3375
E-mail: netzwerk-nahtoderfahrung@t-online.de
Website: http://www.netzwerk-nahtoderfahrung.org

Nour Foundation
Website: http://www.nourfoundation.com

Parapsychologisch Instituut / Parapsychological Institute
Springweg 7
3511 Utrecht
Netherlands
P: +31 (0)30.231.4282
Website: http://www.parapsy.nl

Rhine Research Center
2741 Campus Walk Avenue, Building 500
Durham, NC 27705-8878
United States
P: +1 919.309.4600
Website: http://www.rhine.org

SKEPP VZW

Studiekring voor Kritische Evaluatie van Pseudo-wetenschap en het Para-
    normale /

Study Group for Critical Evaluation of Pseudoscience and the Paranormal

F. Lecharlierlaan 44, bus 10

1090 Brussels

Belgium

E-mail: info@skepp.be

Website: http://skepp.be

Skeptical About Skeptics / Skeptical Investigations

Website: http://www.skepticalaboutskeptics.org/

Society for Psychical Research (SPR)

The SPR

49 Marloes Road

Kensington

London W8 6LA

United Kingdom

P: +44 (0)207.937.8984

Website: http://www.spr.ac.uk

Society for Scientific Exploration (SSE)

Mark Urban-Lurain, PhD

Secretary, SSE

Michigan State University

111 N. Kedzie Lab

East Lansing, MI 48824

United States

P: +1 517.432.2152, ext. 119

Fax: +1 517.432.1356

E-mail: urban@msu.edu

Website: http://www.scientificexploration.org

Stichting Athanasia / Athanasia Foundation
Darrenhof 9
6533 RT Nijmegen
Netherlands
P: +31 (0)24.848.7203
E-mail: stg_athanasia@hotmail.com
Website: http://www.txtxs.nl/artikel.asp?artid=751

Stichting Skepsis / Skepsis Foundation
E-mail: skepsis@wxs.nl
Website: http://skepsis.nl/english/

Pim van Lommel
E-mail: info@pimvanlommel.nl
Website: http://www.pimvanlommel.nl/home_eng

Gerald Woerlee
Website: http://www.neardth.com/

Printed by Amazon Italia Logistica S.r.l.
Torrazza Piemonte (TO), Italy

33038038R00230